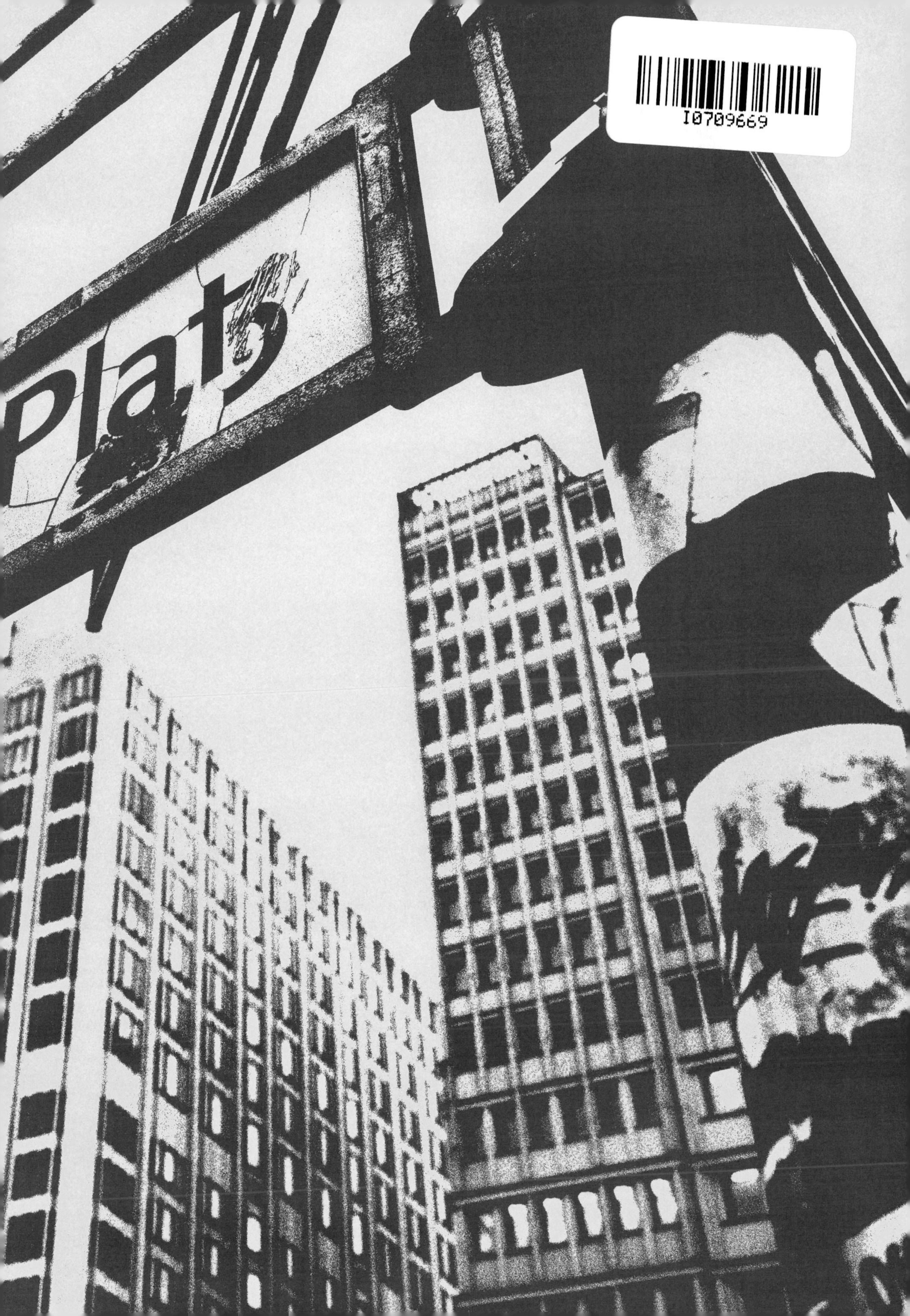

I0709669

DAVID
BOWIE

MIXING
MEMORY
&
DESIRE

DAVID BOWIE

MIXING MEMORY & DESIRE

PHOTOGRAPHS BY
KEVIN CUMMINS

weldon**owen**

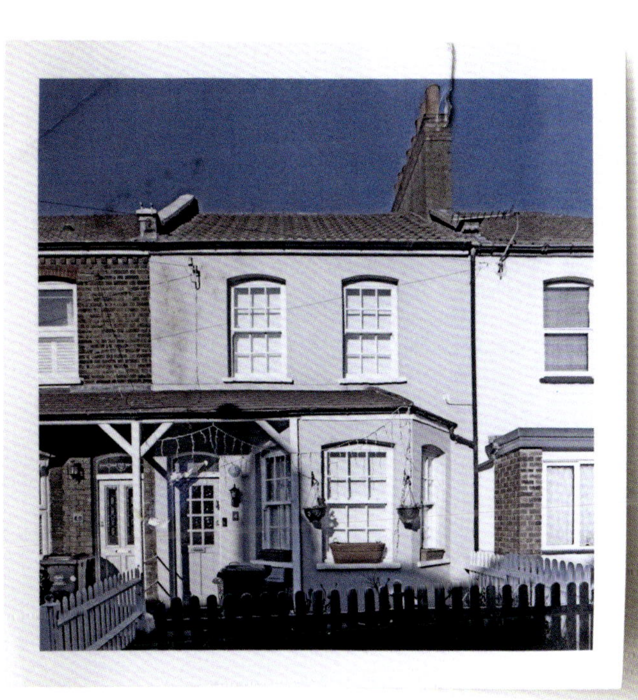

CONTENTS

FOREWORD
JEREMY DELLER

Most people have their own version of David Bowie in their minds – a unique image of him they hold dear, that represents the *true* story of Bowie to them. These versions are intensely personal and provoke, at times, contradictory feelings. For people of my generation in particular the idea of Bowie is not unlike a relationship to a parent, or your country even, in that it becomes integrated into your life in unexpected ways. Omnipresent.

For Kevin Cummins, the image of Bowie is more significant than for most. After all, we have Bowie to thank for Kevin even becoming a photographer. Kevin has not only his own version of Bowie in his imagination, but he also has the photographs to prove it. His relationship with Bowie actually charts his own career as a photographer, starting with his first concert images taken surreptitiously as a teenager at an early Ziggy Stardust gig (it's probably difficult for younger generations to understand that taking photos at gigs would get you thrown out; now it's more or less the opposite). The oeuvre later expands to professional studio appointments as an established photographer and intimate catch-ups in the moments after headlining shows. It's all witnessed here.

My personal favourites are from the *Serious Moonlight* tour at the Milton Keynes Bowl. It's a series of impossibly romantic images taken from the pit showing Bowie looming overhead. With no lighting rig above him, just the ginormous blue sky as the sun begins to fall, the image of Bowie becomes transcendent as the music itself.

In this collection Kevin has shown his versions of Bowie over the years, as well as his own evolution as a photographer. And because Kevin's imagery has become the medium through which many of us benchmark music photography, it creates an opportunity to look back over the evolution of one of the most creative performers ever. The inspiration that Bowie inspires in Kevin is, in turn, inspiration for us all.

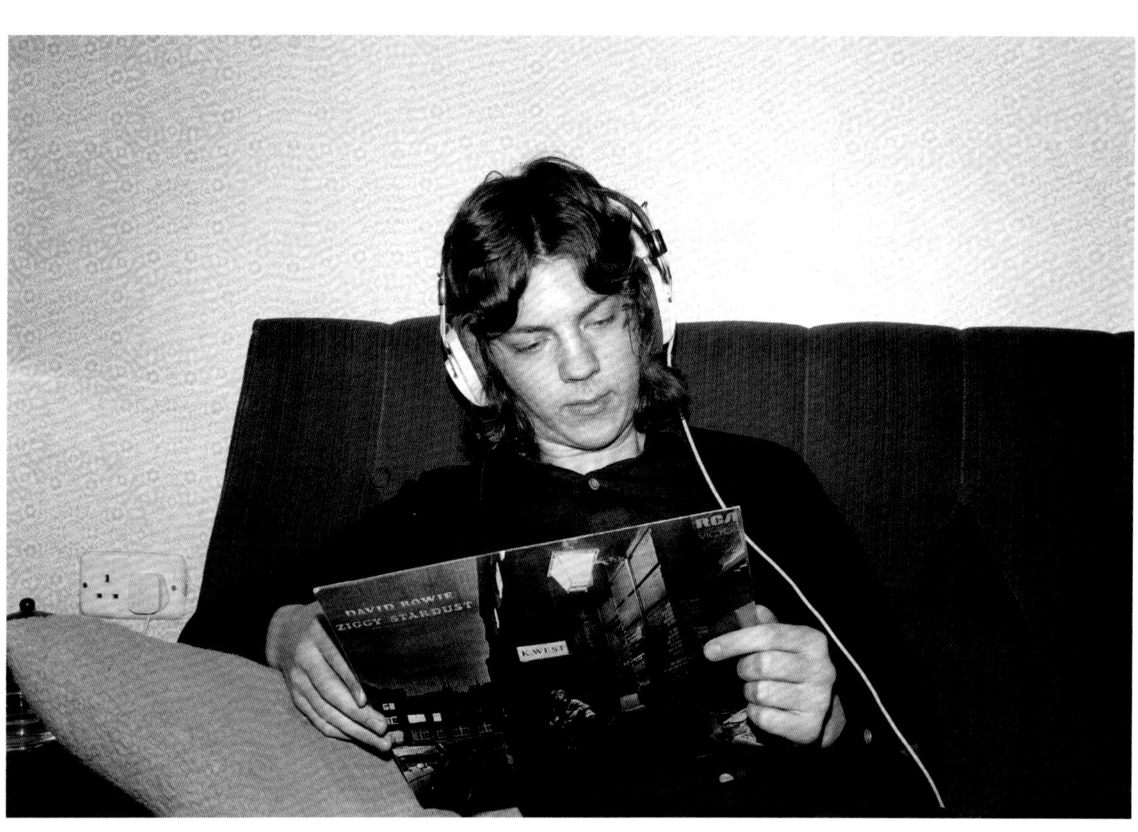

INTRODUCTION
KEVIN CUMMINS

The year is 1969.

On 20 July, the first men landed on the Moon, and I was lying in a typical teenage location, on my bed. While the world seemed space obsessed, the walls around my bed were very much earthbound. There I was full stretch, hands behind my head, surrounded by posters of Man City players pulled from *Jimmy Hill's Football Weekly*, *Goal* and *Charles Buchan's Football Monthly* – Colin Bell, Mike Summerbee and anyone else from City who featured in those pages. At the end of my bed was a window that looked out onto a classic Salford backyard, housing an outside toilet and a bike that I used for my paper round. Nearly all my time was spent checking the fixture lists and working out the various permutations that would need to happen for City to win the league in the forthcoming season. My one non-football concession was a poster of pop singer turned avant-garde jazz singer Julie Driscoll at the side of my bed.

But sometime in July 1969, and I don't remember exactly when, I heard, almost certainly on Radio 1, a song called "Space Oddity" by David Bowie. The luxury of hindsight allows me to check that Bowie released this track five days before Armstrong, Aldrin and crew even left Earth for the Moon, which ensured that everyone would be listening to it by the time they arrived. I certainly was. I like to think it was on my transistor radio that I used to take on my paper round, or on a radio at school in the playground, or on the bus to school, because ever since BBC Radio 1 had

launched a couple of years earlier, suddenly we all had access to pop music in a whole new way. But whenever and wherever I heard it, I realized that I was listening to something different. For a start, in comparison with other pop songs that tended to last for less than three minutes, this song felt epic, topping five minutes in length. And then there was the theatricality of it: a small, lone man blasting into vast space, spinning in a tin can above the Moon. As much as I loved Julie Driscoll's *Streetnoise*, released the same month, "Space Oddity" had something a bit different going on. Part of the attraction for me was the grandiose pomp of it all. My mother had introduced me to musicals and light opera, and I immediately fell in love with the drama and spectacle of Bowie. But on top of that, unlike many other singers at the time, he actually wrote his own songs.

Looking back, there really is something quite astonishing about me in my Salford bedroom, a pupil at an all-boys Roman Catholic grammar school, encountering David Bowie for the first time. It's probably the same astonishment that lots of people in 1969 felt when they saw exactly who was singing this music. In my world there was absolutely no room for self-expression and defiance. If you grew your hair to hit the top of your shirt collar, this was the height of rebellion. Being faced with someone – a man – who wore flowered shirts and make-up was, to sadly use a cliché often attached to Bowie, like encountering an otherworldly being. But the reality is that Bowie *was* different, which meant that lots of us discovering him for the first time were able to live vicariously through him and his daring.

So, along with the posters of Colin Bell and Julie Driscoll, I pulled out a headshot of Bowie from *Fabulous* magazine and pinned it up on my bedroom wall. We all spoke about him at school. We all spoke about the Moon landings. We knew there was a world beyond the one that we lived in, but I am not sure any of us thought about how we might reach it.

At this age, I assumed I would become an English teacher. That is what my school friends saw as their future and, until a little later, I just accepted this. We were never taken on school trips to art galleries. We were never really introduced to visual culture at all. But humming away in the background of my upbringing were my father and grandfather, who were self-taught photographers. They never had big projects, it was never anything huge or life-changing, but they were fascinated to learn about cameras and film, and how to take a photograph and then process it: holidays, family events, scenes from around Manchester, nothing out of the ordinary. My father converted a small cupboard-like space into a darkroom and, even as a child, I loved the smell and feel of the process that unfolded there. I was gifted my first camera at five years old. But, like all children, what I was surrounded by was my norm; I had no thoughts of becoming a photographer and I was so obsessed with whether City would win the league or

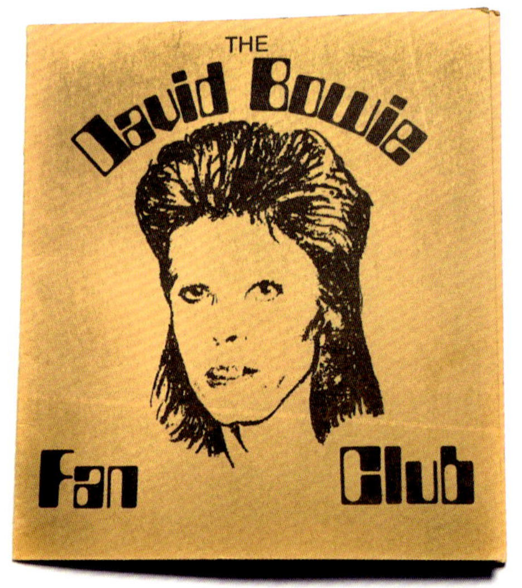

not that I didn't much focus on anything else. That's not to say that I wasn't interested in photography because I was. I loved photographs in the press that were able to transport you to another world, whether that was a particular place or fashion. But I did see a huge gap between those sorts of images and the ones that my father and I and my grandfather were producing. They seemed completely different entities, and this was not a gap that I ever anticipated bridging myself. But, despite this, I do think it is fair to say that I saw the visionary potential in photography, even if at that stage it wasn't something that I thought had anything to do with me. At the time I was too young, and way too clueless, to think that my trajectory would in any way run alongside David Bowie, who was pinned up on my bedroom wall and seemed to be perpetually floating in the most peculiar way.

The thing is, I don't have an epic life-changing story about hearing Bowie for the first time. I did listen to him, and I liked him a lot, and I loved the melodic songs that he wrote himself, but then I kind of forgot about him for a couple of years. I was busy spending all my money watching City and ripping pages out of my school exercise book to create *Kevin's Top Ten*, where I attempted to predict what would make the charts the following week and triumphantly ticked off the entries that were correct. I wasn't old enough to go to clubs, and even when I was, I often wasn't allowed in because I looked 15 for most of my teenage years and had no ID to prove otherwise.

When I was 17, I listened to *The Man Who Sold the World*, and when I was 18, I listened to *Hunky Dory*. The following year (1972) I set up a tripod and camera to take a photograph of me sitting wearing headphones and holding *The Rise and Fall of Ziggy Stardust and the Spiders from Mars*. Every signifier in the photo screamed 1970s, from my by now quite daring shoulder-length hair to the white headphones and functional sofa. A tantalizing hint of glamour is offered by the picture on the album cover: Bowie standing in an impossibly cool position with his guitar under a light on Heddon Street, London. My photo is black and white, so it does no justice to the yellowy and red-brick hues of the album cover designed by Terry Pastor, who airbrushed and coloured the photo of Bowie to give it that illustrated look.

Over the previous couple of years, as we had listened more and more to Bowie, we became obsessed with the references in his songs. Names such as Andy Warhol and Kahlil Gibran had us venturing to Manchester Central Library to look these characters up. It inspired us to read more, we looked at art, we wanted to know what was inspiring him. And this opened up another world for so many of us. As Bowie progressed from David to Ziggy to Aladdin Sane, we were progressing from hapless teenagers to young students who gradually understood that teaching English was not where it was at for us. As I hit my later teen years I became increasingly interested in the visual arts, initially while still at school. Then, when I had to decide where to go after that, I chose art college. These were those crucial formative years when you start being influenced by certain things and people around you, soaking up information, learning new things, craving different experiences.

I suppose all these transformations converged when I heard that Bowie was playing a gig at the Hardrock in Stretford in September 1972. I couldn't afford to go. But then he added two more dates in December of that year, and I went to one of them armed with a small point-and-shoot camera. By the time he returned to Manchester in June 1973 at the Free Trade Hall, his fame had exploded. The press began building the mythology of Bowie as an ethereal, otherworldly being, and I, along with many others, was swept along by this narrative. Even the national tabloids were giving away posters of him. I took some more photos at a couple of gigs on this tour, starting to hone my craft and photographic eye. One of the shots from a night in Leeds would eventually sell to the V&A Museum four years later.

Having recently started at art college, but still with no thoughts about what sort of photographer I wanted to be, I had become increasingly interested in what Bowie had to say about the visual arts. His belief was that it was possible to feel something inside that needed to be manifested, and if it could be, then you would not only understand more about yourself but also how you operate in the world around you. I had always seen photography as a window onto the world, but a window that required art, craft and skill. When it came to taking a photograph, it always seemed important to ask: out of all the people and places it the world, why capture this one right now at this moment? I believed then, and I believe now, that it is to communicate something. Images, or at least good images, tell us something significant about the place and time at which they were taken. They are not merely recording a scene or revealing a piece of knowledge, they show something beyond the physical limits of the frame. And if they are exceptionally good, they can add and build into mythology and stories. Bowie understood how visual art worked, and I was gradually learning. I had seen my father and grandfather teach themselves how to take a photograph, playing about with different types of film, trying and often failing to frame a certain scene, so trying again. They would process film in different ways, using different techniques. It was all about experimentation. And it seemed to me, so was Bowie. Always changing, always flitting from one transformation to another, bold and fearless.

It was probably around 1973 when I decided that photographing musicians might be something that I wanted to do permanently. But there seemed so much to learn. Over the next few years, I began to get commissions. A memorable one was for the *NME* in August 1977, when I got to spend two or three days with Marc Bolan during the filming of his TV show *Marc* at Granada Studios in Manchester. Paul Morley

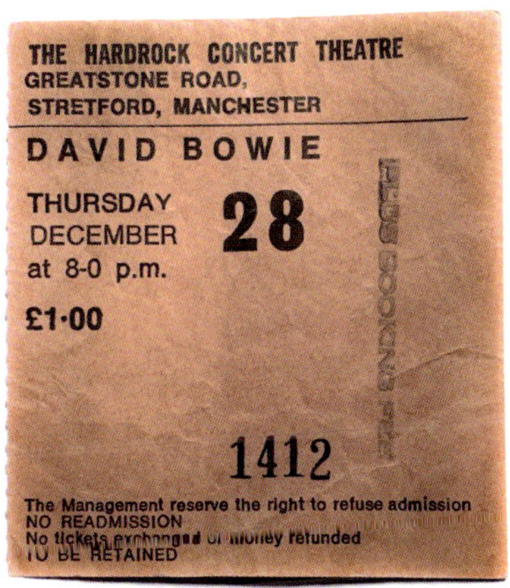

would do the writing; I would take the pictures. We spent our time talking to Marc about the sort of music that we loved (Bowie obviously came up), and he was an attentive listener. In fact, he was just a really nice person. At the end of our time with him, he invited us to go back to his show the following week with a peculiar smile. We left excited, but then were devastated to get another commission that we had to take – this time with a minor Manchester artiste – leaving us unable to attend Marc's show. That was the week that Bowie appeared. Marc had intended for us to meet him. Tragically, within a month, Marc, who had been filled with so much life and energy, was dead. What a devastating loss.

Despite becoming a leading expert on him, Paul Morley never again got the chance to interview Bowie. And despite photographing Bowie at various concerts over the coming years, I would have to wait another 14 years before I met him in person for our first studio portrait session. This meeting took place on 4 August 1991 at a warehouse rehearsal space and studio in Dublin. It was during Bowie's Tin Machine period. Even though I had already shot quite a few *NME* covers by this stage, I was in such a nervous-excited state that what should have been a momentous highlight for me became professionally depressing. I was hamstrung with nerves. I felt like a teenager lying on his bed daydreaming and thinking about his idol. Only now, that very idol was right in front of me and expecting me to know exactly what I was doing. Which I did in theory. It just felt a bit trickier to execute in practice. When you look at the series of photos taken from this shoot later in the book, and read the accompanying story, I think it becomes obvious when that paralysing moment disappeared. Happily, the day ended with me getting some of my favourite shots of Bowie.

As ever, though, when you are photographing someone who is probably one of the most photographed musicians in the world, the unique challenge is to get something different. I often liken it to photographing the Eiffel Tower. Everyone who goes to Paris takes almost the same shot; the landmark is so well known that it is hard to do something different or unexpected with it. Bowie was exactly the same. Over the coming years, as I grew more confident in my art and less nervous of meeting him, I was more playful, and certainly more experimental with some of the images that I captured.

But this book is not a tidy chronology of unsure images taken by me as a student through to successful later shots when my career was established. Photography doesn't always work like that, and neither does art. Sometimes the light just isn't quite right, sometimes someone is wearing the wrong thing, but then sometimes, after much planning, you find yourself positioned in exactly the right place at the right moment to capture a truly magical image. One of my earliest pictures of Bowie (1973) with his arms outstretched in "The Width of a Circle" mime is one of my best-known and best-selling shots. Likewise, a picture I took 24 years later (1997) of Bowie in a New York street, looking completely different and much less theatrical, is also popular.

I never photographed Bowie again after 1997. But when I was in New York during the summer of 2016, I walked by his apartment on Lafayette Street where he had died just six months earlier, shocking the world into disbelief. I was moved to see a makeshift memorial. LET'S DANCE was painted on the railings of the building, messages of thanks and devotion, flowers, gifts and memento mori laid on the sidewalk. It was incredible and telling that, in a city such as New York, this shrine had been allowed to remain and grow since the beginning of the year. I took some photographs, mostly to remember what he meant to me, to all of us. I couldn't help but think back to the first time I met him in 1991, nervous and feeling 15 all over again. After taking his photograph, I asked him if he would sign the picture I had taken of him, arms outstretched on stage. He agreed. "You are the reason I became a photographer," I blurted out. He laughed. "I get blamed for lots of things," he said, "but I'm barely responsible for my own career, I don't want to be responsible for yours too."

But he was, and he is, and this book is proof.

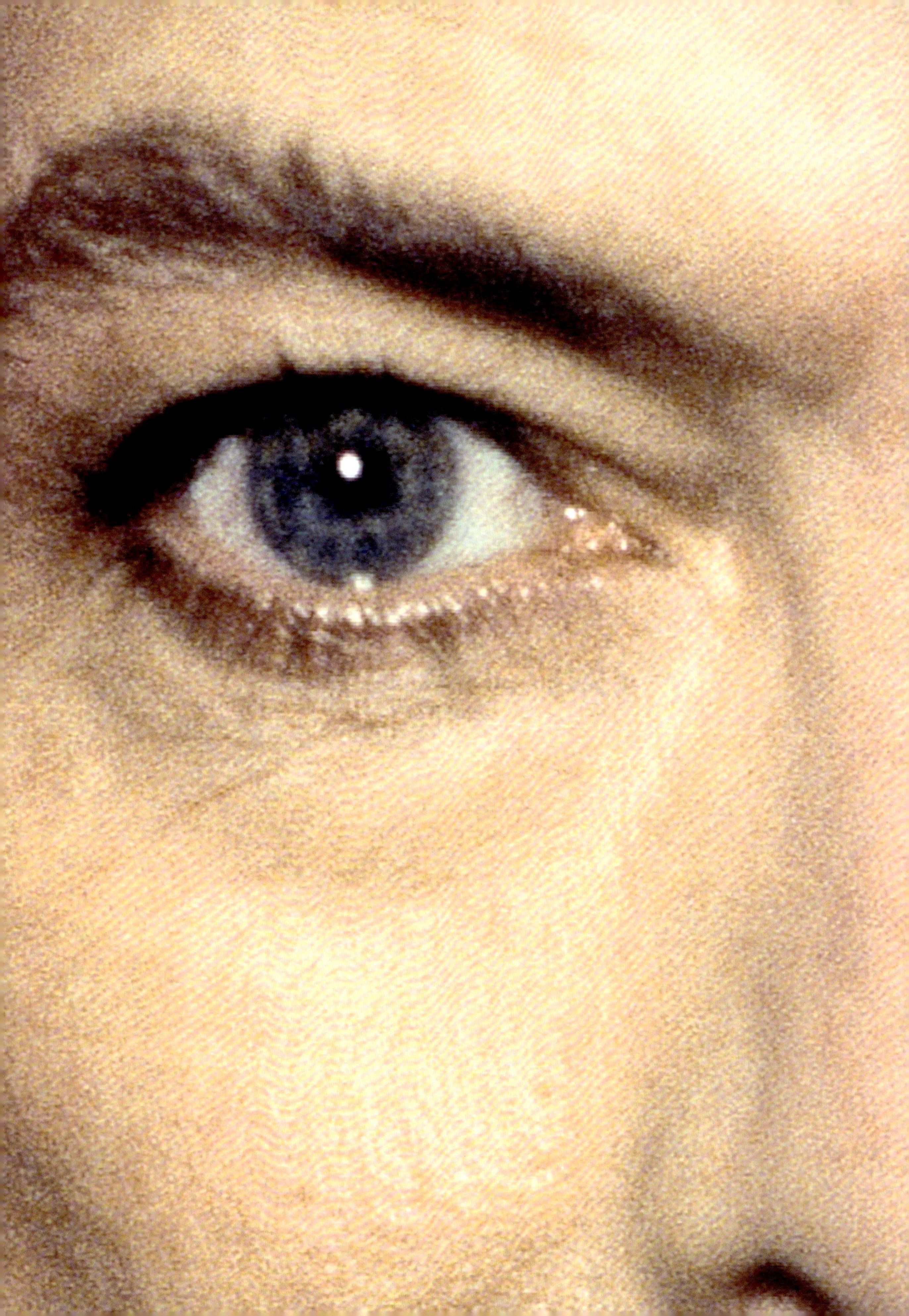

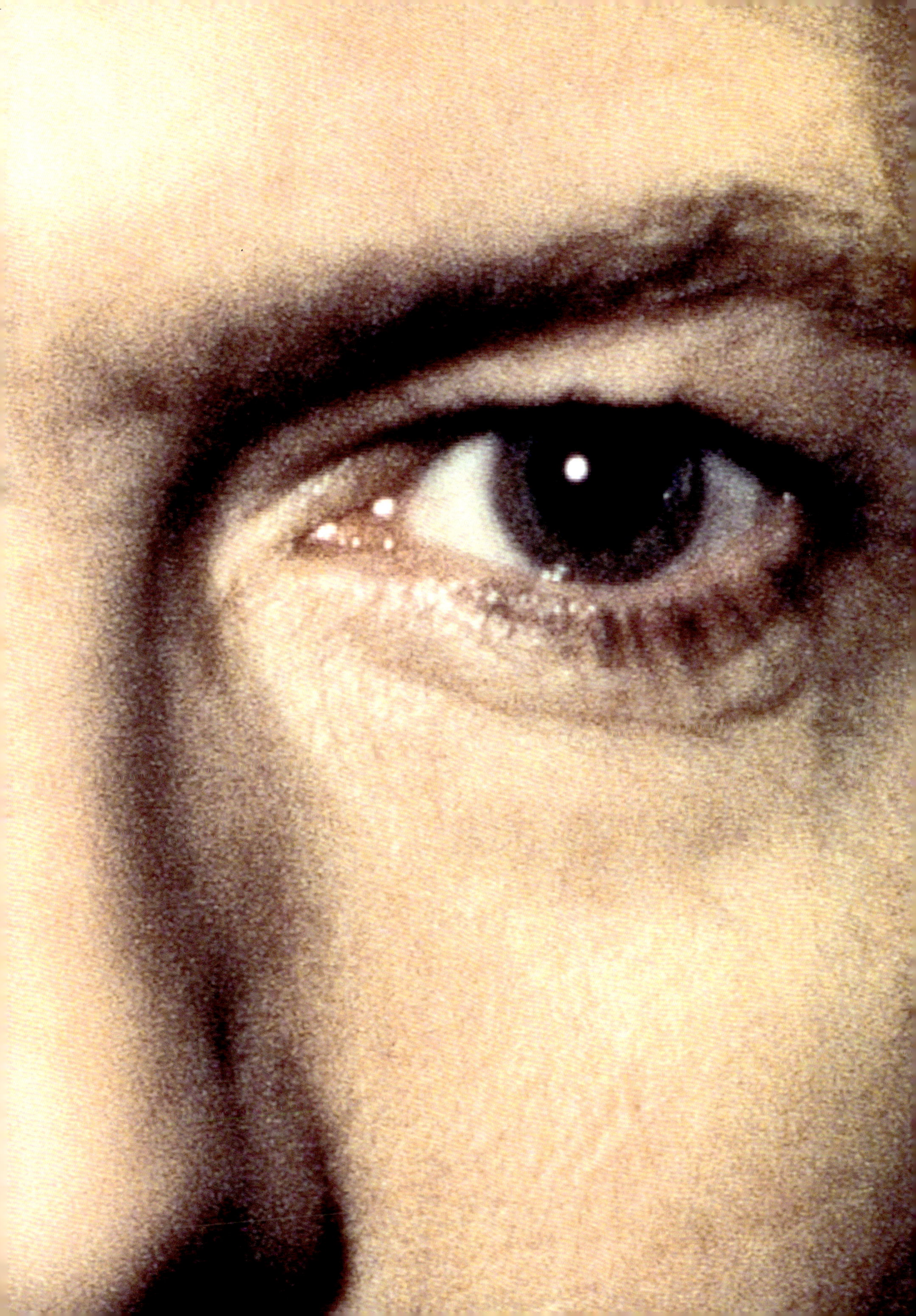

28 DECEMBER 1972
HARDROCK, STRETFORD, GREATER MANCHESTER

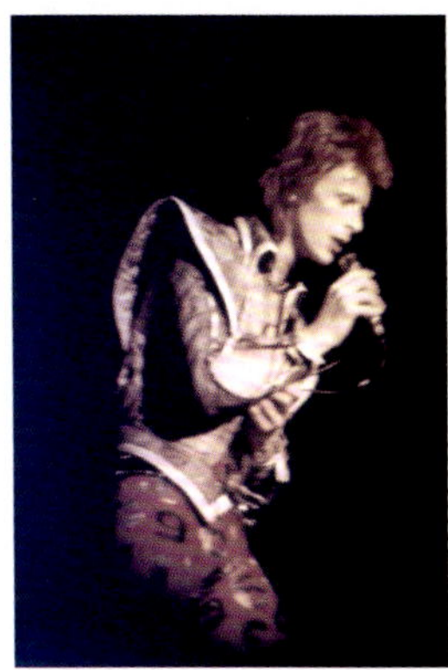

I think we all have pivotal moments in our lives, a day or experience that stays with you for ever. These colour photographs of Bowie captured one of those moments. This cold December night in Stretford in 1972 was the first time that I saw Bowie live. I had taken a point-and-shoot camera with me, primarily because I was desperate to try out a roll of GAF 500 colour film that I had seen fashion photographers such as Sarah Moon use. Studying certain images at college, mostly taken in daylight, I was able to see that this particular film was especially grainy, and I was keen to see how it performed under different light conditions. I had never shot under stage lights before, so the combination of experimenting with new film while seeing Bowie for the first time was fairly monumental.

When the film was processed, I thought the pictures were a little too red, too warm, but I was pleased to stick them on my moodboard at college. What is odd, looking back, is how differently I viewed the camera then. I was confident handling it and I knew how it worked, but as a student I had not quite realized just how permeable a viewfinder can be. I had not yet discovered that, far from the lens being a barrier, it is possible to almost make it disappear, so that there is an invisible connection between you and whomever you are photographing. The French essayist Roland Barthes wrote about this in *Camera Lucida* as "a sort of umbilical cord" that "links the body of the photographed thing to my gaze...is here a carnal medium, a skin I share with anyone who has been photographed."

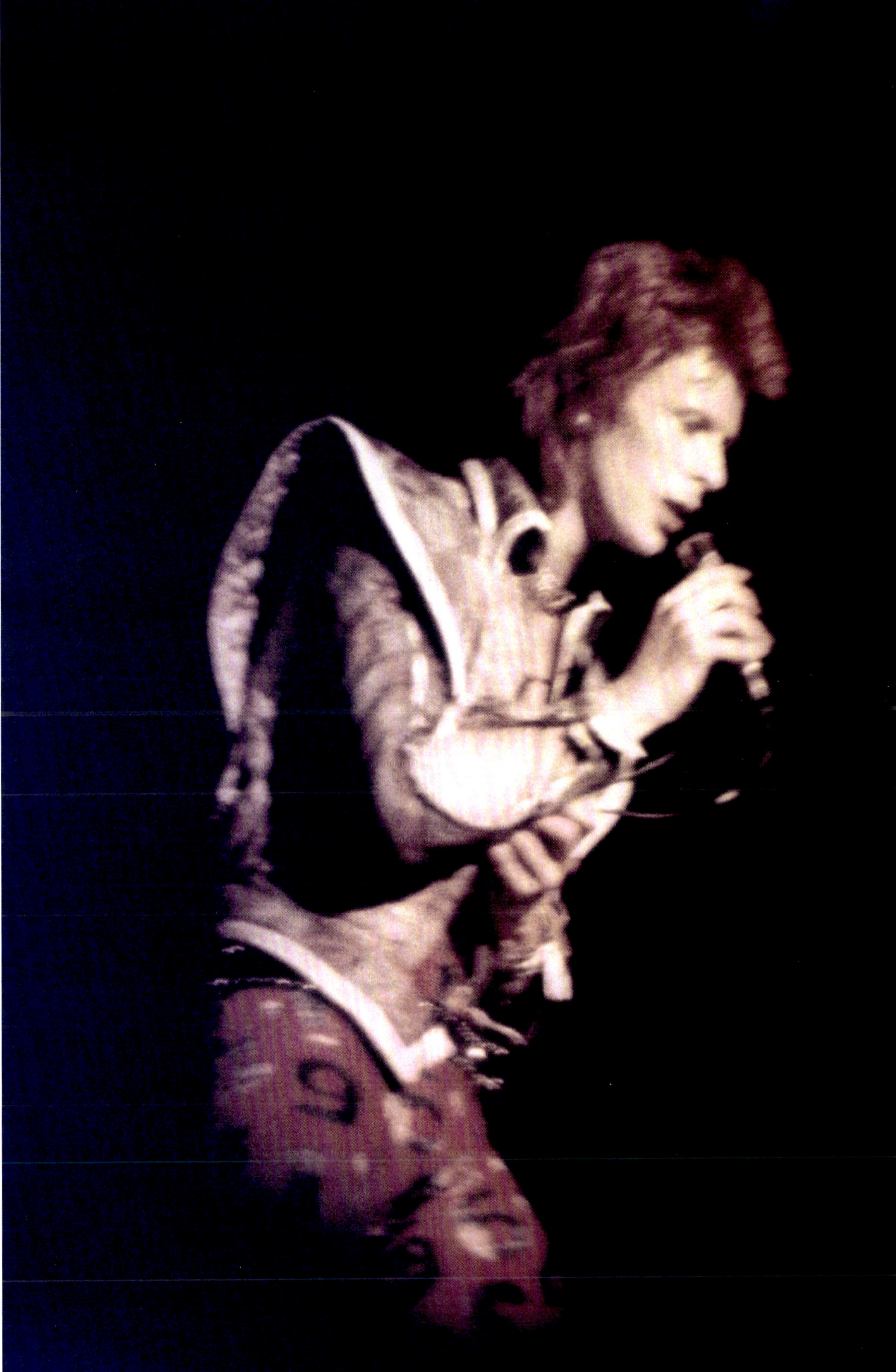

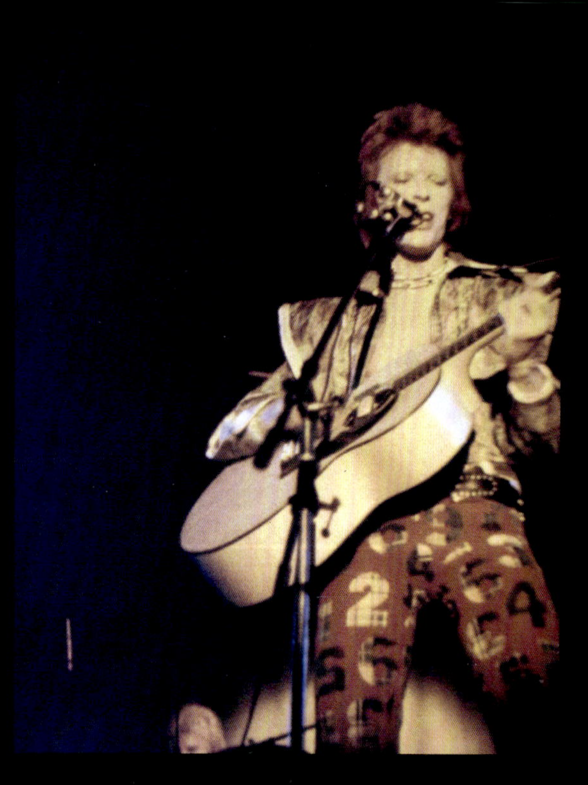

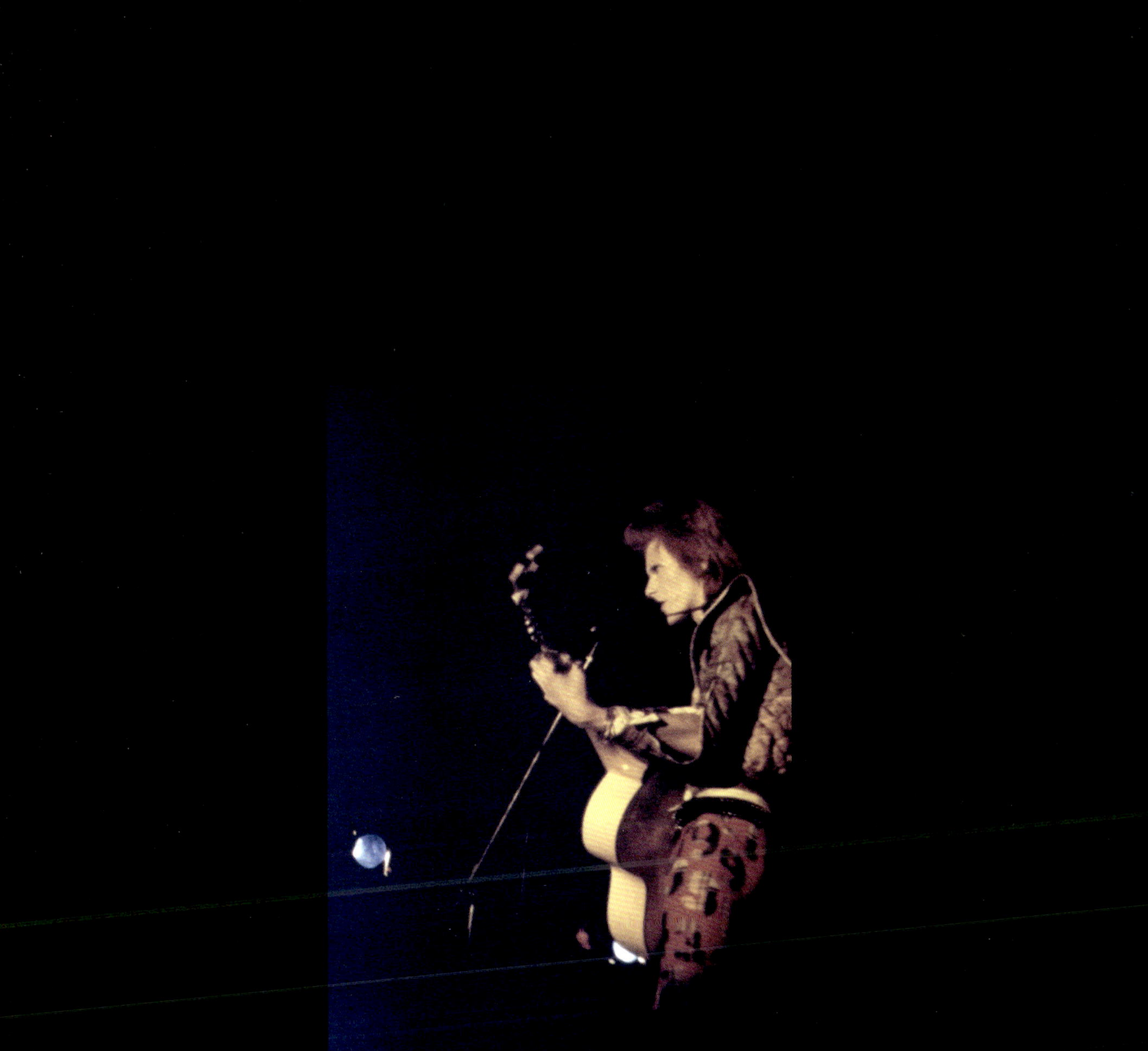

7 JUNE 1973

MANCHESTER FREE TRADE HALL

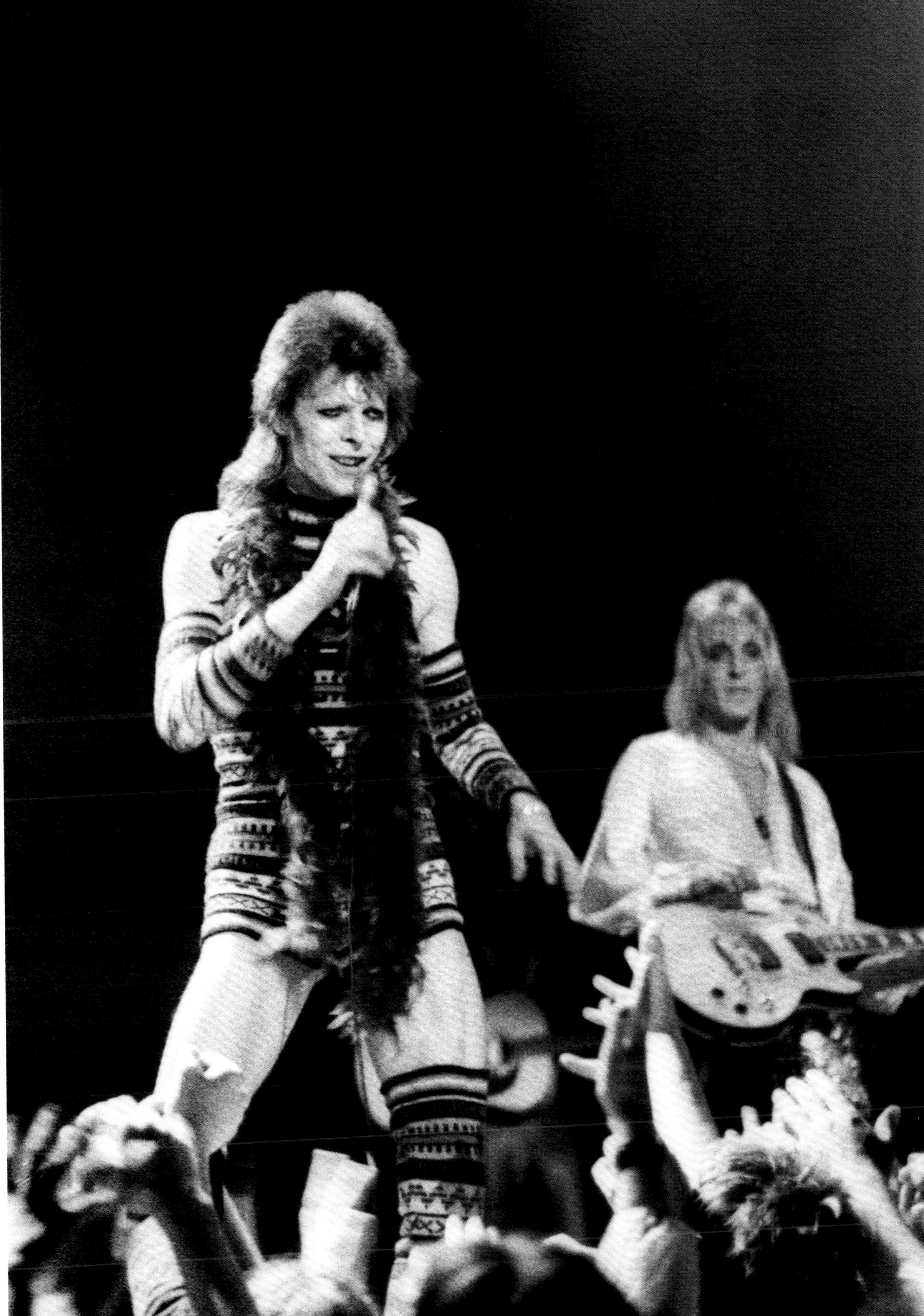

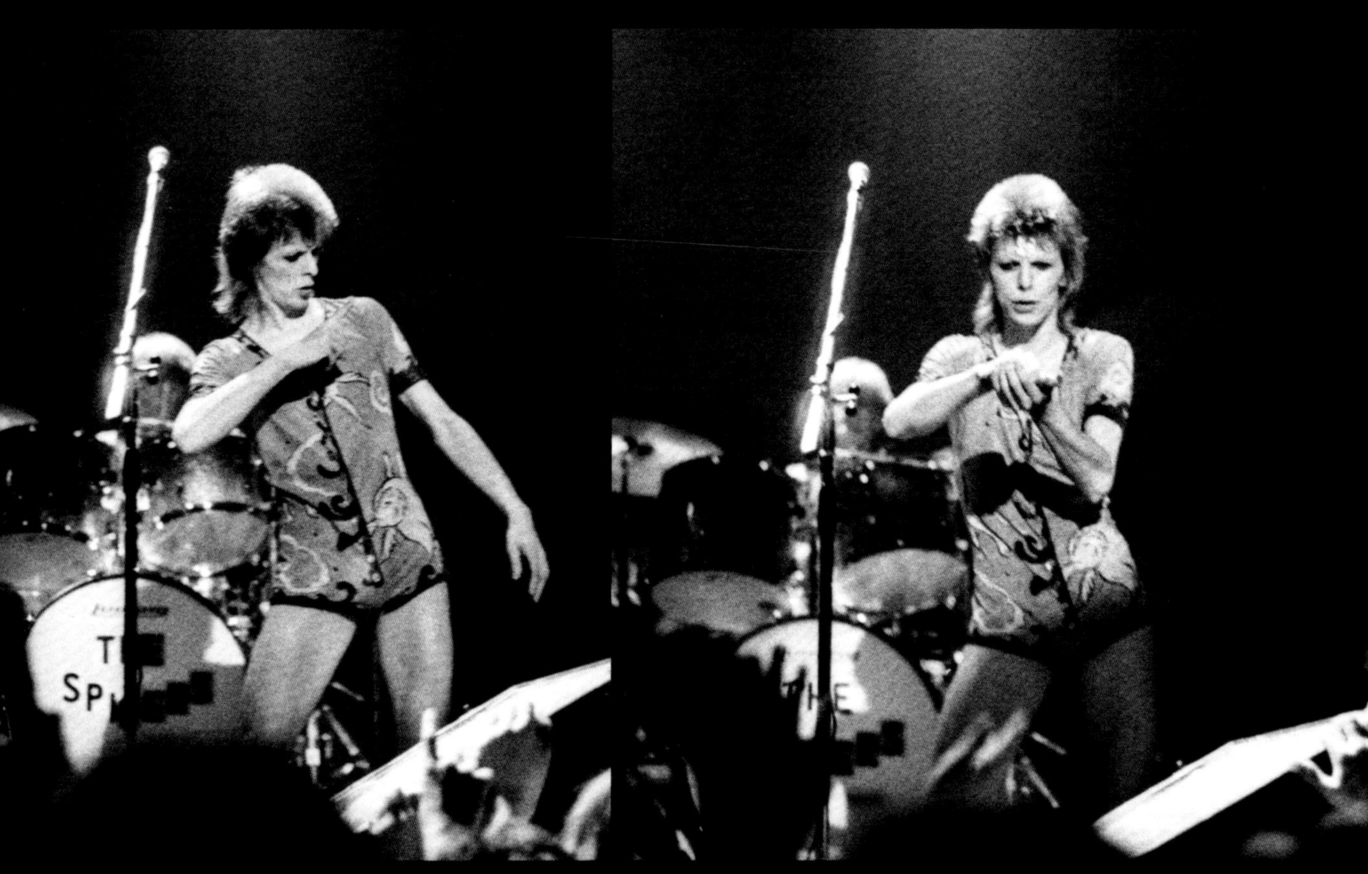

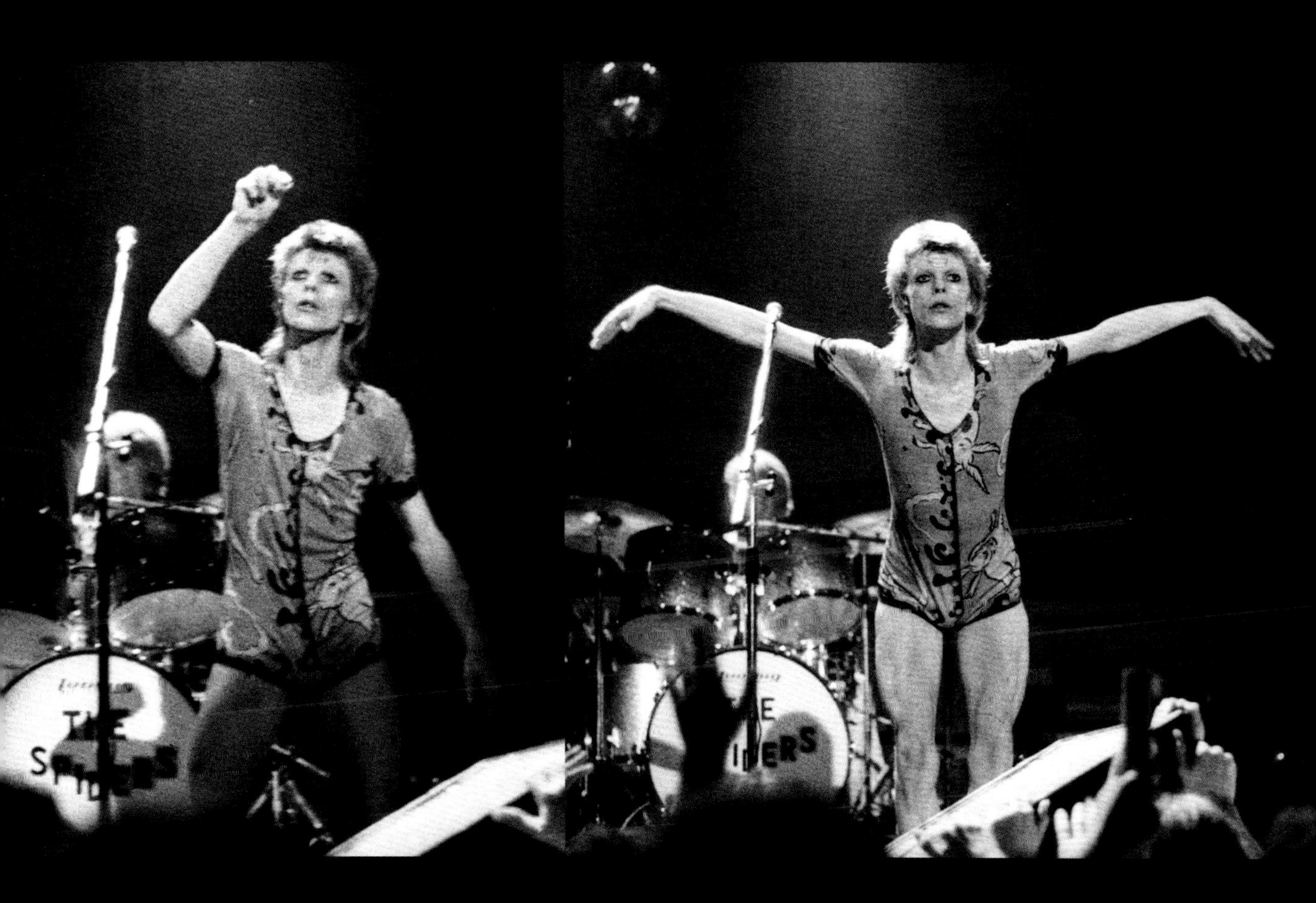

THE SPIDERS

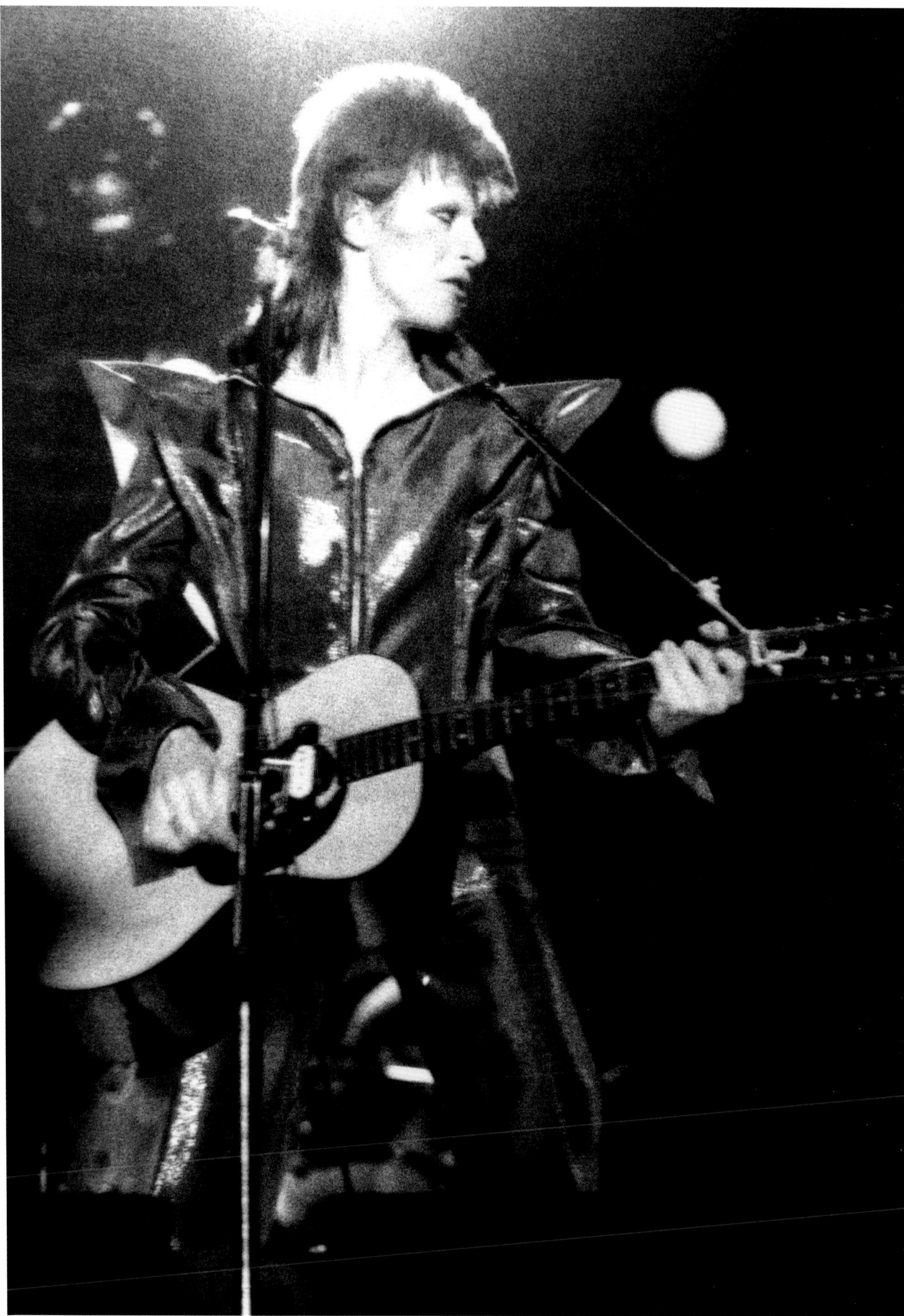

29 JUNE 1973
ROLARENA, LEEDS

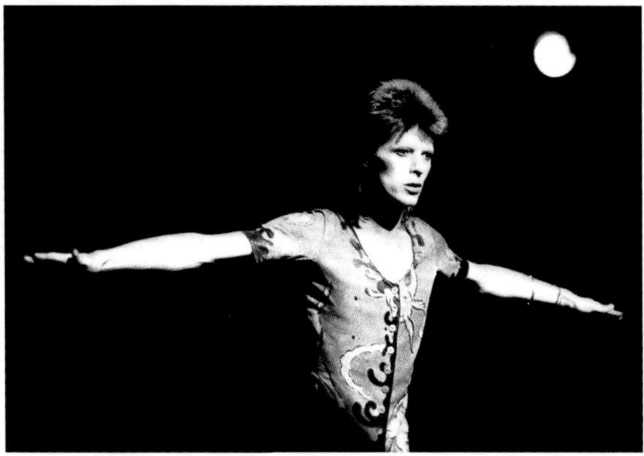

After my initial experimentation with colour film in December 1972, when Bowie returned to Manchester six months later, I decided to capture some publishable shots. Armed with a better camera, I went along to the Free Trade Hall and took a series of pictures that I processed the next day at college. Although I liked them, the moment in "The Width of a Circle" mime when Bowie stretches out his arms just wasn't quite captured from the optimum position, so I decided to try again. Even at this early point in my career, I understood that it was never a good thing to settle for a shot if you felt you could better it.

I bought a ticket for Bowie's gig in Leeds and began some of my earliest experiments with the relationships between stage, lighting, movement and position. I figured out exactly where I would need to stand to best capture the moment in the mime when Bowie's arms reach out to the side. In my picture Bowie is lit perfectly, a shadow just cutting across his lower torso, a stage light a little like the Moon hangs in the top right of the frame. Getting a shot like this is not luck or being in the right place at the right time; it requires learning a craft, knowing how to look at and frame a scene. When I was younger, it was also about trying different things until I understood the art of photography. Because photography is an art and, like any other discipline, it requires intense study. In 1973 I was in the early days of my study, but these shots of Bowie from Manchester and Leeds made me realize that it was something I wanted to take further. In 1977 this image sold to the V&A Museum; it was my first sale to a gallery and remains part of its permanent collection.

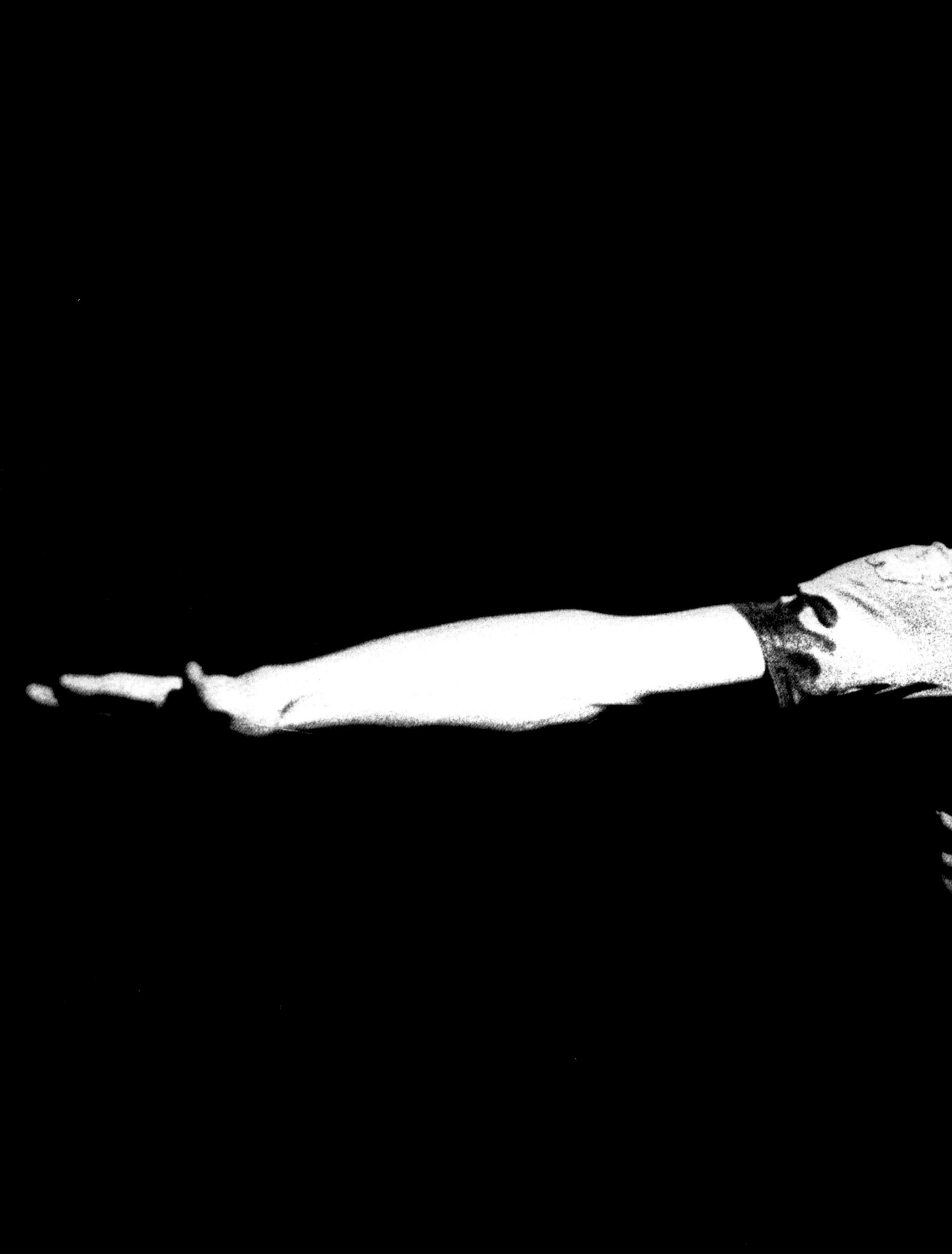

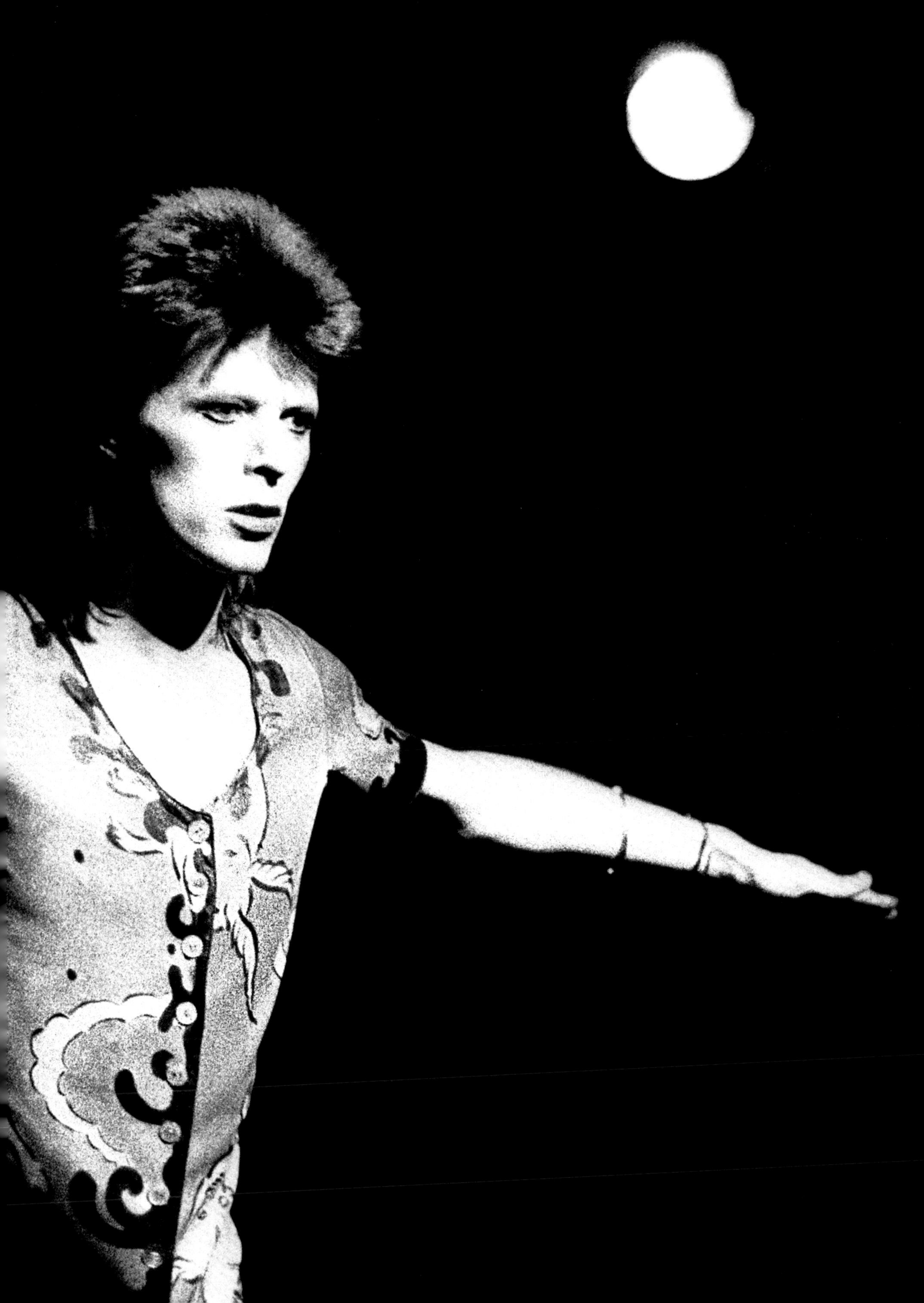

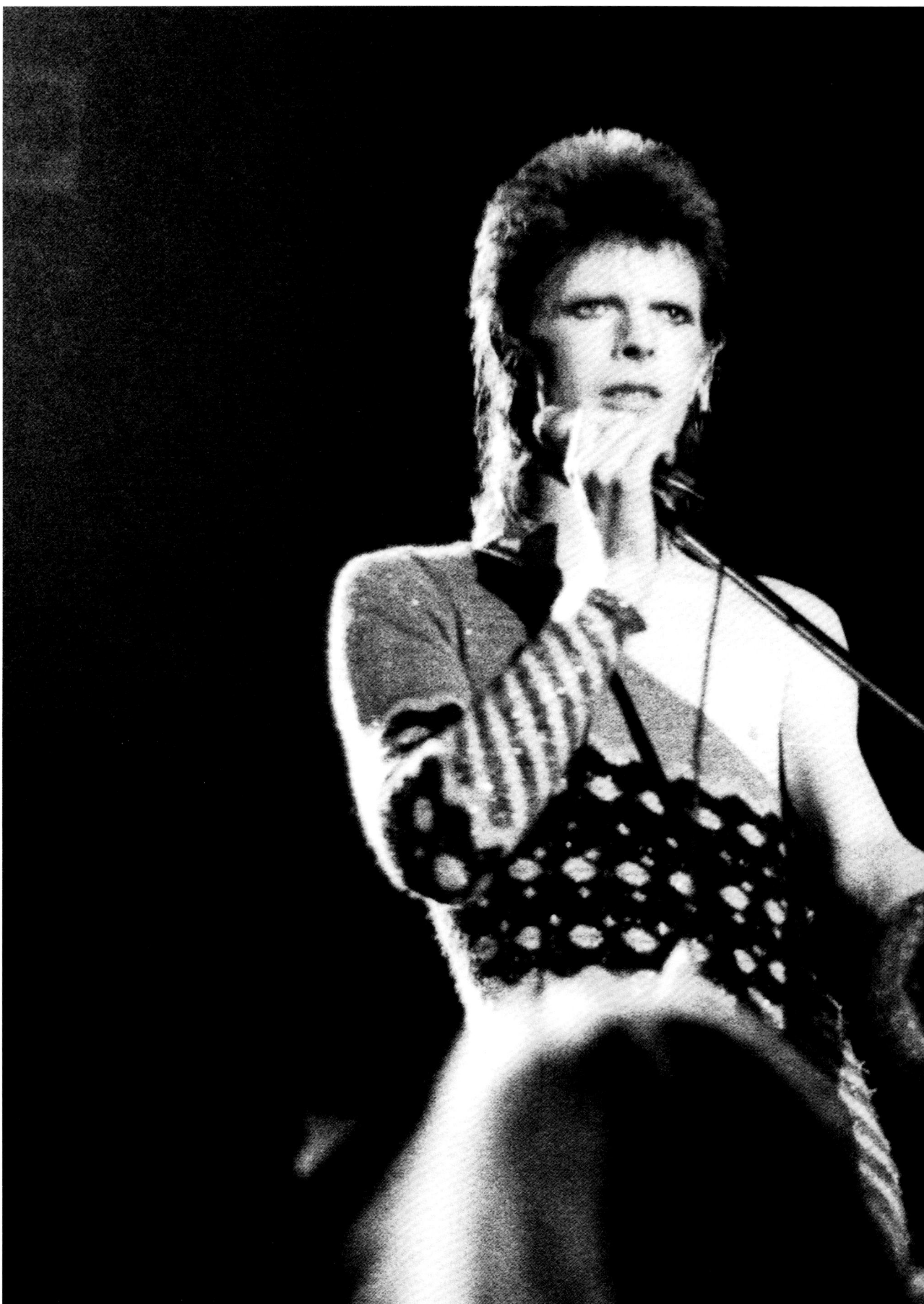

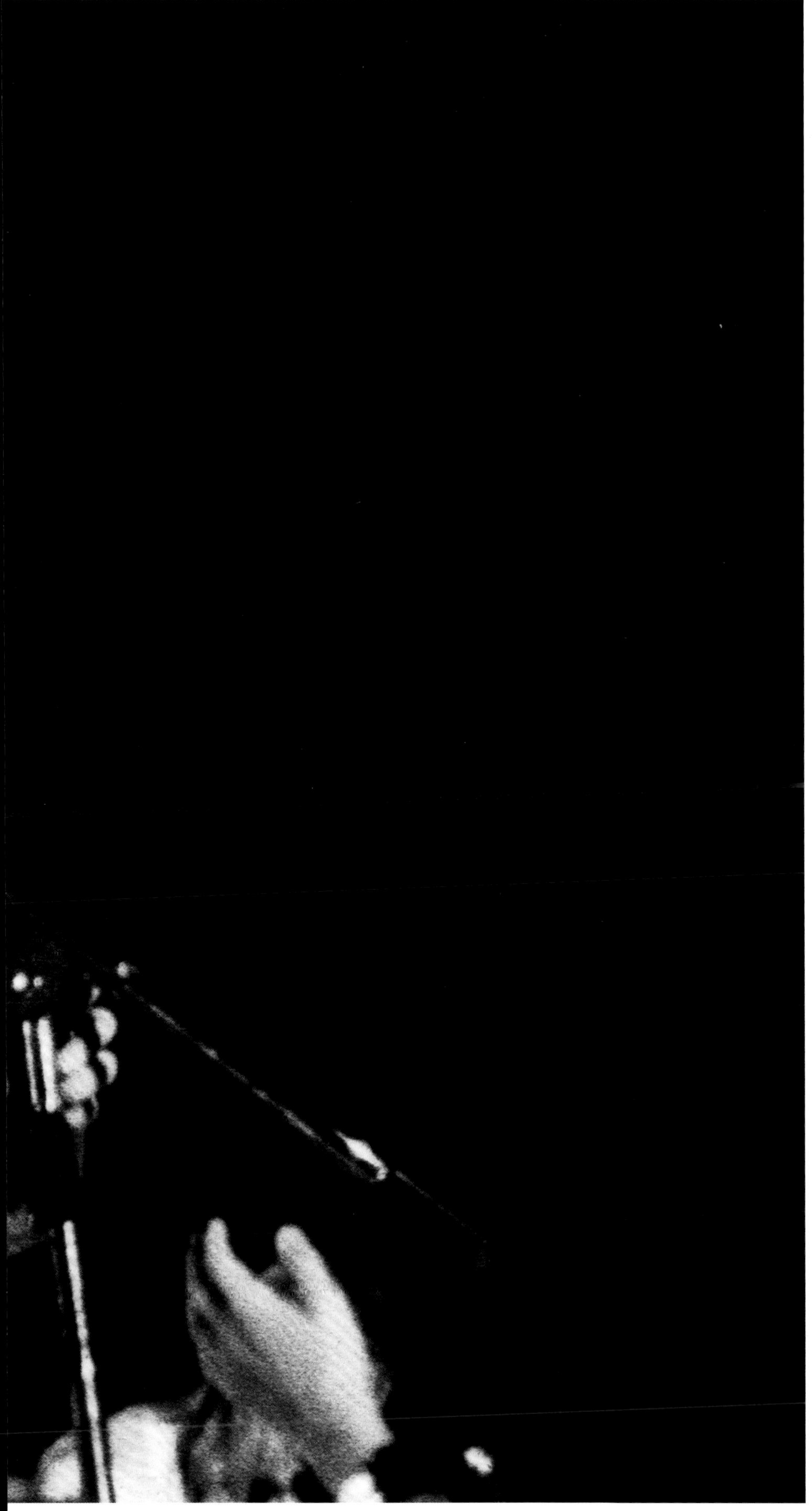

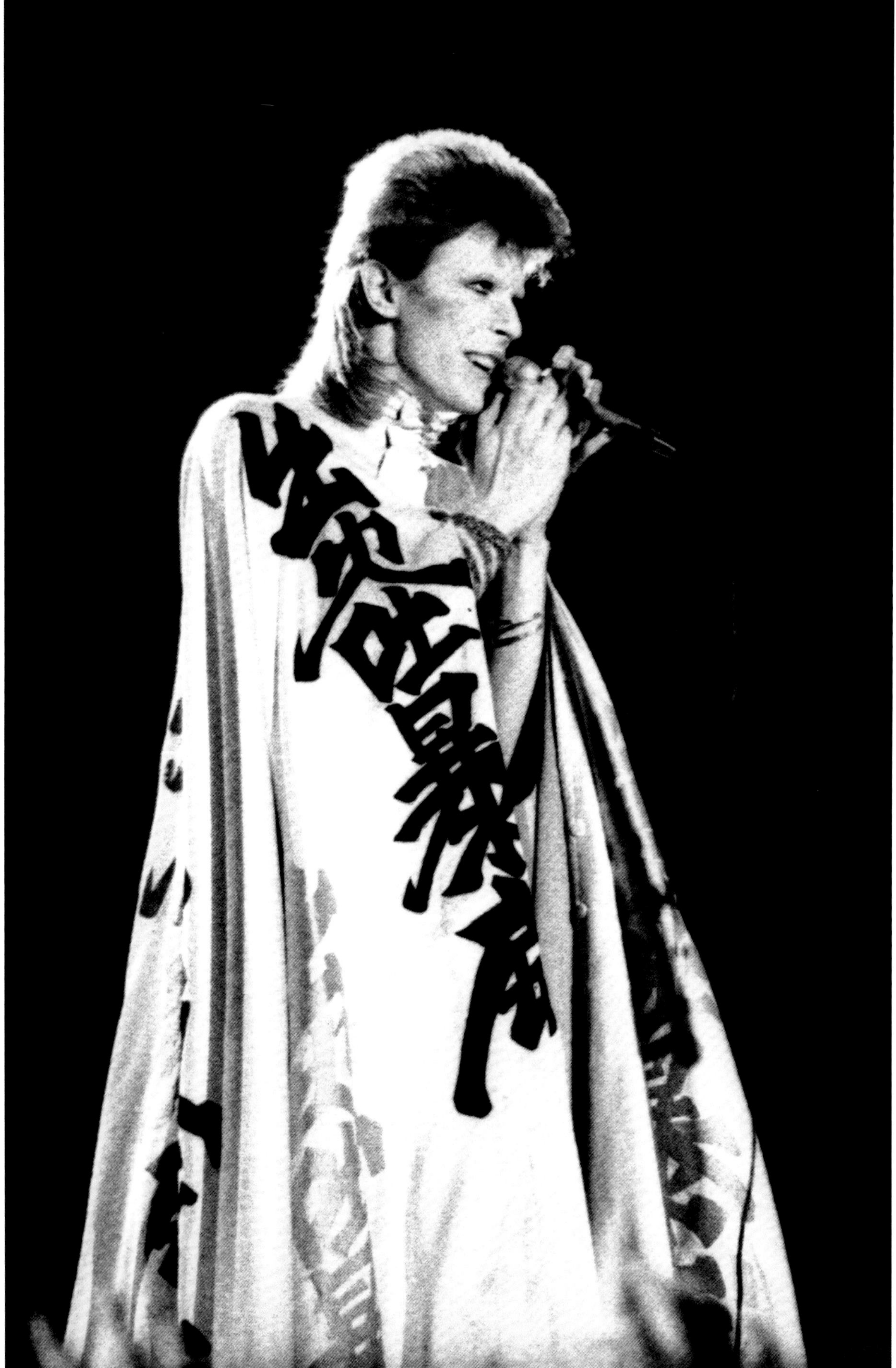

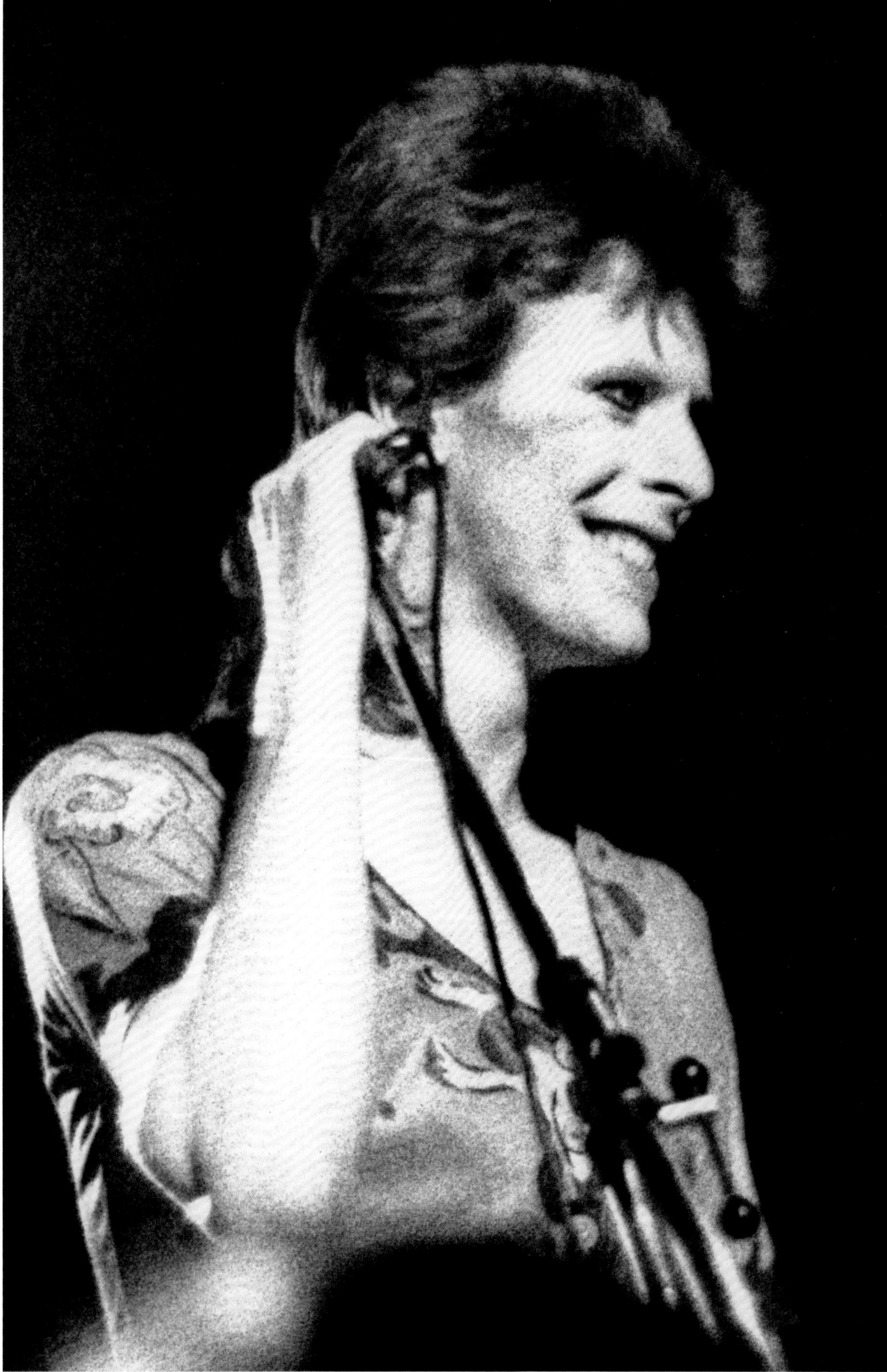

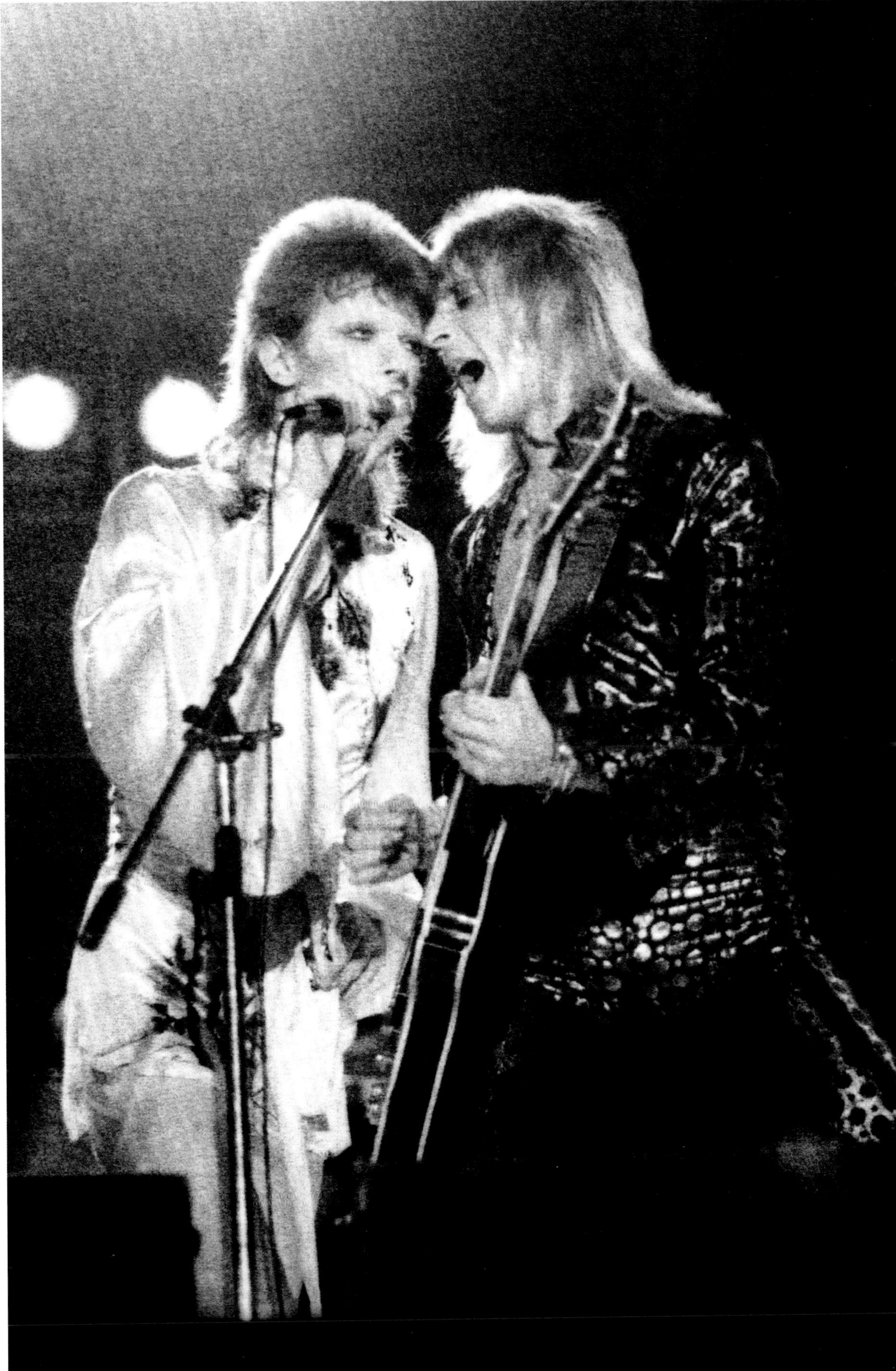

4 NOVEMBER 1975

SOUL TRAIN

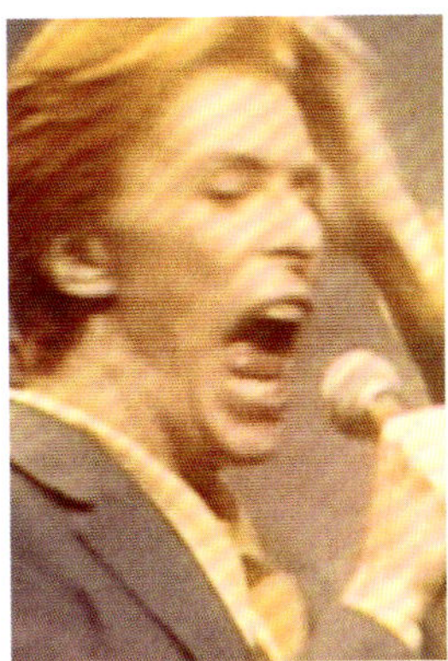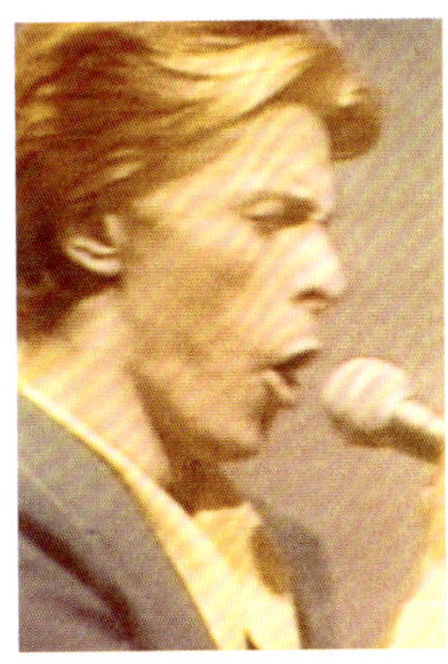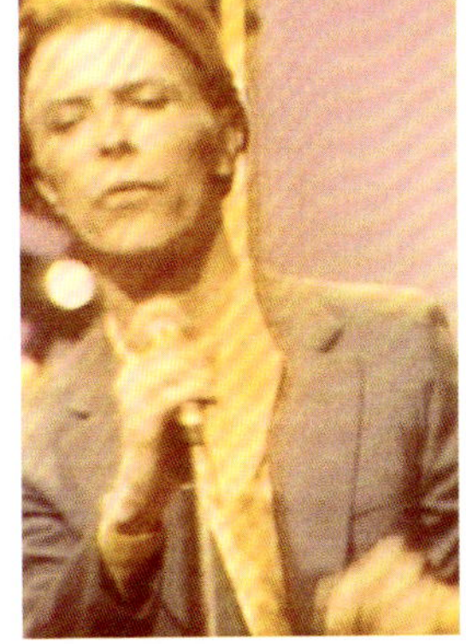

These three images were taken from the TV one evening in November 1975. Bowie had disappeared for years to play in America, so when it was announced that British TV was going to air a clip of him performing on a Black music programme called *Soul Train*, I decided I wanted to capture some up-to-date pictures. In 1975 there was no ability to pause TV, or to record and rewatch it, so taking these photographs was like being at a live concert. And because it had been so long since I had seen him, there was the same level of excitement and anticipation too.

I set my camera up on a tripod in my parents' living room in front of the TV and only had one chance to get the images. At college we had covered how to photograph footage from the TV and the particular challenges it posed. These images were just for me and my moodboard at college, so I used a standard colour film and then rushed it to Dixon's to get it processed quickly. You can see the images are slightly too yellowy orange. This is partly to do with the processing technique and the machine used, but it is partly to do with time as well. Over the years the colour has shifted and drained, exactly like it does in old family photographs. Bowie's yellow shirt seems almost the same colour as the front of his hair.

The memory of what he performed had long gone, though while I was working on this book I managed to find this actual performance on YouTube. Bowie sang "Golden Years" and "Fame" and gave an awkwardly shy interview answering questions from the audience. "Is it true you are going to be teaming up with Elizabeth Taylor to do a film?" "No," answered Bowie. He was the second white artist to appear on *Soul Train* (Elton John had appeared a few months earlier) and he answered a question about his love of soul music, describing how he had discovered it as a teenager on street corners ("We have street corners in London" – laughs awkwardly) and "James Brown was very popular in the French clubs."

These photographs are a particularly treasured part of my personal archive. They ignite memories of the sheer excitement of seeing your favourite singer on TV, and they form a social document of the few ways in which we were able to access performances in America during the 1970s. I also liked the double challenge of not only having to pierce the camera lens but the TV screen too, to make Bowie ever-present, as if he were there, standing in front of me, singing.

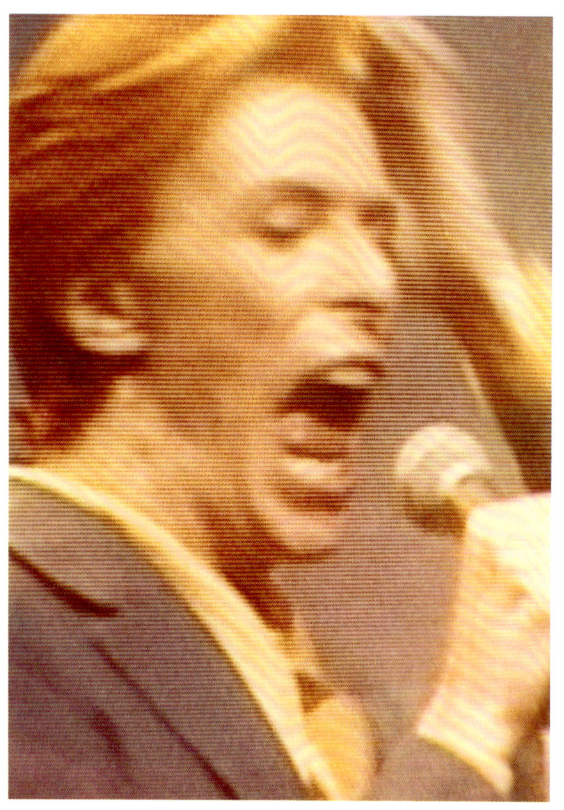
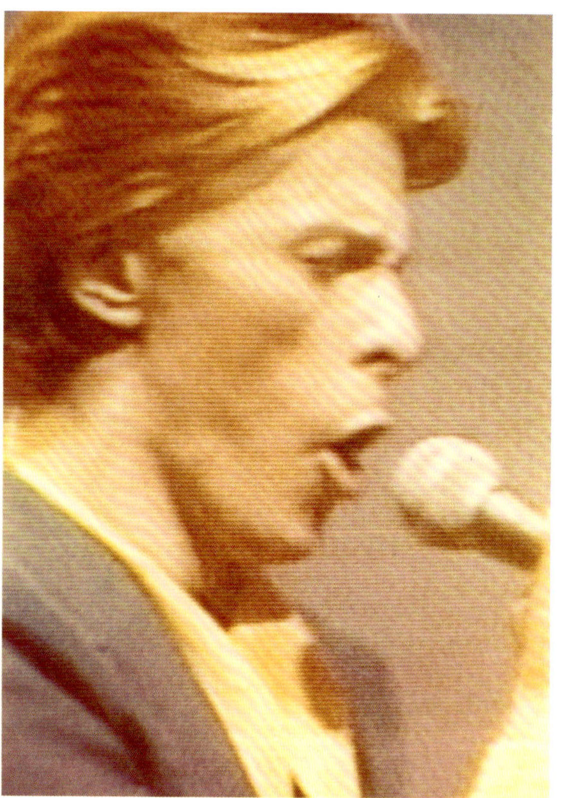

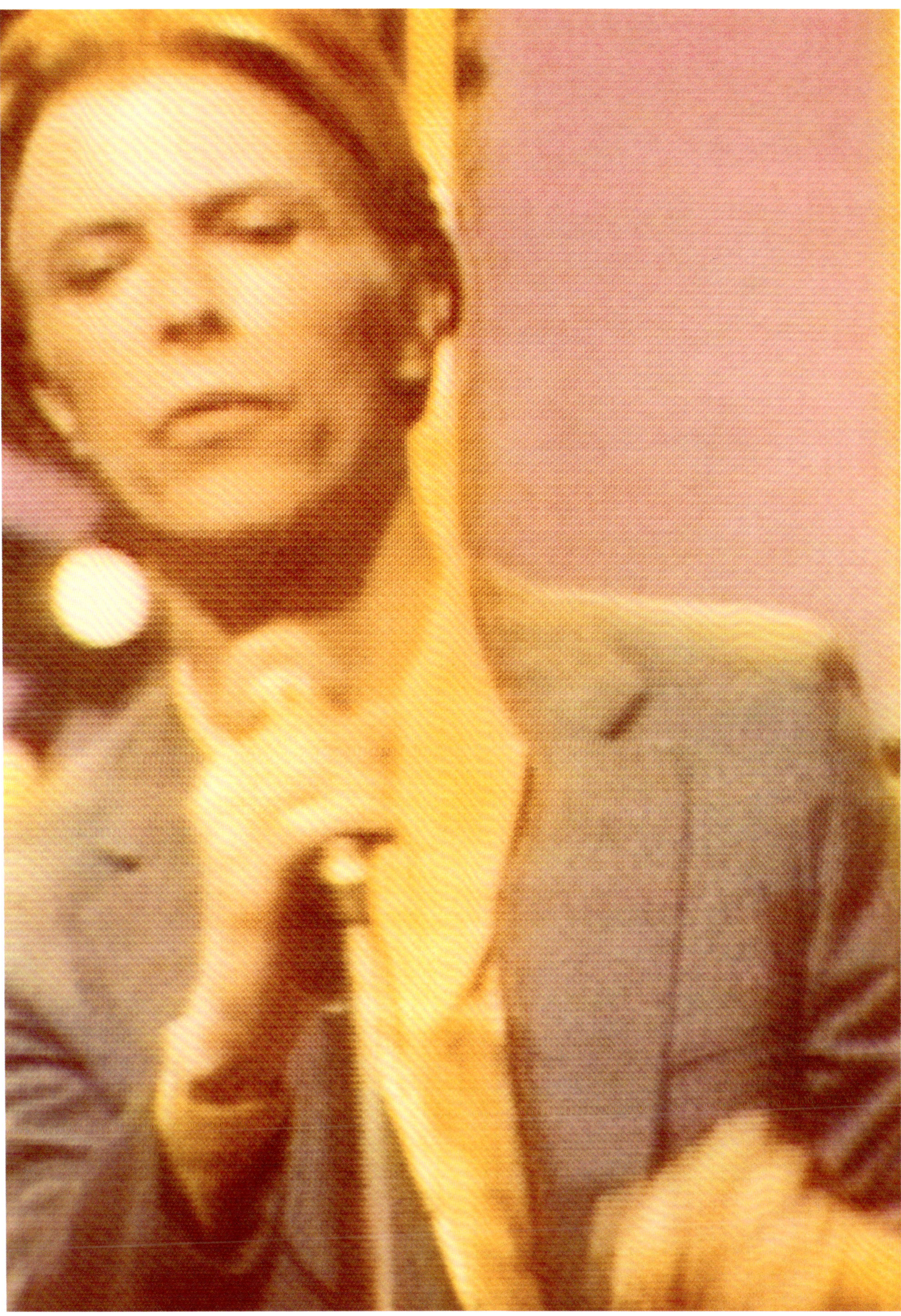

8 MAY 1976
EMPIRE POOL, WEMBLEY,
LONDON

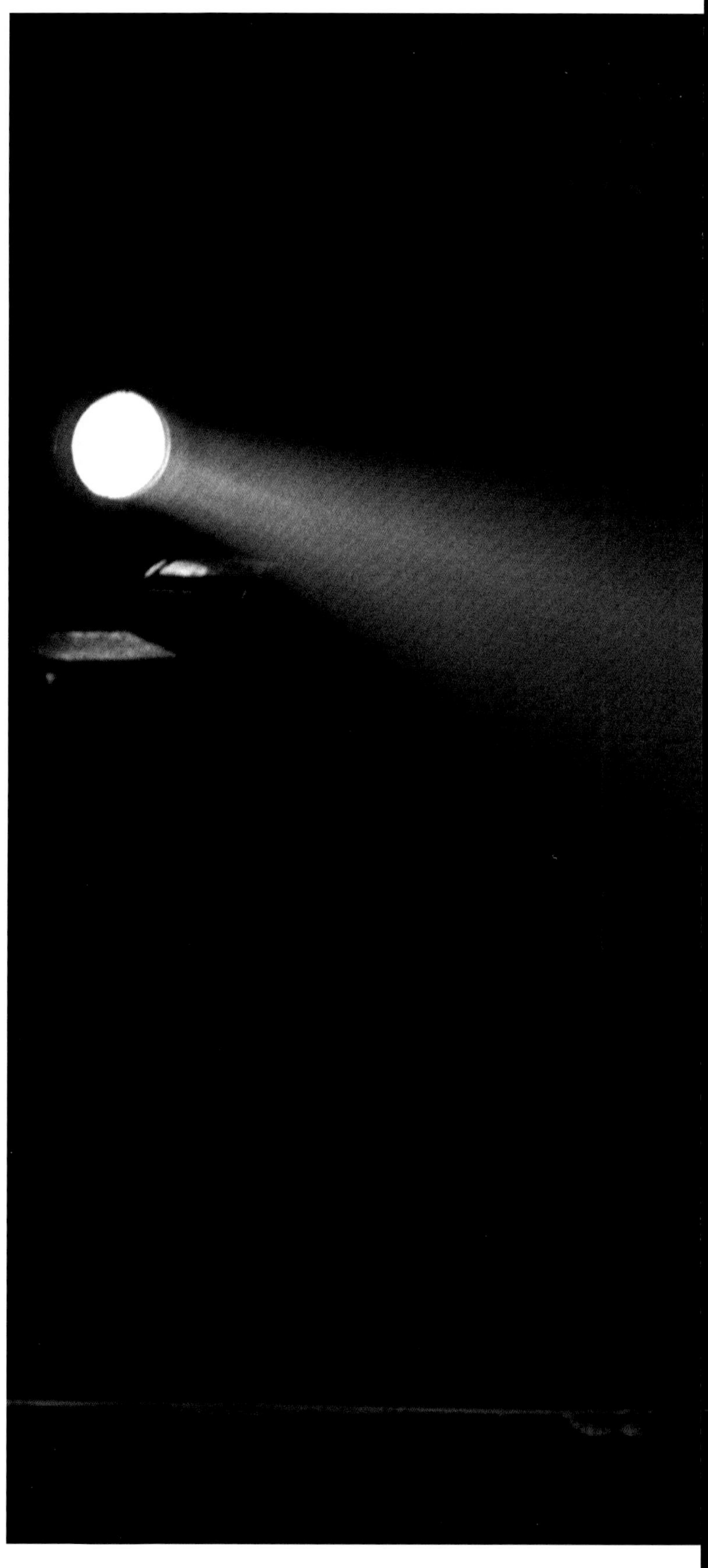

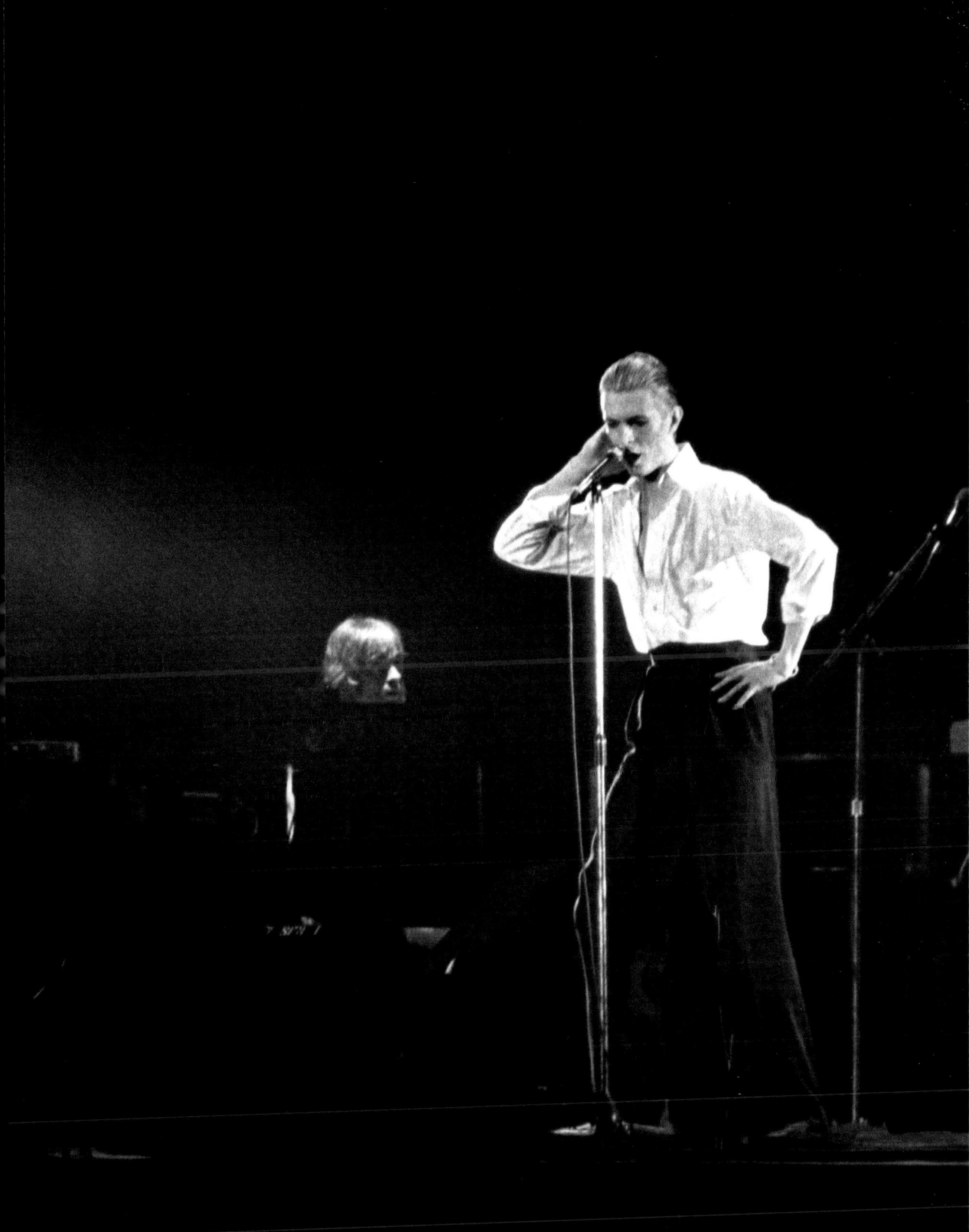

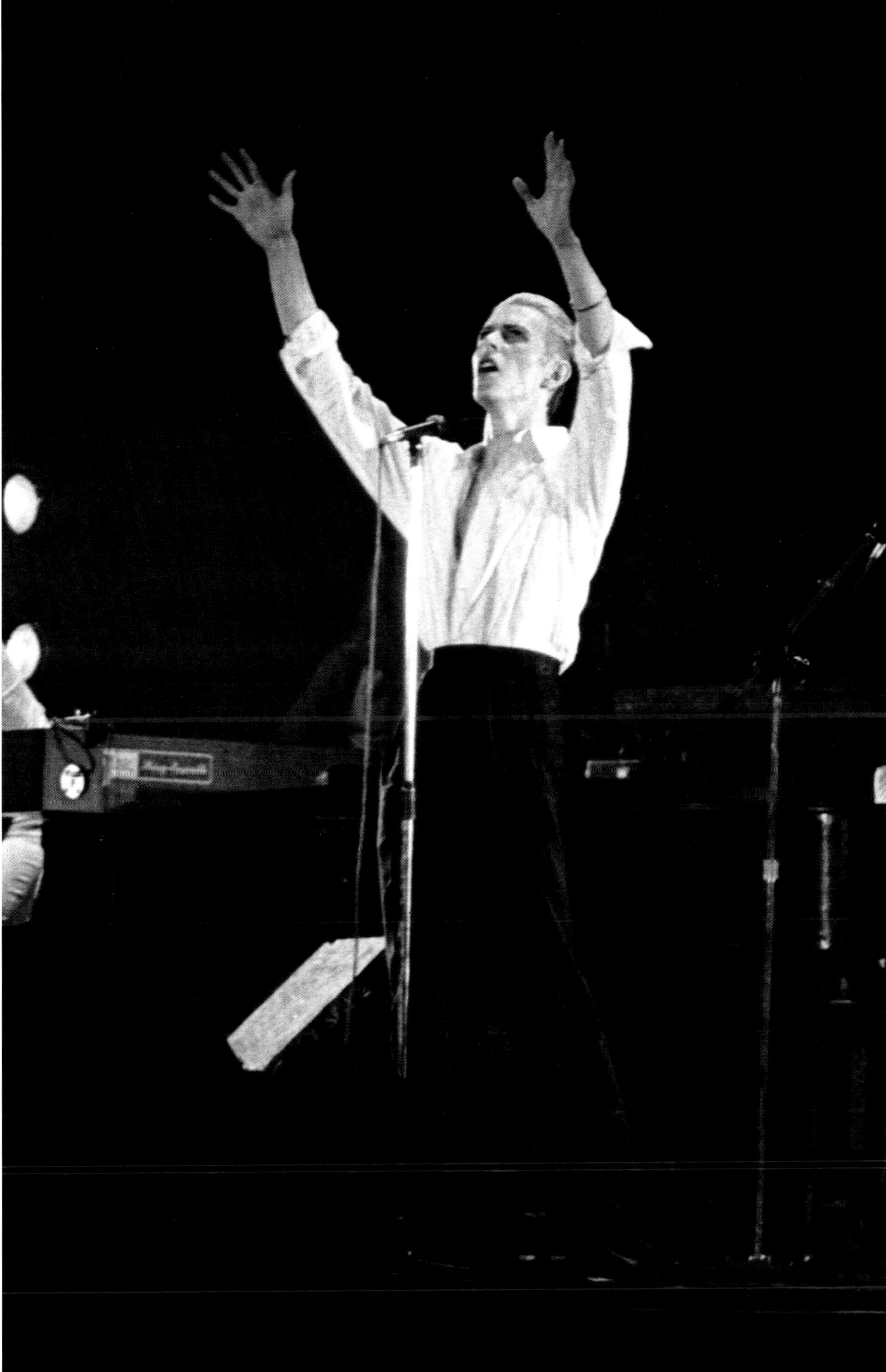

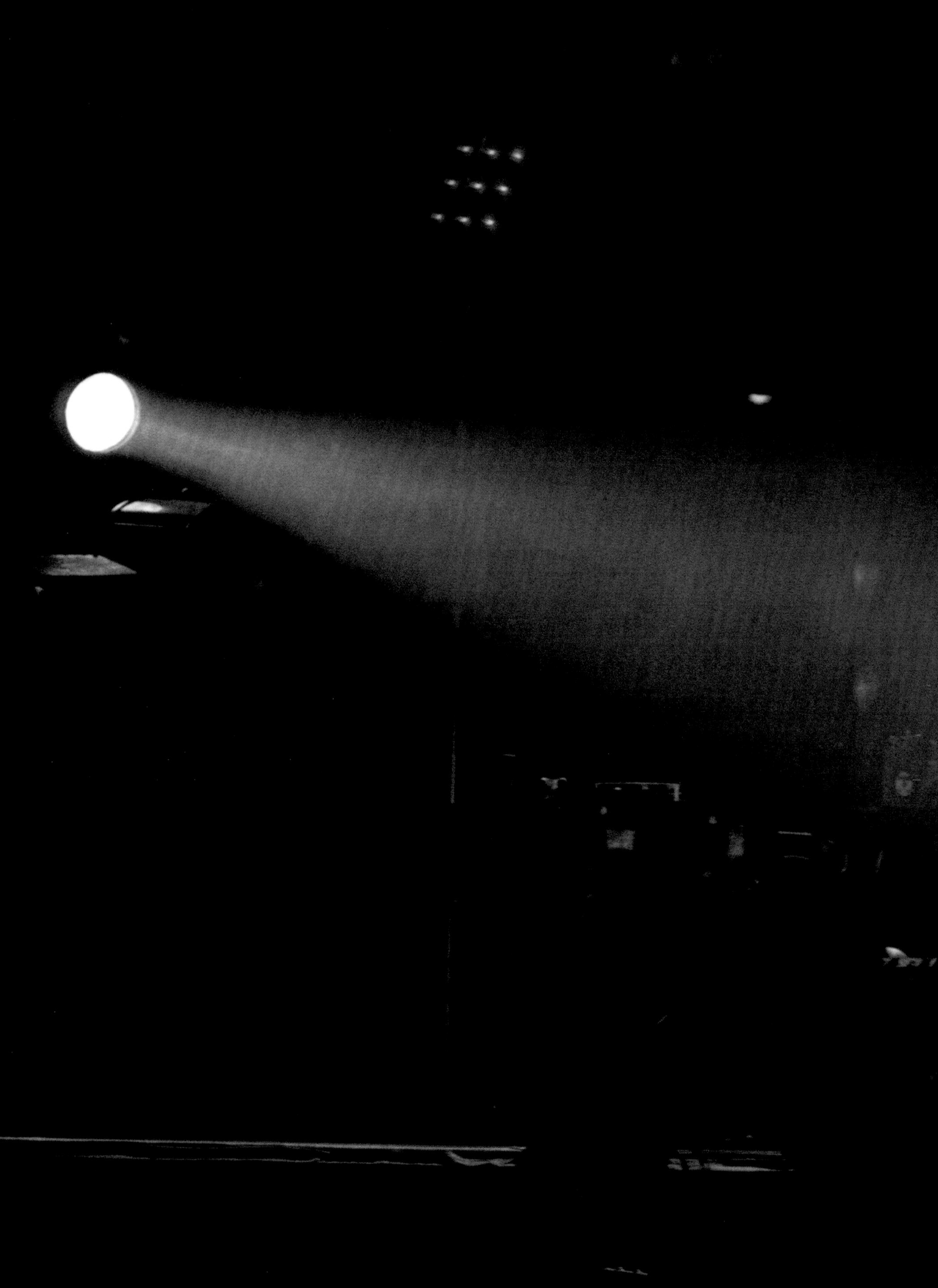

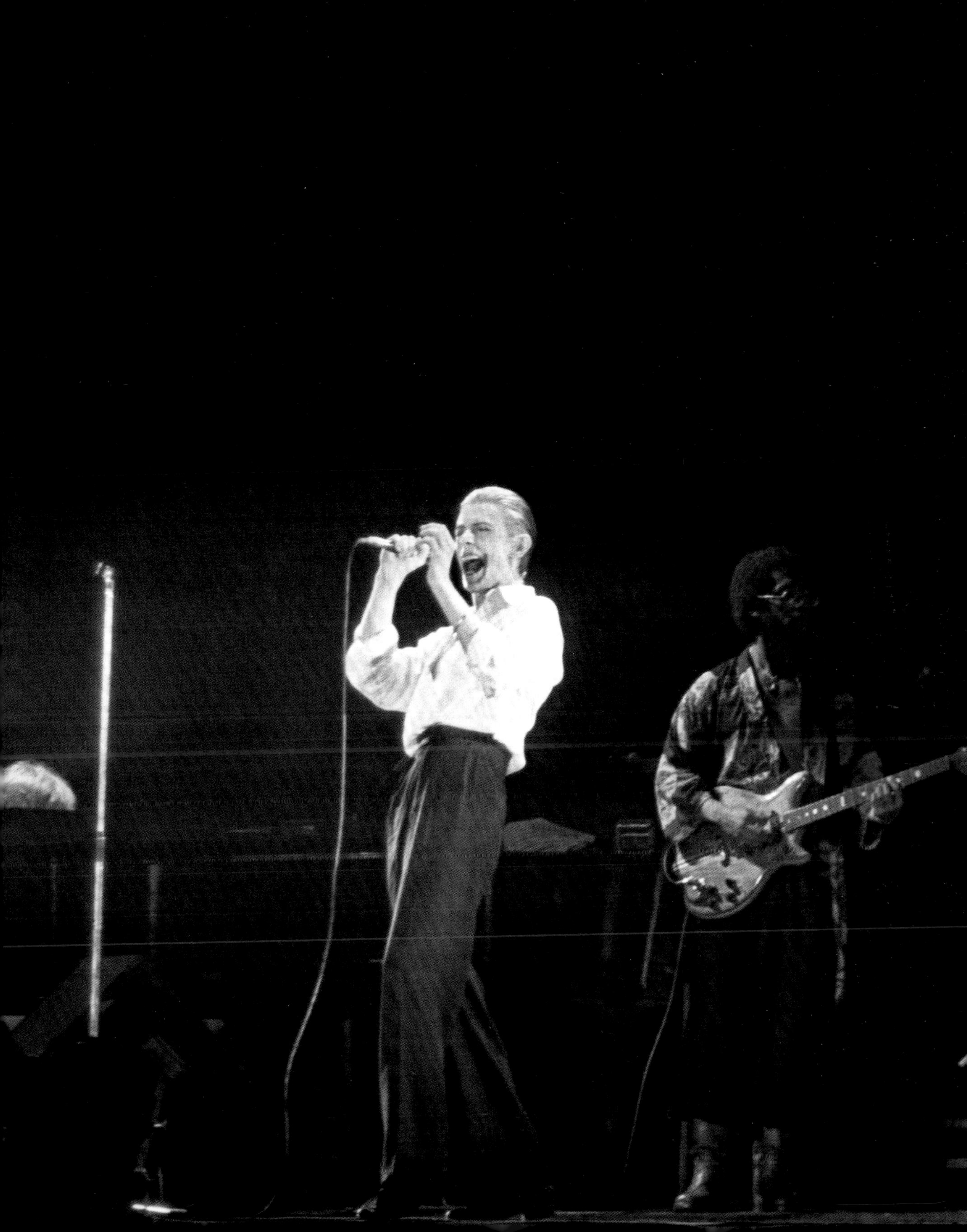

3 MARCH 1977

BOWIE ON KEYBOARDS FOR IGGY POP, APOLLO THEATRE, MANCHESTER

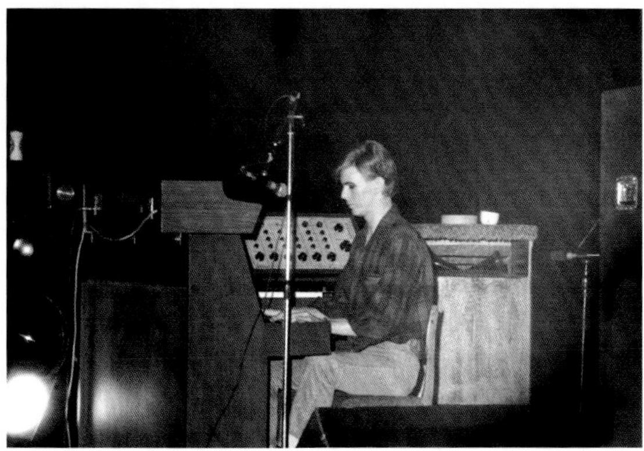

In March 1977 Bowie had not played in Manchester for almost four years. He had recently produced Iggy Pop's new album, *The Idiot*, and there was a rumour that he would be playing on keyboards when Iggy toured. Nobody really believed this. After 1973 when Bowie's fame simply went colossal, it was hard to imagine him playing in the shadows. This moment became the stuff of music myth. Much like the Sex Pistols at the Lesser Free Trade Hall in the previous year, Bowie on keyboards for Iggy was one of those will-he-won't-he, did-he-didn't-he moments. Of course, he did, and we know this because I was there and photographed it, though I could hardly believe it myself. But Bowie was there, at the back with no light on him at all. And as if to make himself even more invisible than he already was, he was sitting down behind the keyboards and wearing a dark,

checked shirt. I always hated using a flash to take photographs, but I had no choice; Bowie was so in the dark that I had to rely on a flashgun to light the shot myself. This image perfectly captures how inconspicuous he was. Centre-placed in the frame, he is engulfed by stage equipment and a microphone. A lone can of Heineken lager sits to the far left of the frame.

I think, for music in Manchester, this moment was as, if not more, important than the Sex Pistols at the Lesser Free Trade Hall. Punk in Manchester had a completely different lineage to punk in London. Most of the punk in Manchester came out of glam – Bowie, Iggy and Roxy Music. Once Bowie had appeared with Iggy, it really appeared to galvanize musicians in Manchester, and it was at this point that so many bands formed and everything really took off.

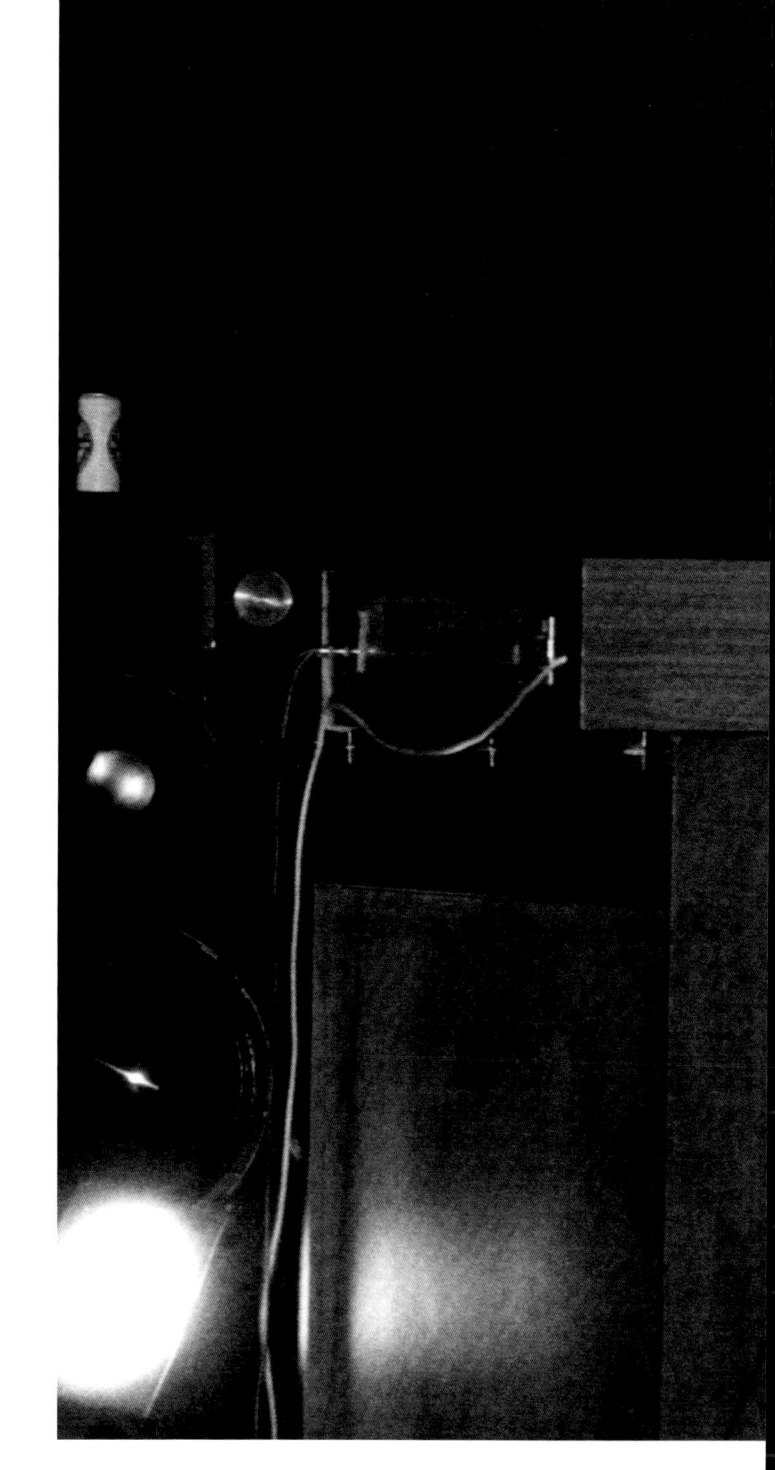

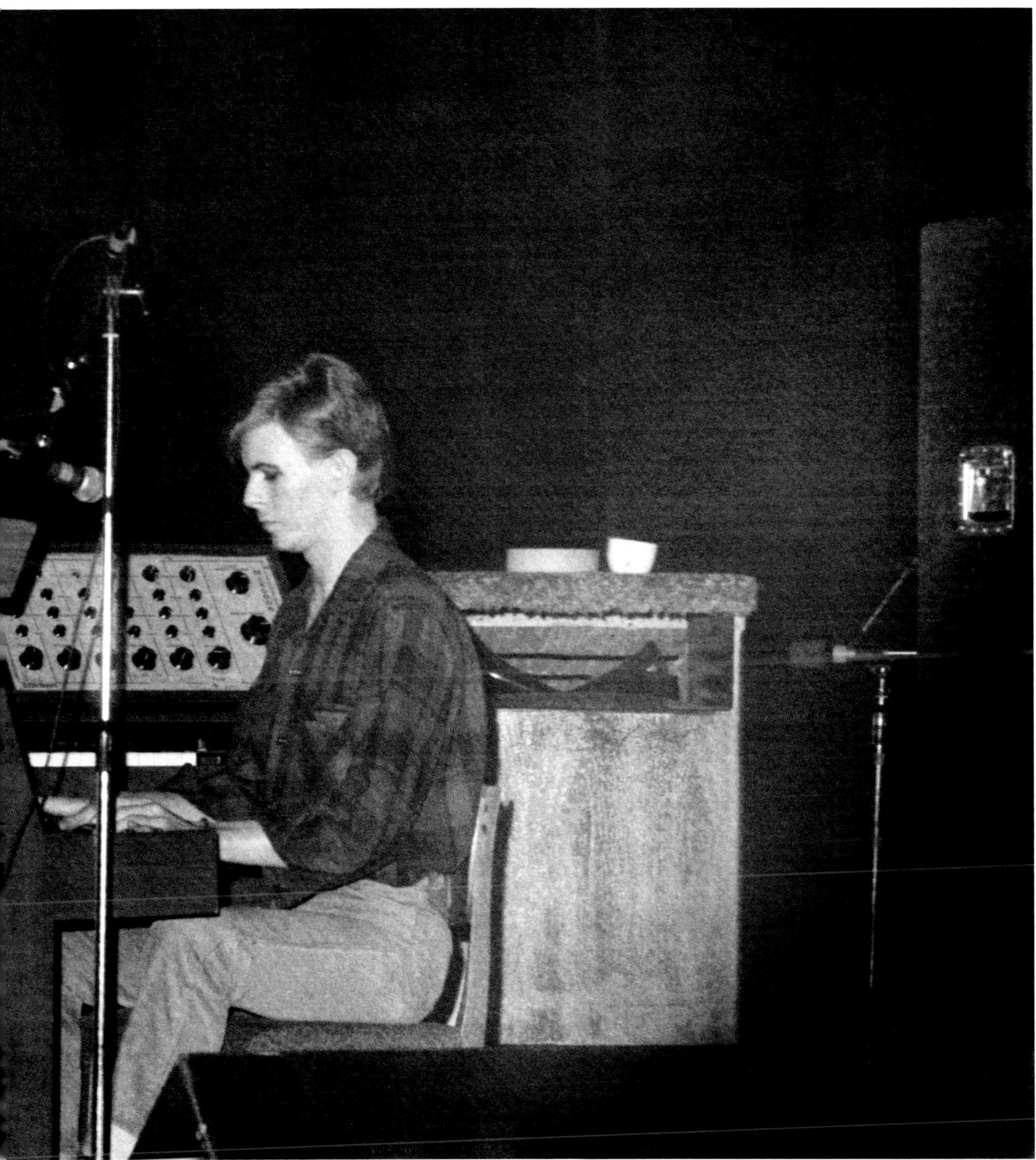

15 JUNE 1978
CITY HALL, NEWCASTLE

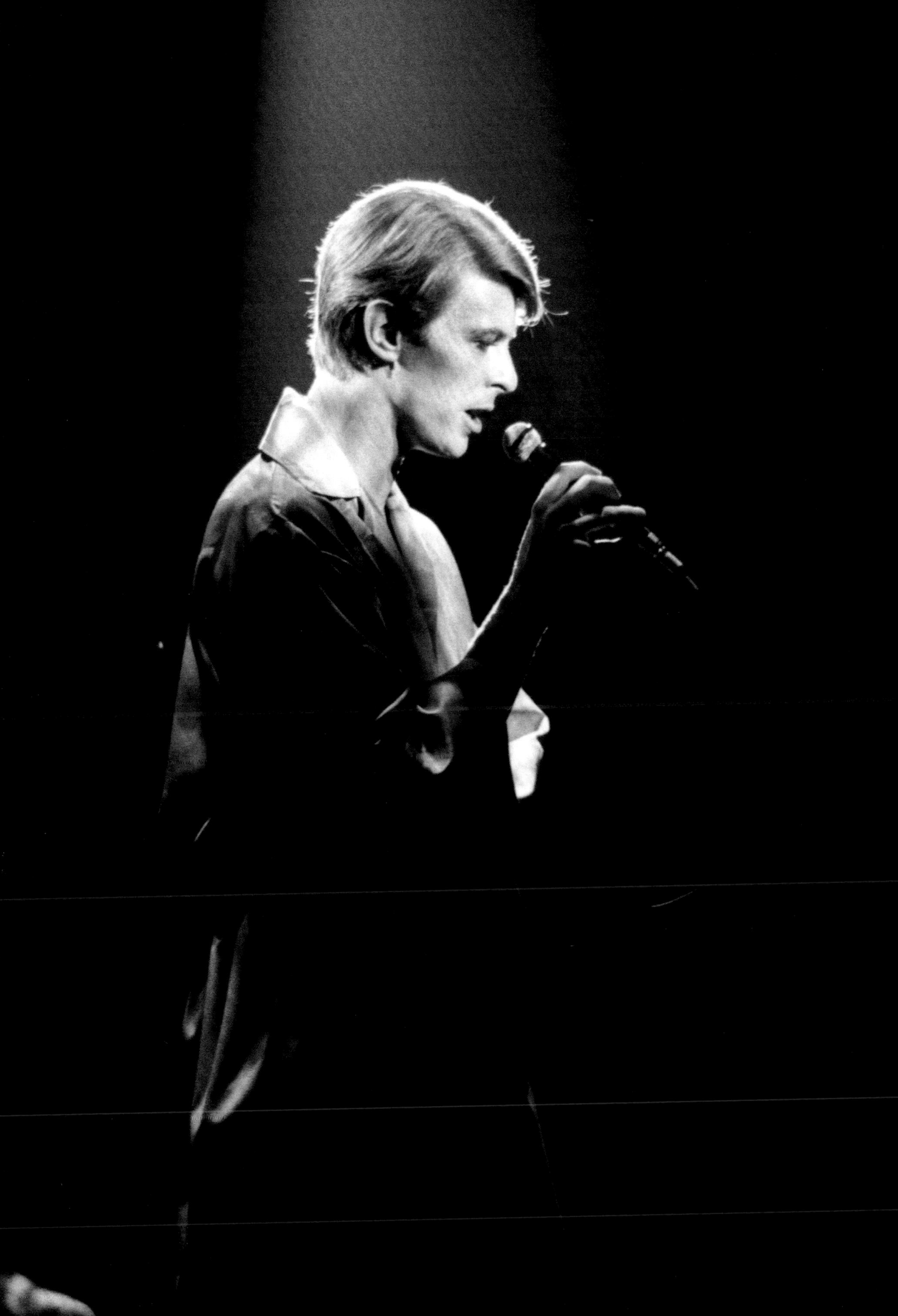

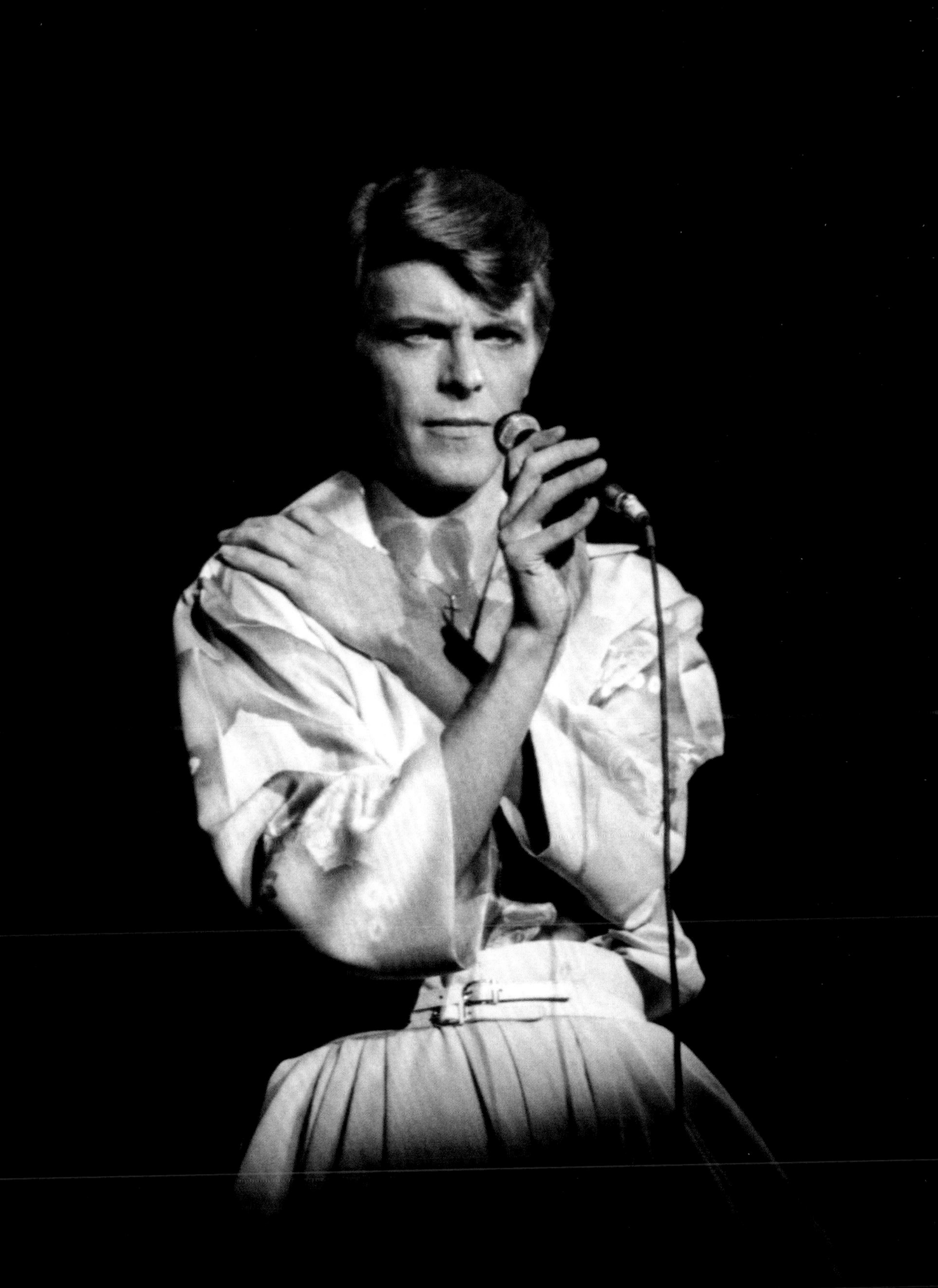

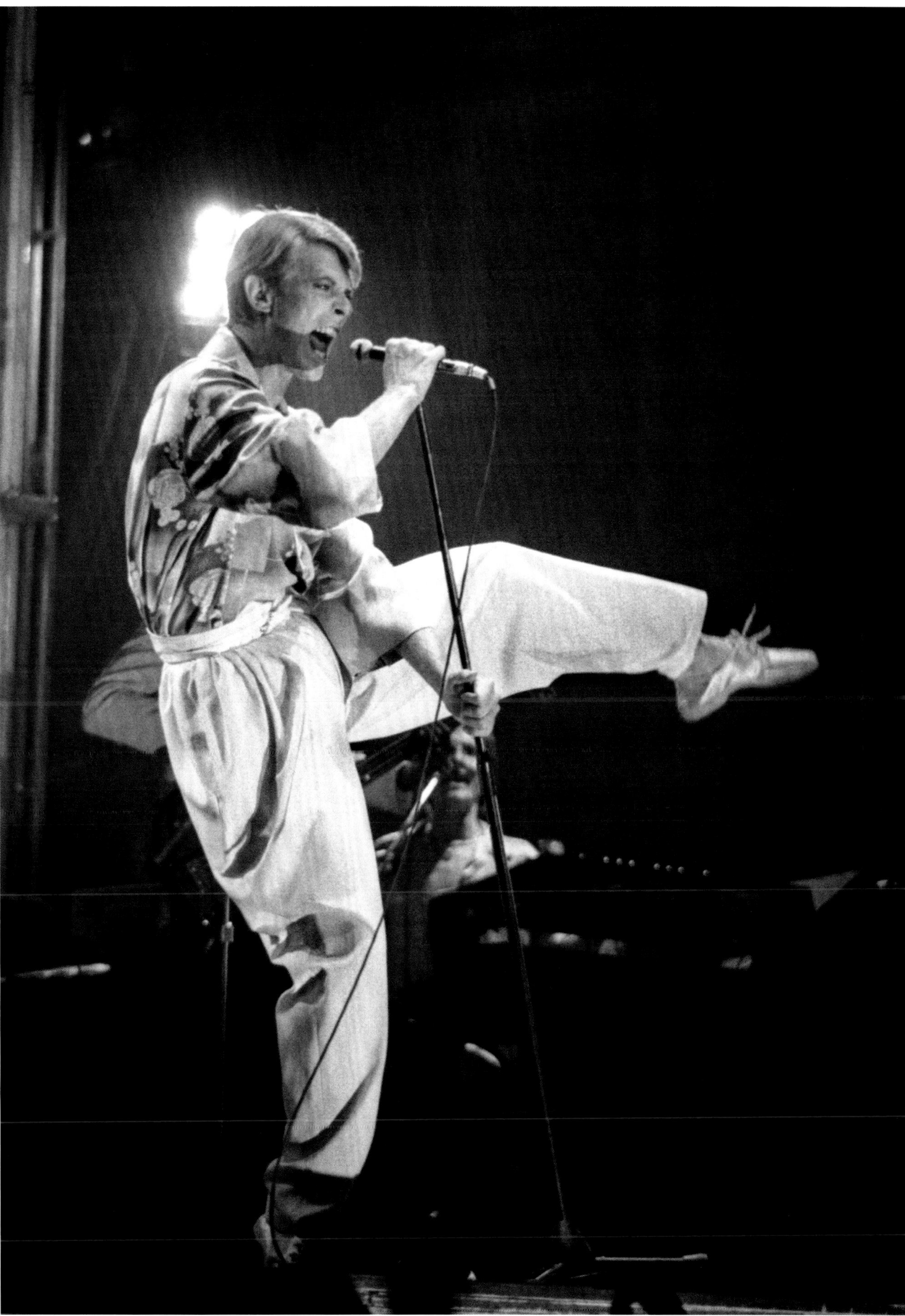

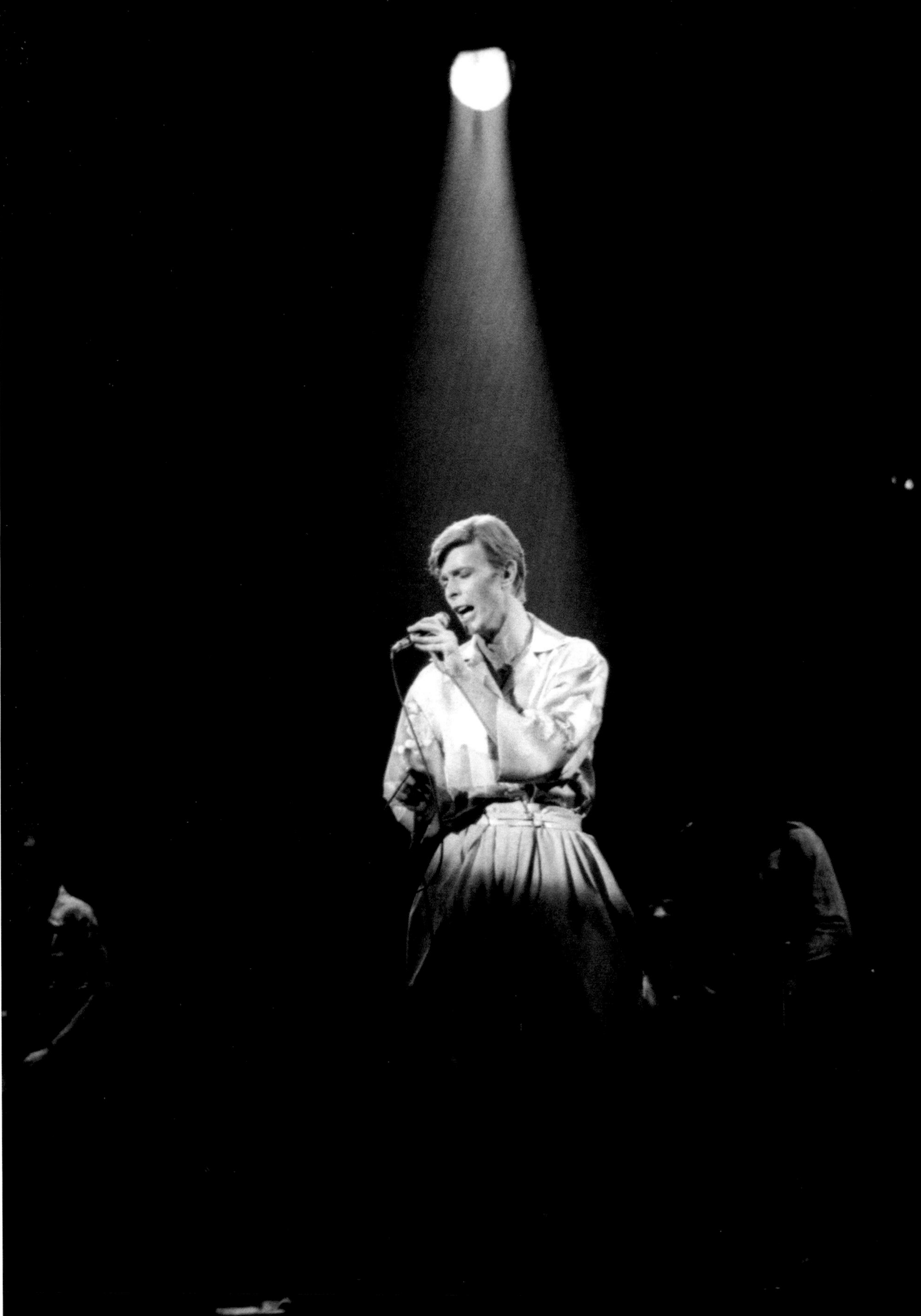

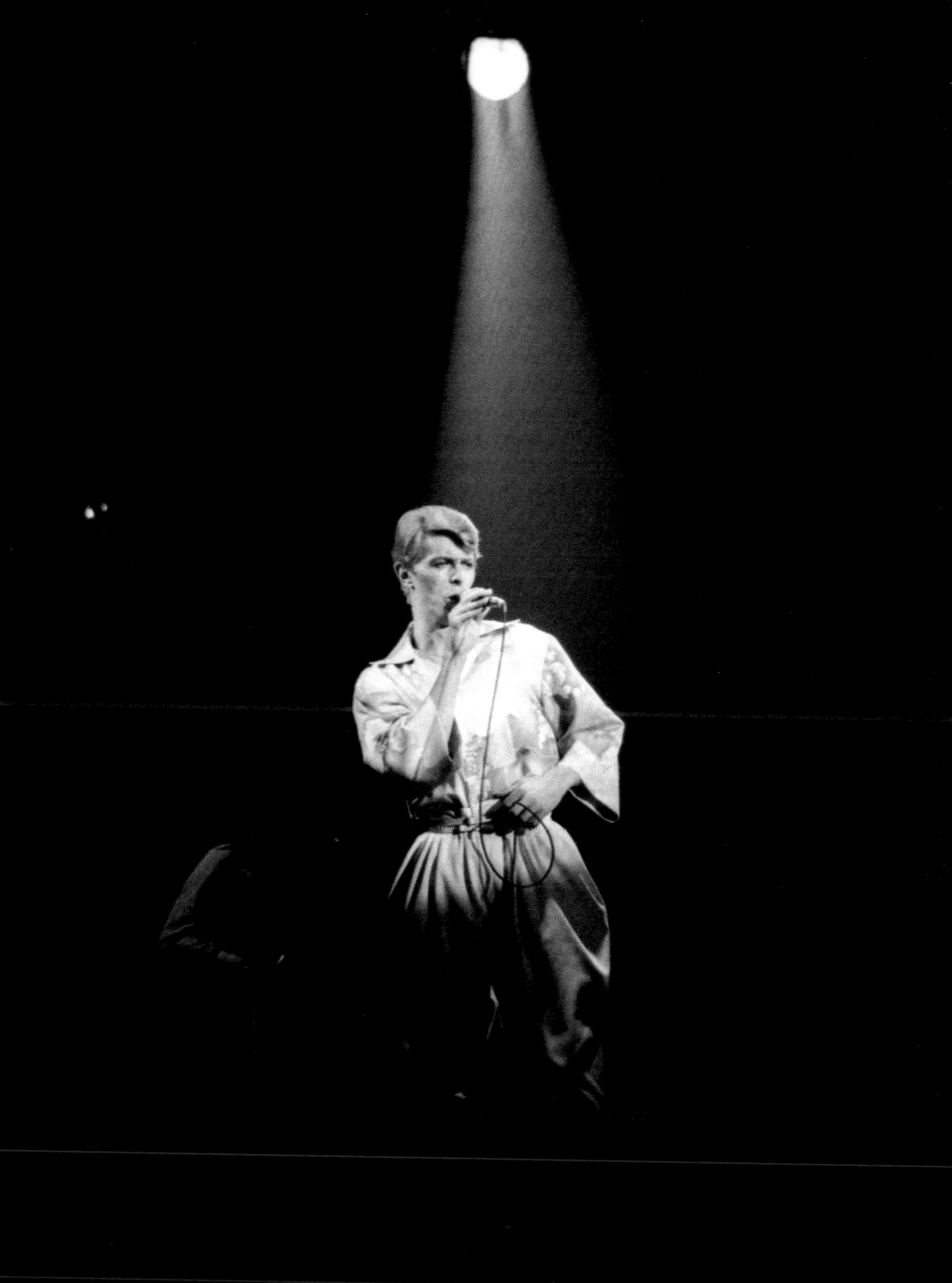

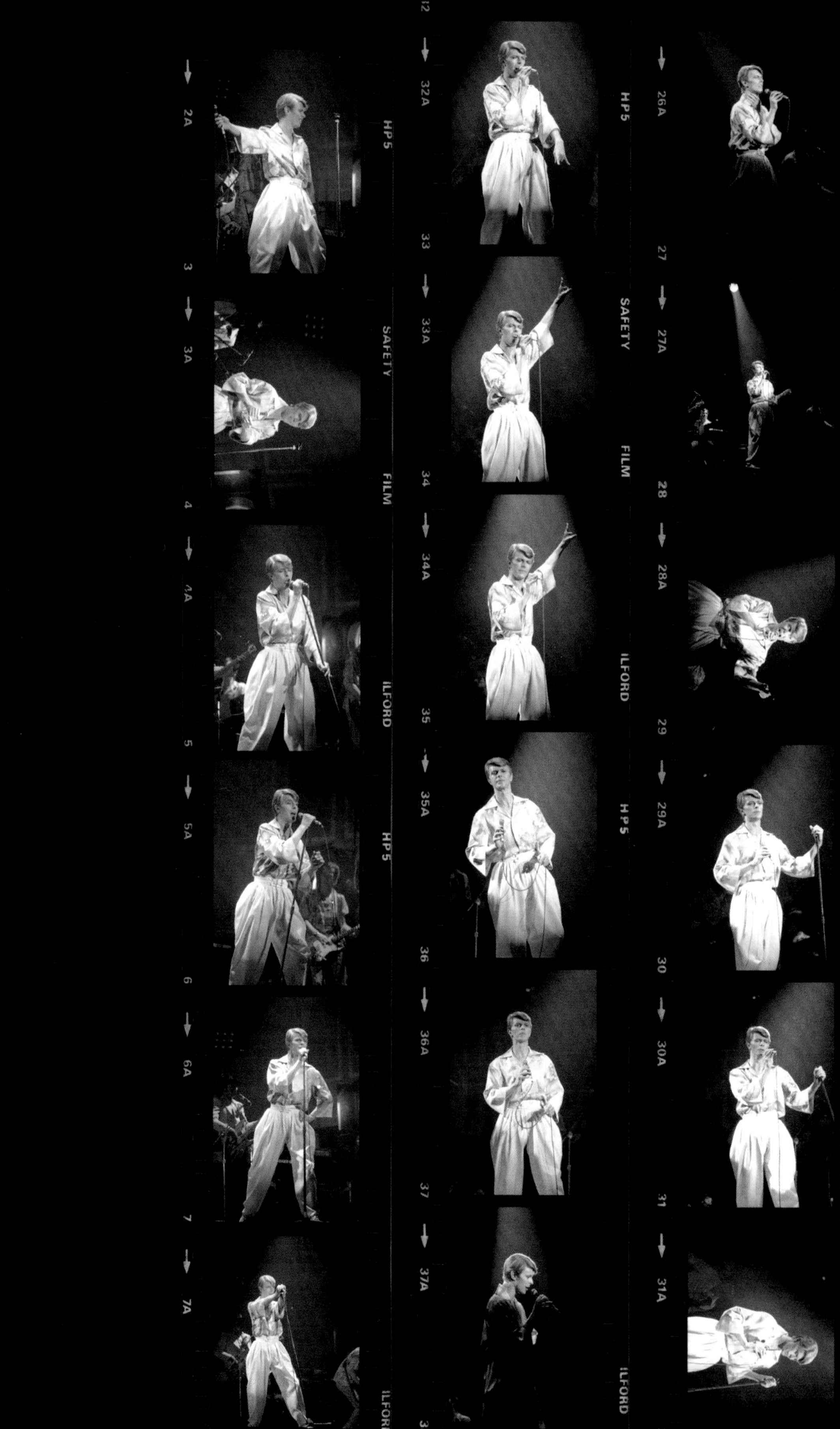

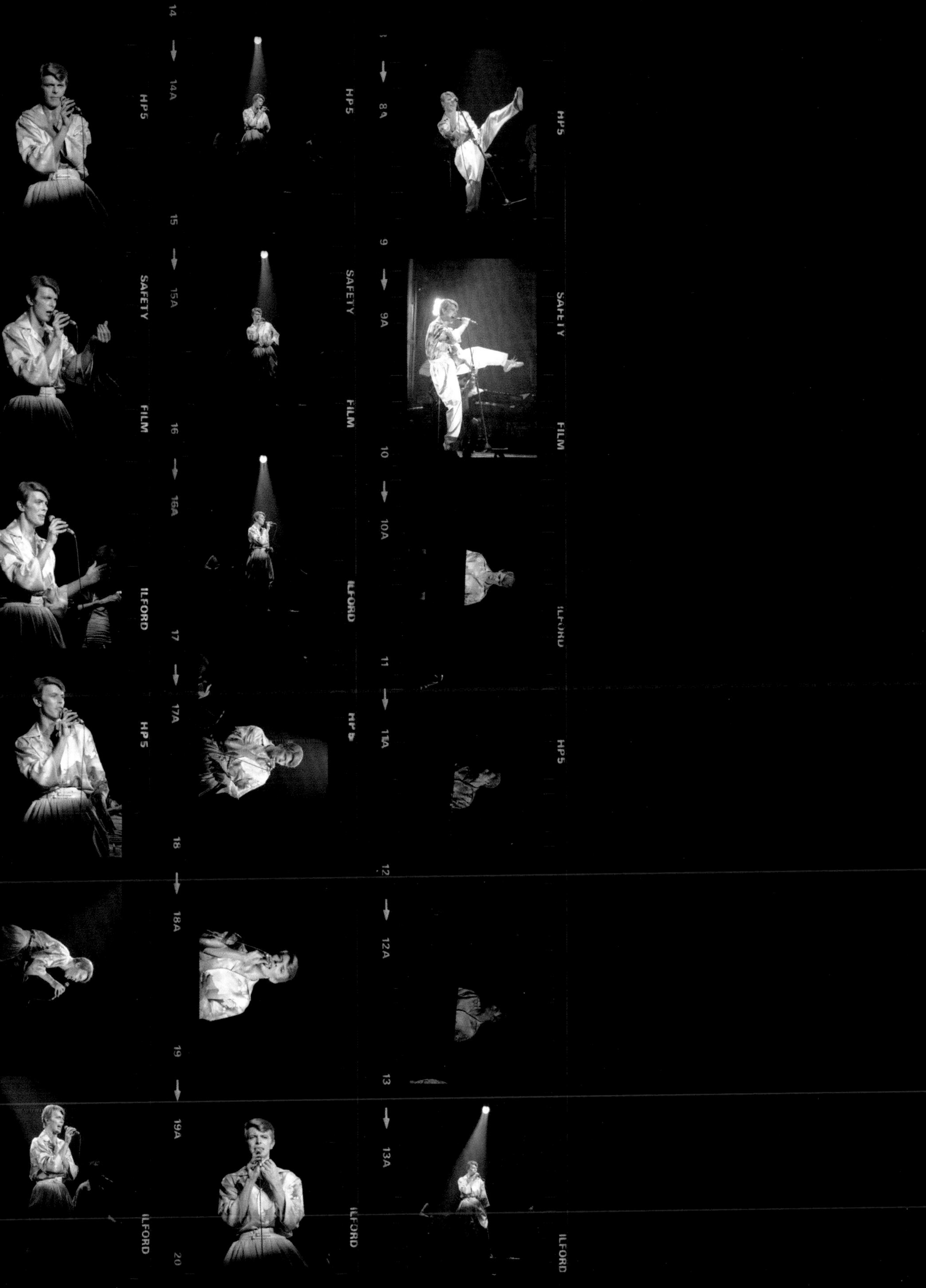

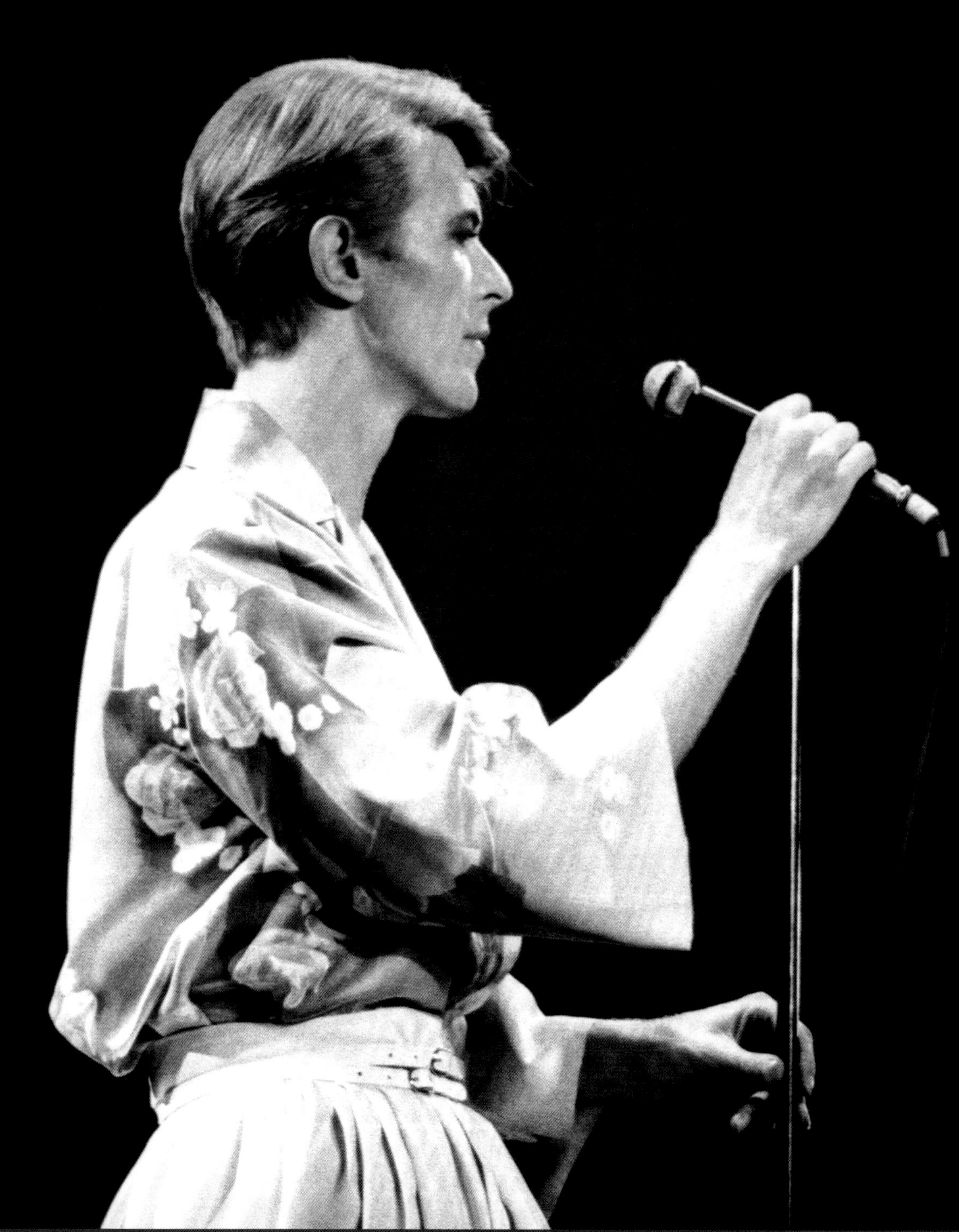

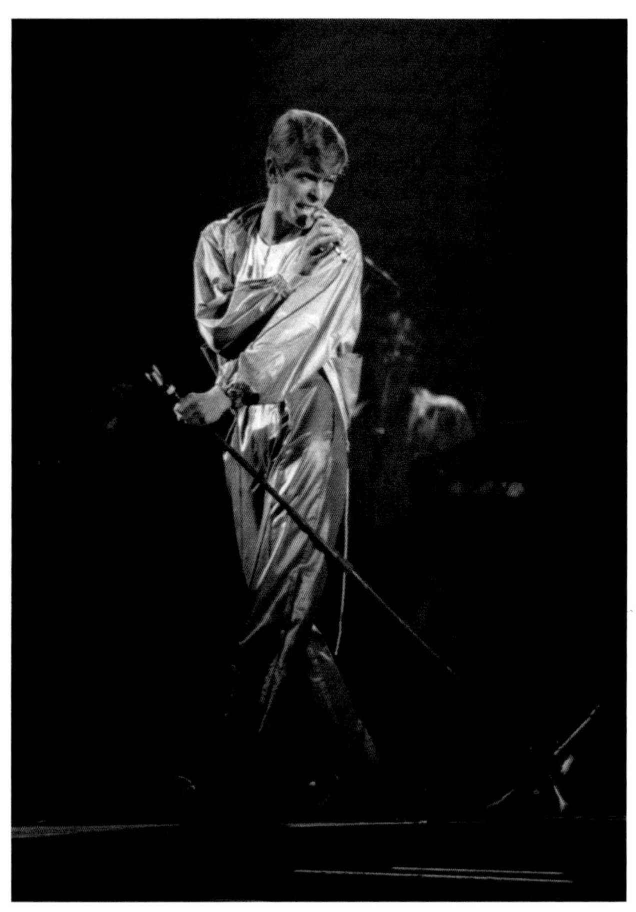 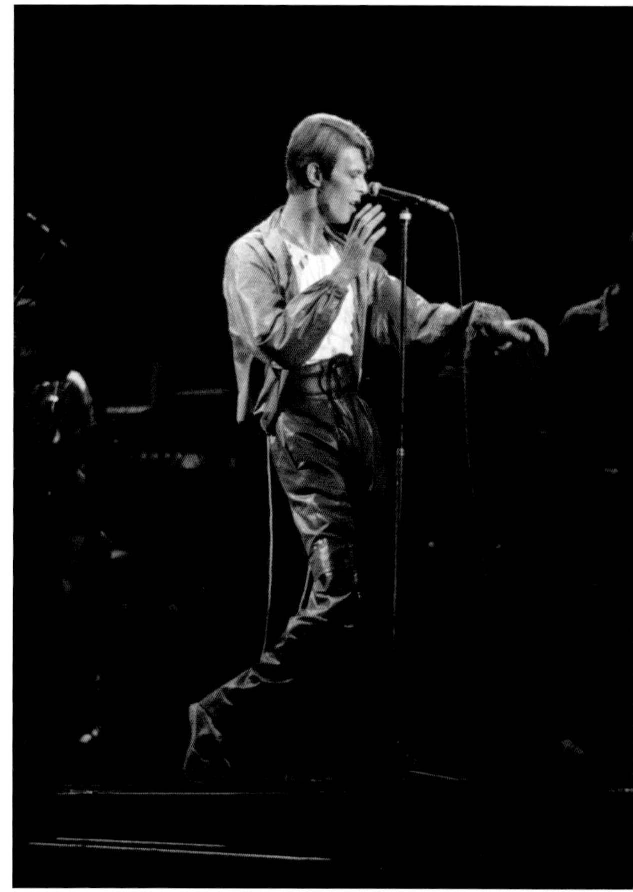

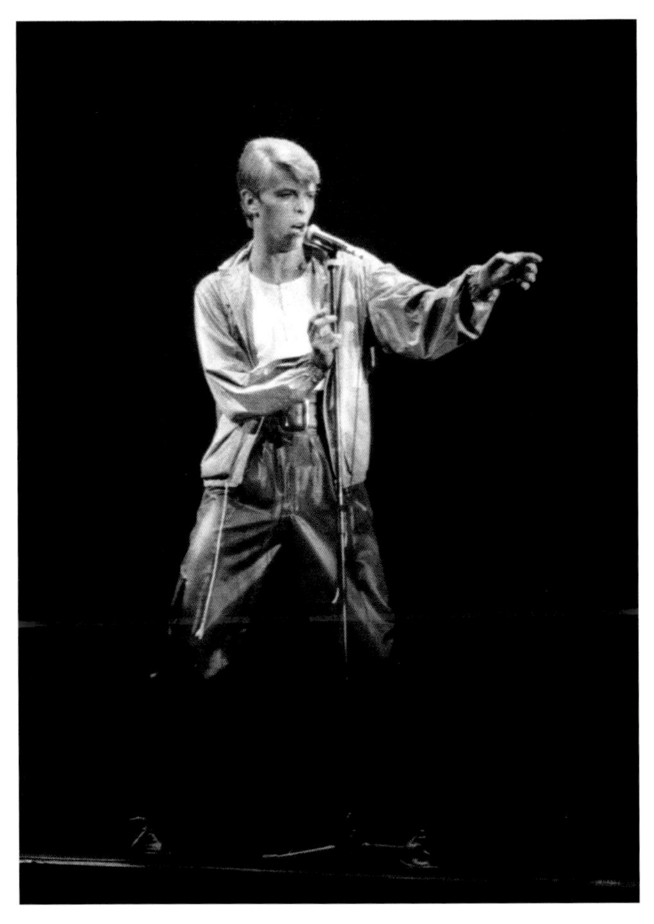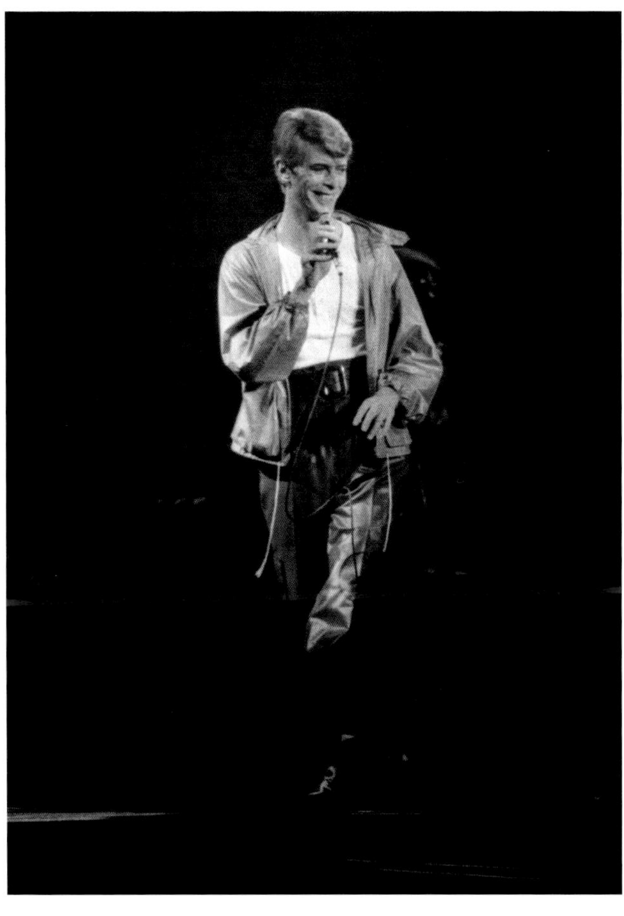

24 JUNE 1978
BINGLEY HALL, STAFFORD

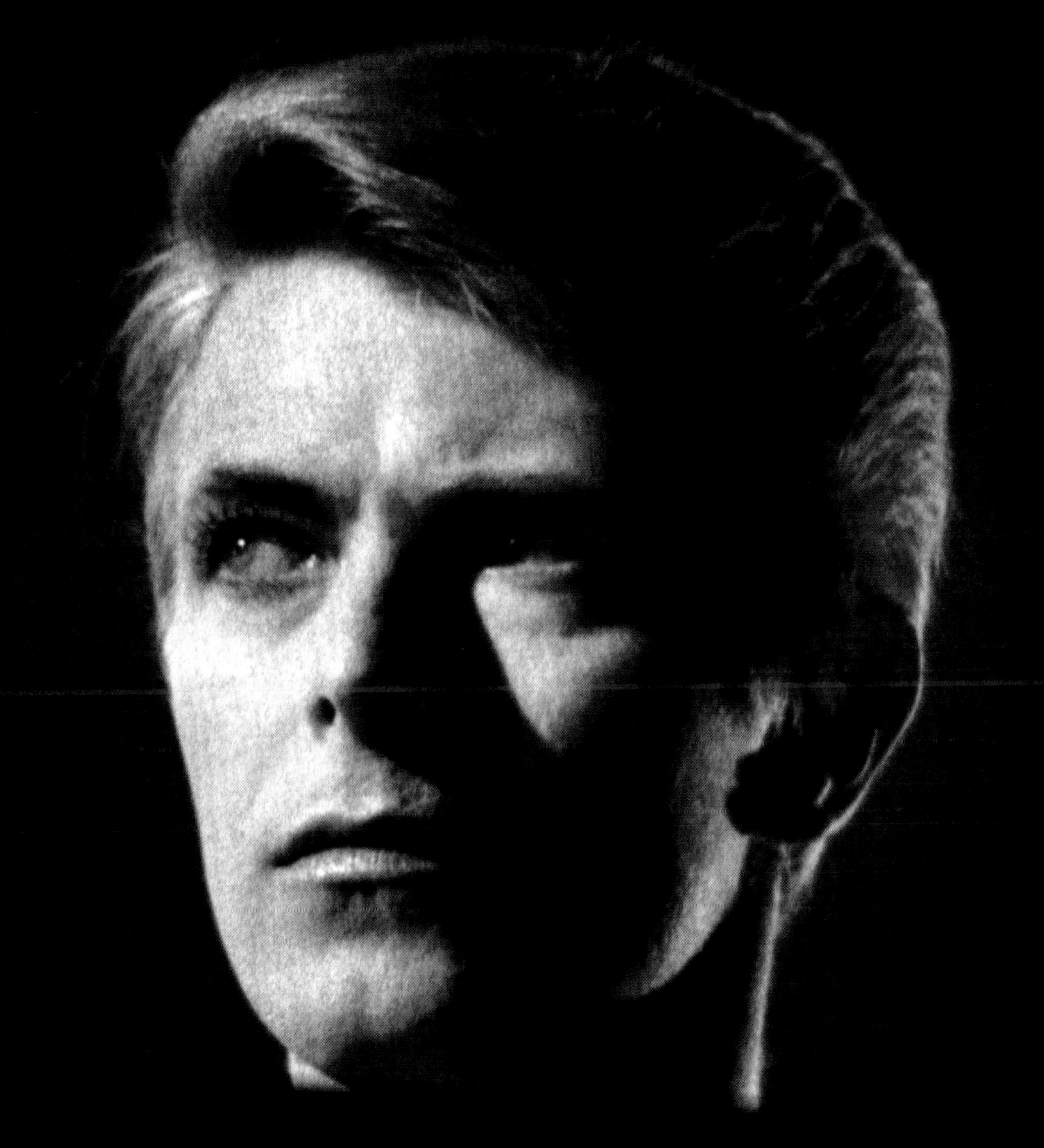

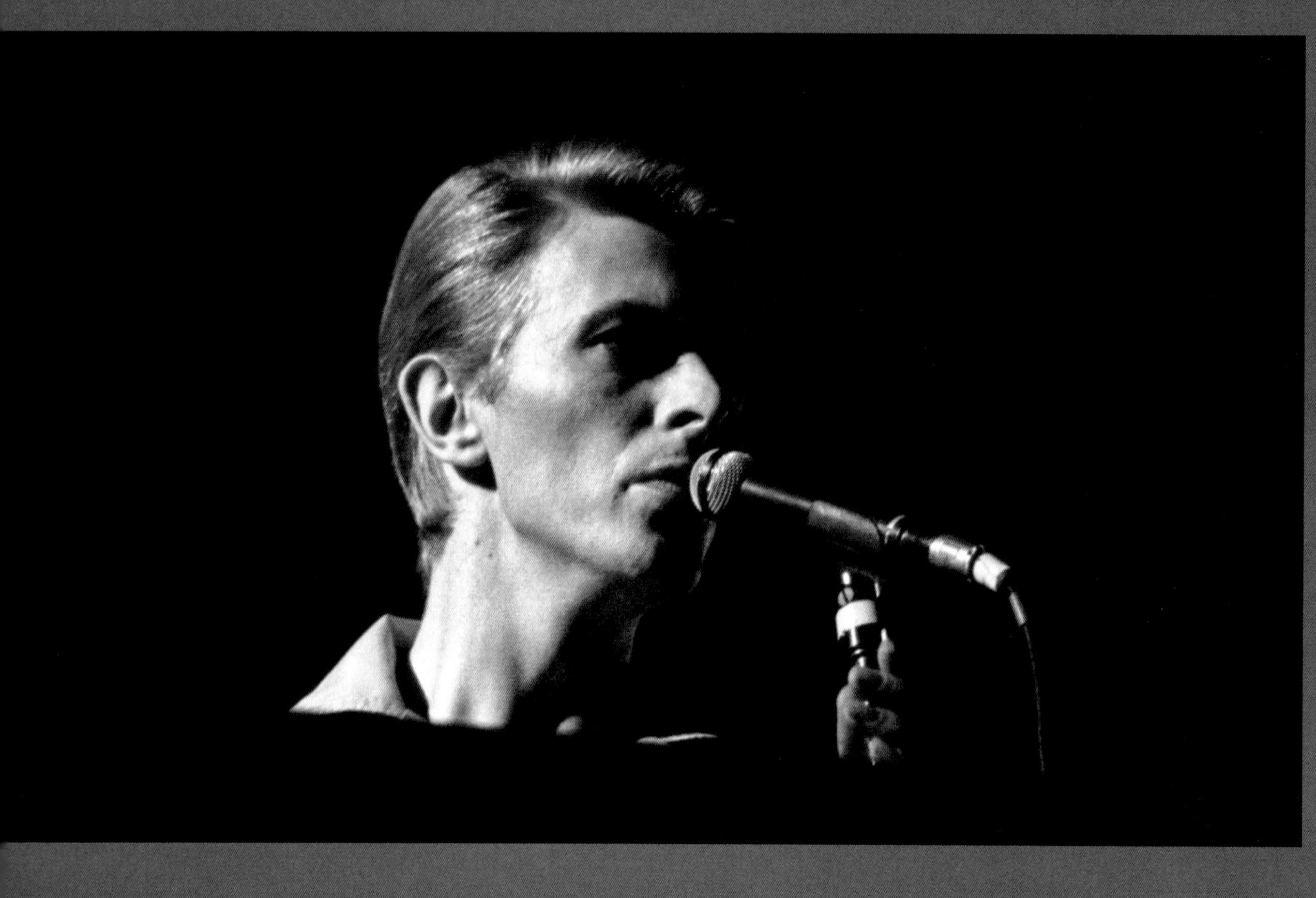

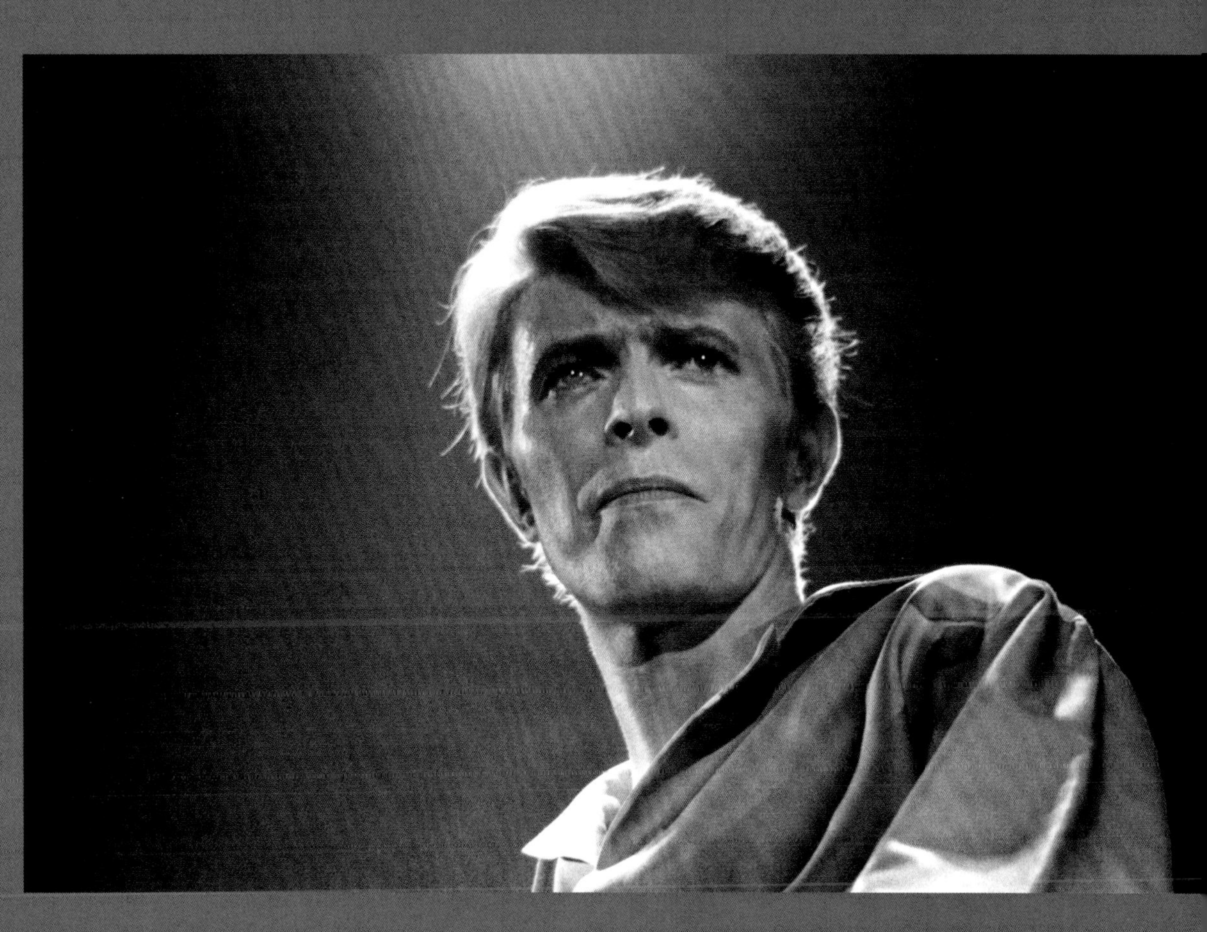

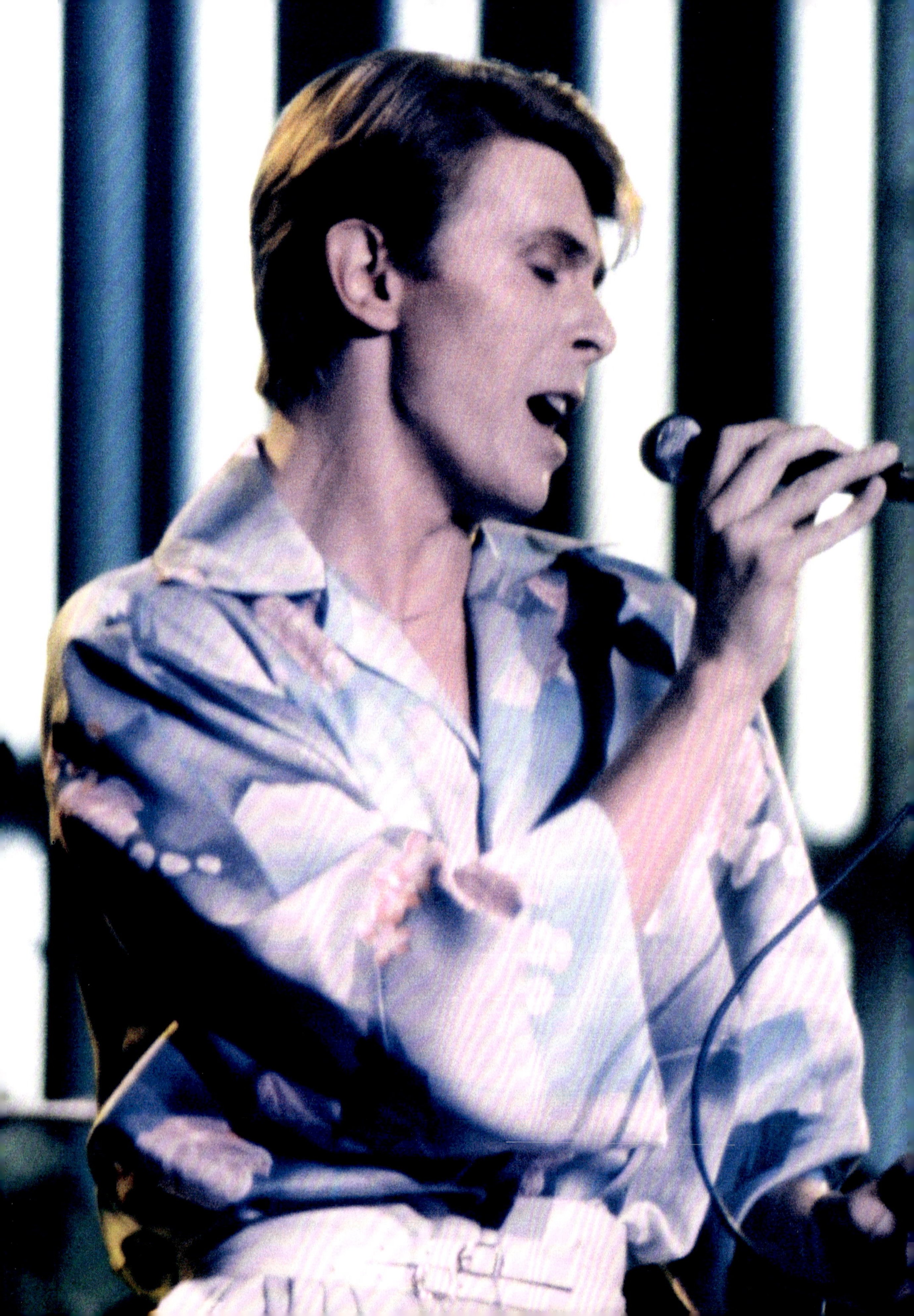

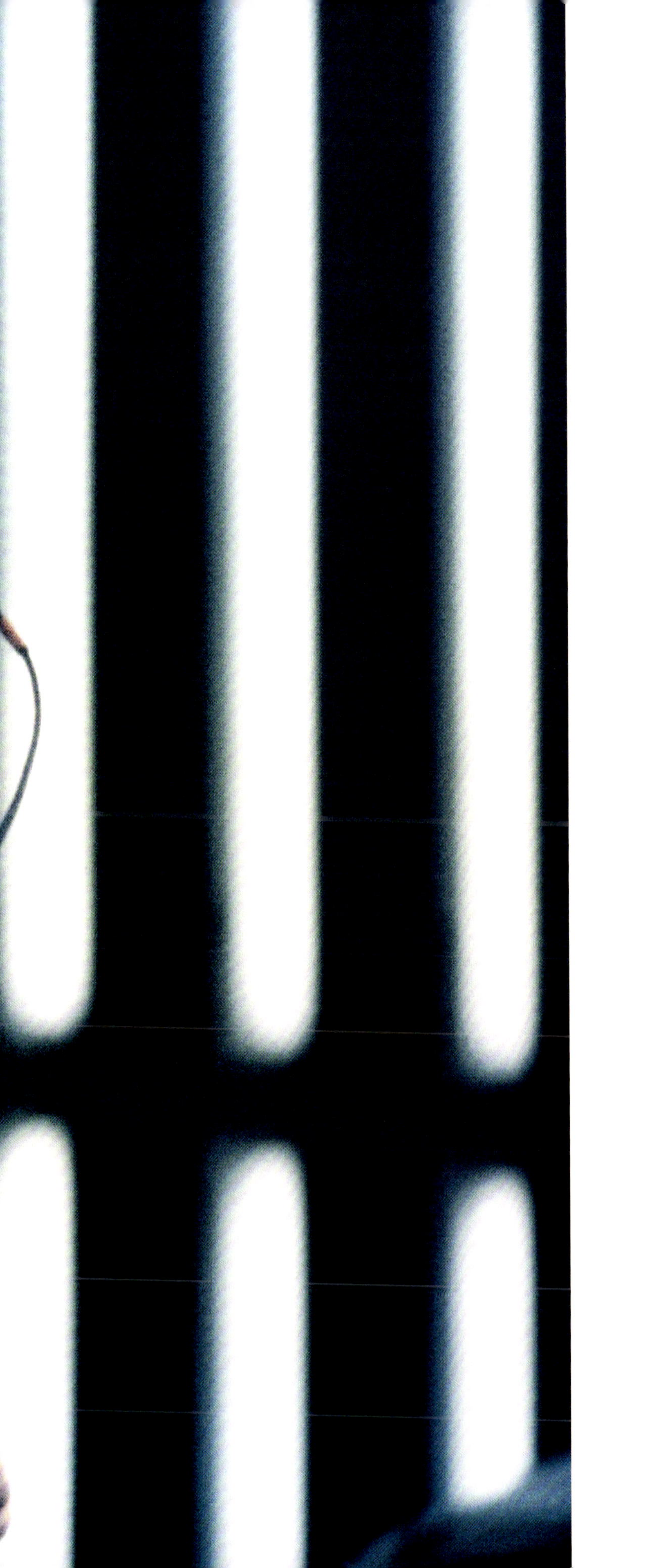

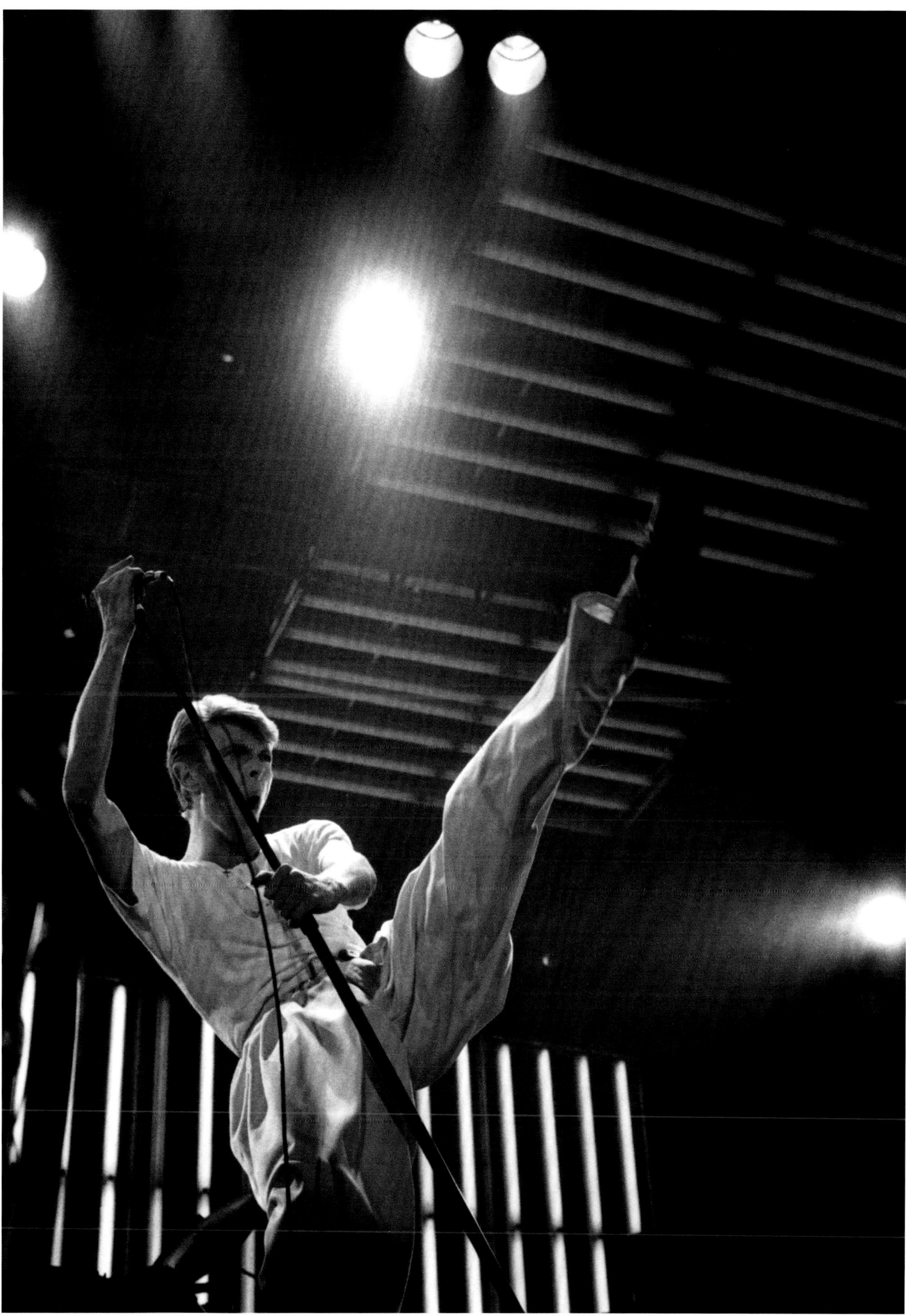

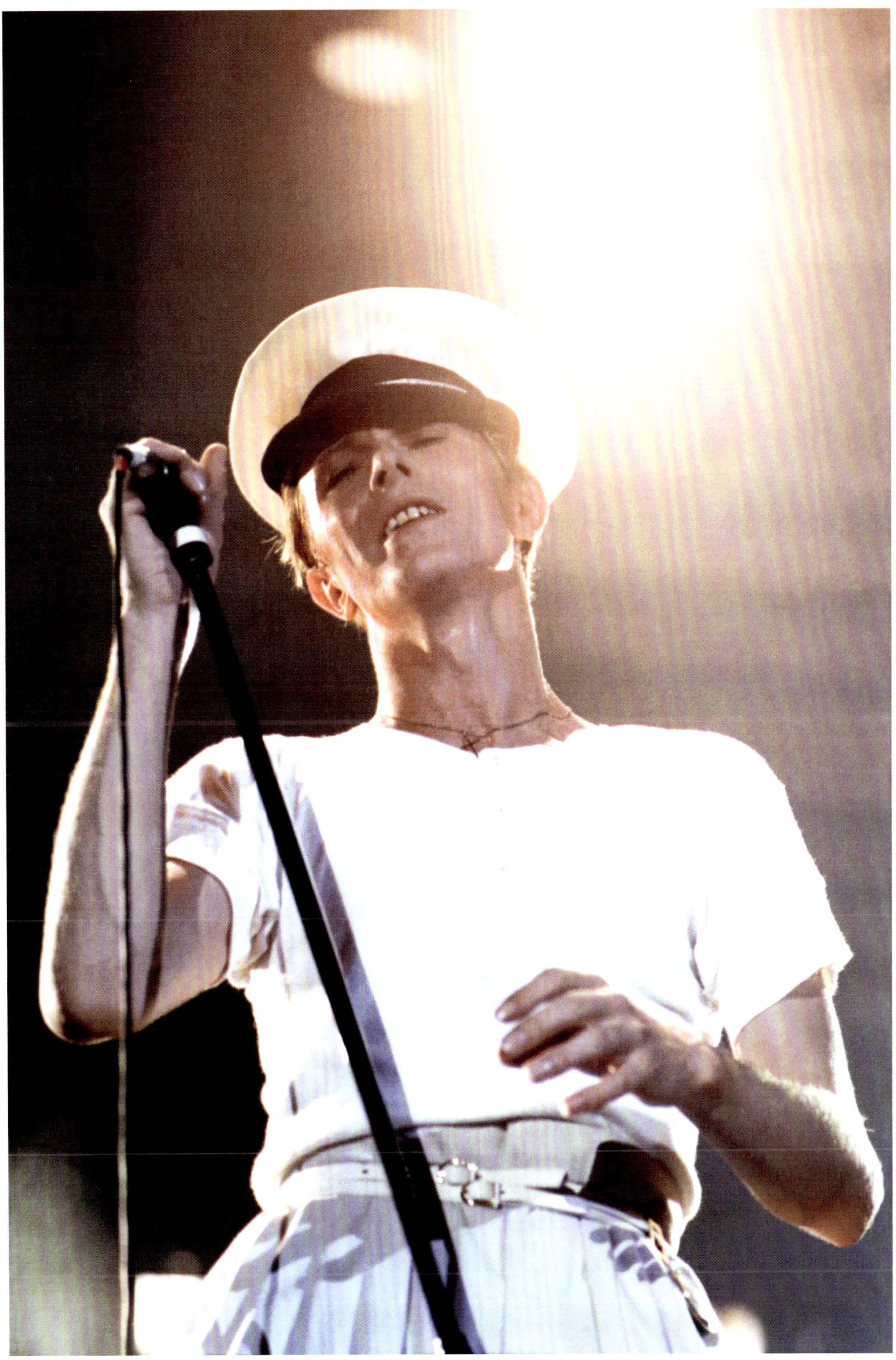

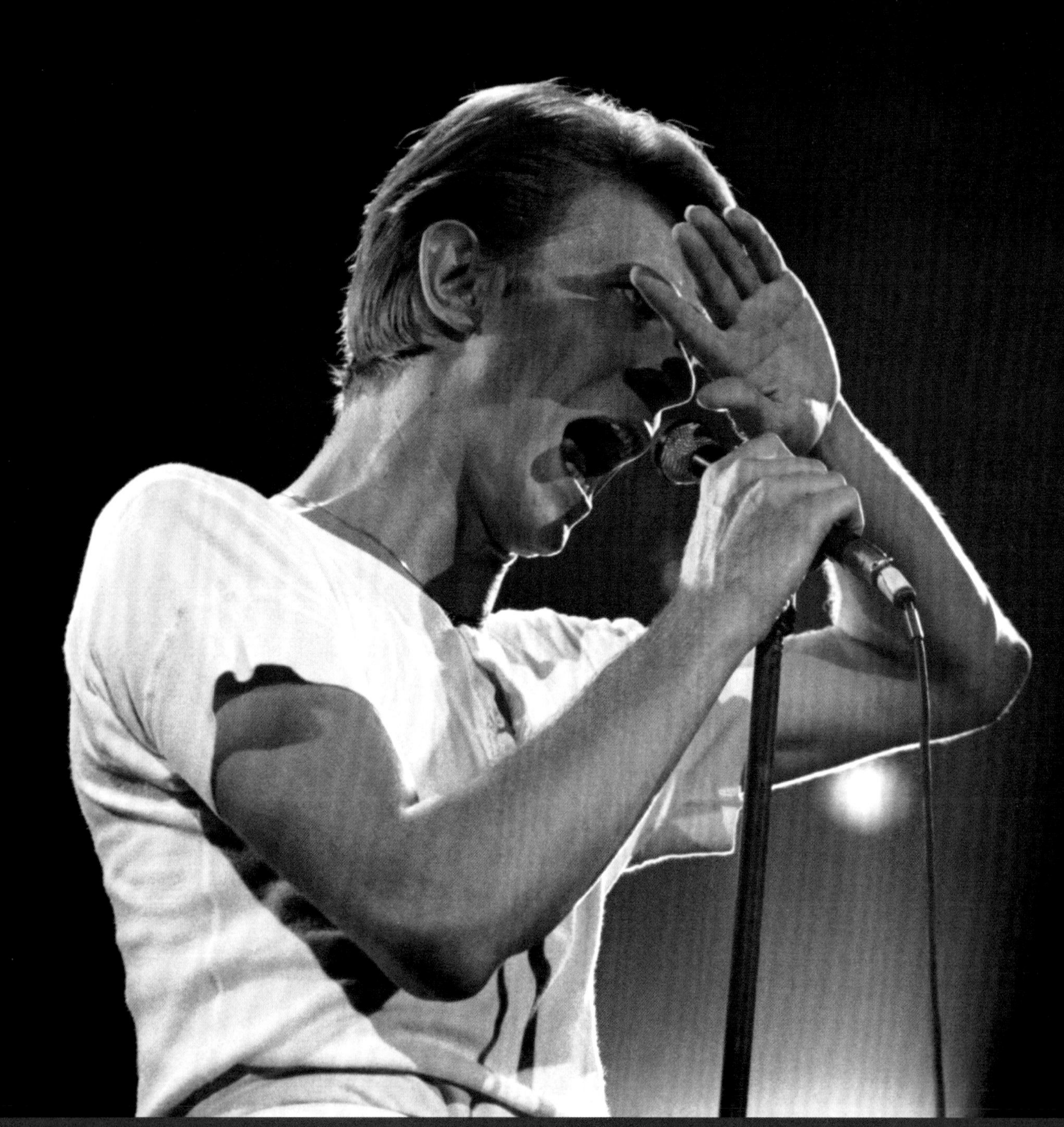

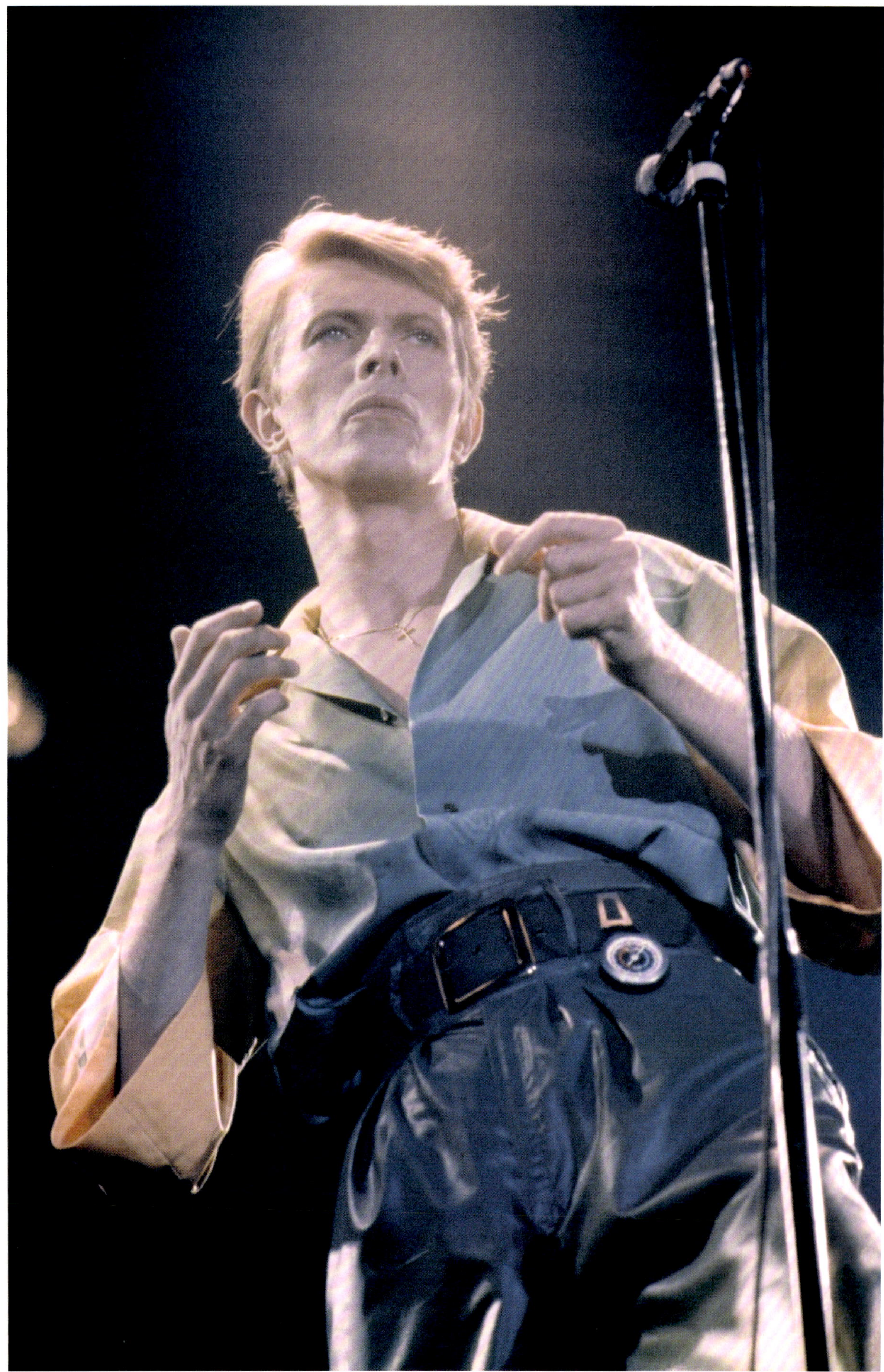

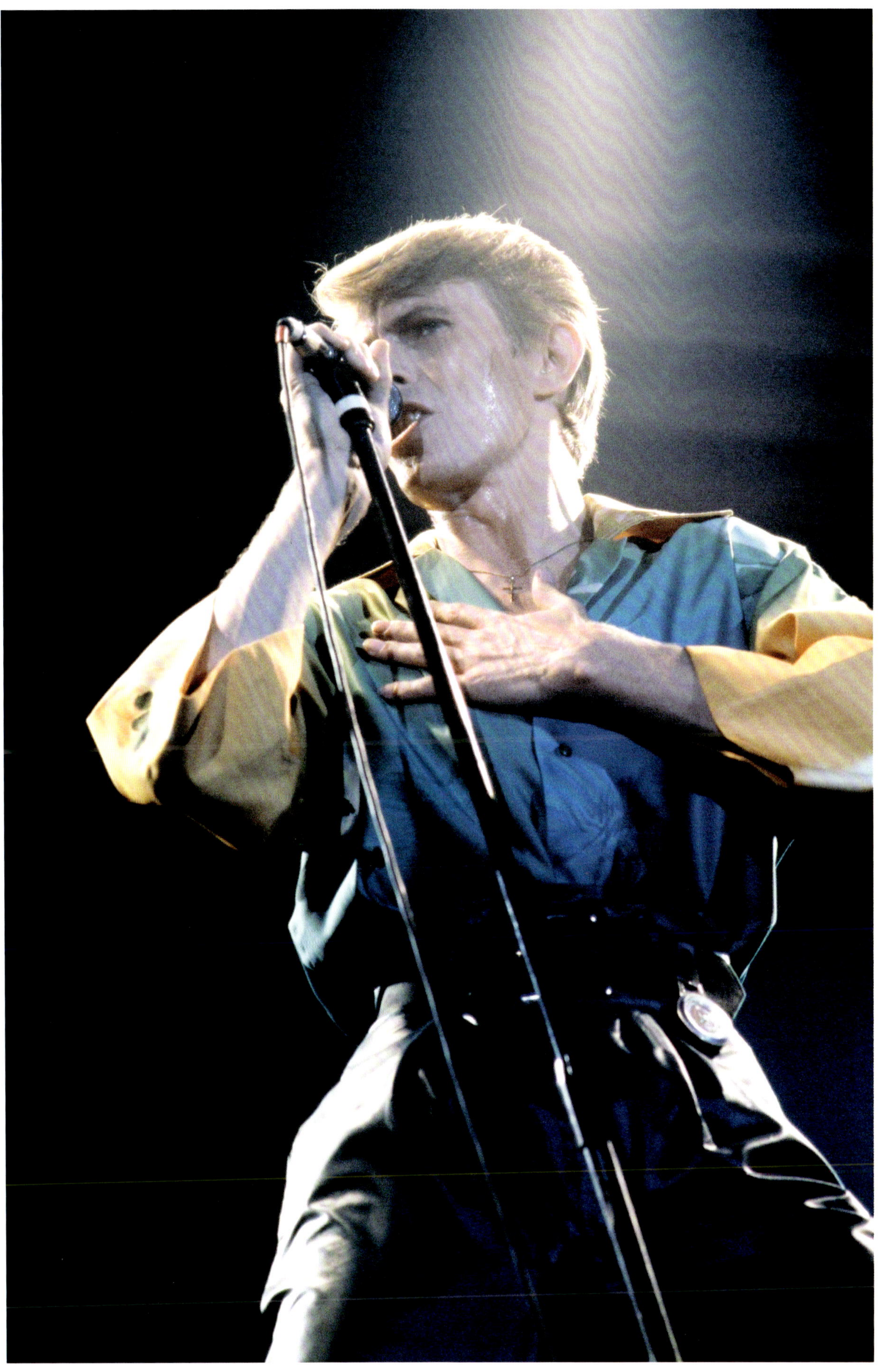

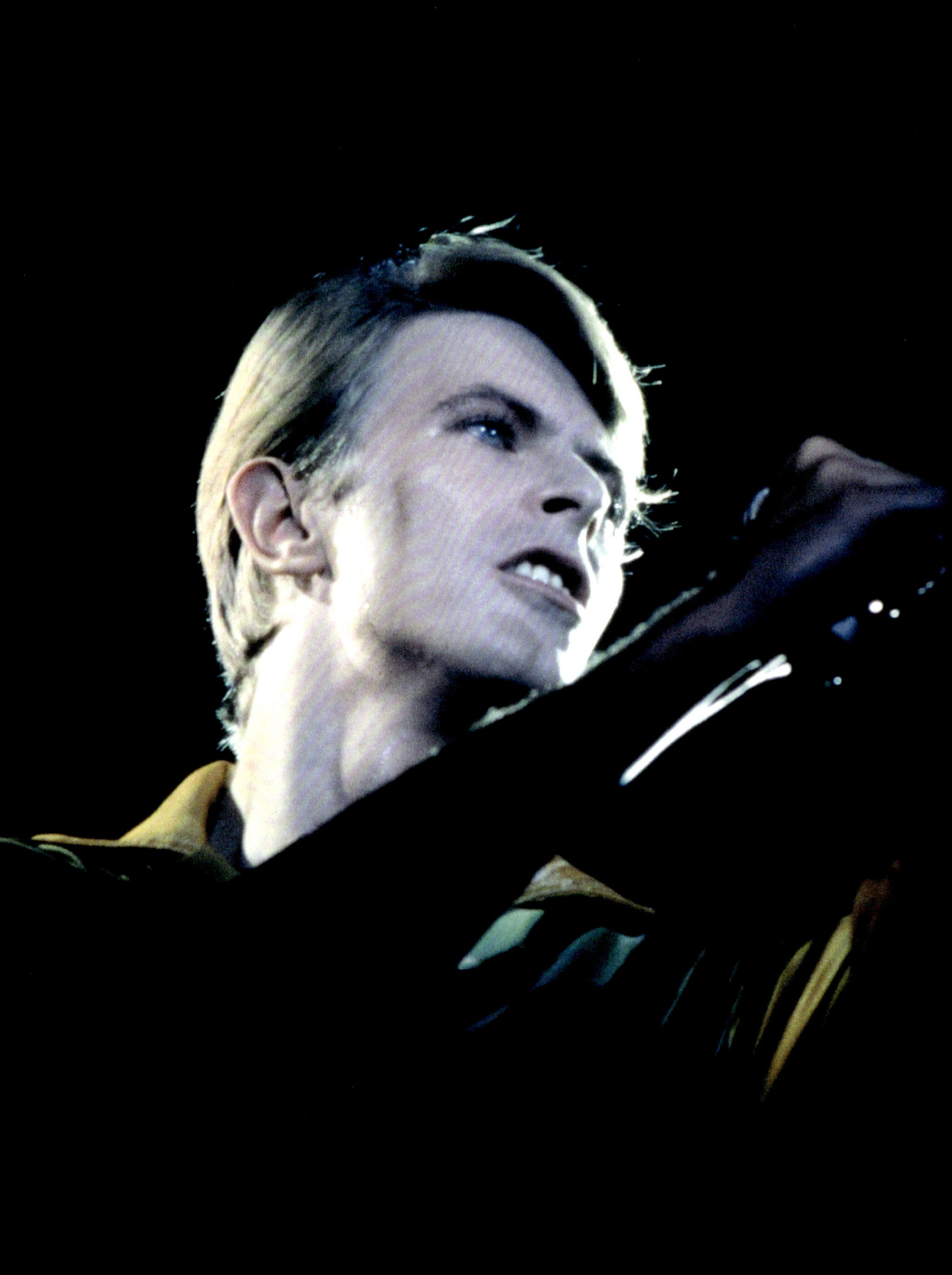

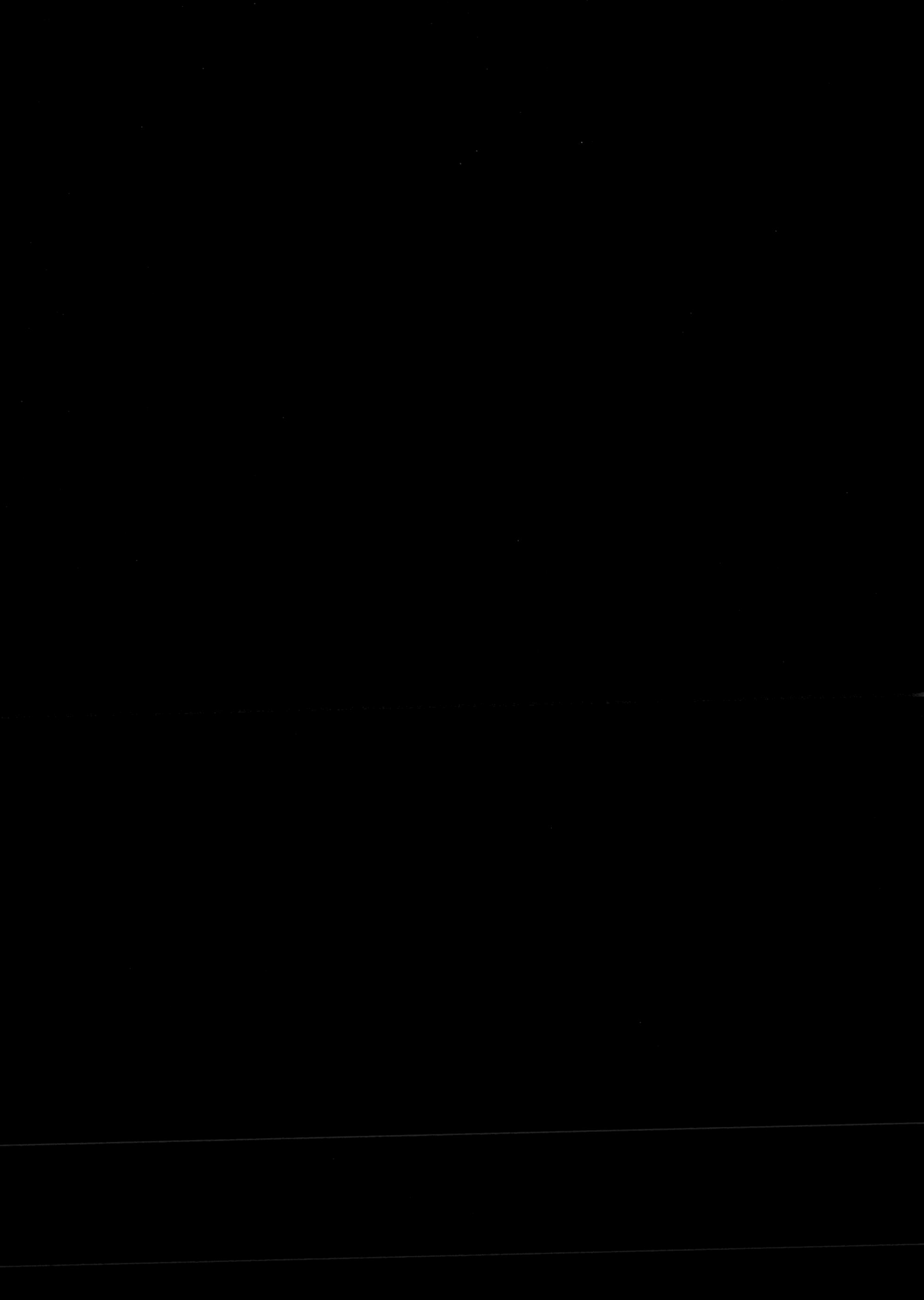

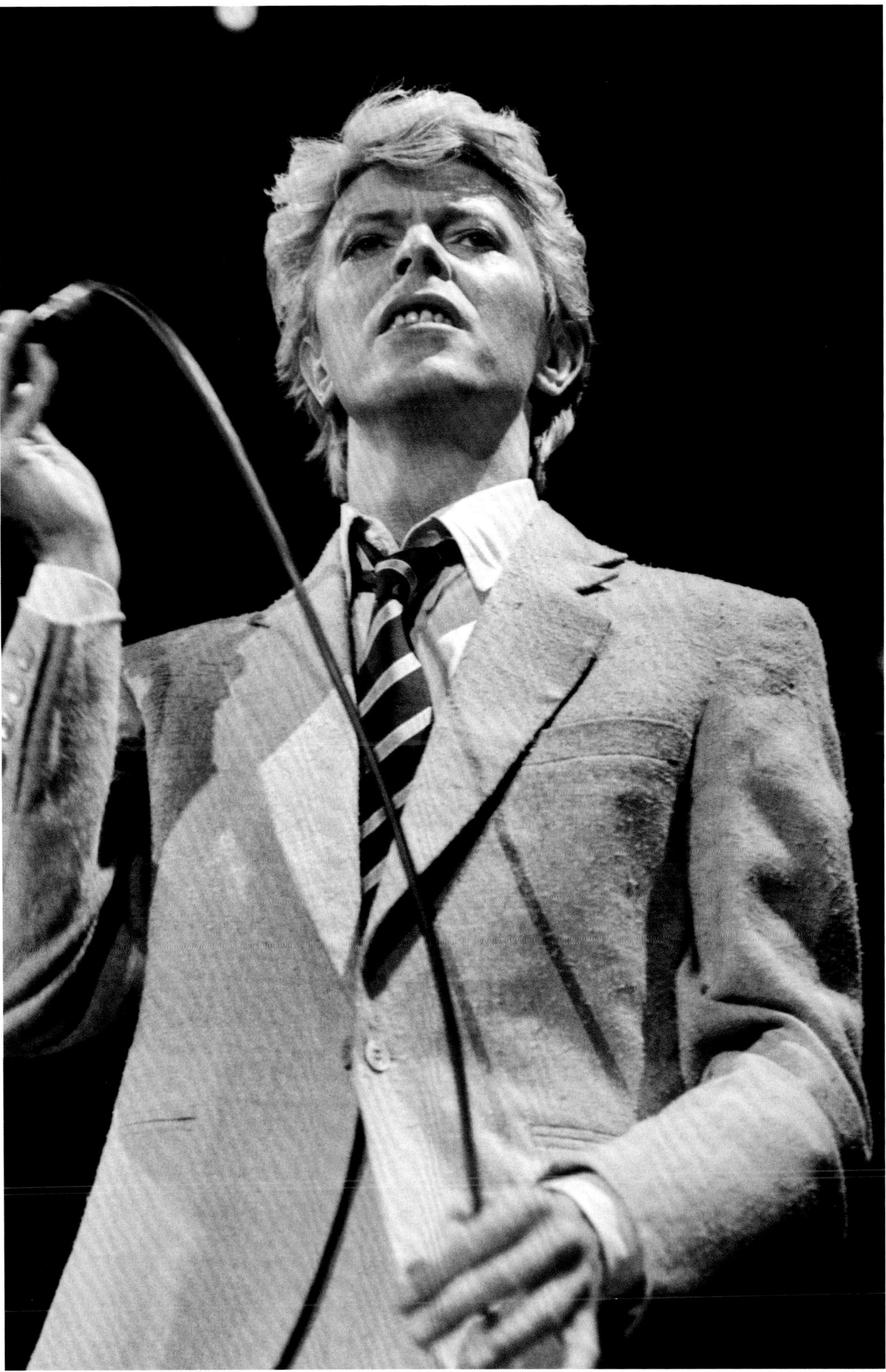

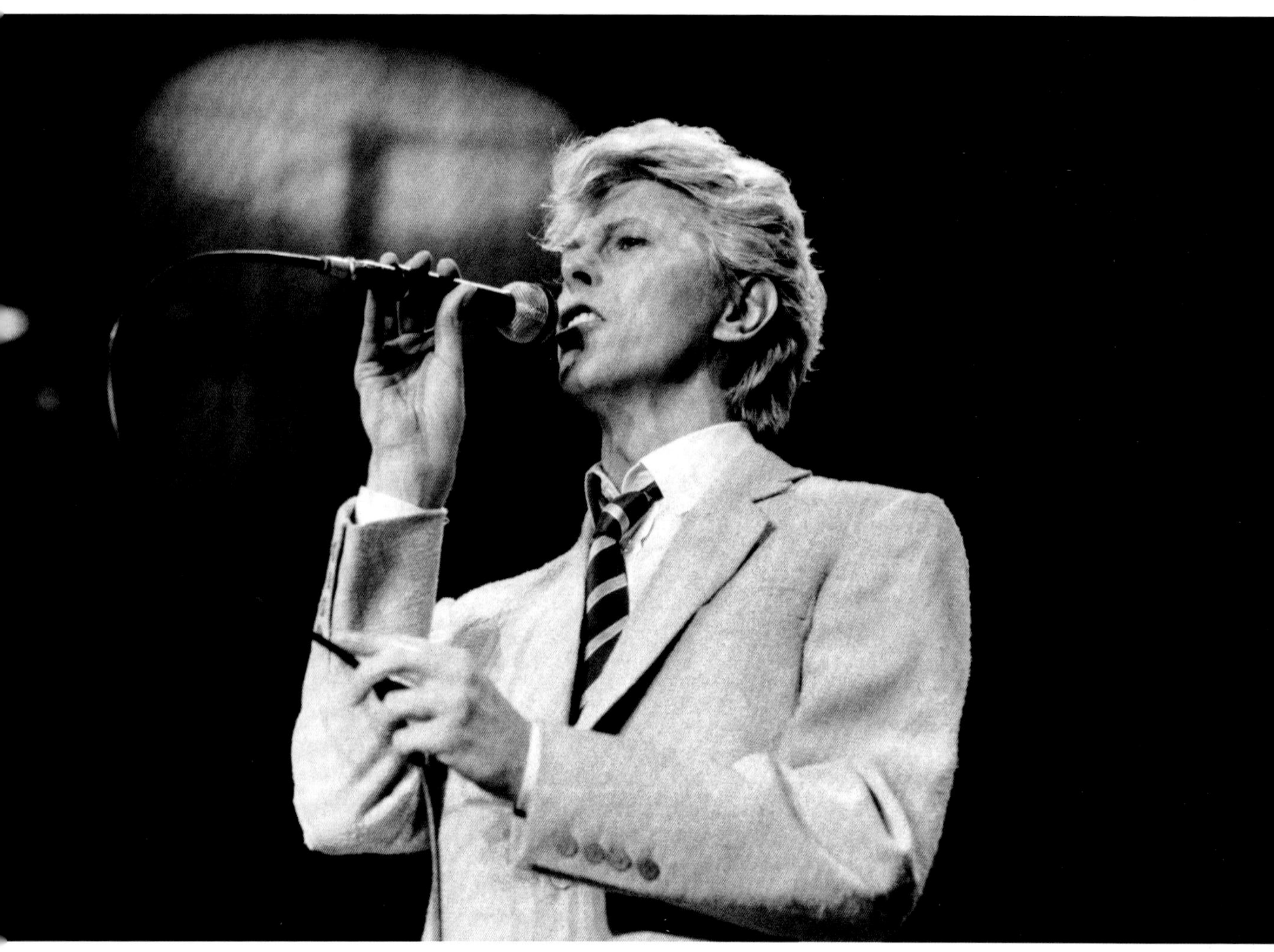

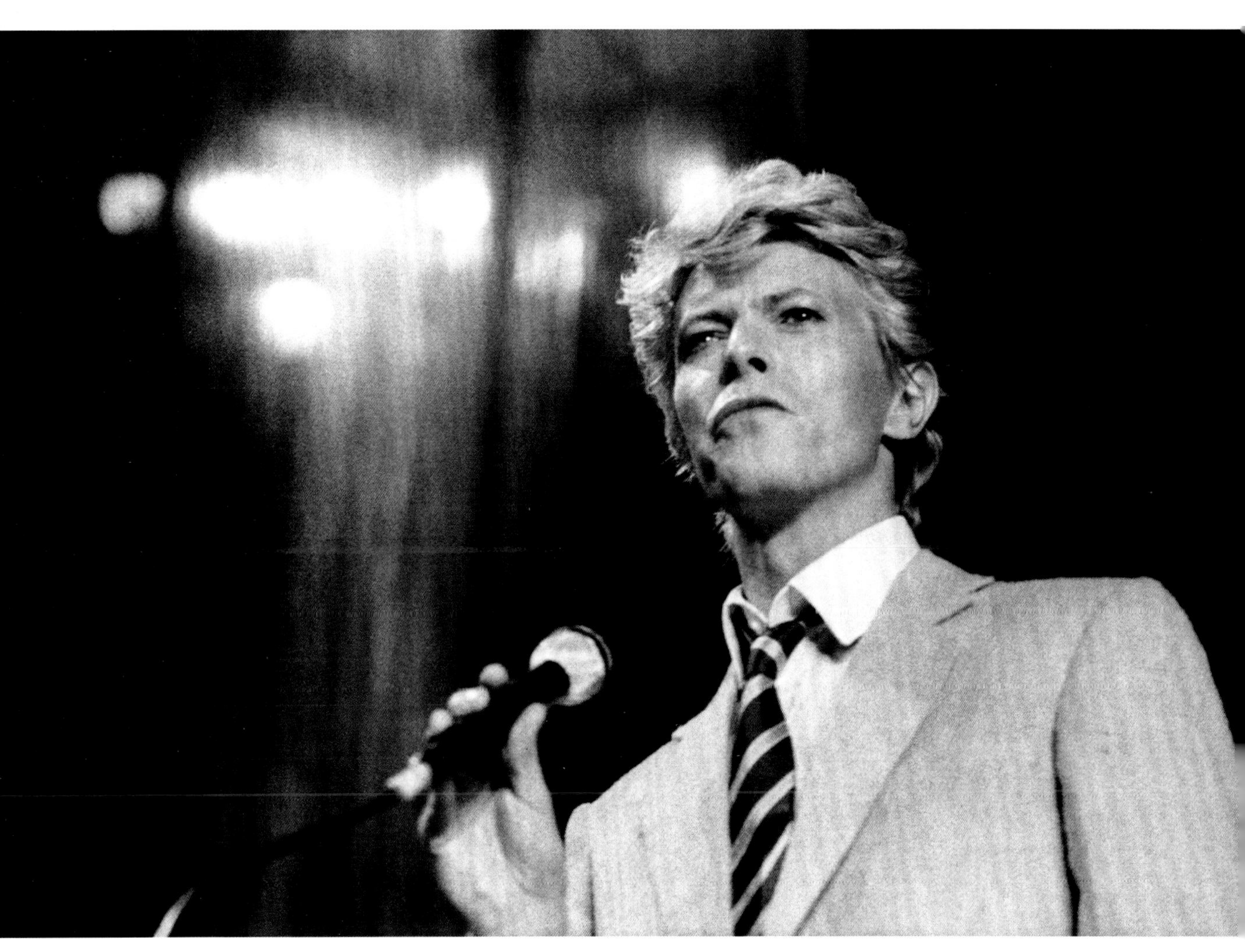

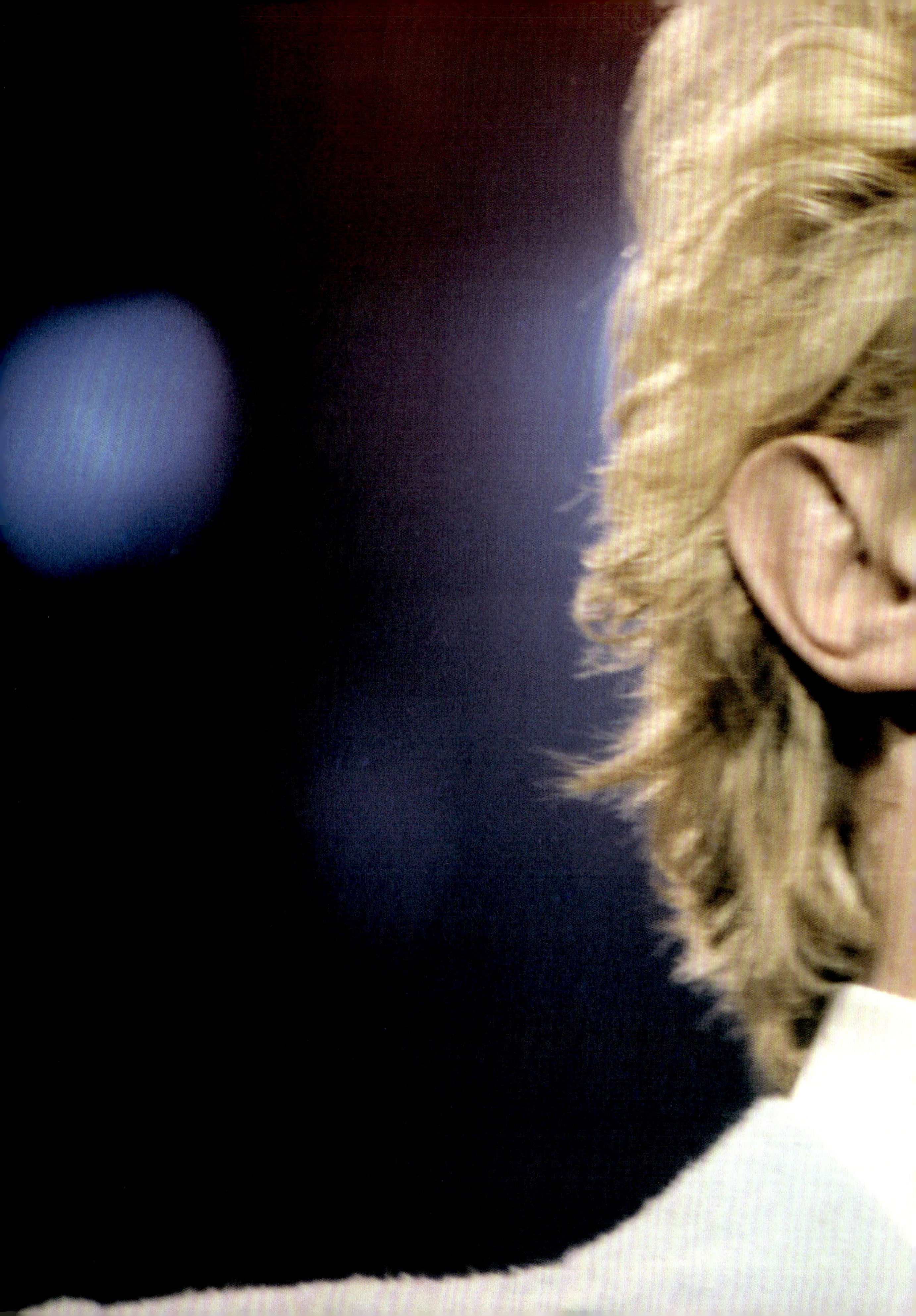

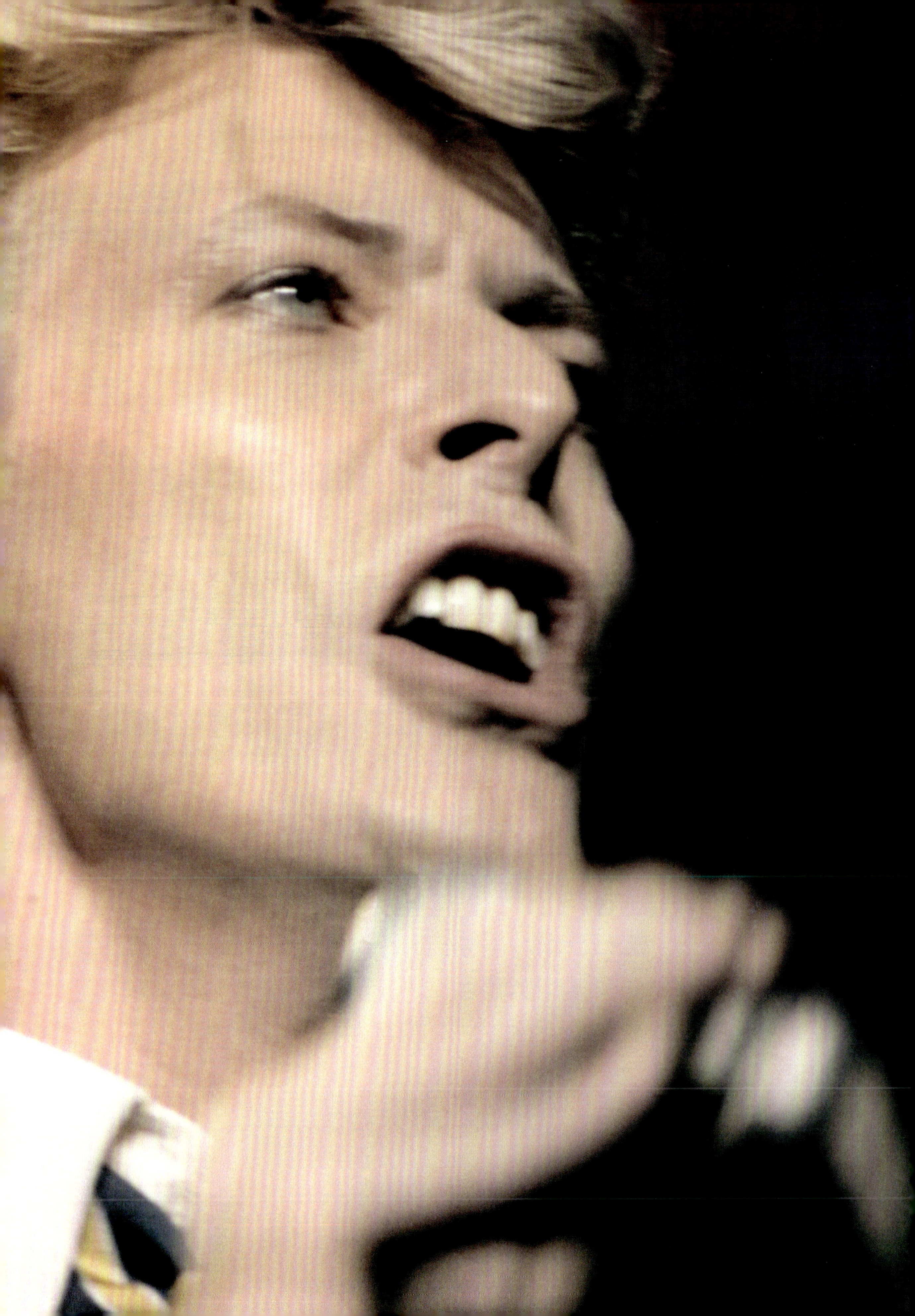

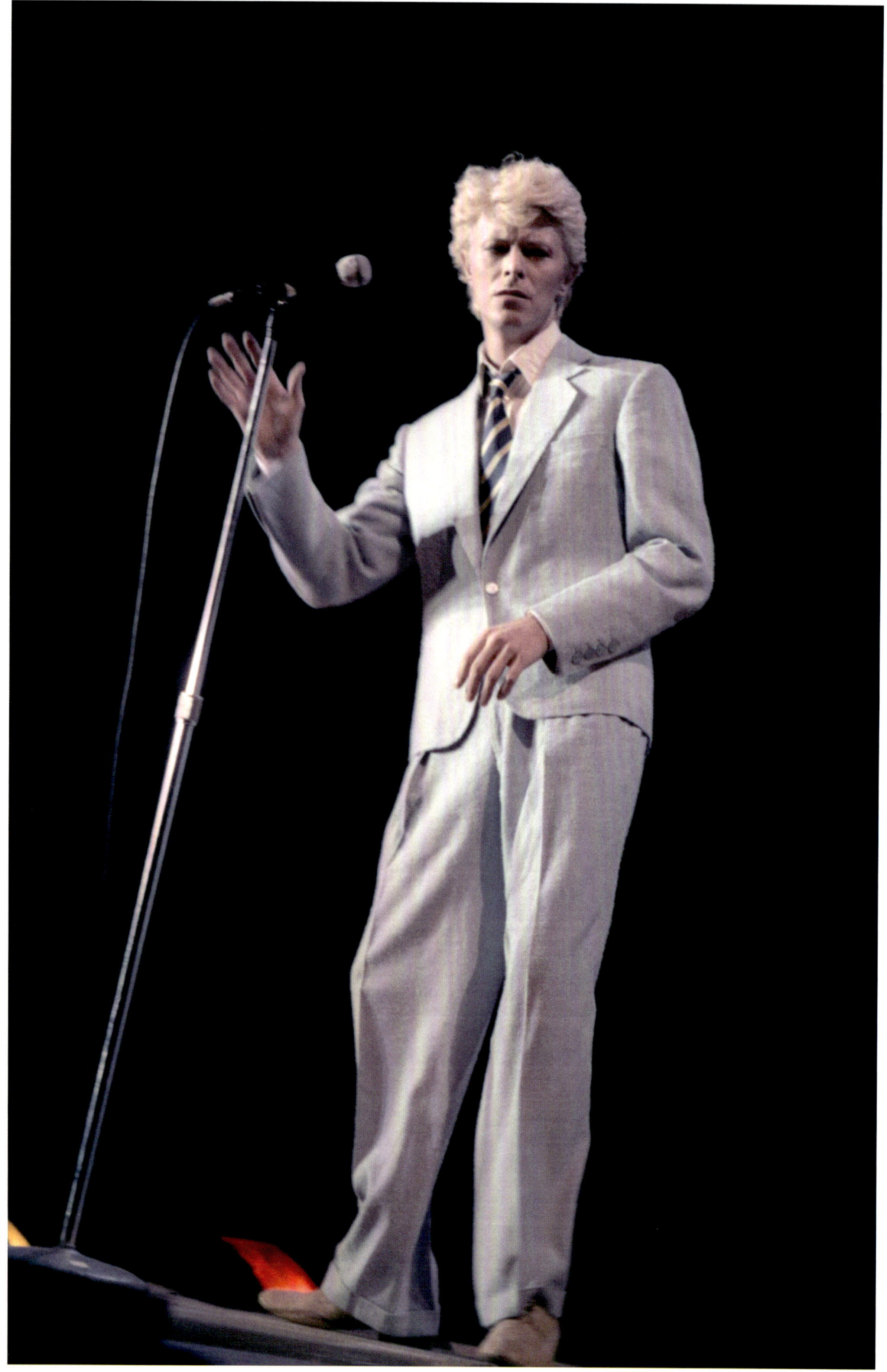

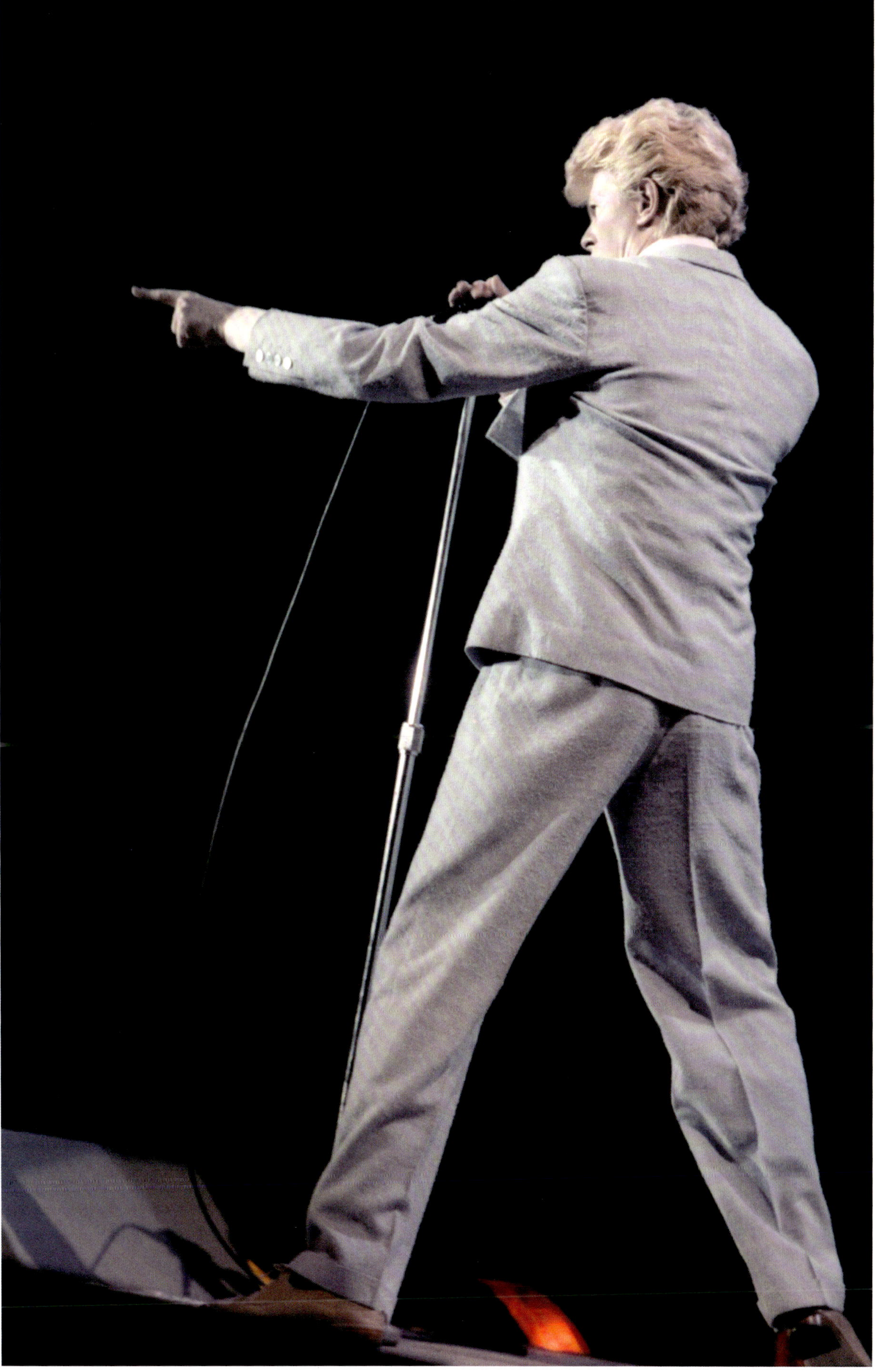

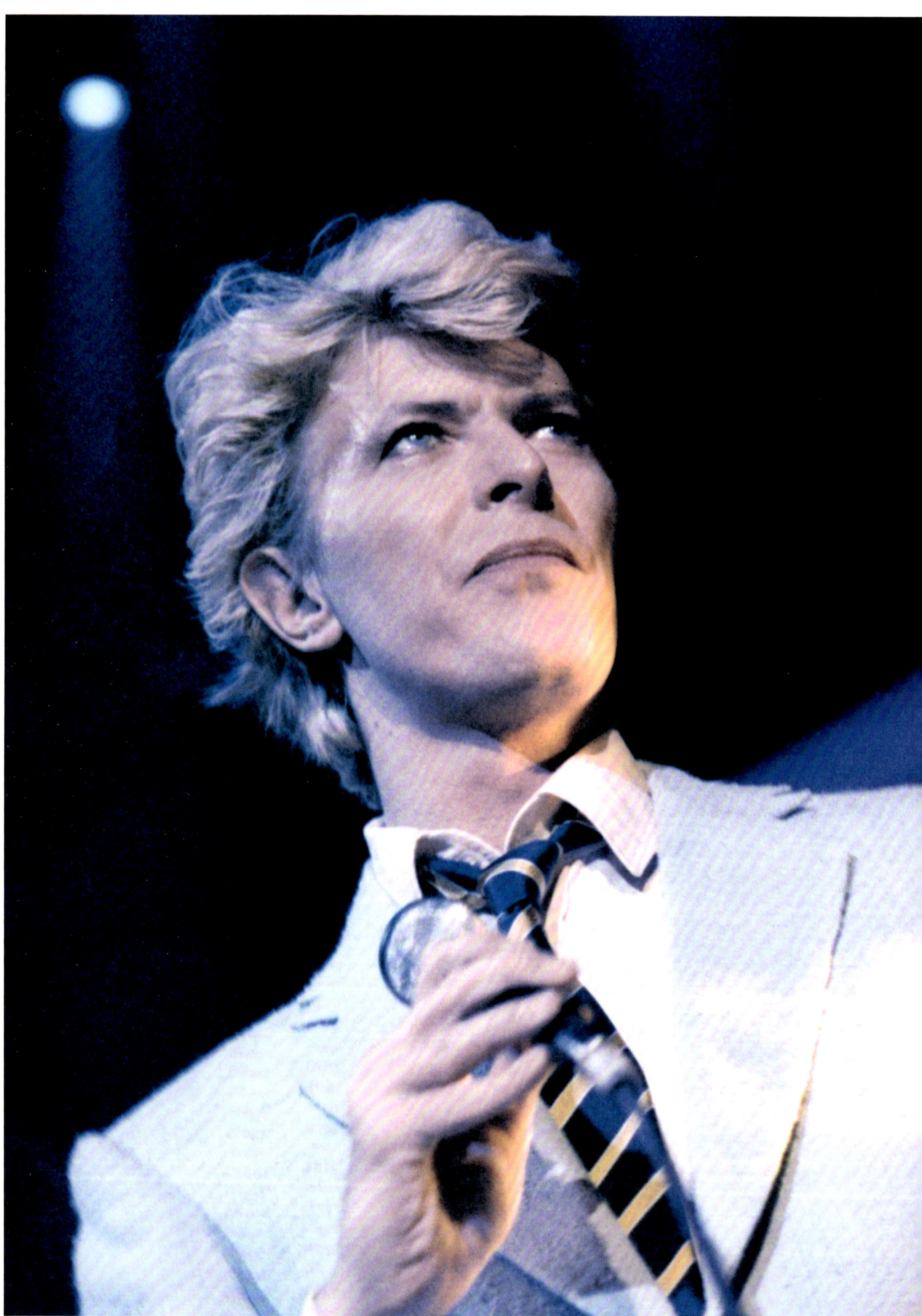

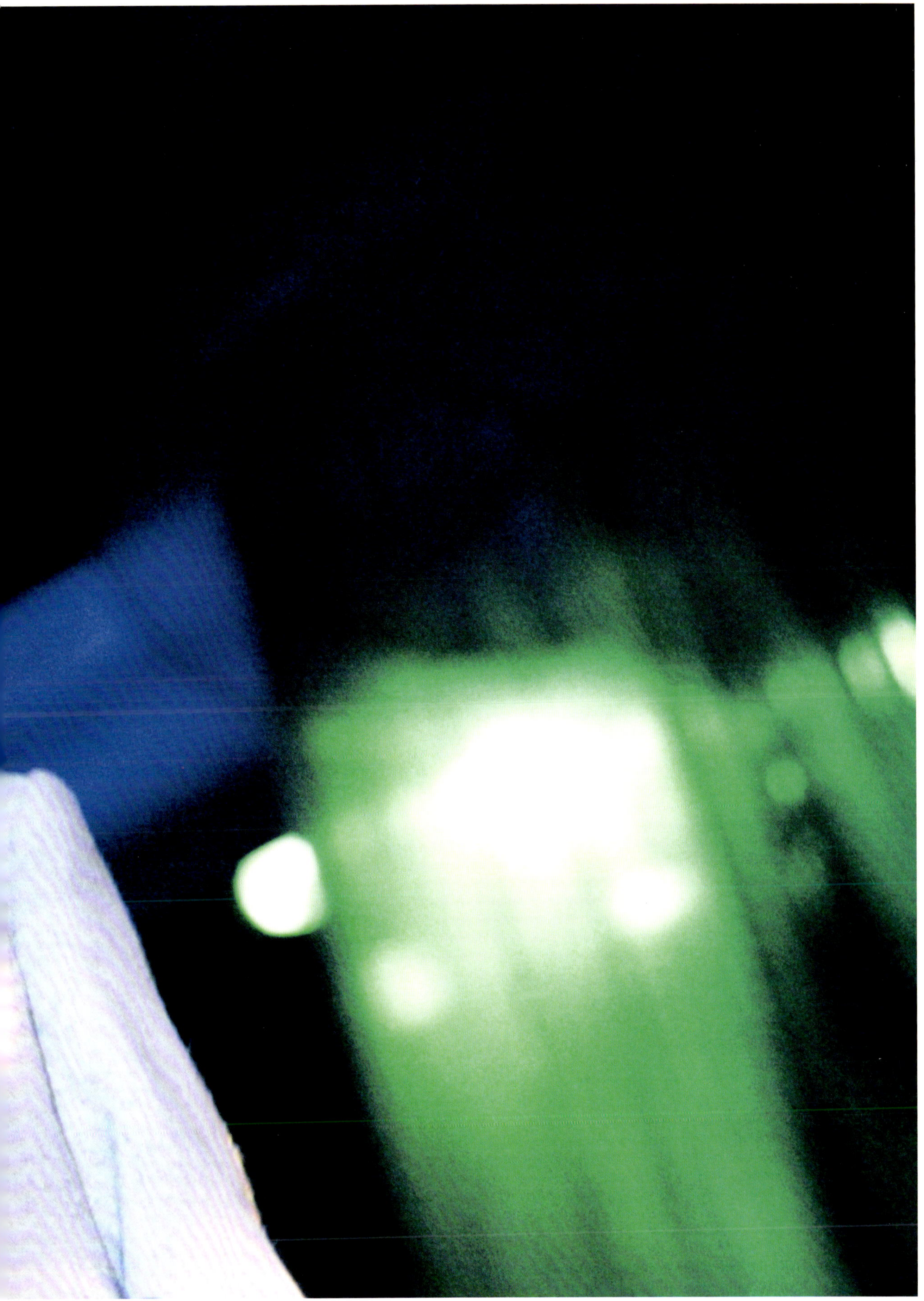

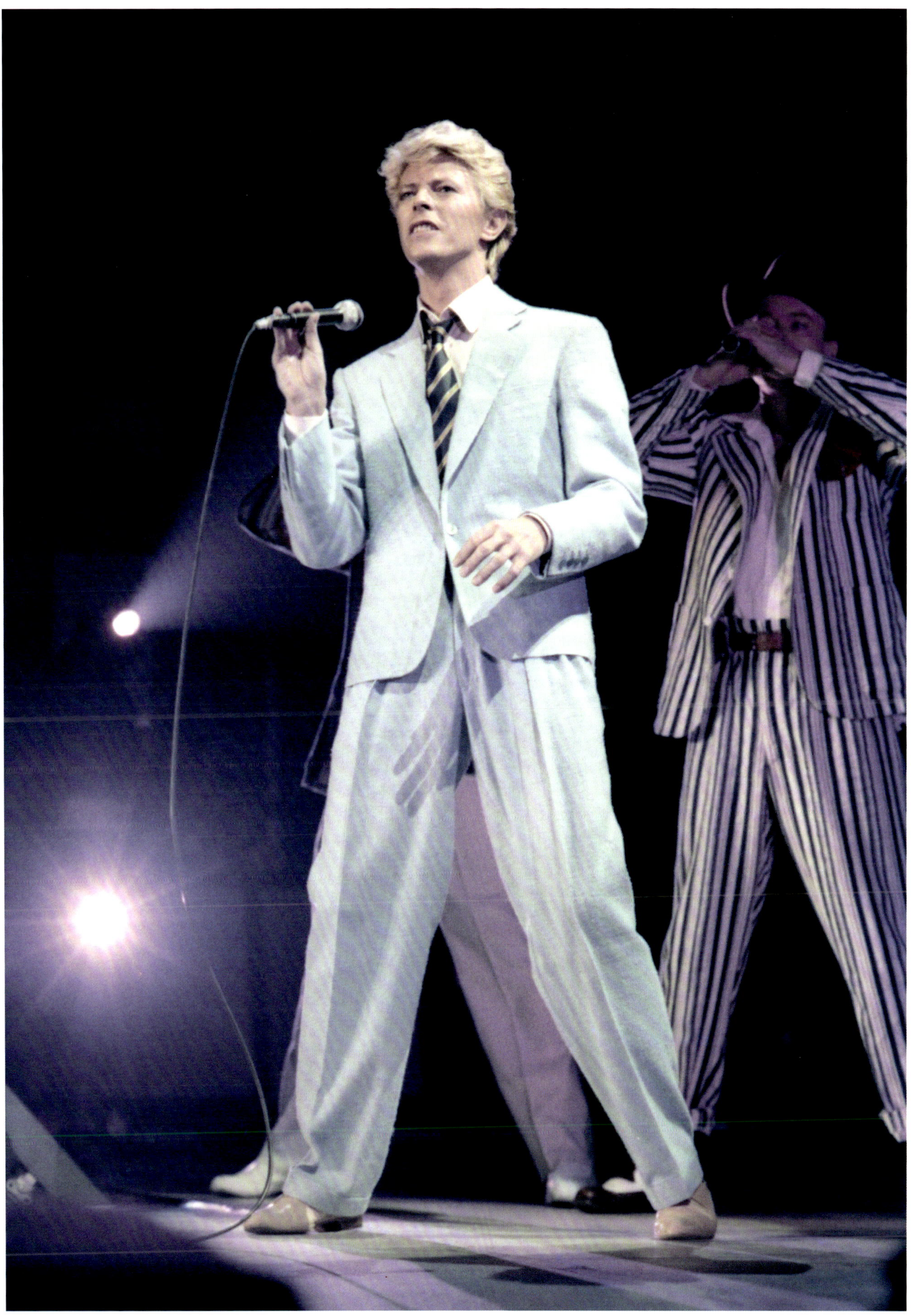

2 JULY 1983
NATIONAL BOWL, MILTON KEYNES

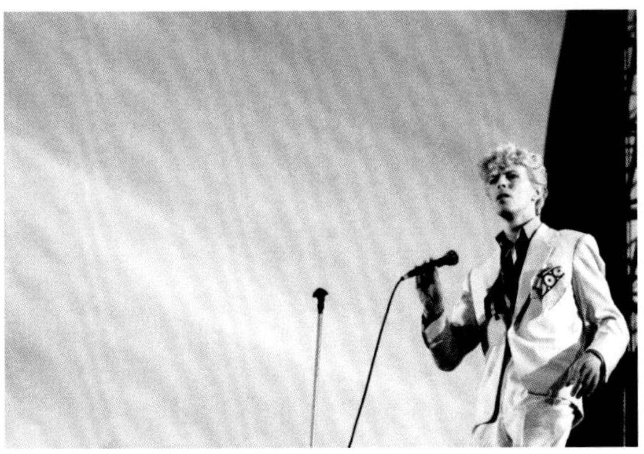

By 1983, on the Serious Moonlight tour, Bowie was massive commercially. He was playing big venues and selling out stadiums, and was easily one of the most photographed musicians in the world. For a photographer, there is always a unique challenge with such an exposed subject, to capture something a bit different in a live setting. Often at these gigs, quite a few photographers are lined up, all facing the same way. In my own head I was competitive. I wanted to get the best live shot, an image that captured something differently, something that stood out. Sometimes it could be hard to get a picture editor to understand what I was trying to do, but thankfully the *NME* usually gave me free rein.

When it came to Bowie at the Milton Keynes Bowl, I wanted a shot that had a vastness to it. At outdoor gigs there can be so much space and so much sky, yet so many photographers just focus in on the band. Sometimes it isn't even possible to tell whether it is shot inside or out. For me, there was something about the size of Bowie's career at this point, and the size of the sky he was playing under, that worked very well together. My main aim was to show just how big both were. This is a photograph with a lot of space in the frame. In fact, it is the space that draws you into the shot. The sky takes up half of what you can see, and from that empty, cloudless sky the eye is drawn, right down to Bowie beneath it, mid-song, with a flamboyant pocket square. It is a big photograph in every sense of the word, and you feel as though the sky and Bowie could both just go on for ever.

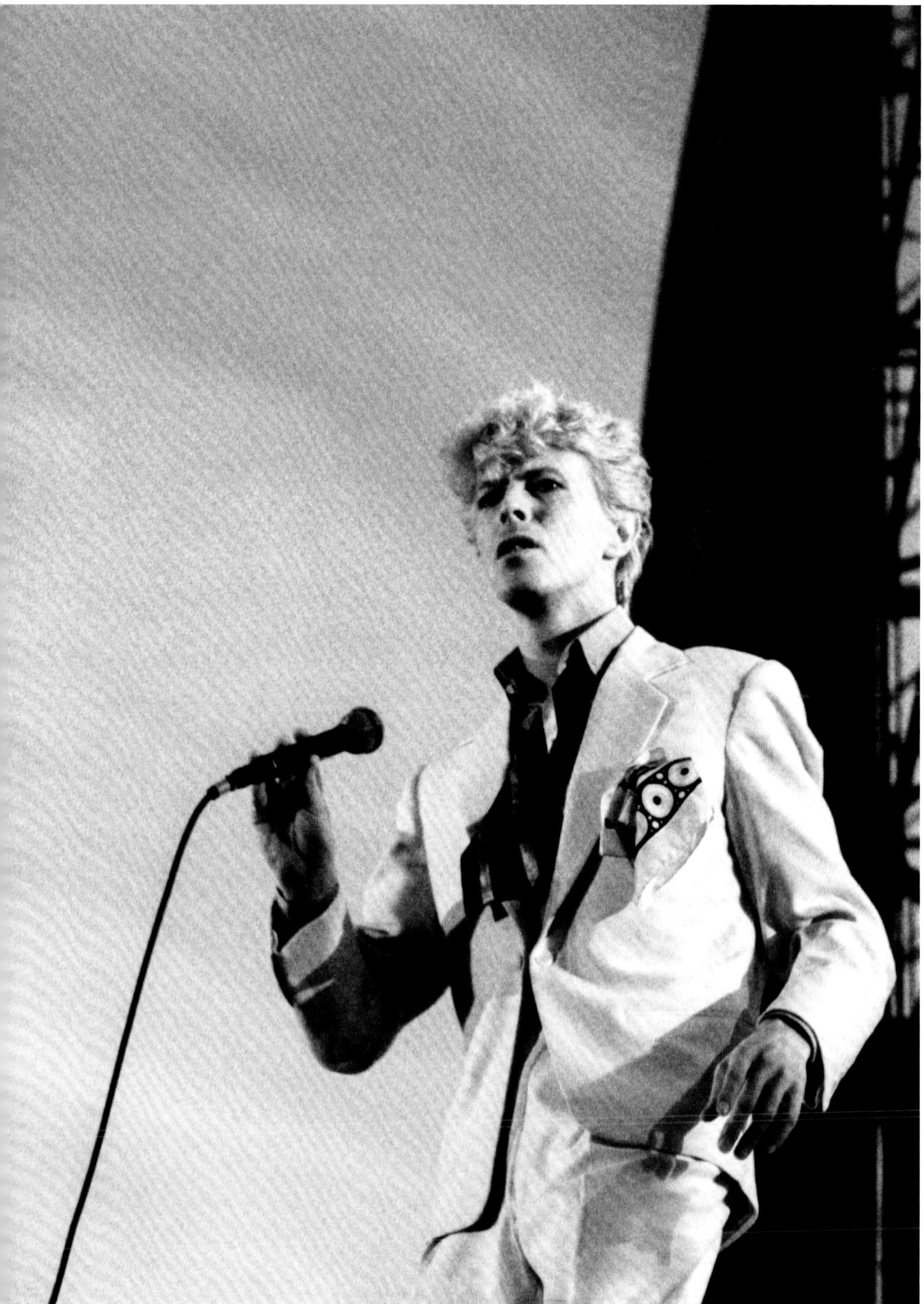

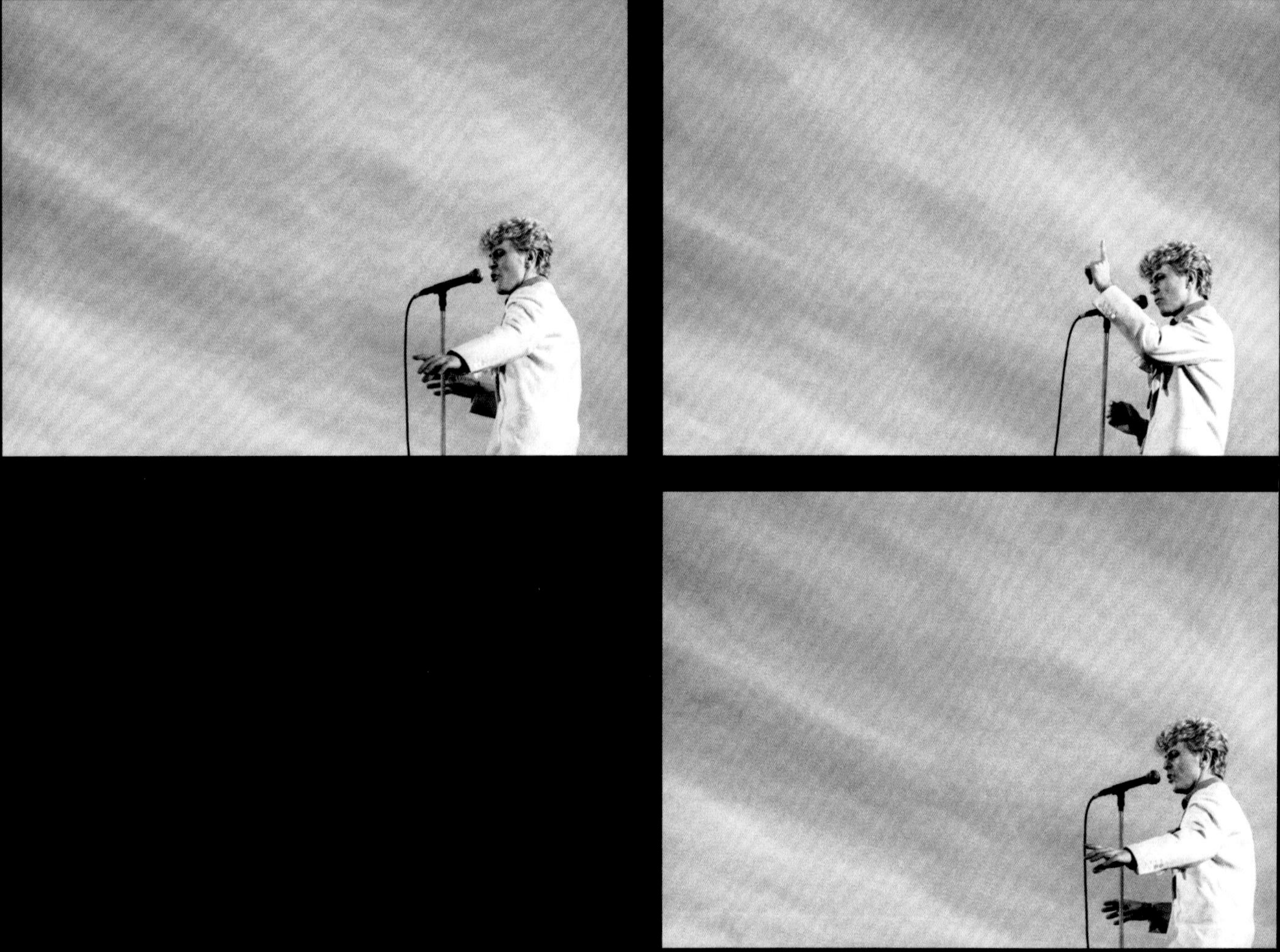

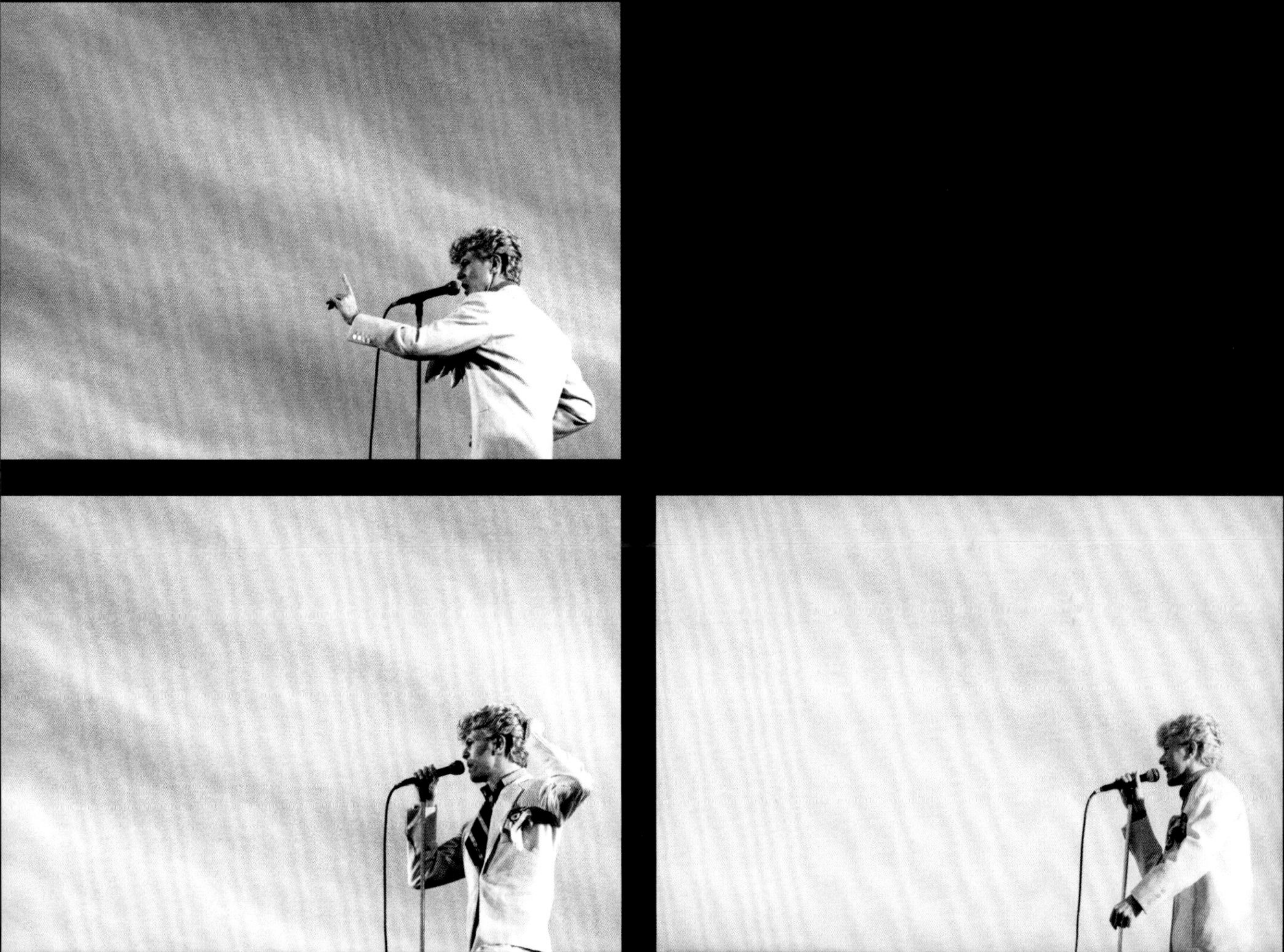

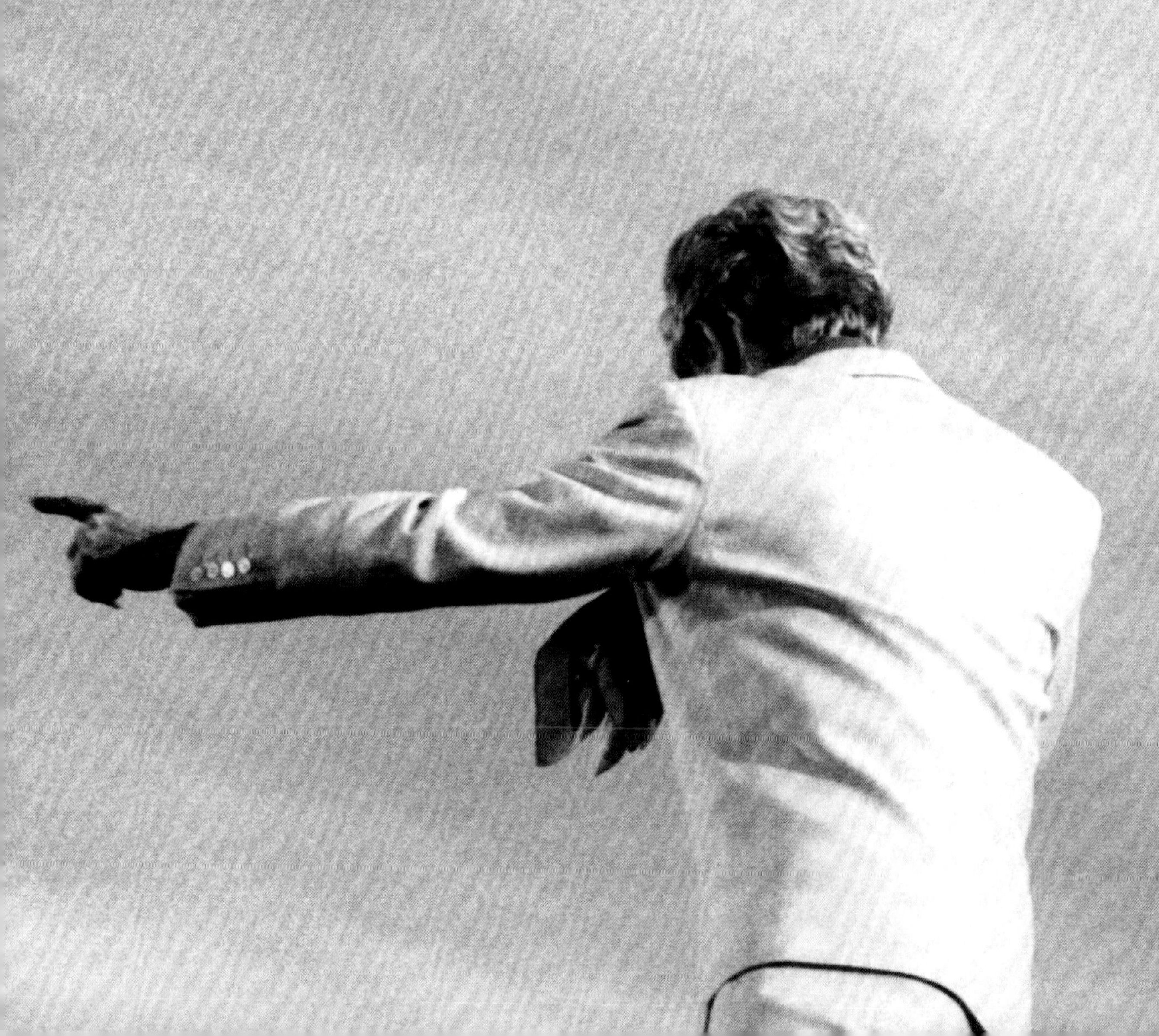

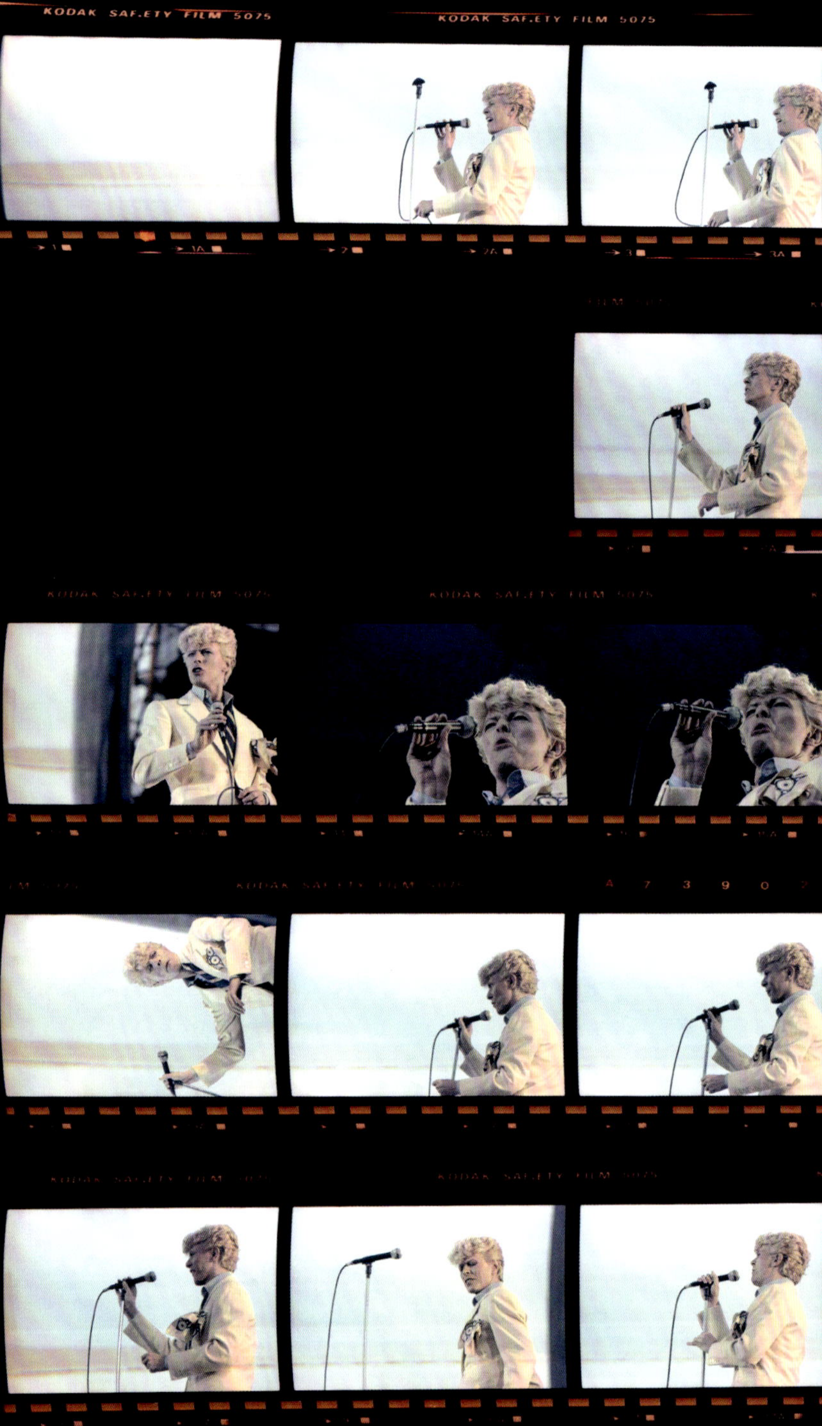

KODAK SAF.ETY FILM 5075
KODAK SAF.ETY FILM 5075
KODAK SAFETY FILM 5075
KODAK SAFETY FILM 5075
A 7 3 9 0 2

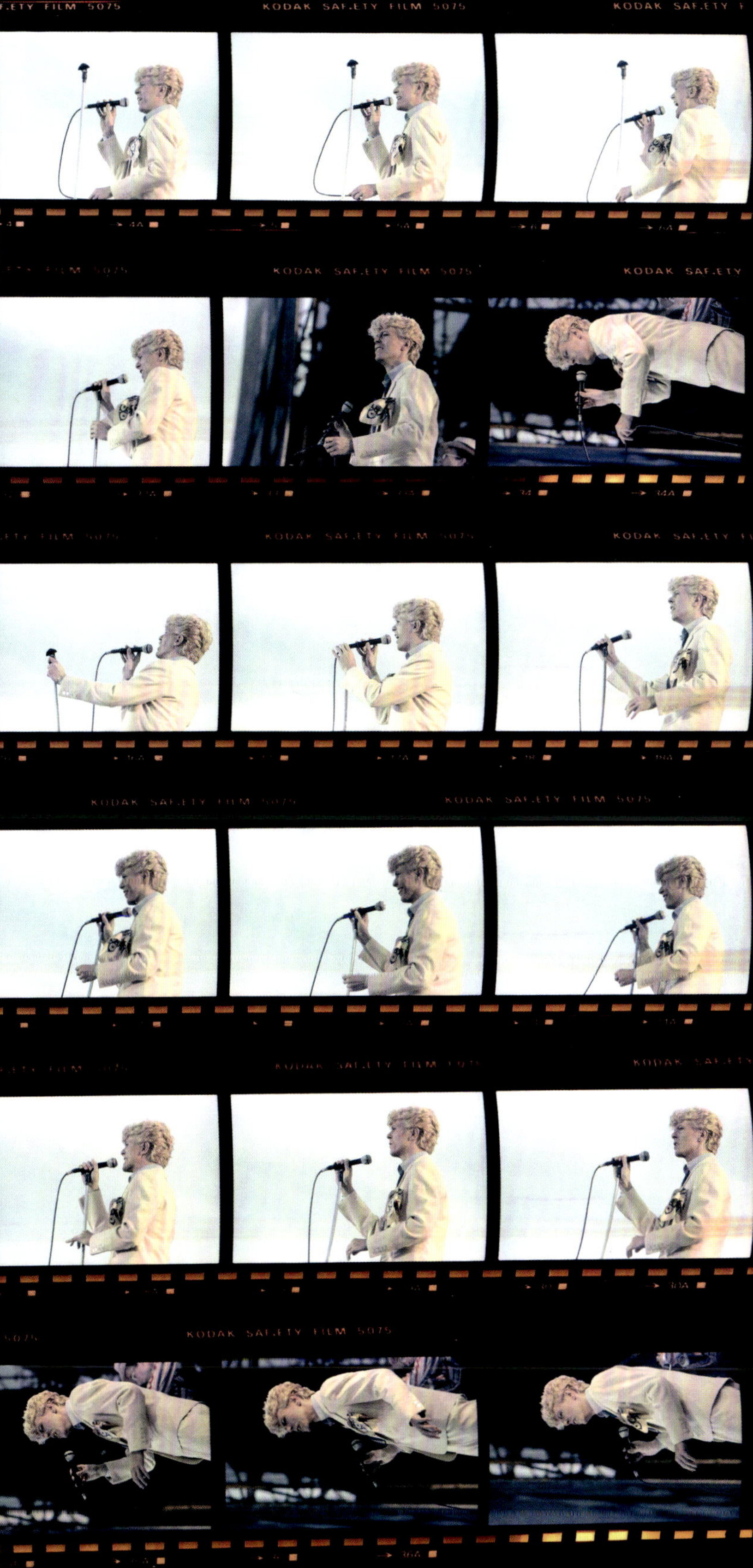

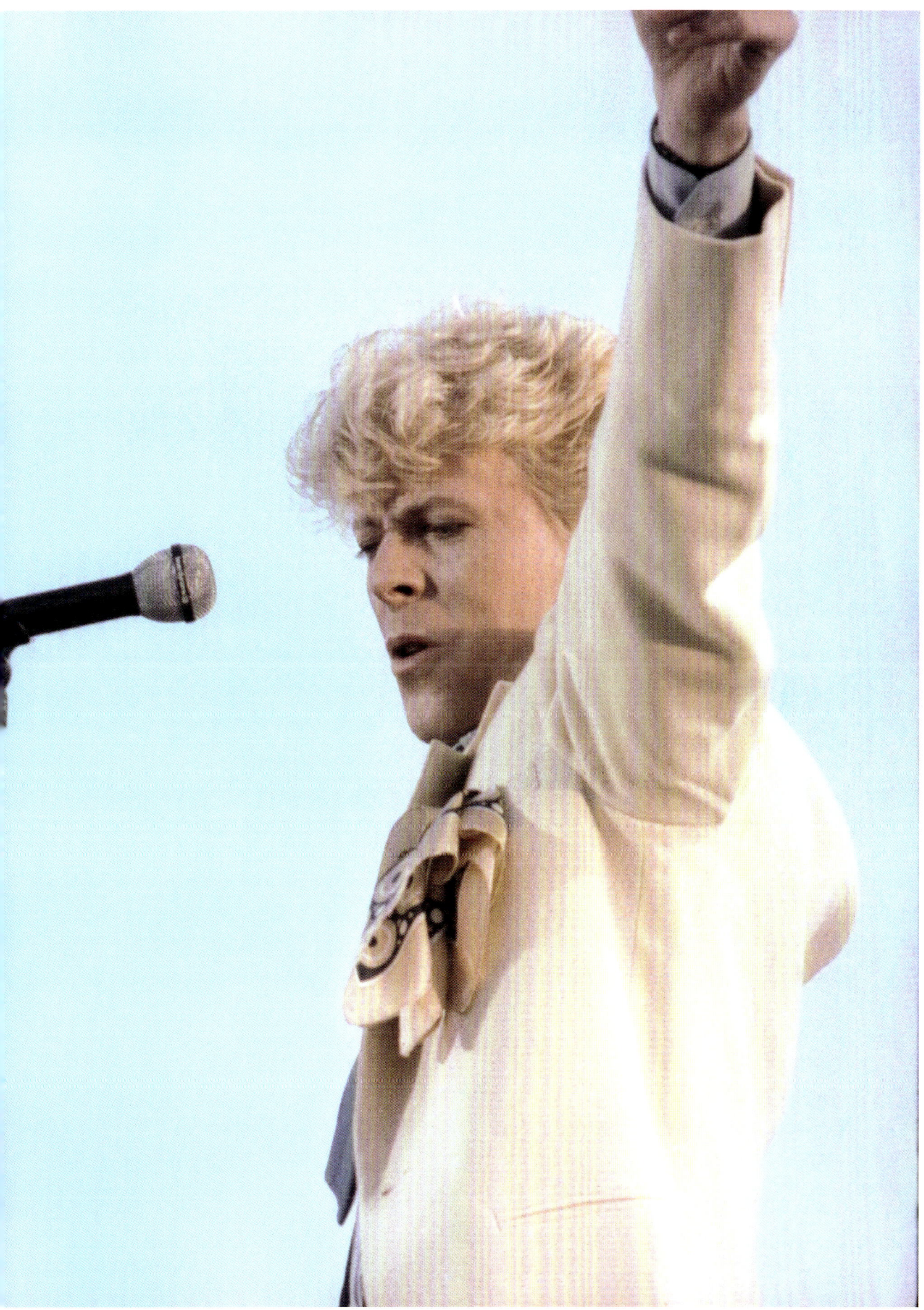

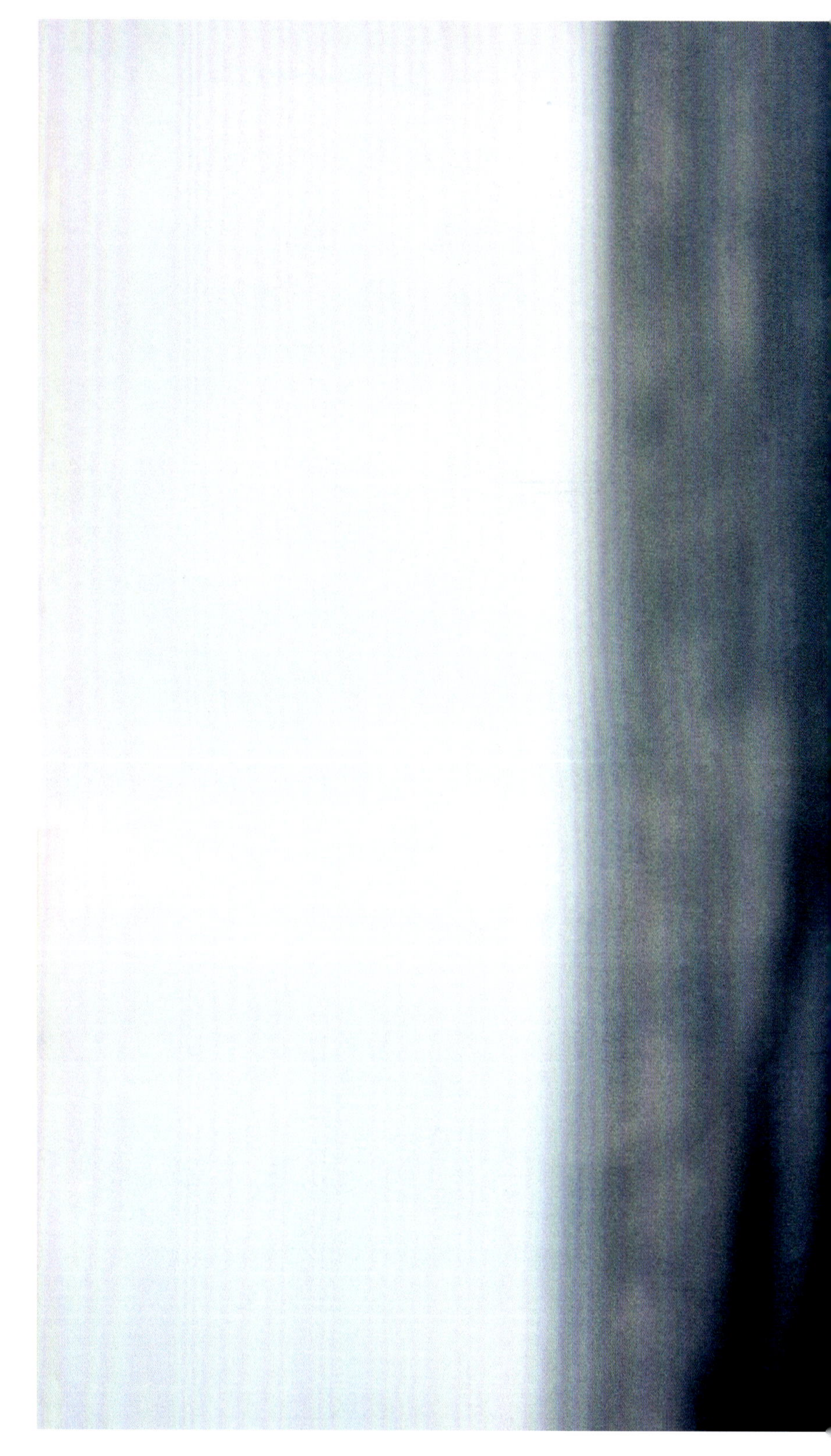

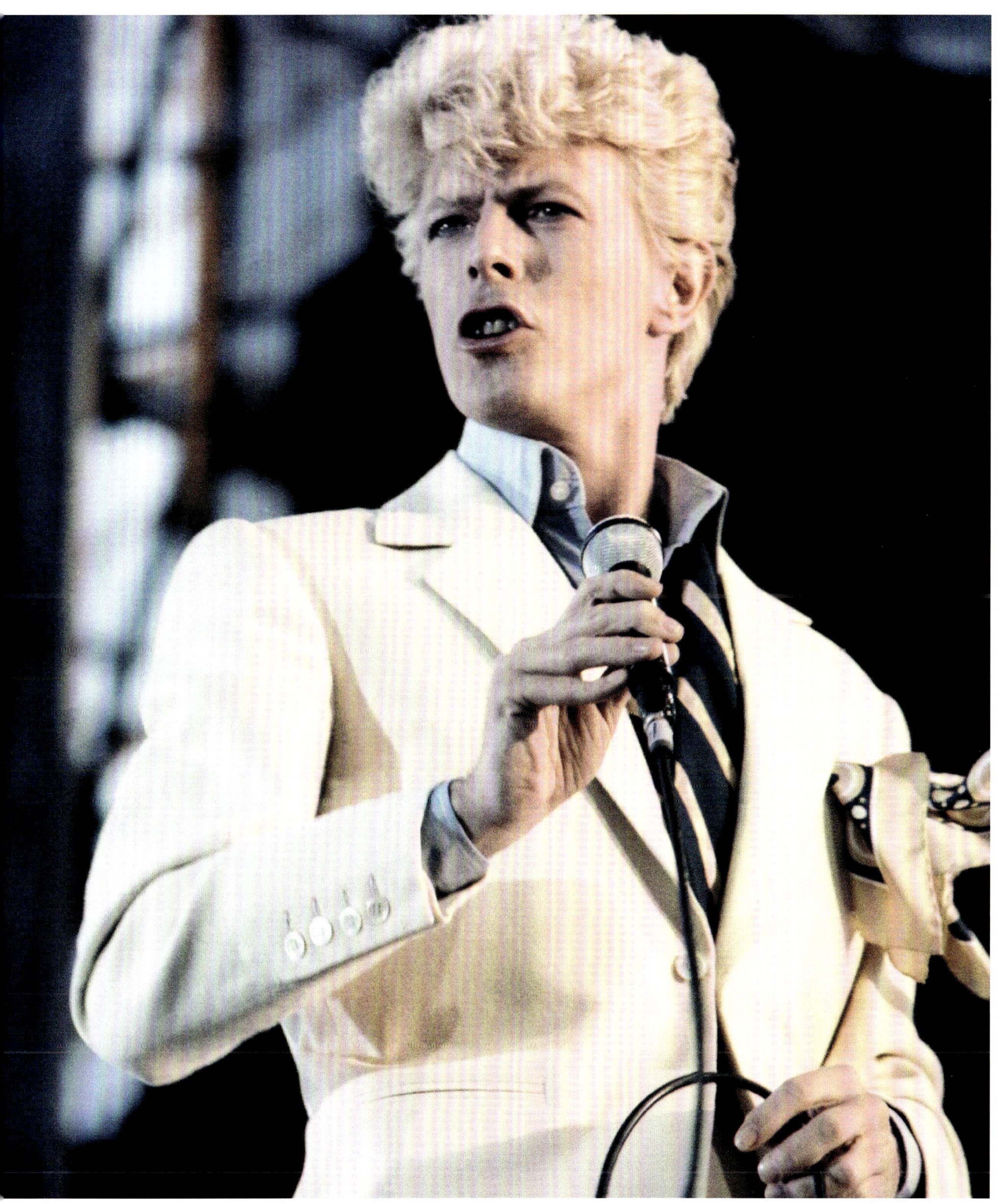

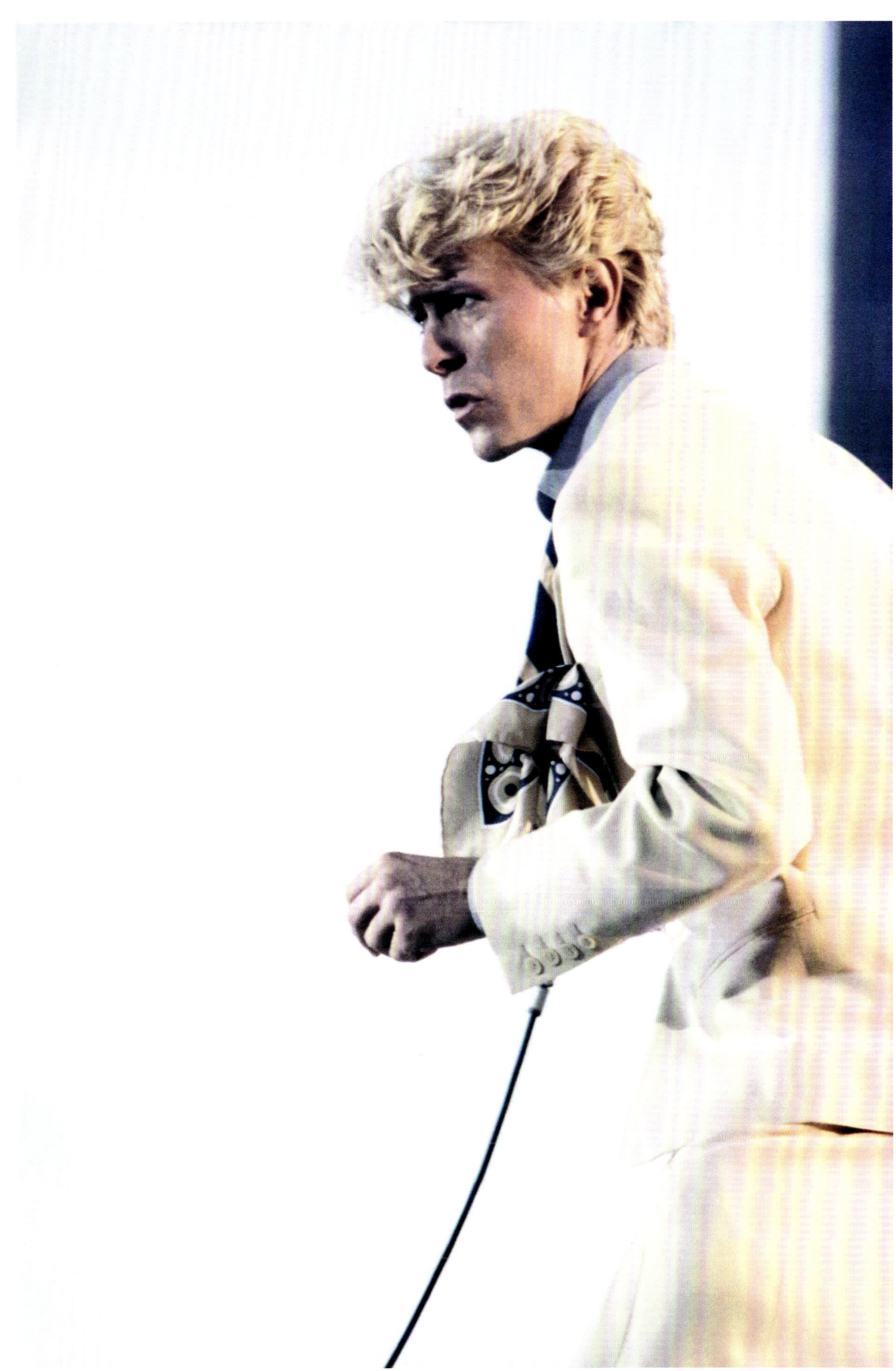

27 JUNE 1989

TIN MACHINE GIG, THE TOWN AND COUNTRY CLUB, LONDON

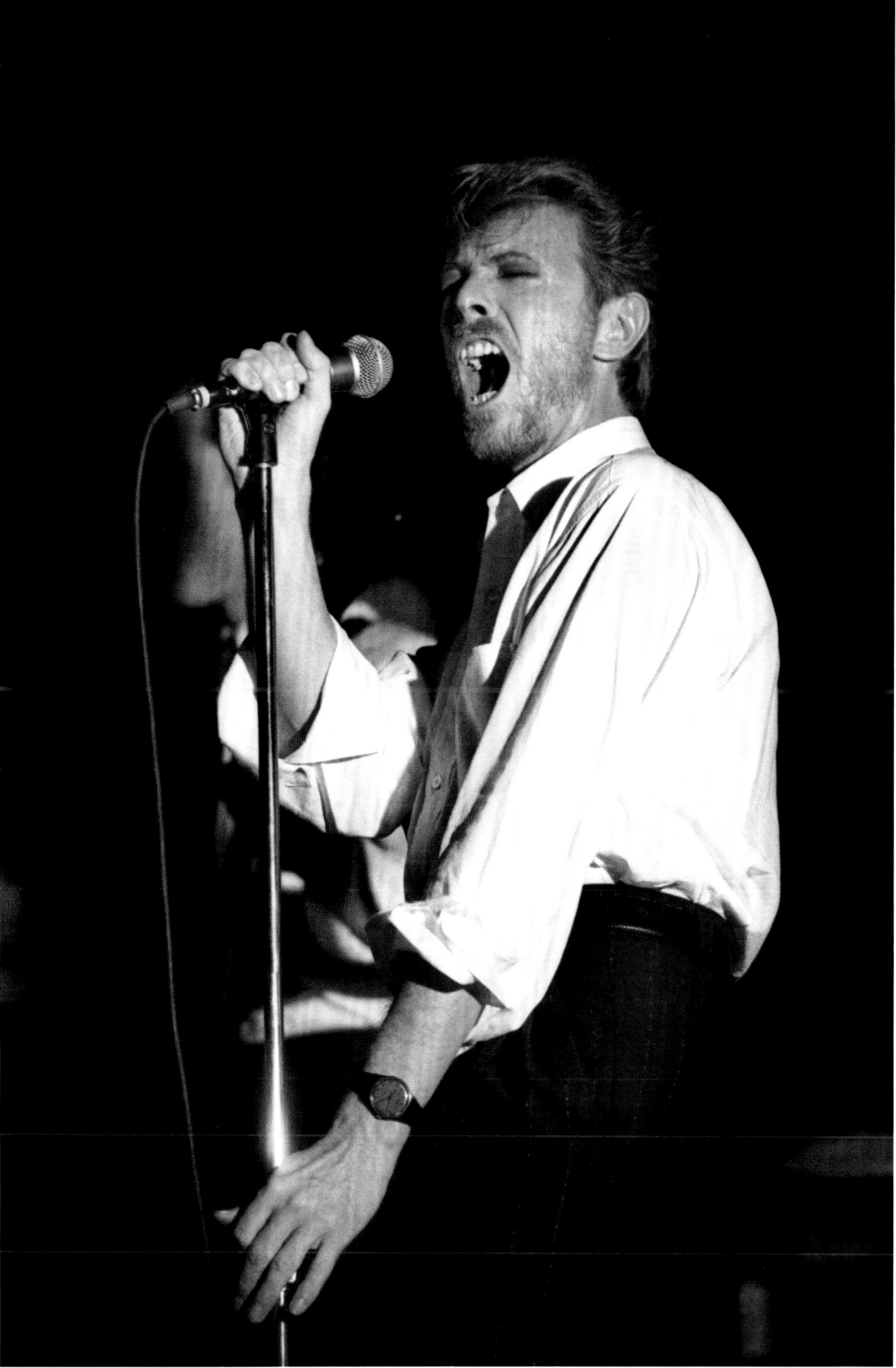

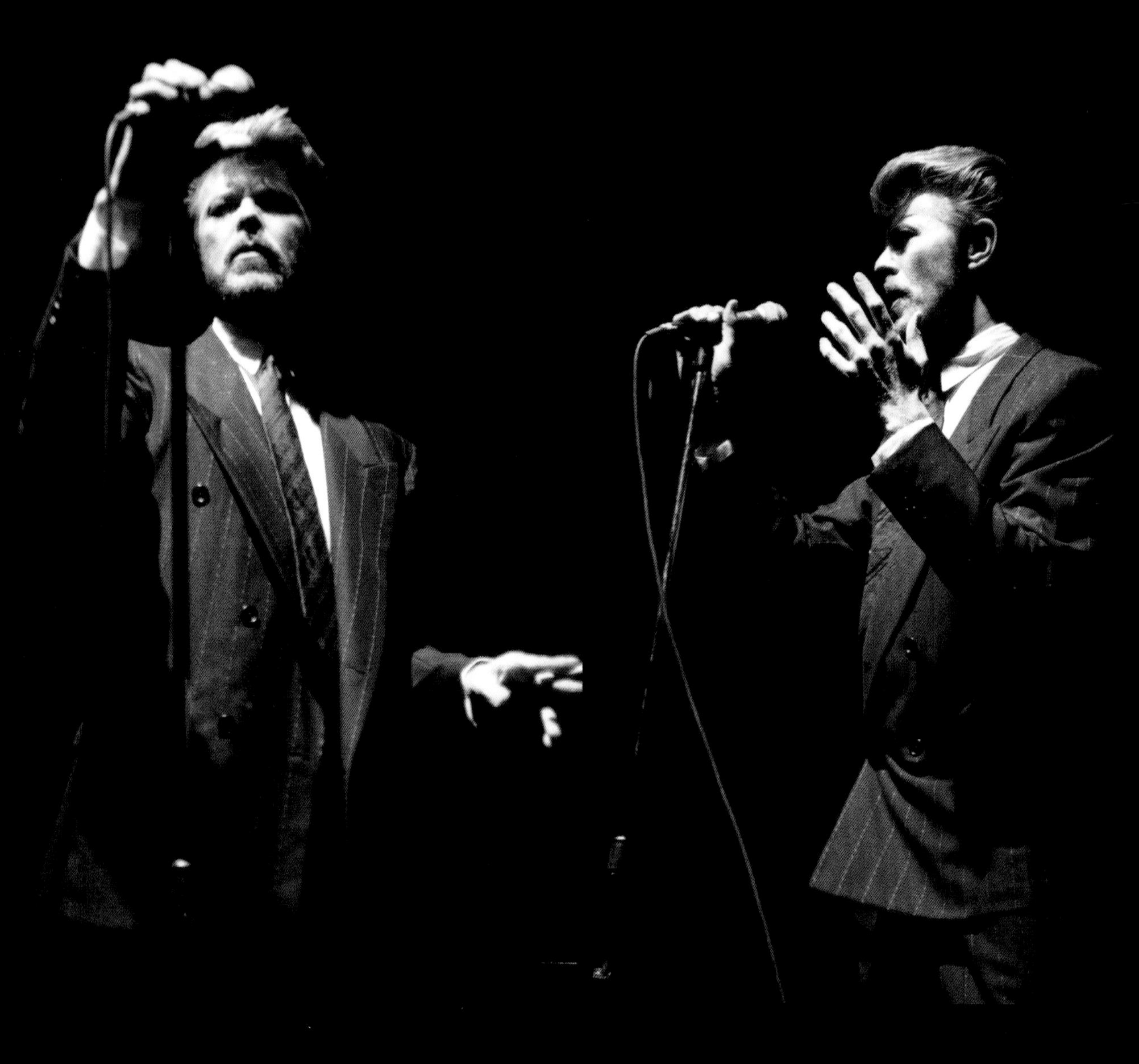

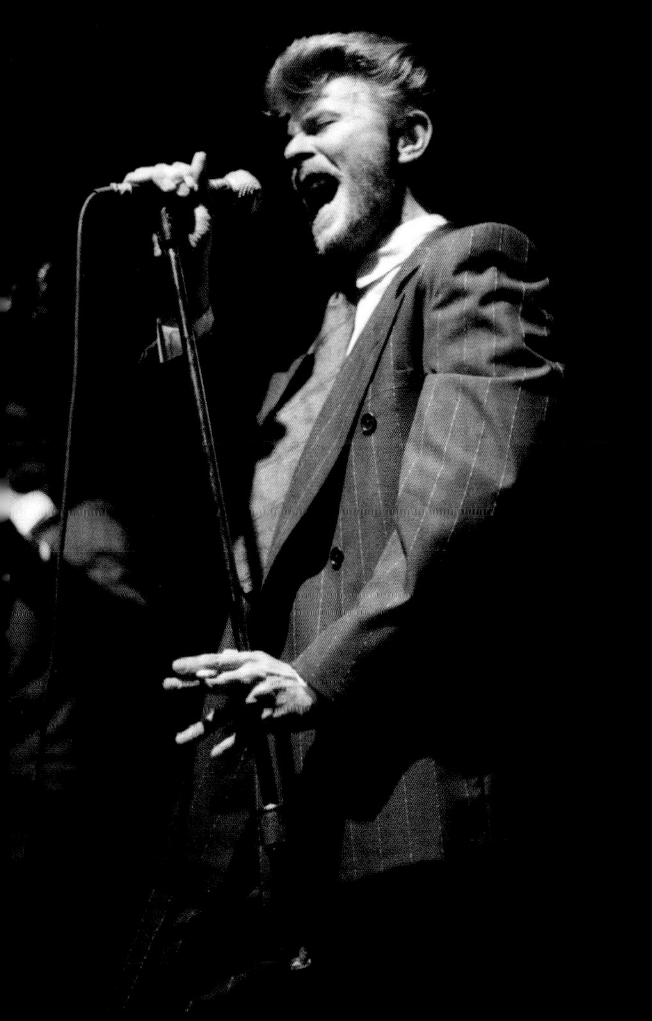
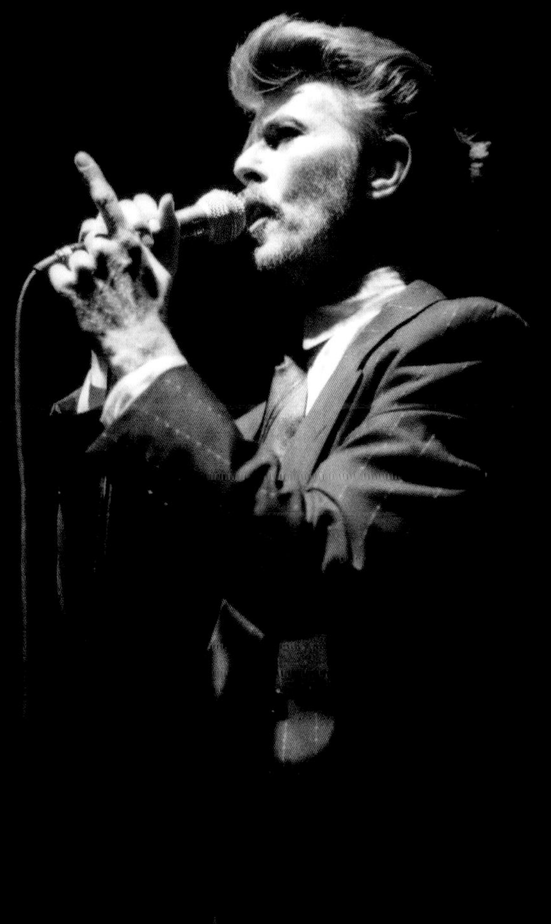

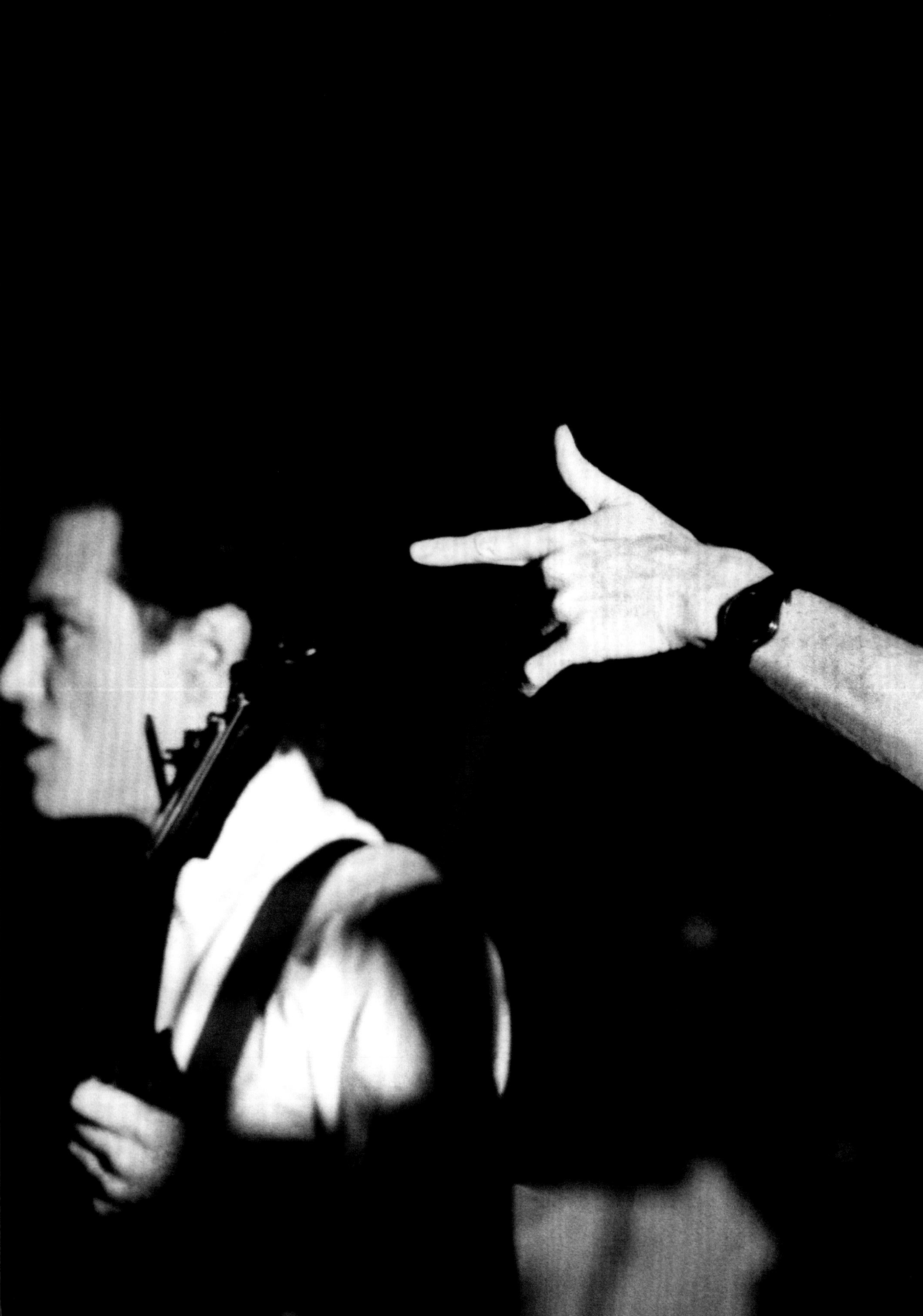

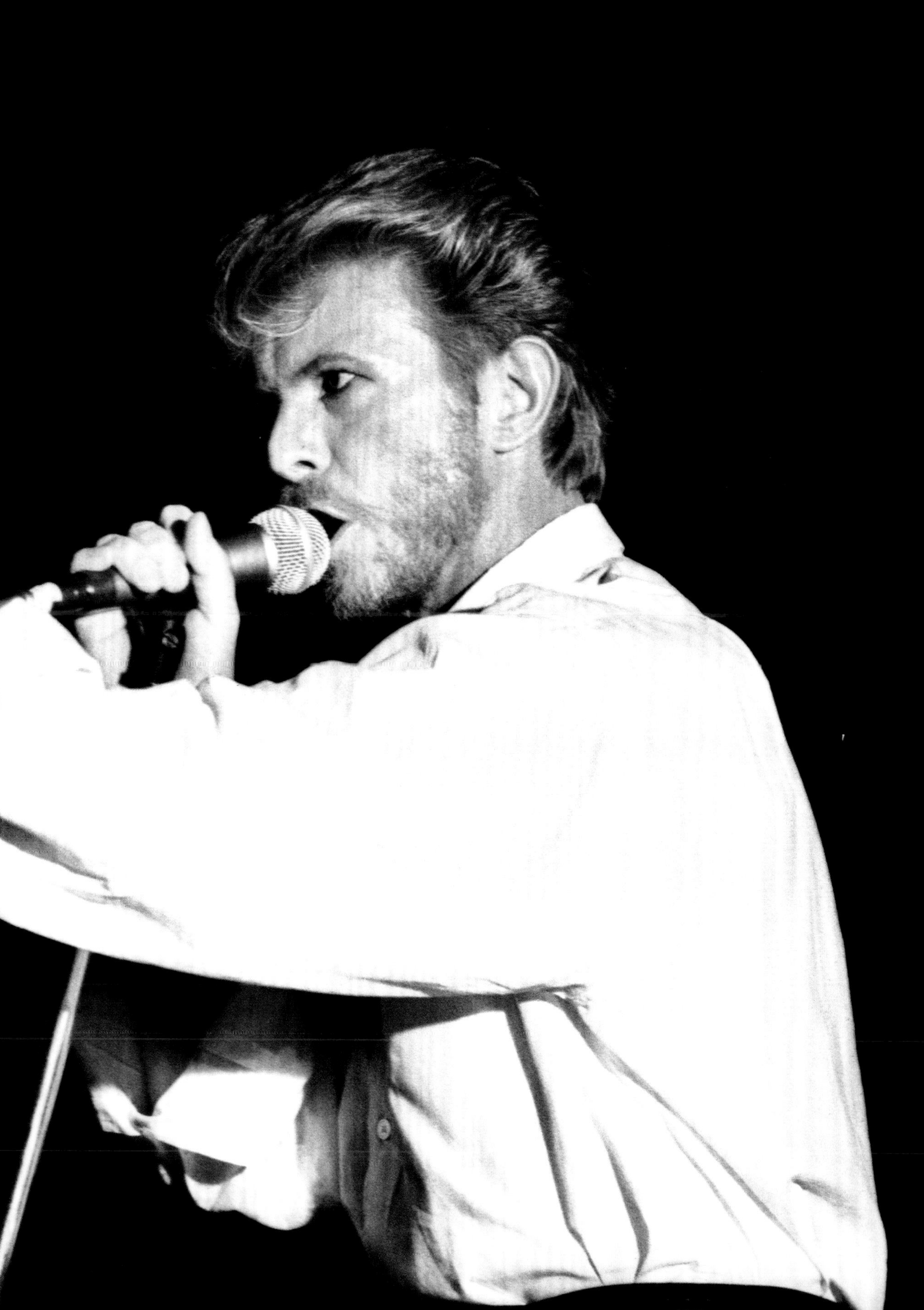

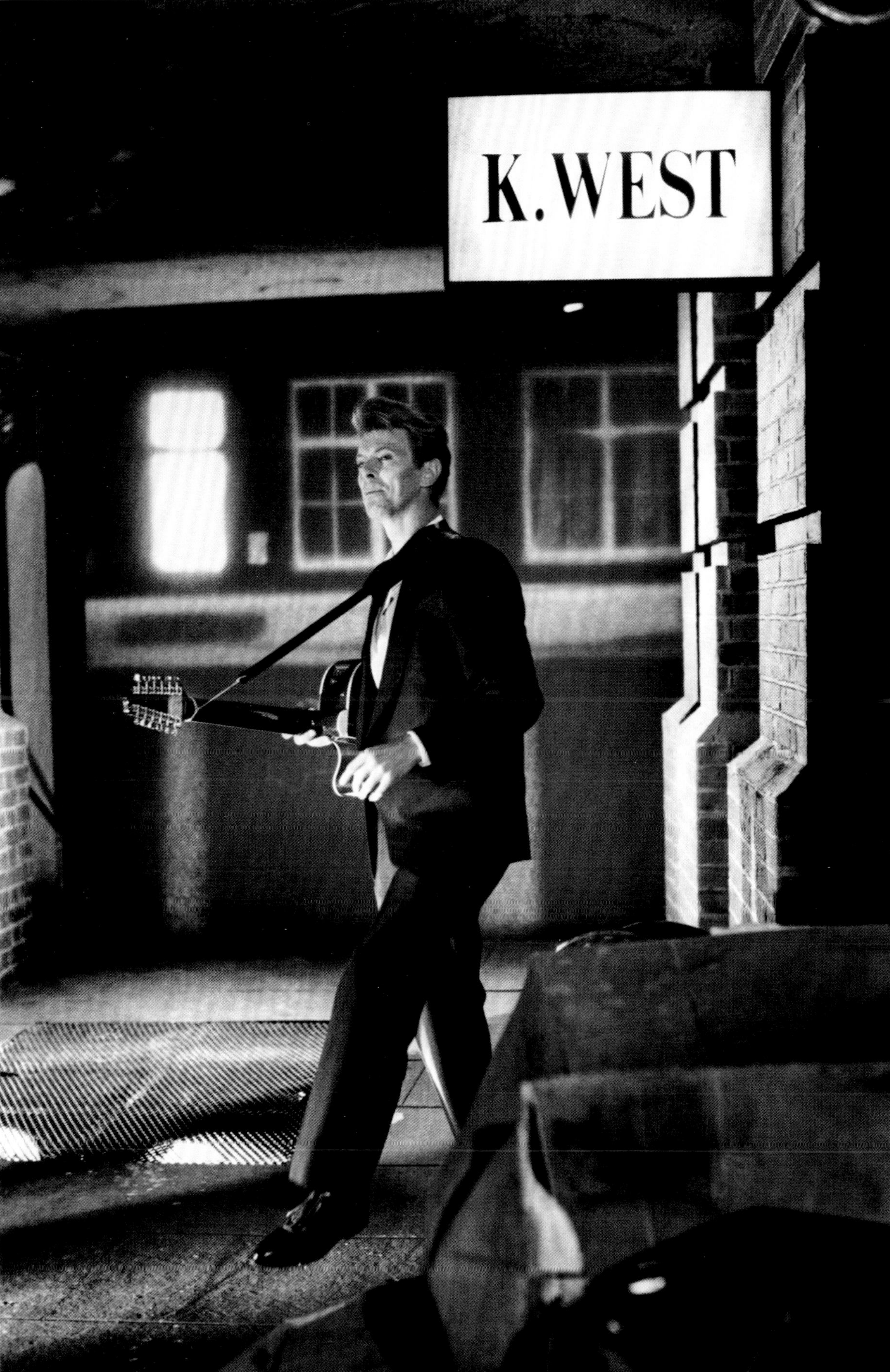
K.WEST

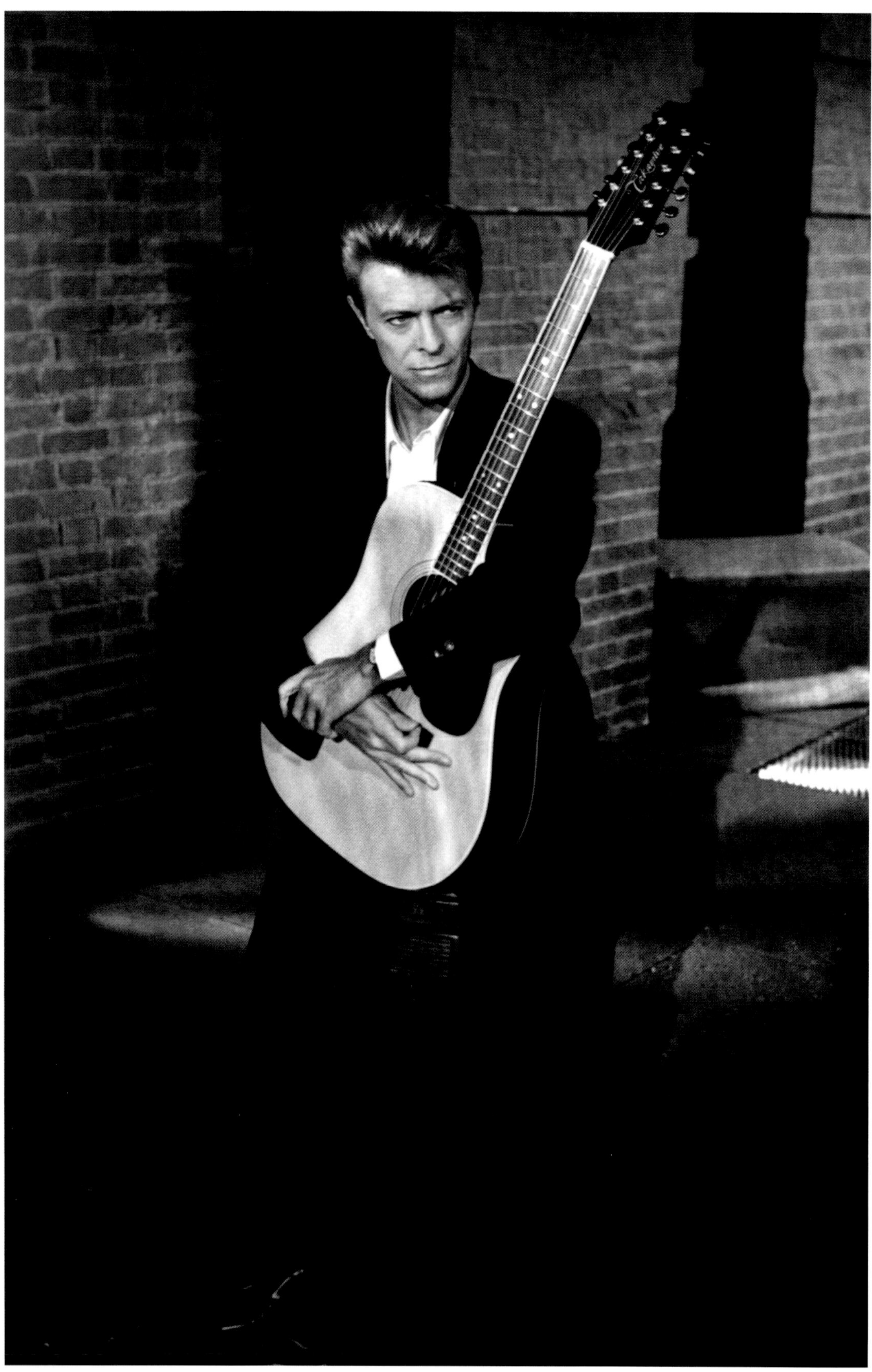

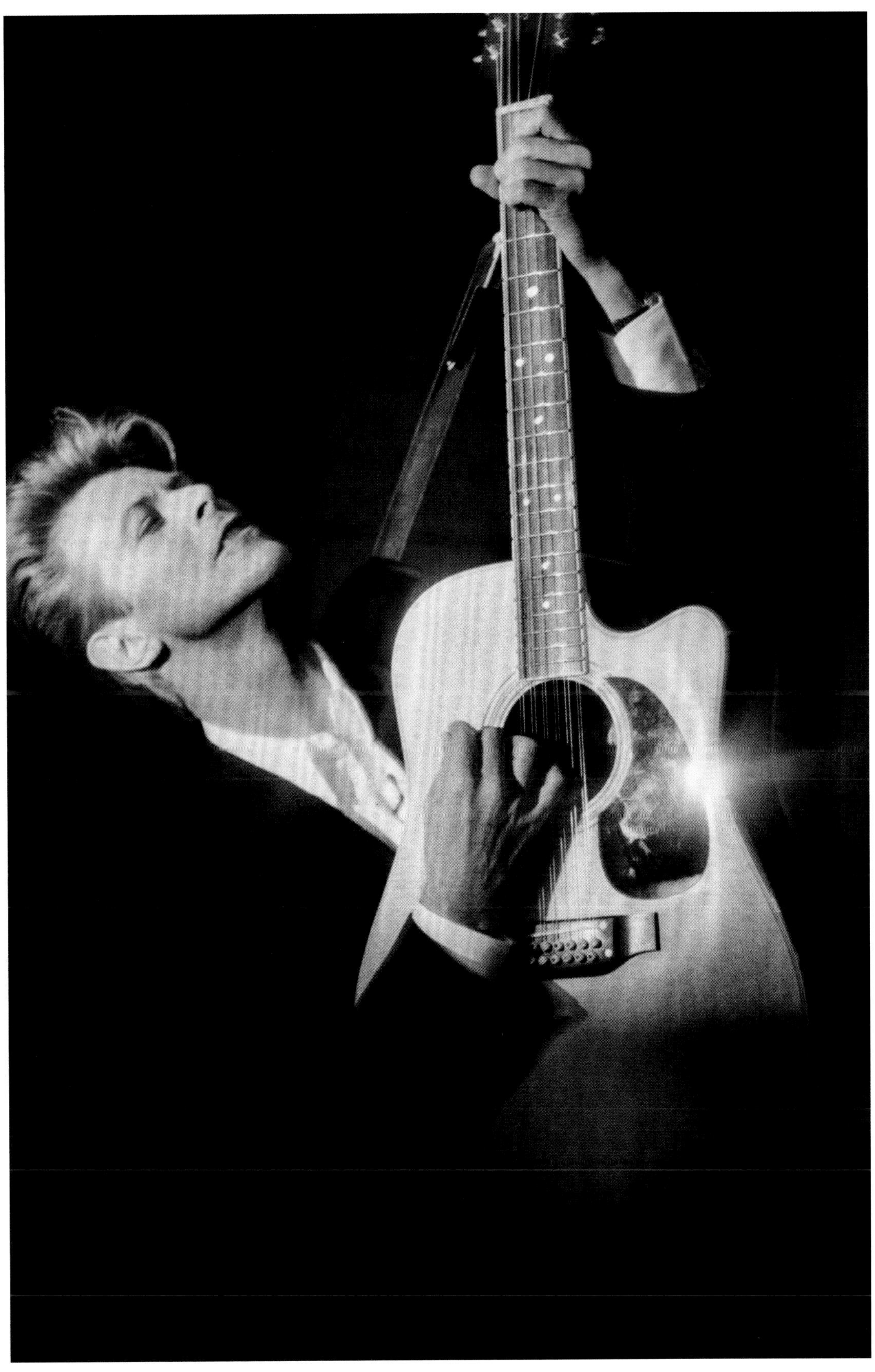

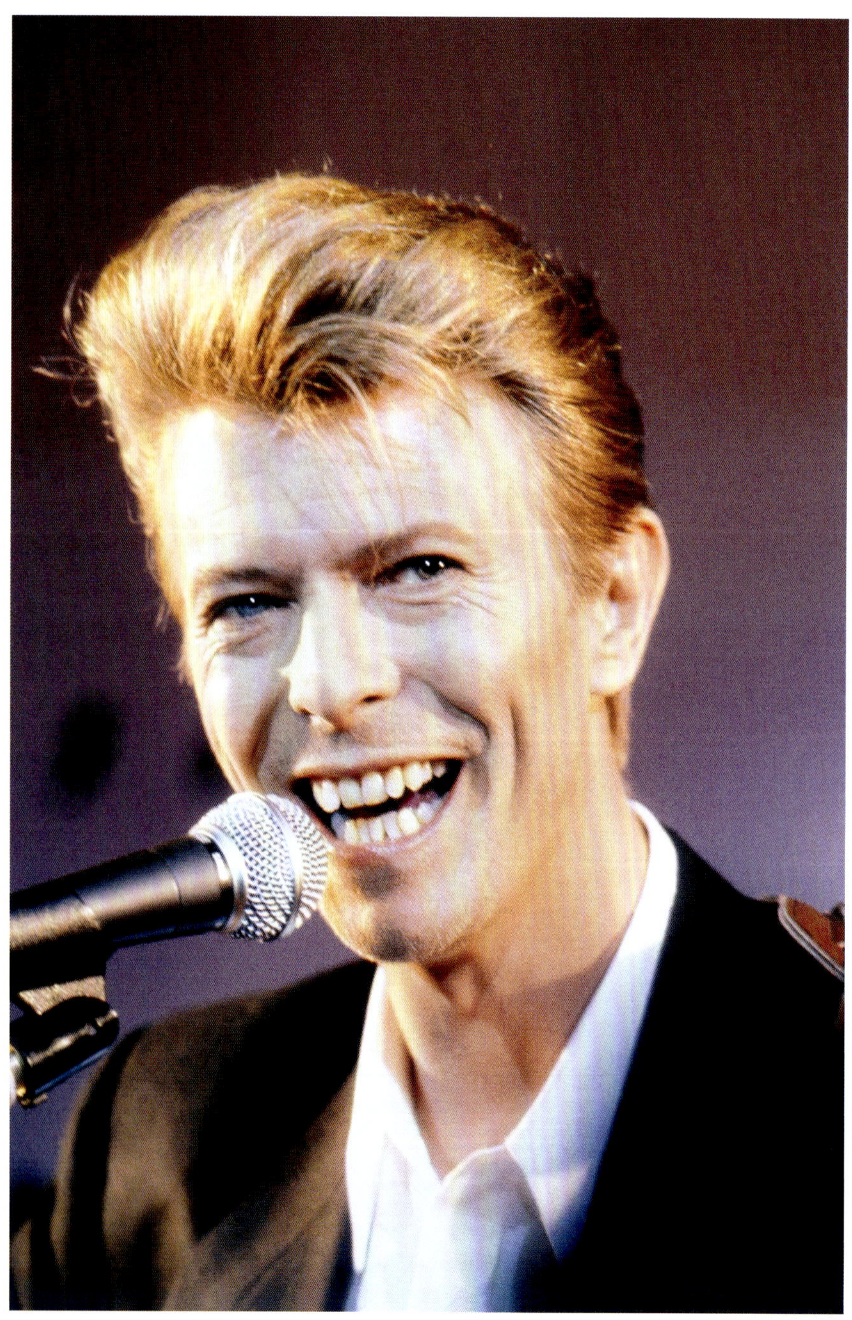

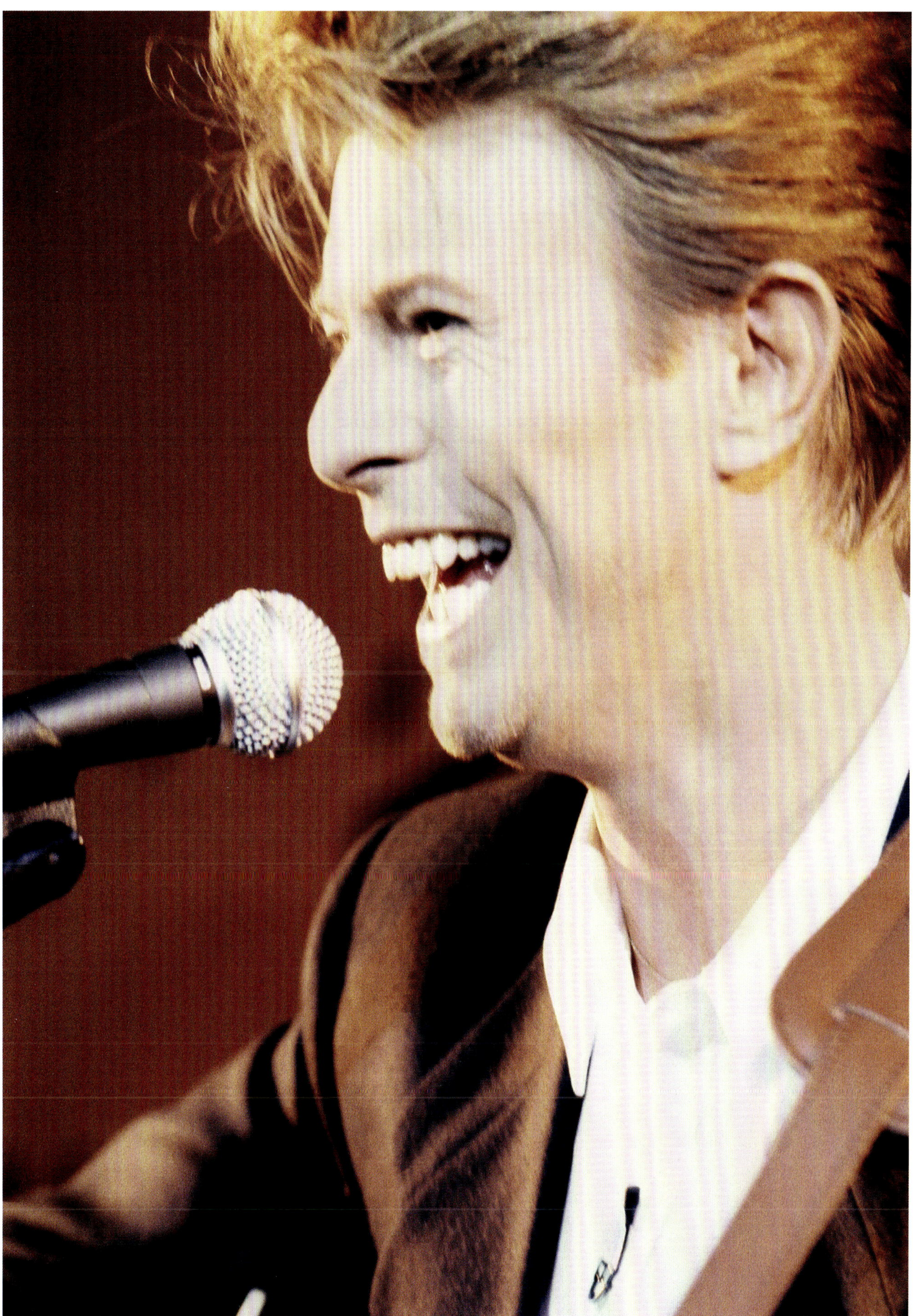

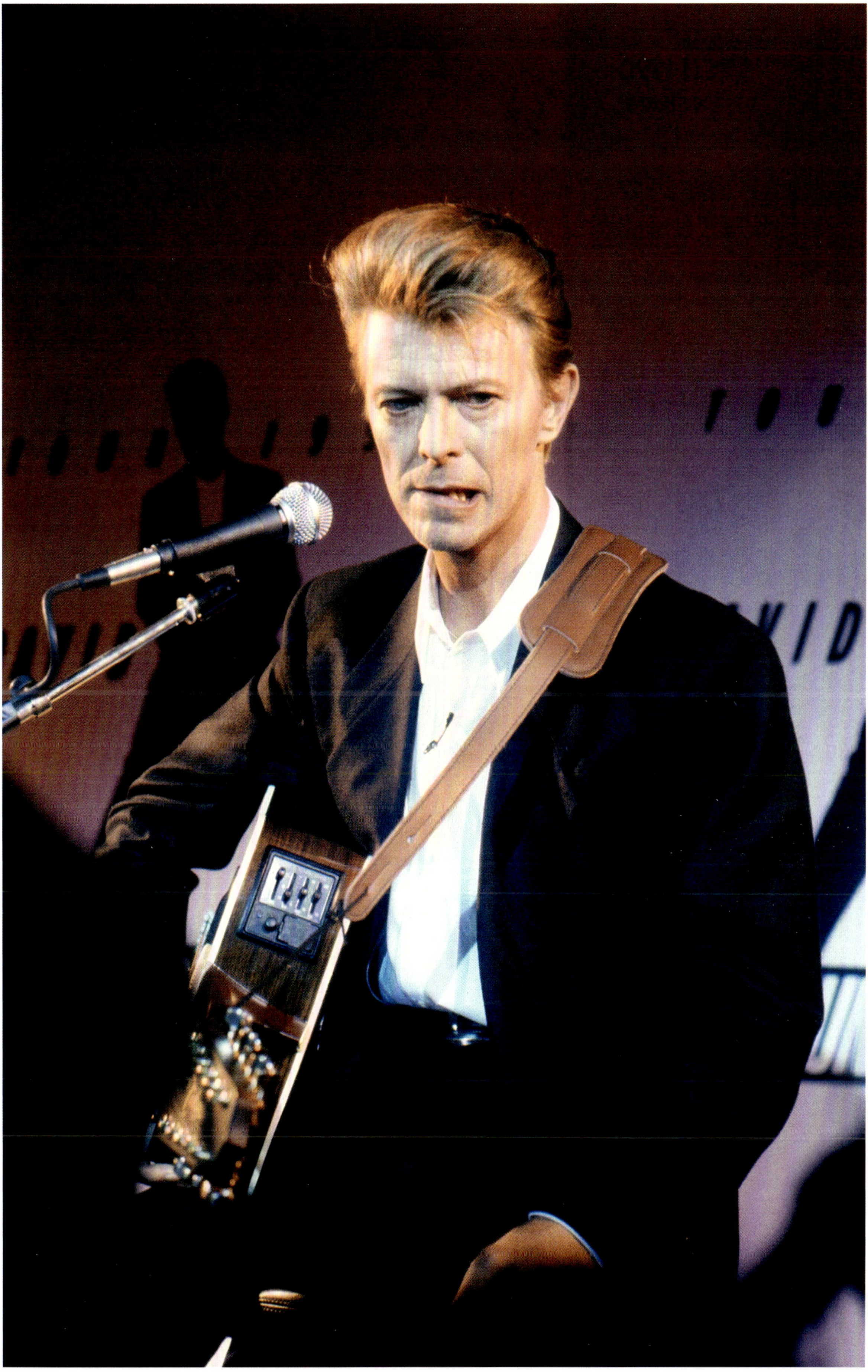

19 MARCH 1990
NEC, BIRMINGHAM

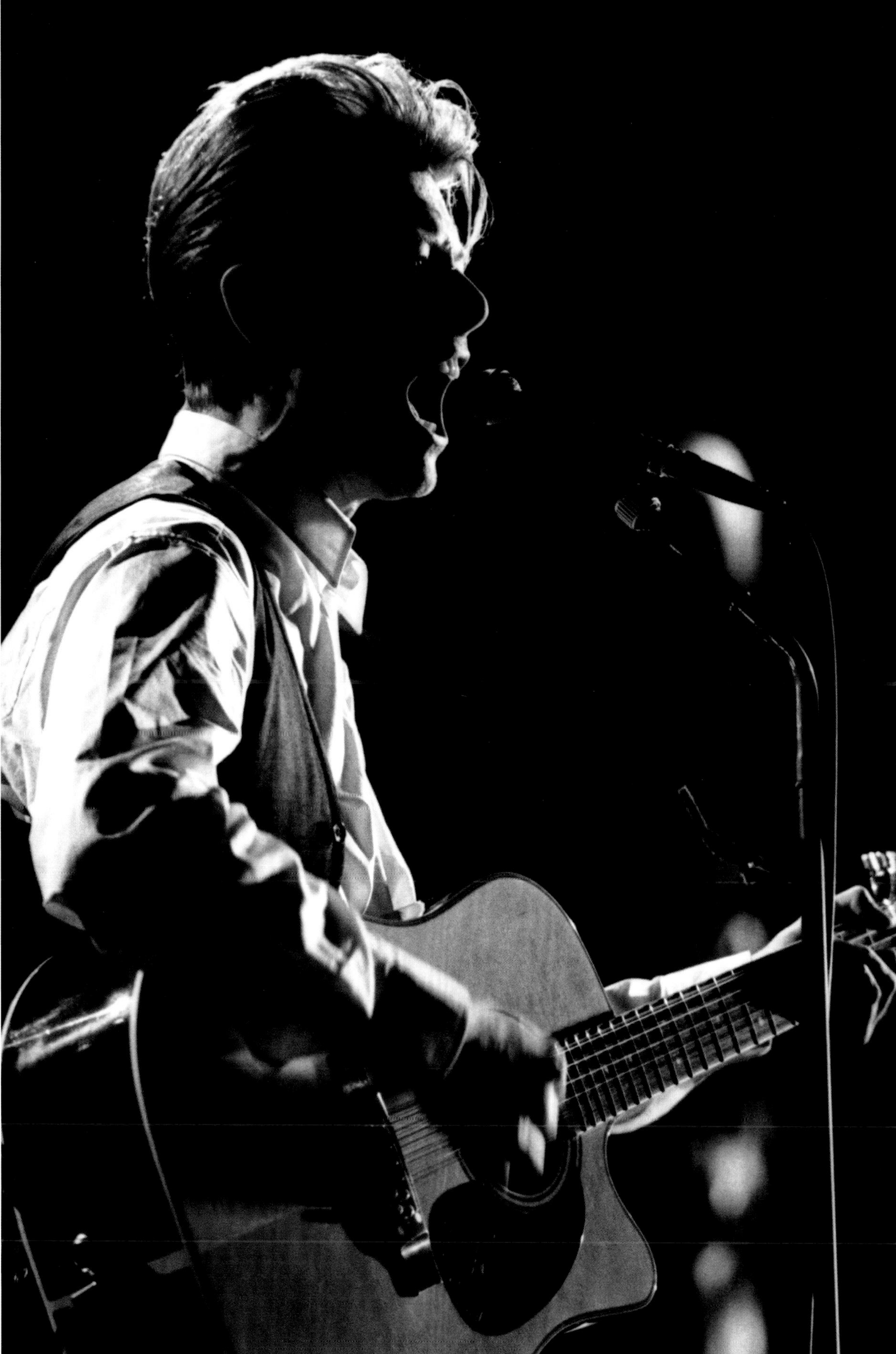

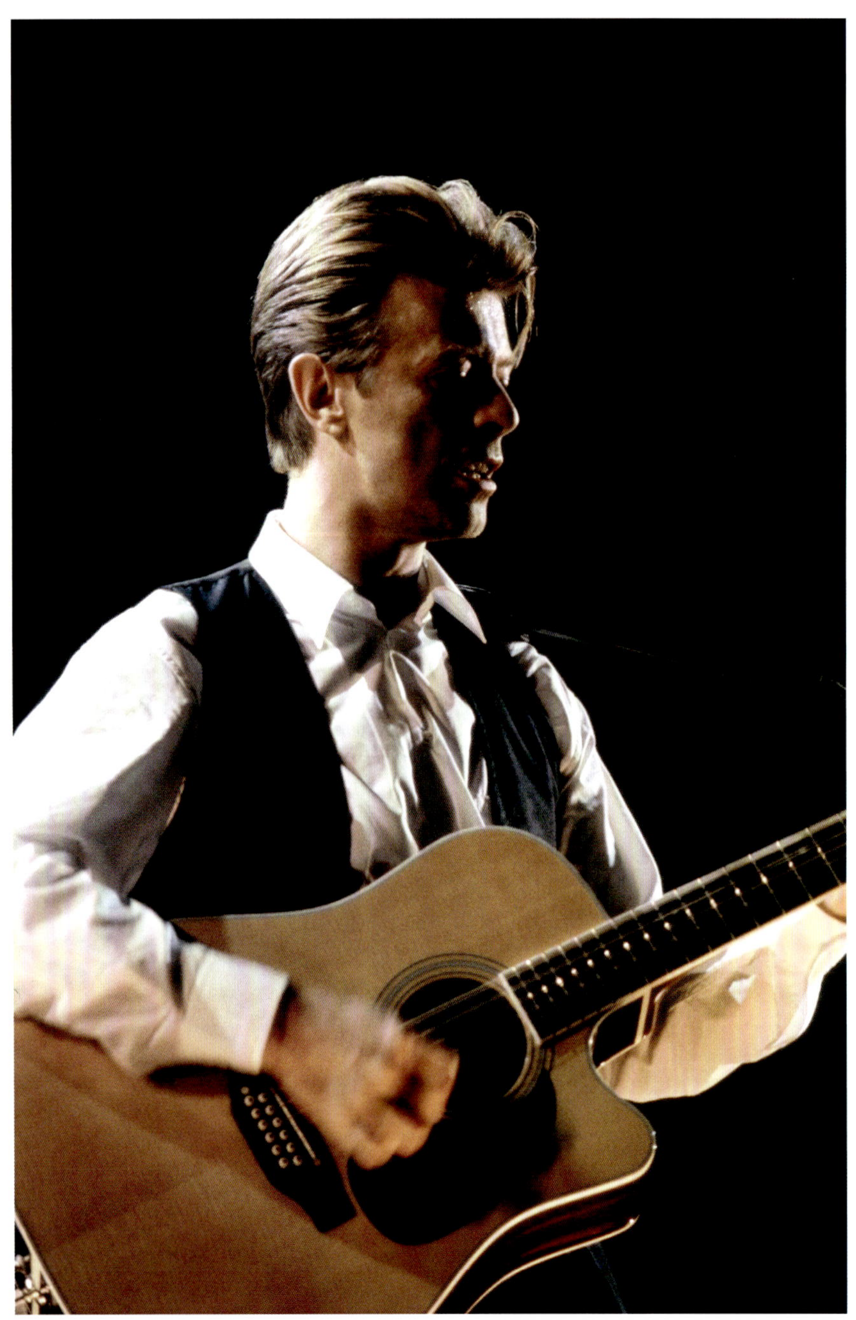

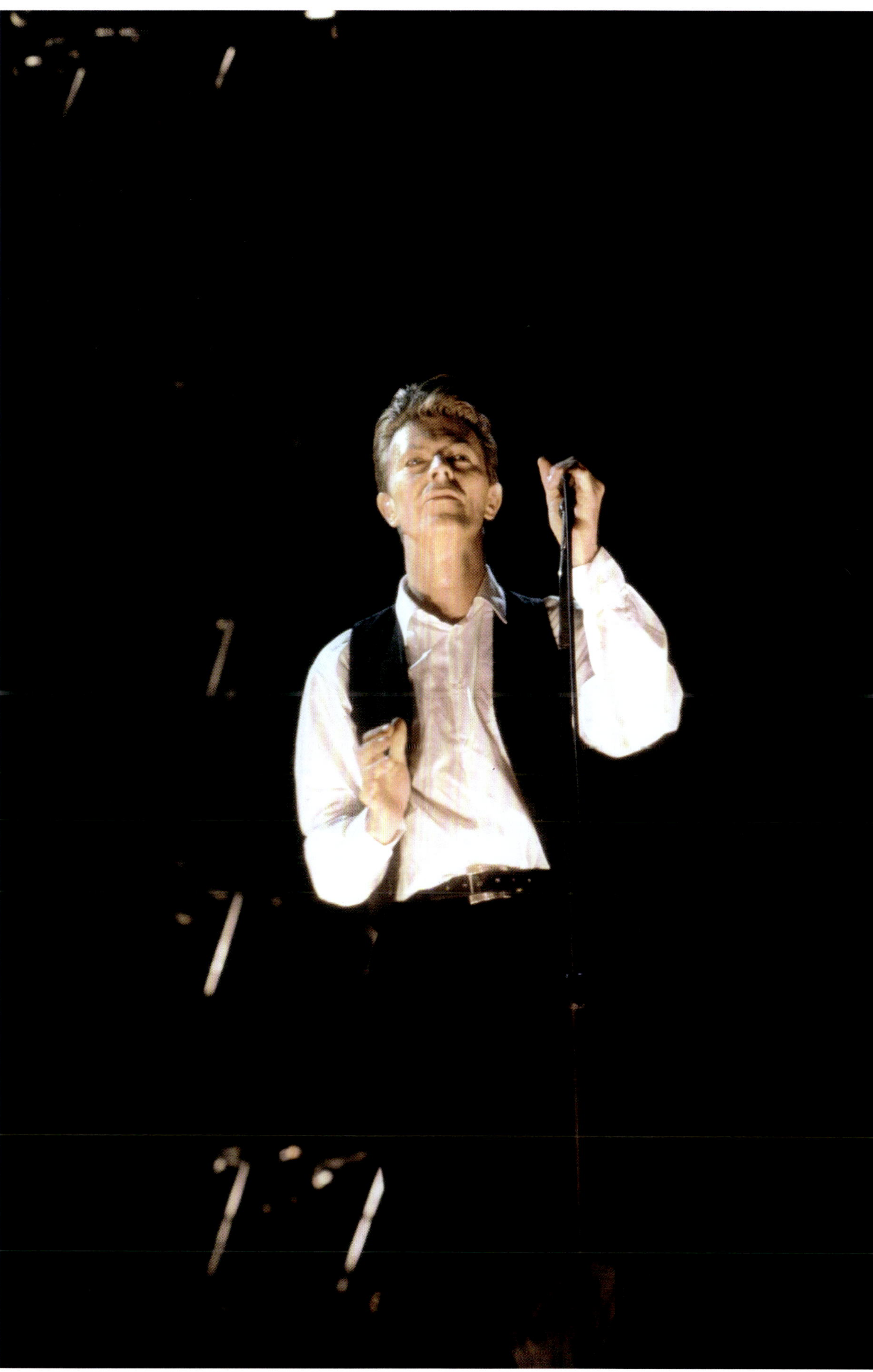

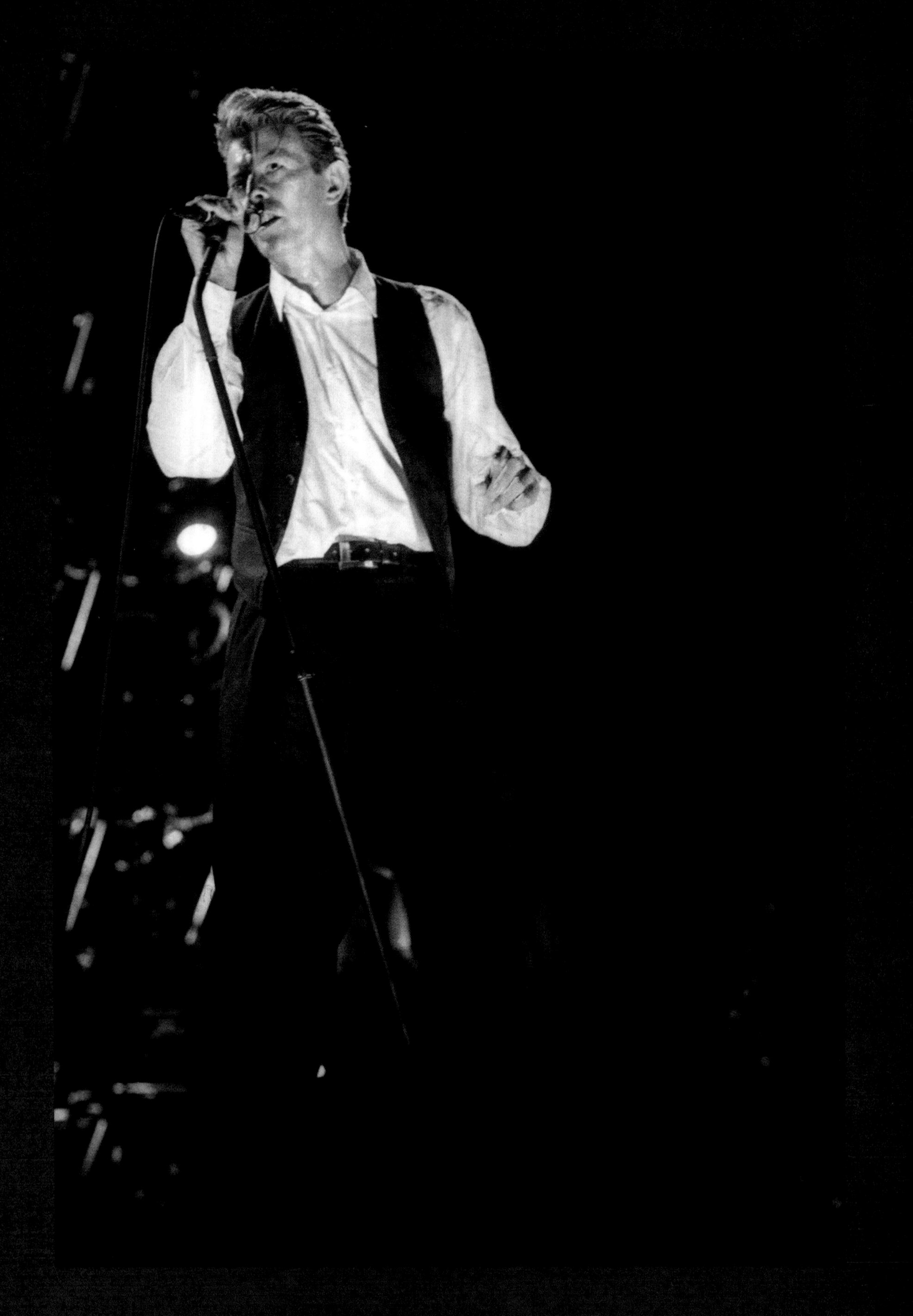

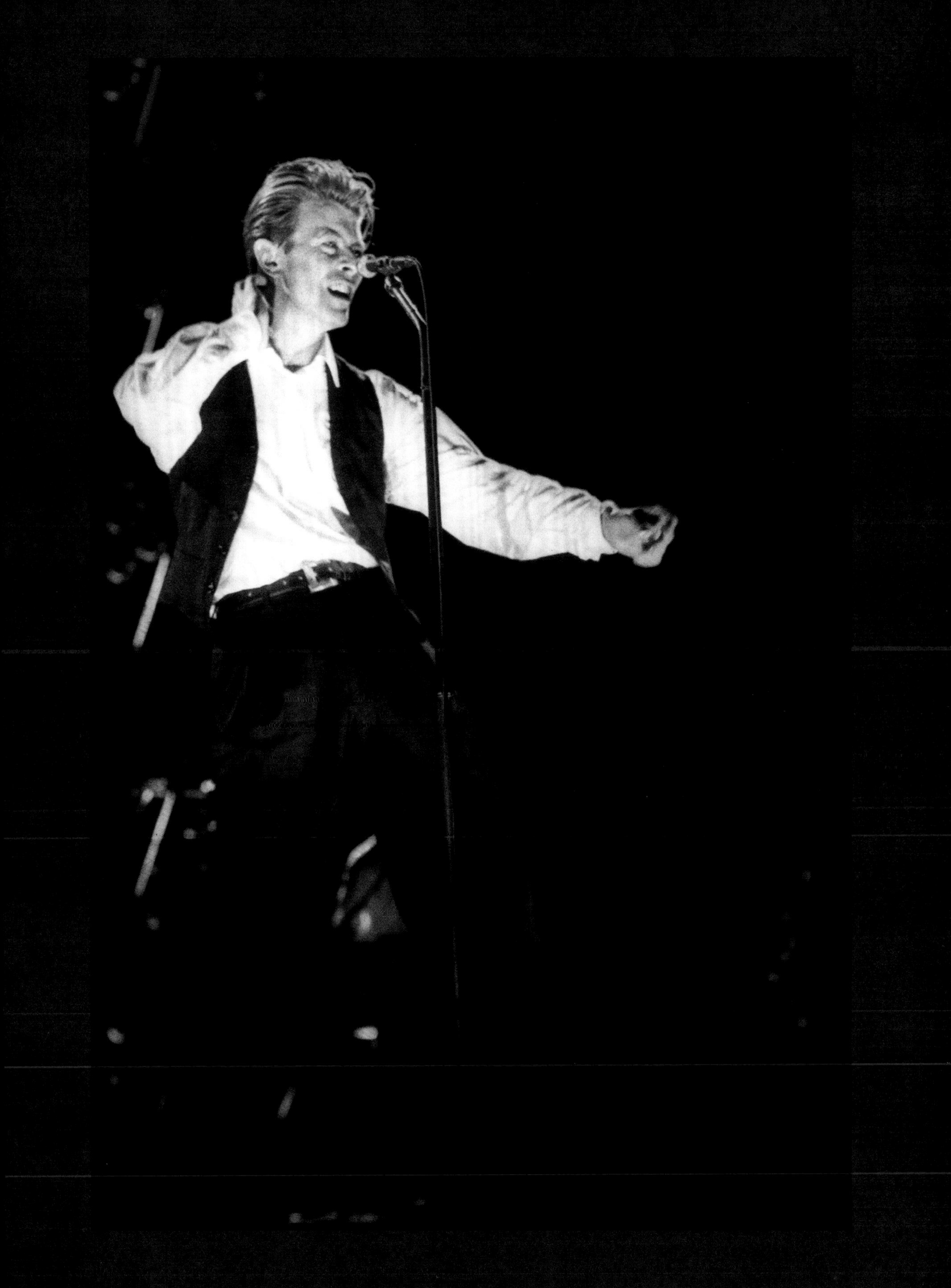

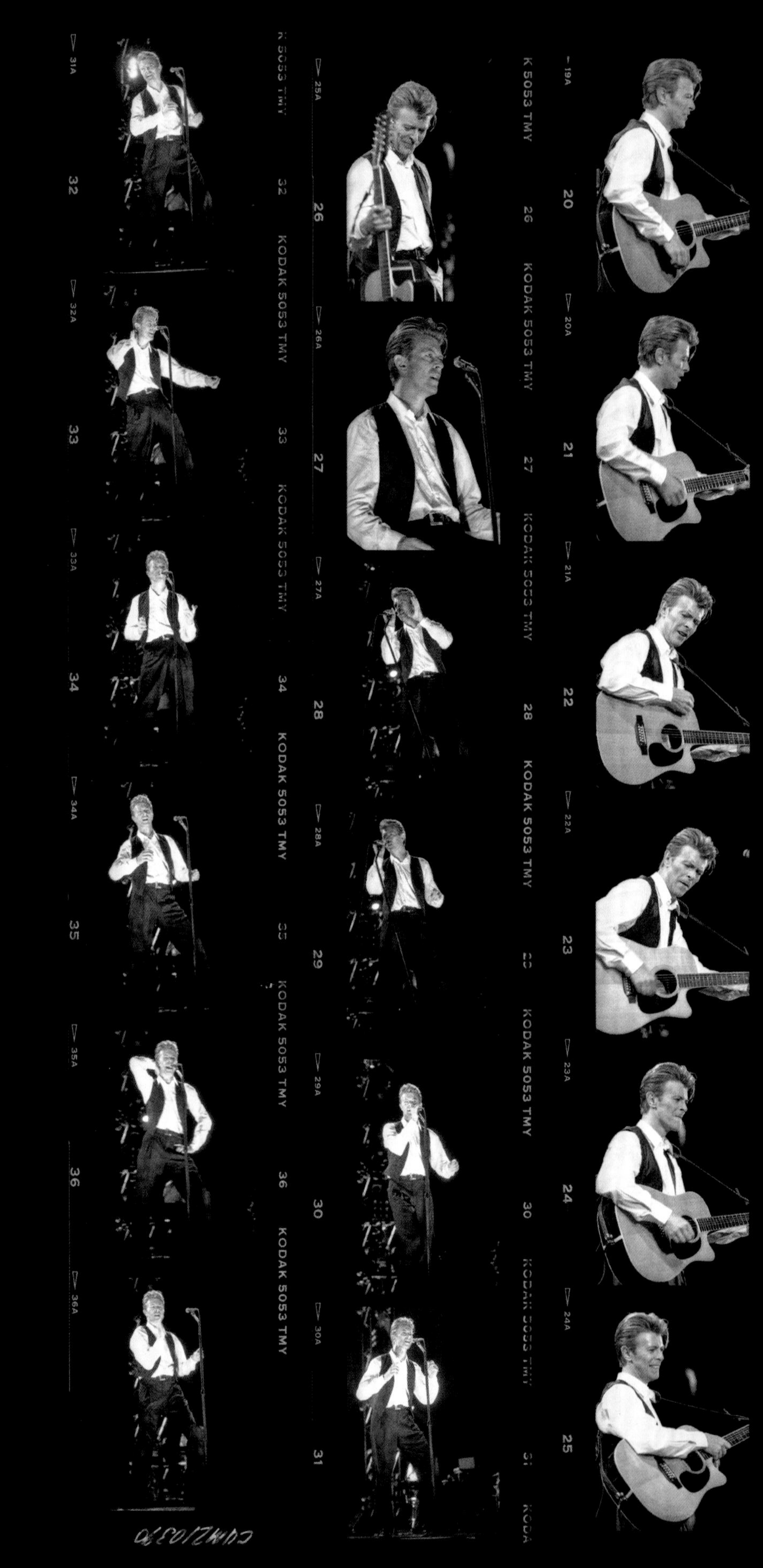

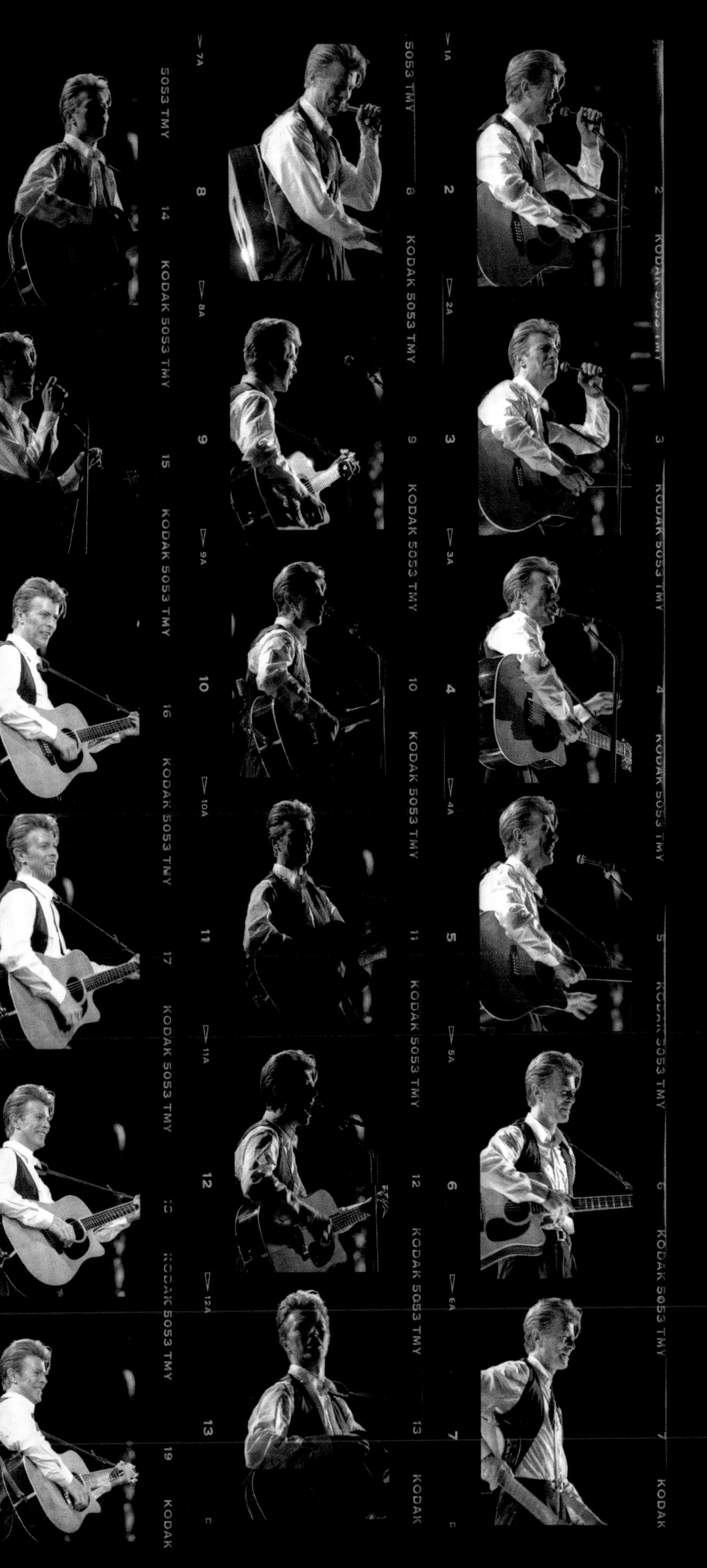

4 AUGUST 1991
FACTORY STUDIOS, DUBLIN

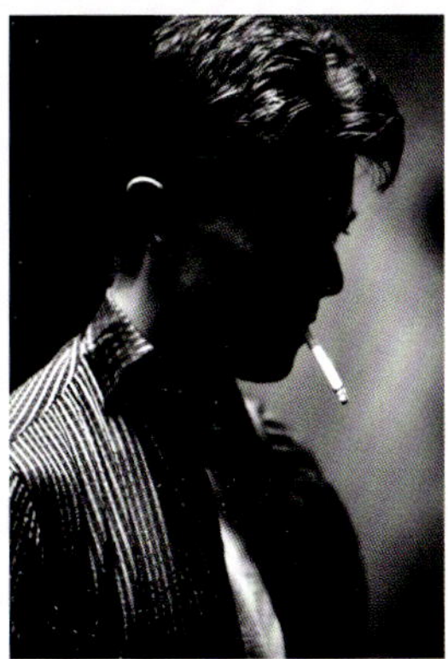
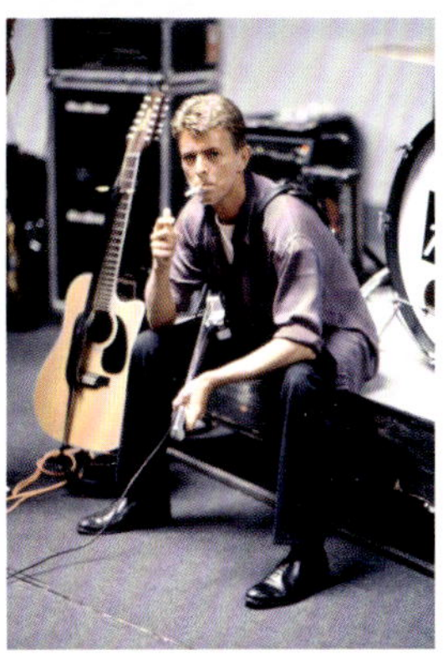

The first time I met Bowie was in Dublin in 1991, during the Tin Machine era. I had been commissioned by the *NME* to photograph him while they were rehearsing and recording, and it had been agreed by his PR that the cover shot of the magazine would definitely feature Tin Machine. Not that any of this was at the forefront of my mind because I was about to meet Bowie for the first time in person and I was a mix of overwhelmed, excited and terrified. It hasn't happened often in my career that I've felt slightly intimidated, but this was one occasion when initially nerves got the better of me. The shoot started in an unsatisfactory way. Bowie was wearing a, shall we say, not entirely aesthetically pleasing Versace blouson jacket. I didn't like how it photographed and I didn't like how it made the photographs look. The problem was, I was too scared to ask him to take it off. So I continued shooting, becoming increasingly frustrated, knowing that none of the shots would work for a cover but too paralysed to tell Bowie his jacket was horrible.

When we finished the posed pictures, I asked if I could stay and watch the rehearsals. Happily, I was told no problem. Bowie was standing around chatting to the band, smoking. But even better, now that the official photo shoot was over, he had removed his awful jacket. There were two perfect moments that I captured. In one, Bowie is casually sitting on the drum riser, elbows on knees, smoking, wearing jeans and a blissfully unfancy shirt. A guitar is standing to the left of him and he has another slung over his shoulder. Briefly, he glanced up towards me, and that was the moment.

In the second, he was standing against an illuminated wall in the rehearsal room, as ever, smoking. There was no light on him at all and his position was perfect, so I moved myself slightly to frame the picture better. This was when I captured him in silhouette – that utterly distinctive profile. The frame draws you in via the brightest, most central point, the cigarette, which allows your gaze to travel up to his face. He is in shadow, but it is unmistakeably Bowie.

The end of this story is that the *NME* cover featured the shot of Bowie sitting on the drum riser. When his PR complained that the agreement was that Tin Machine would be on the cover, the editor assured him that Tin Machine were on the cover and directed him to the caption accompanying the photograph, which read, "David Bowie out of Tin Machine (not pictured)."

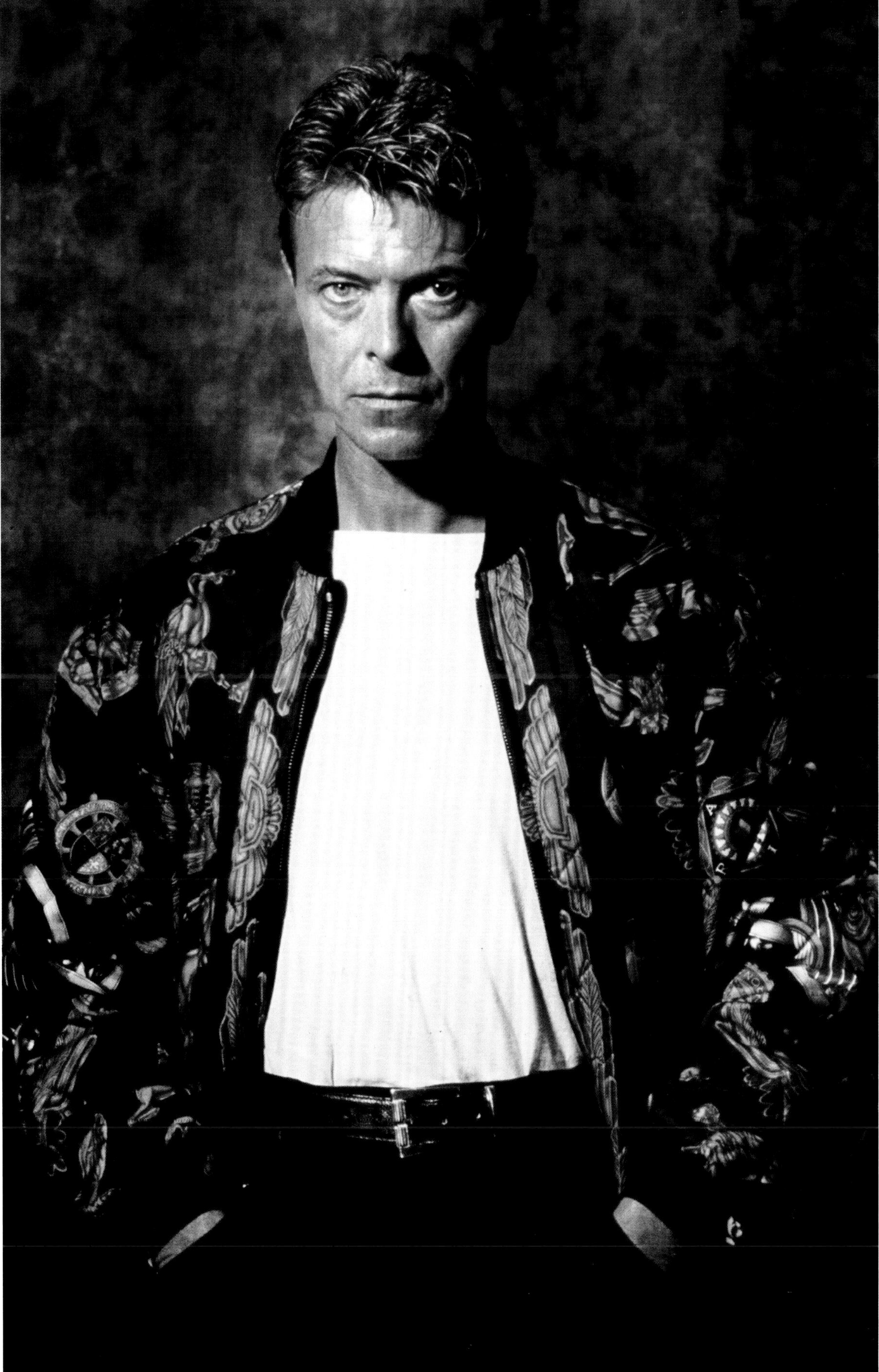

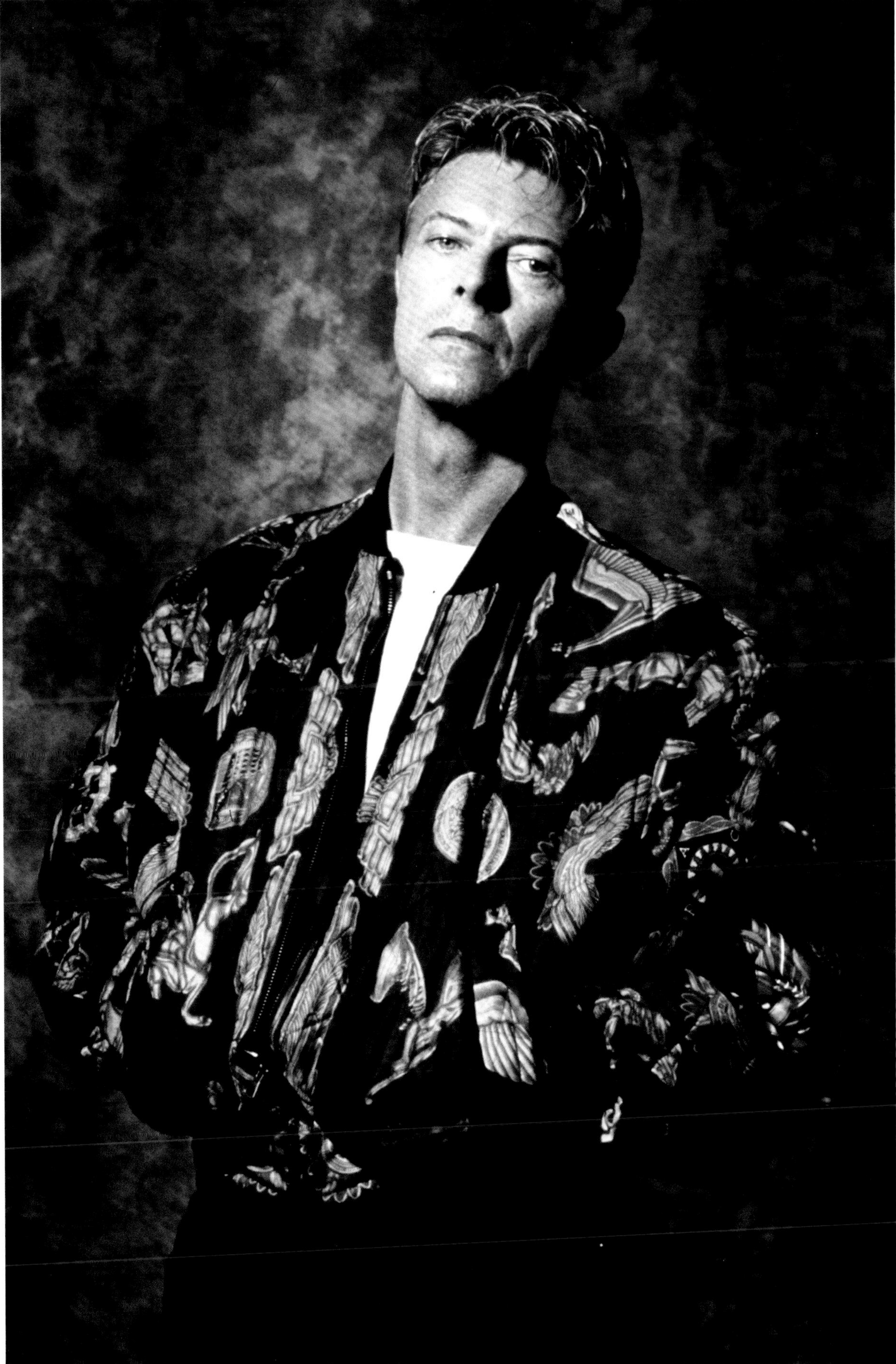

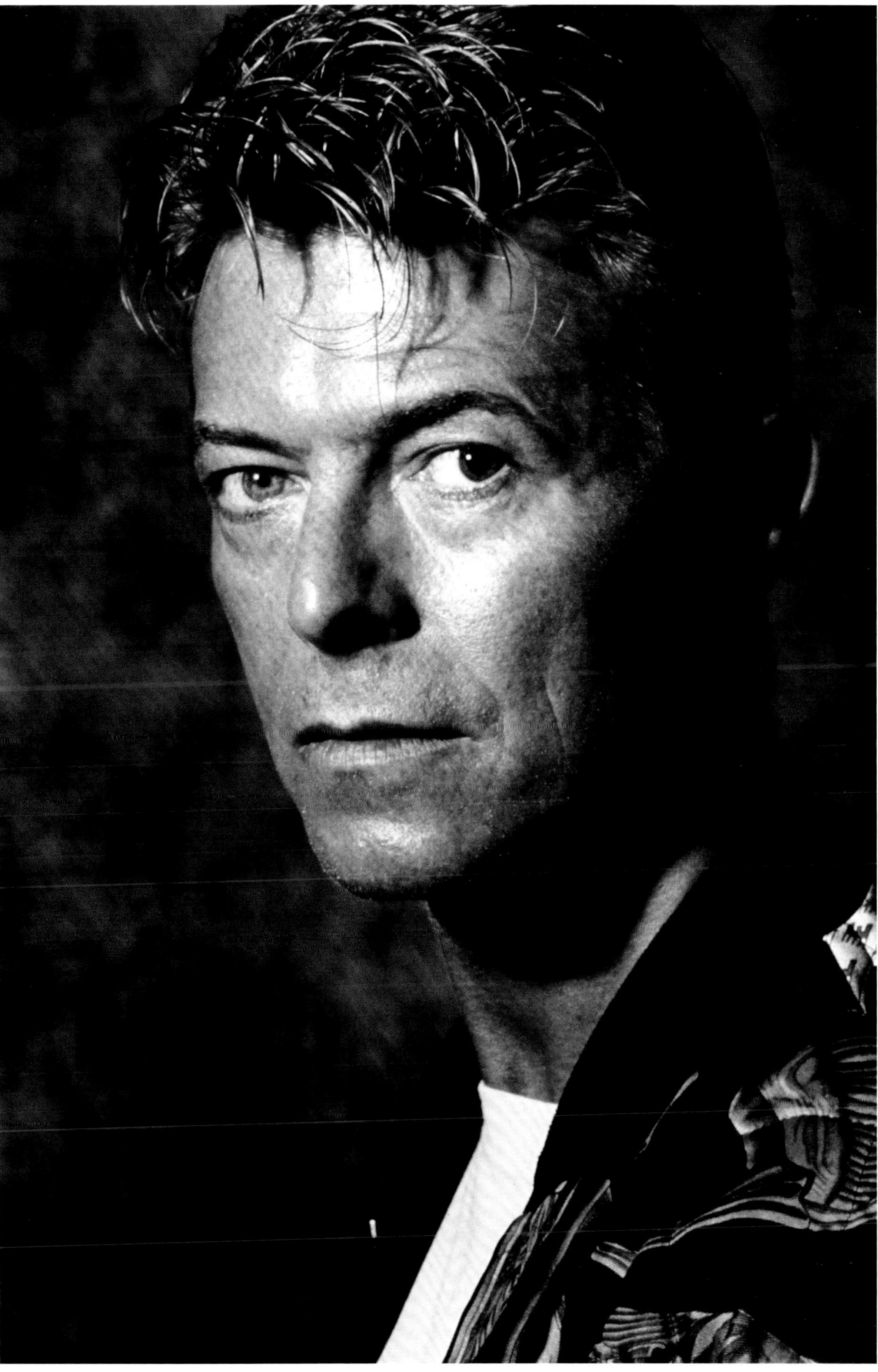

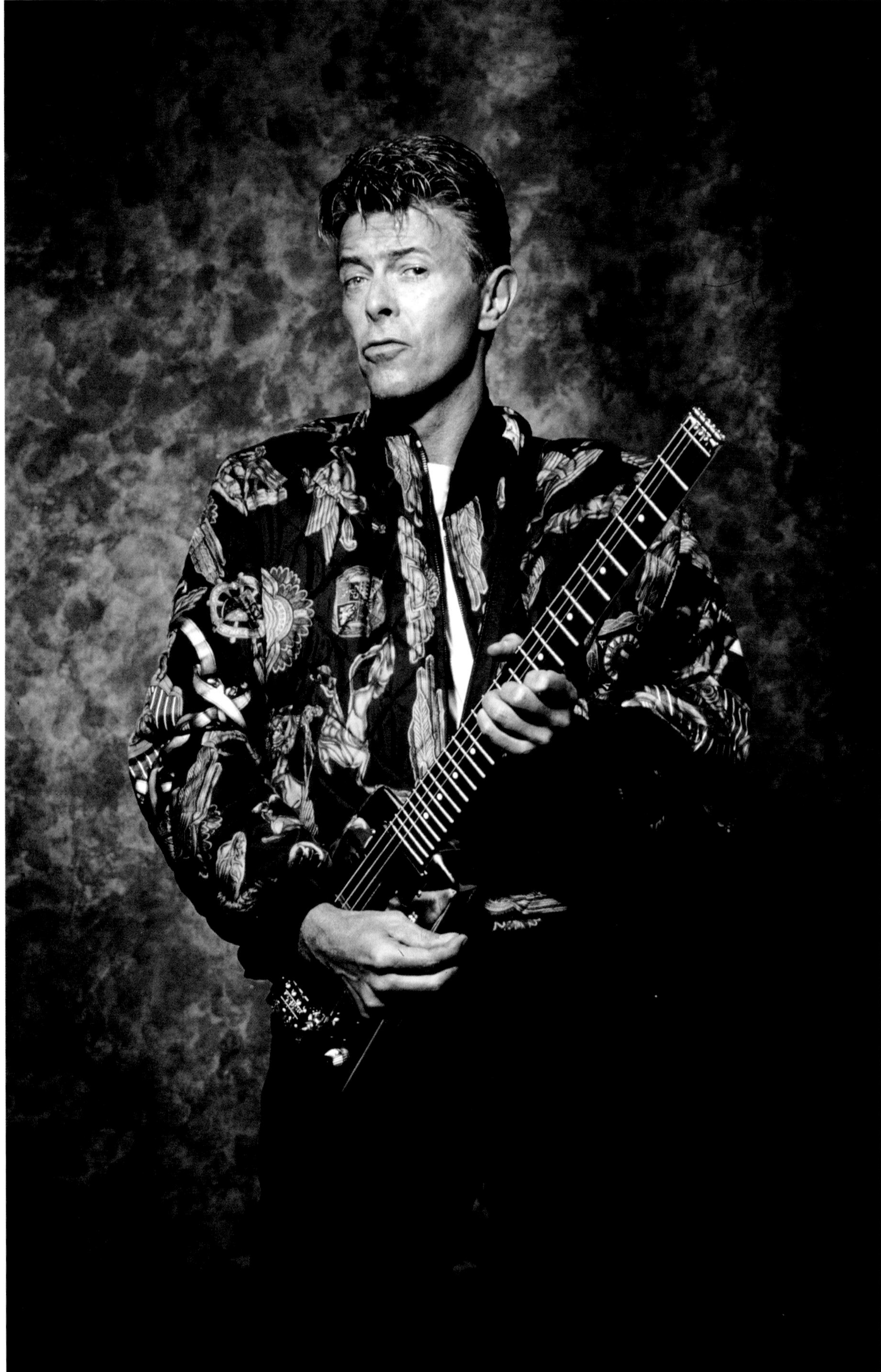

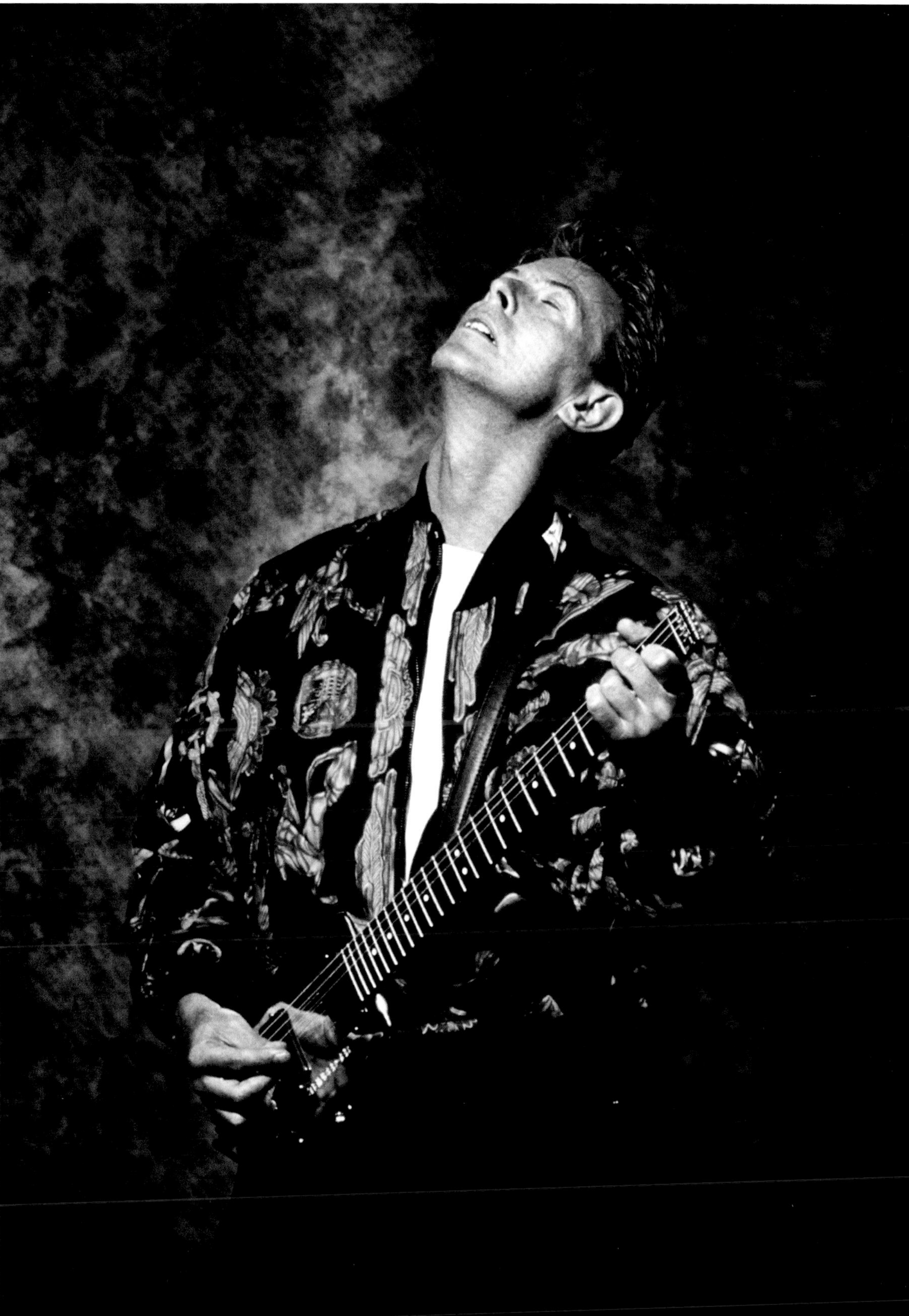

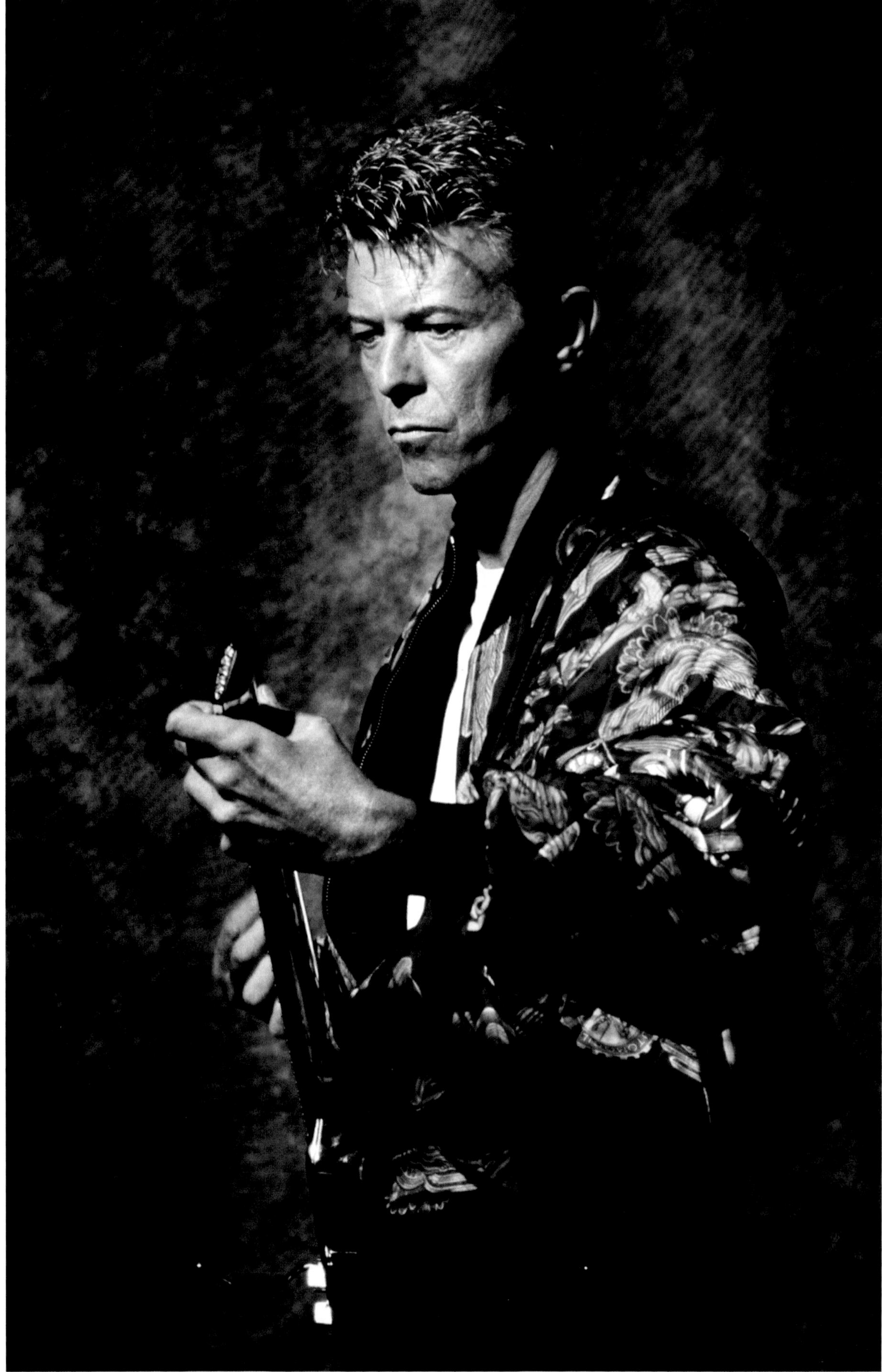

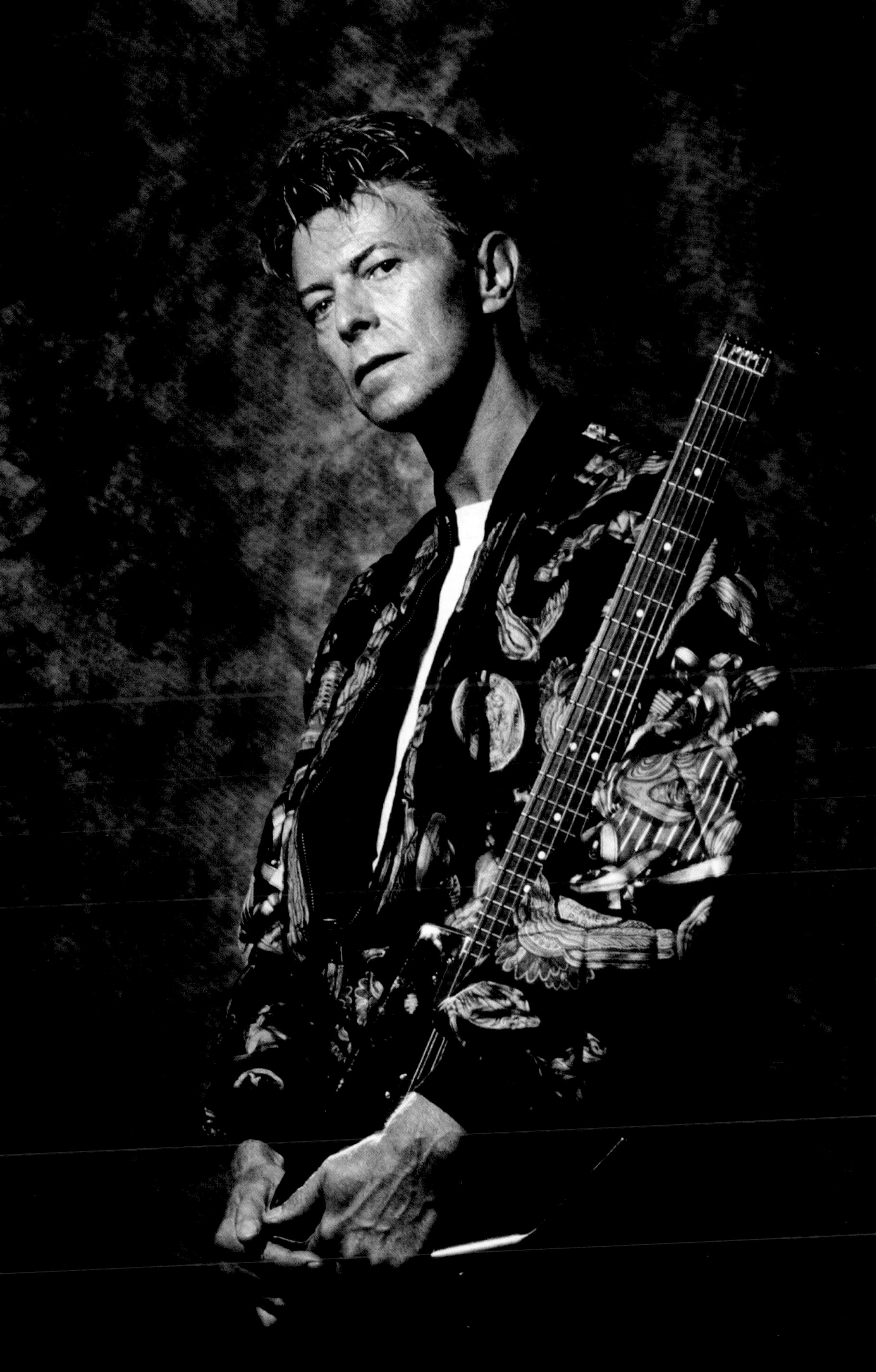

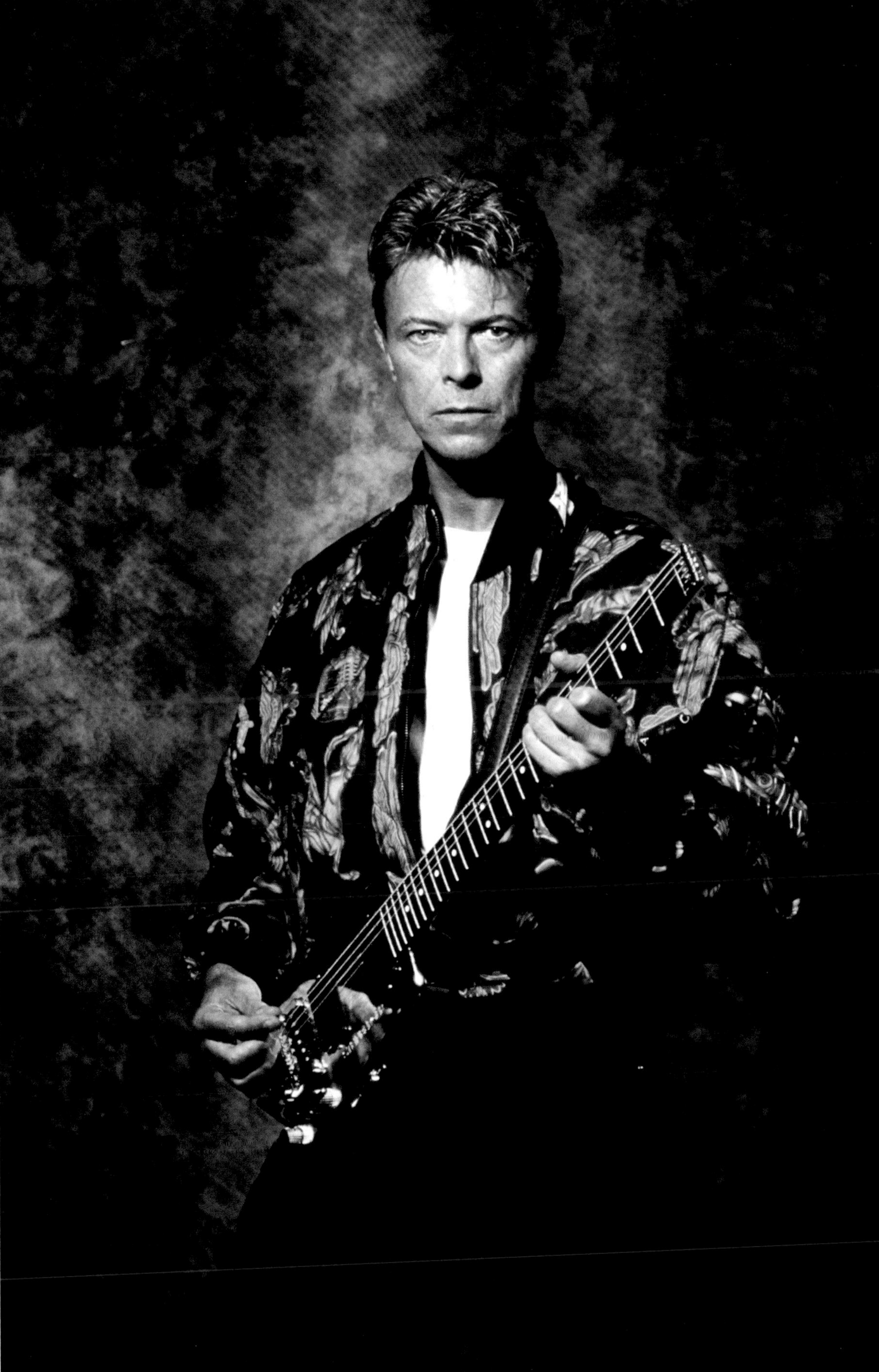

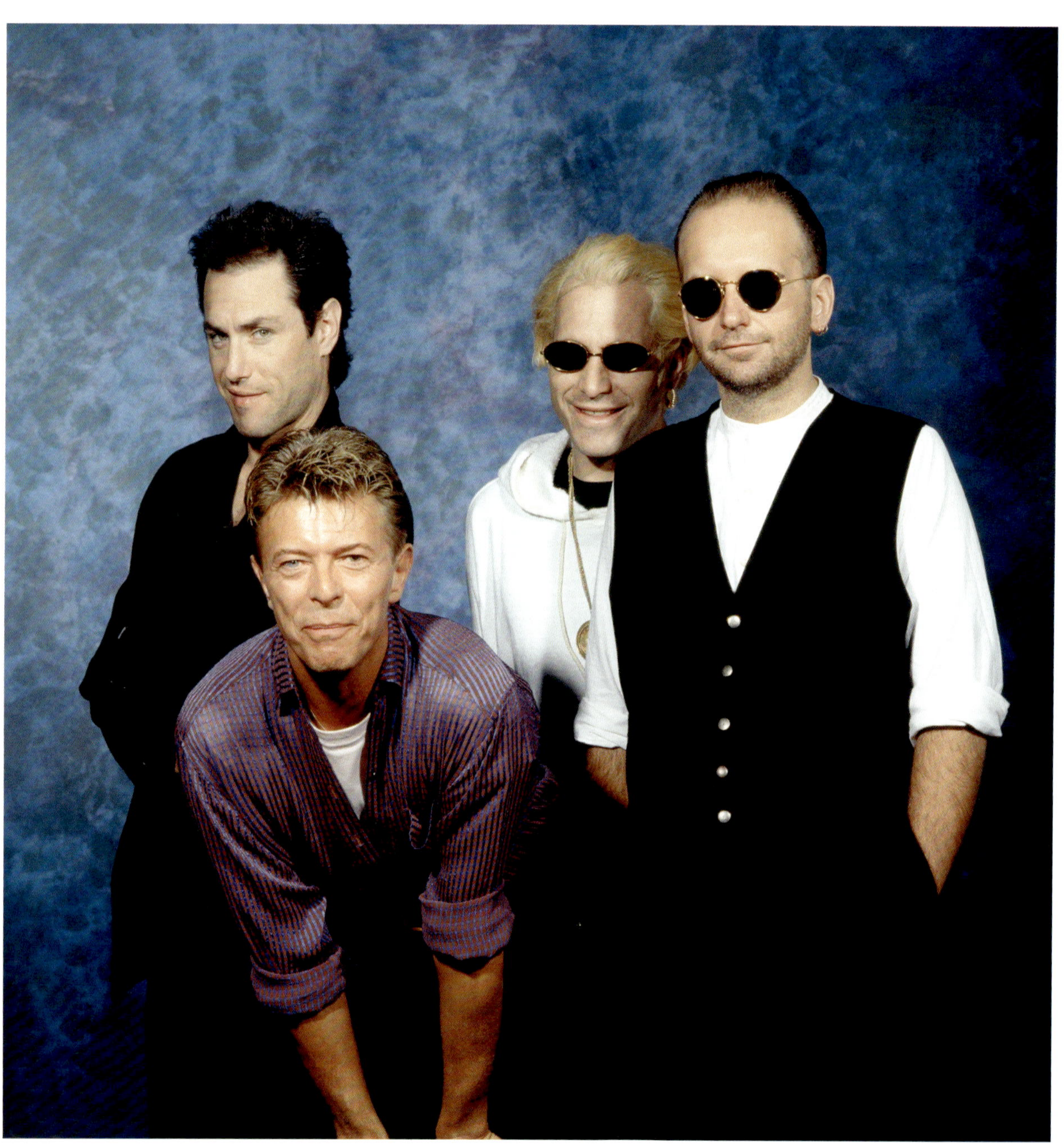

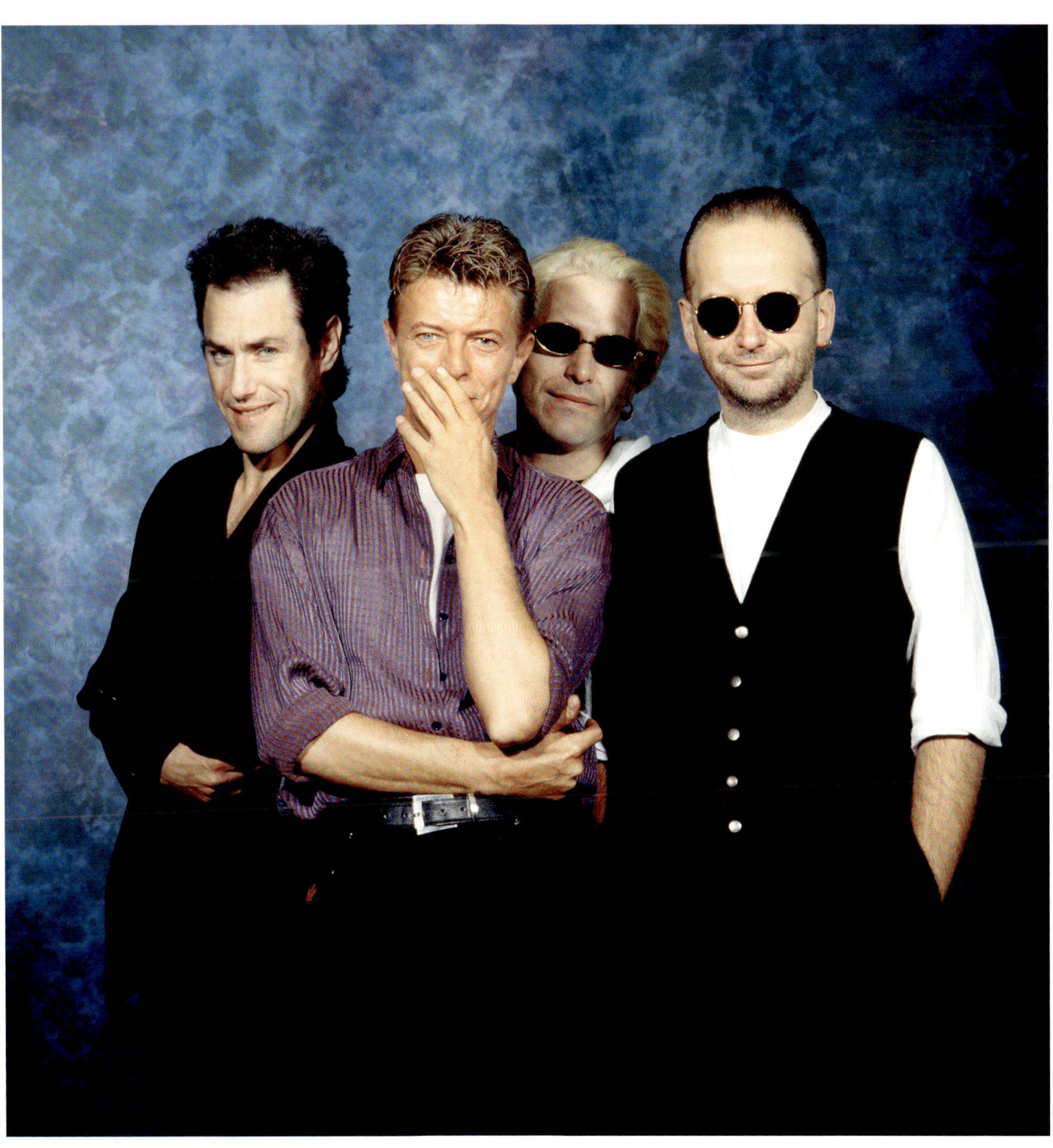

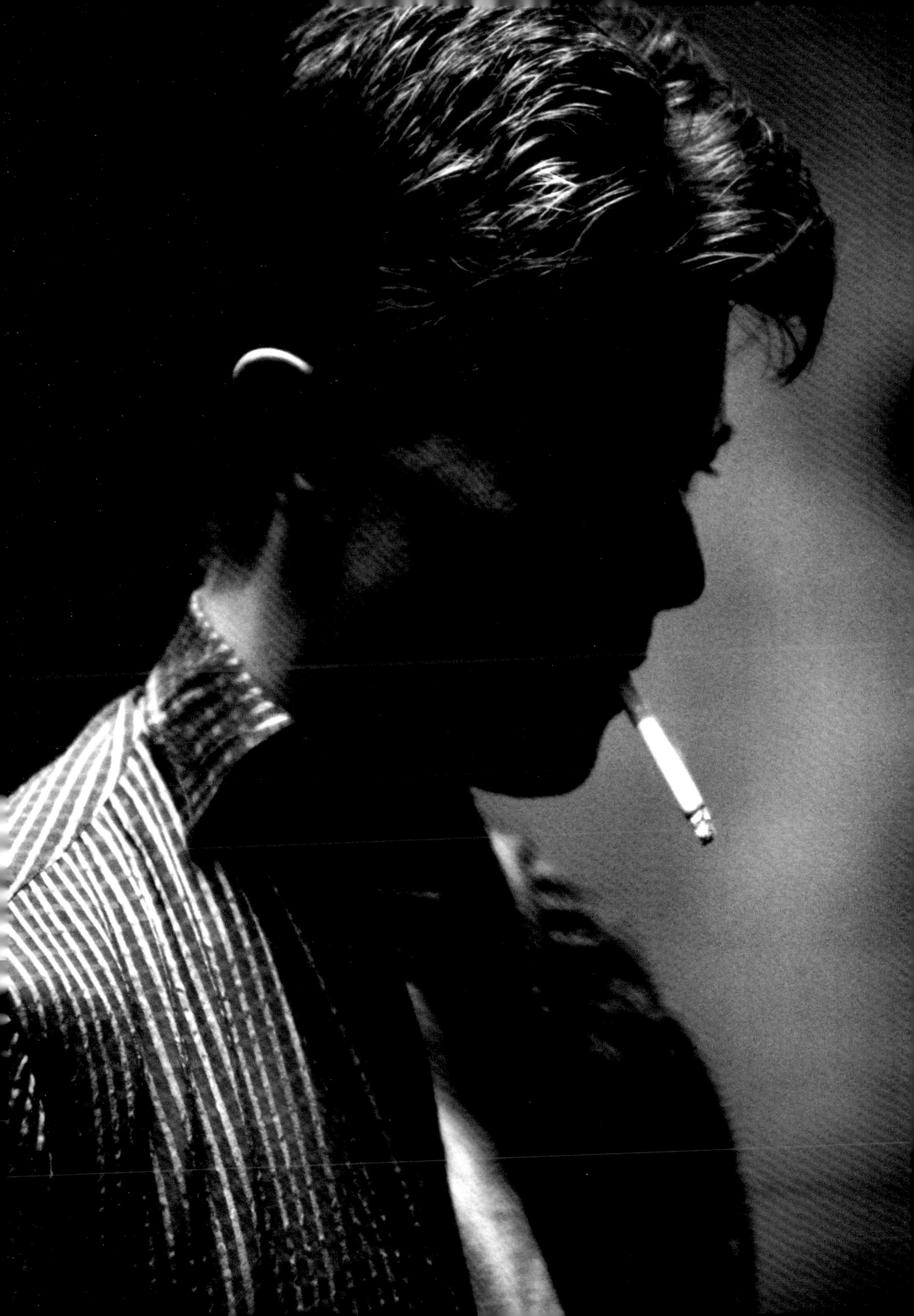

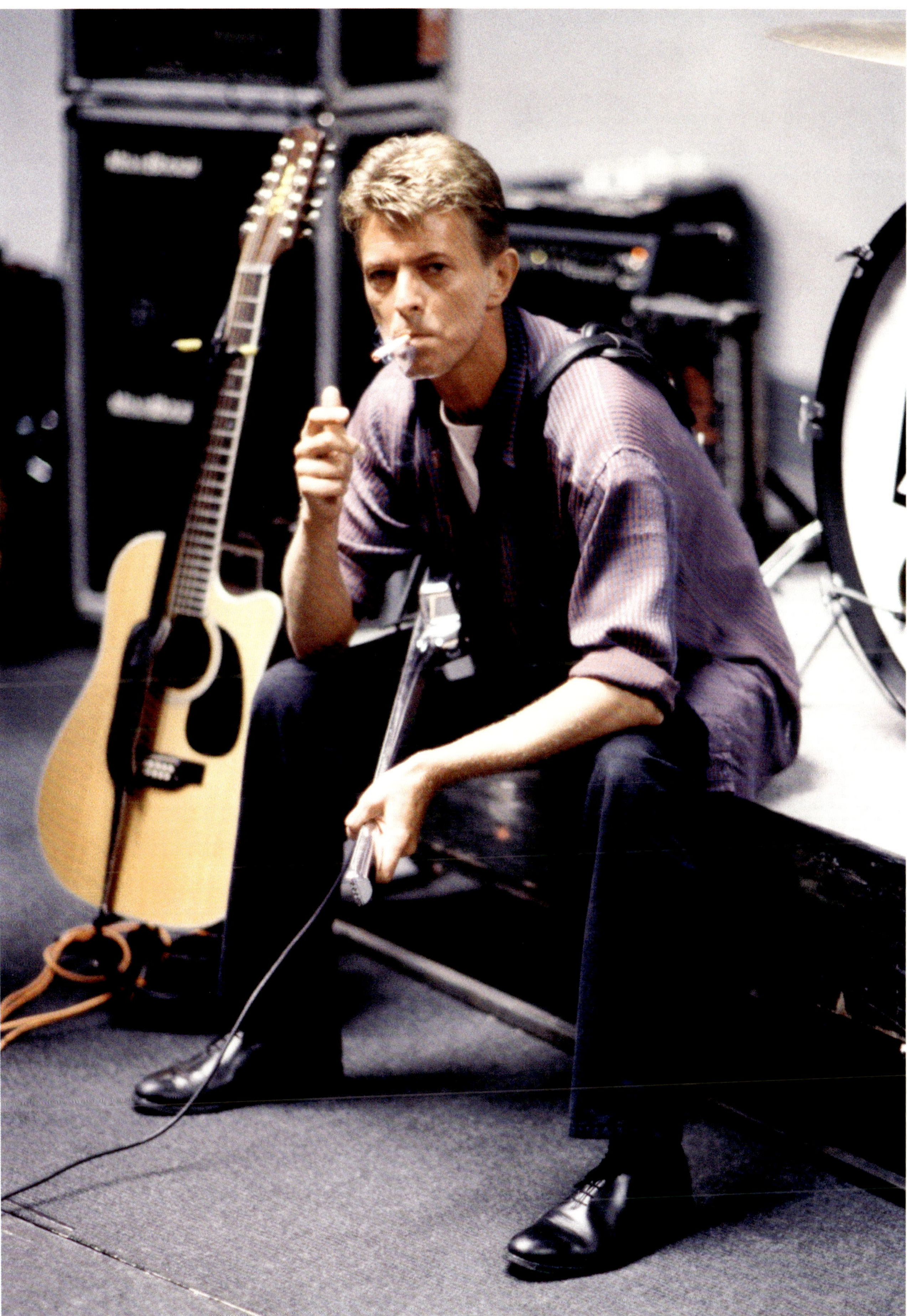

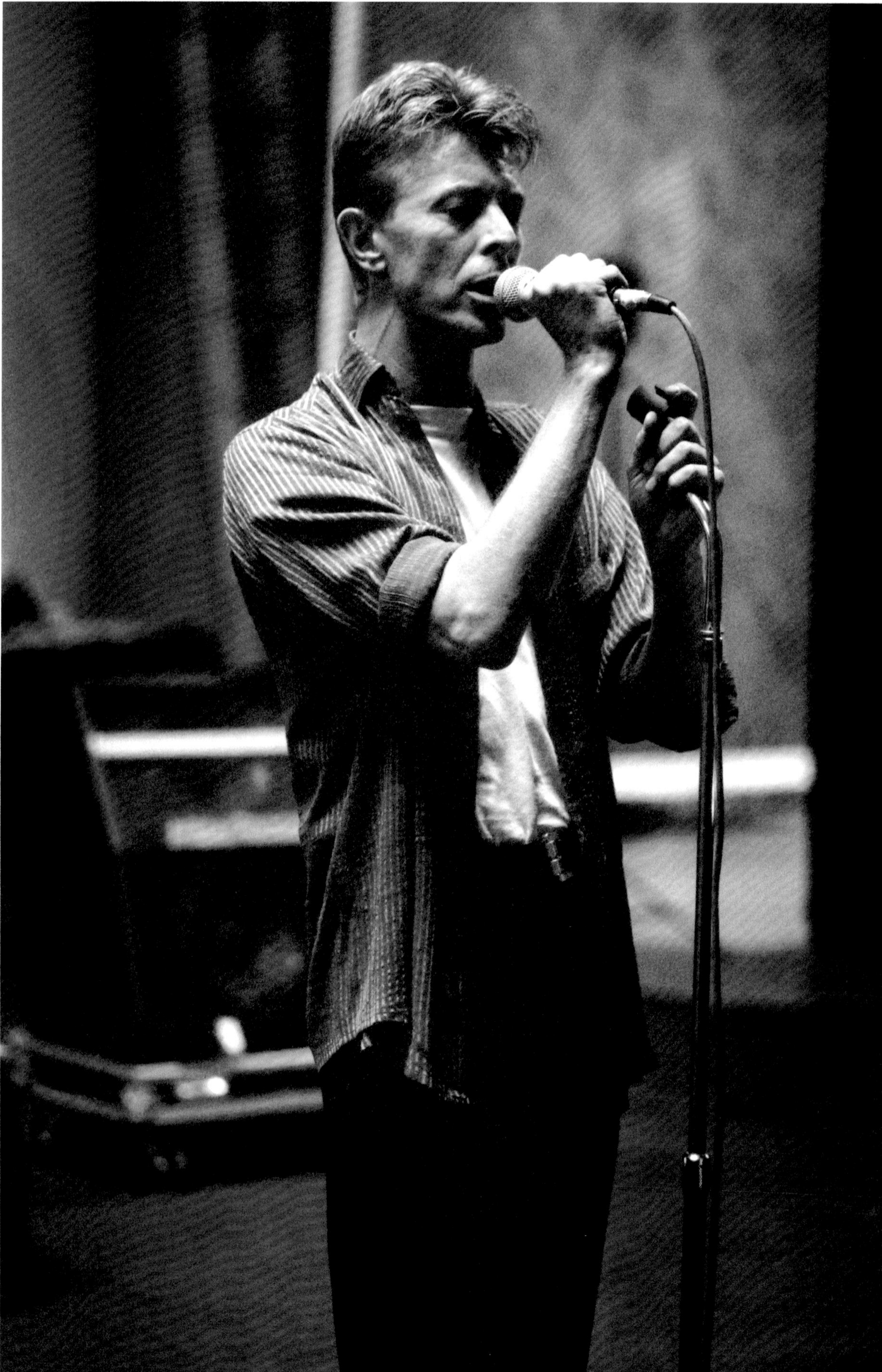

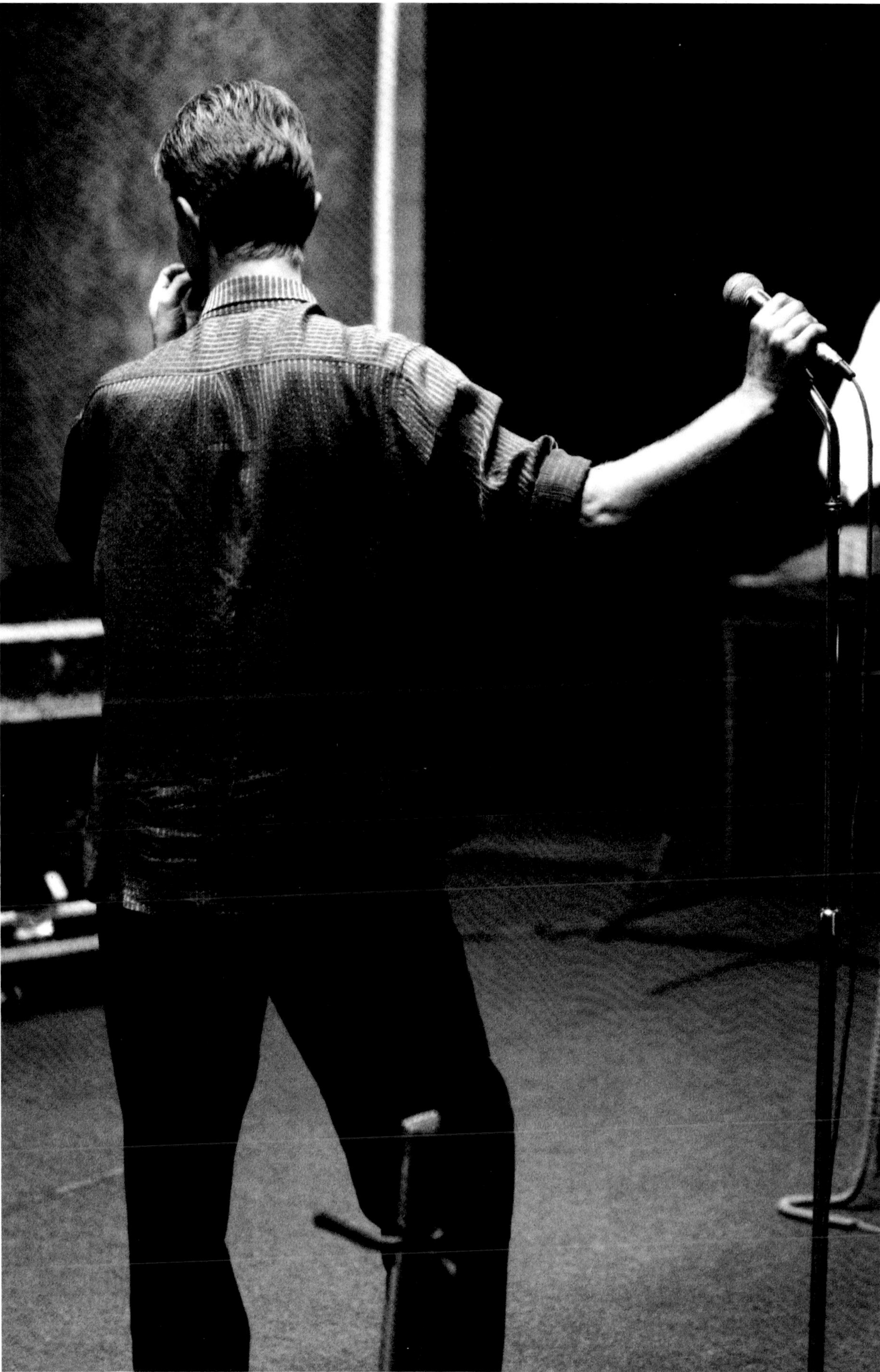

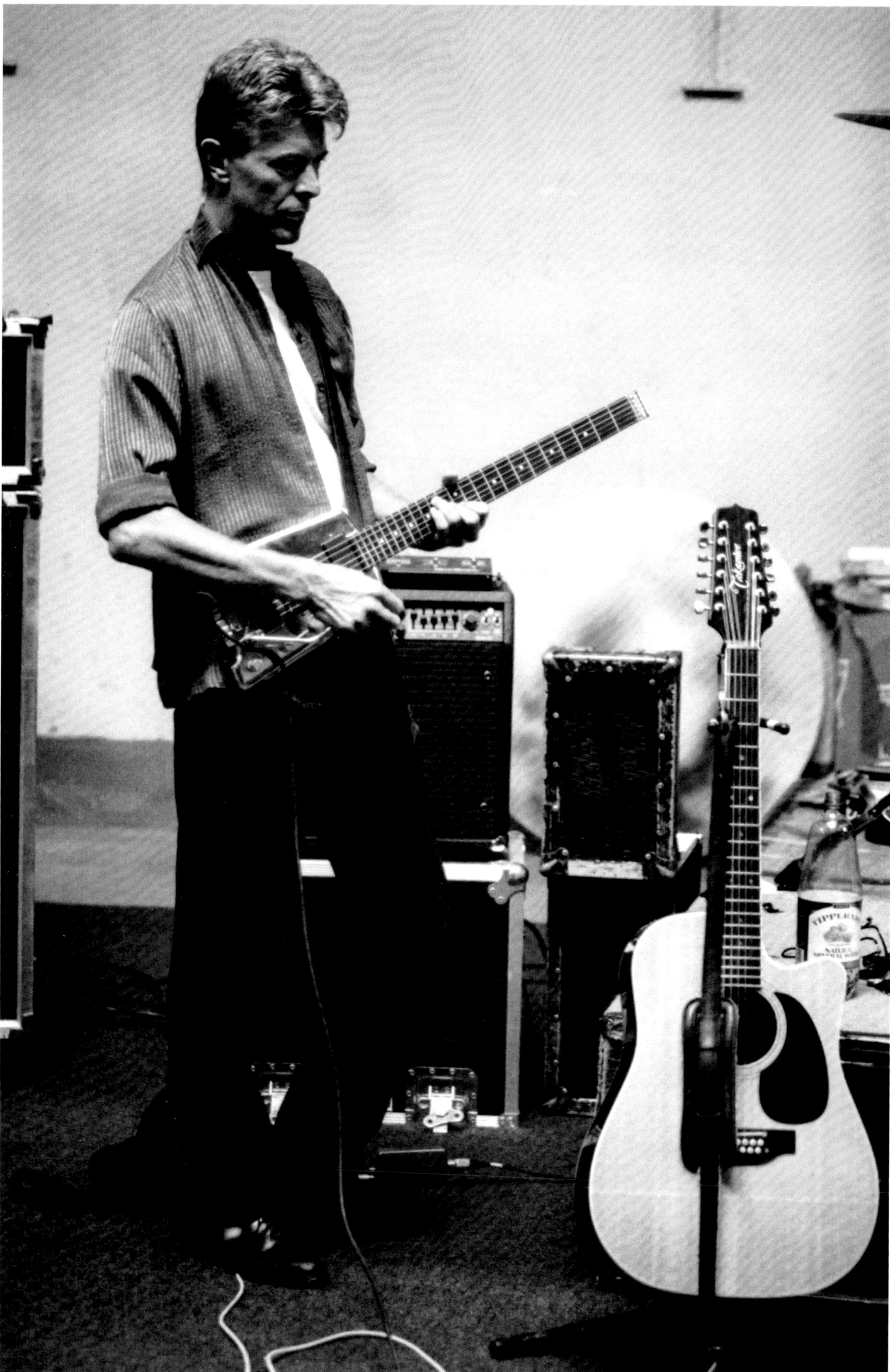

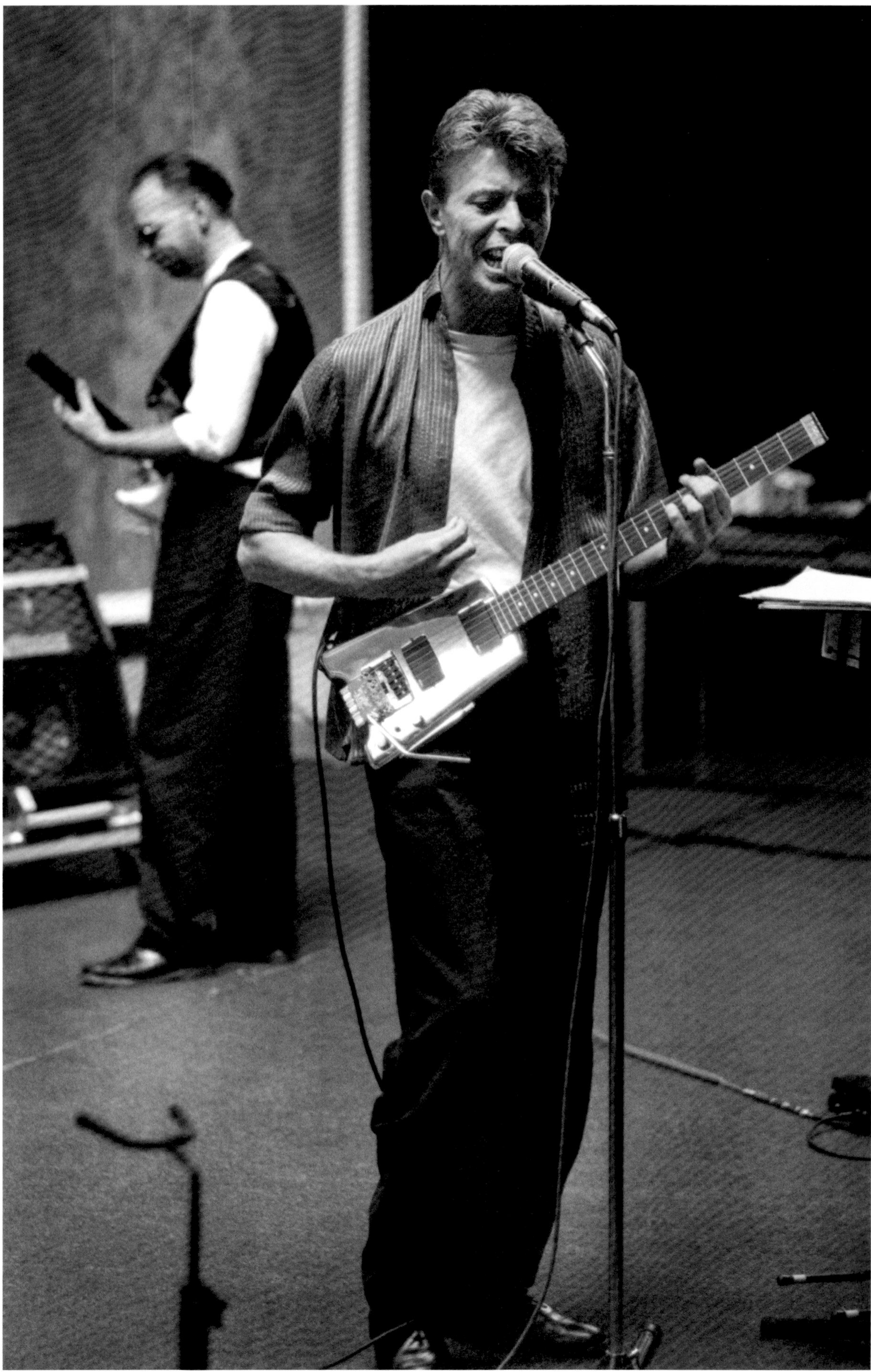

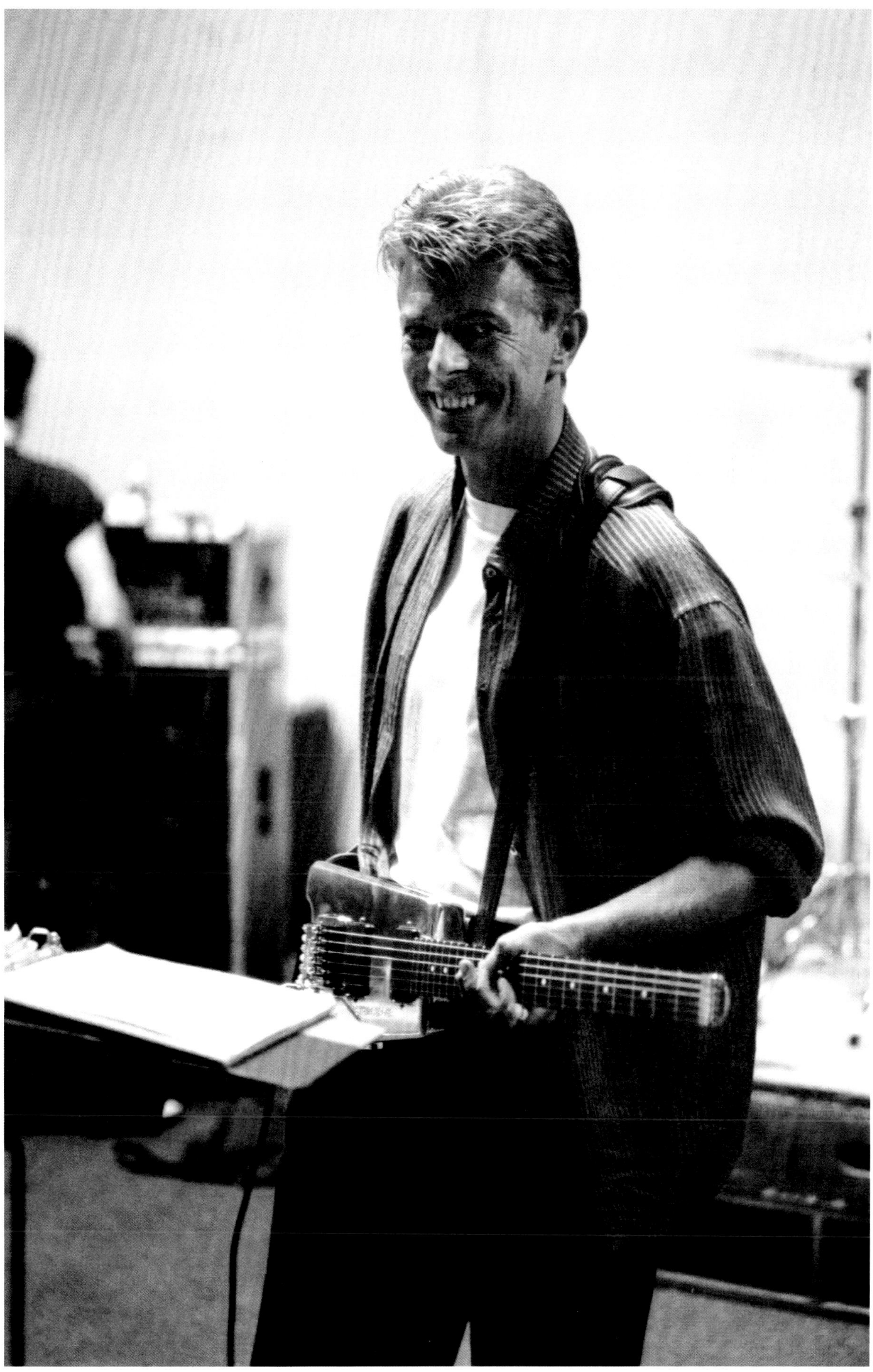

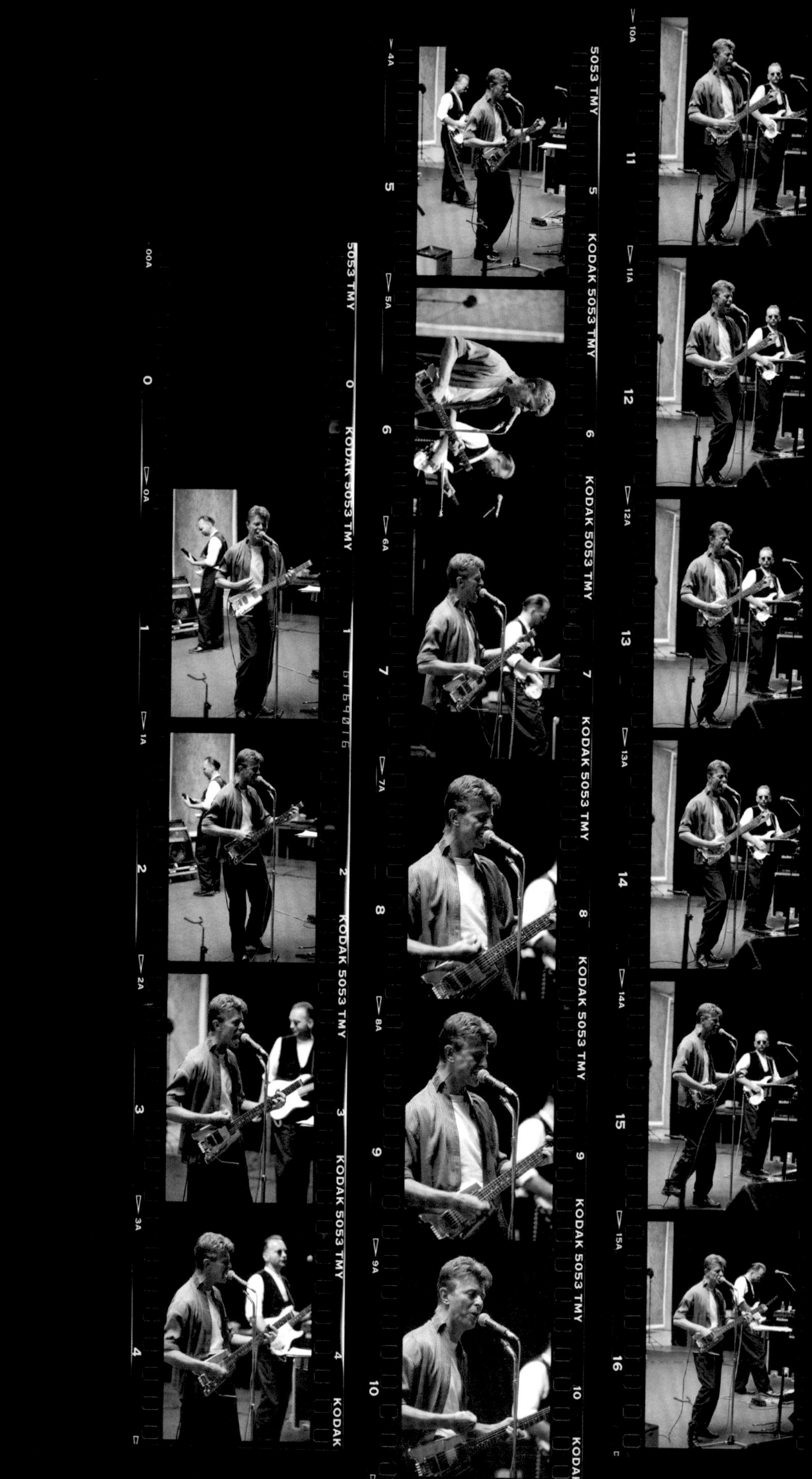

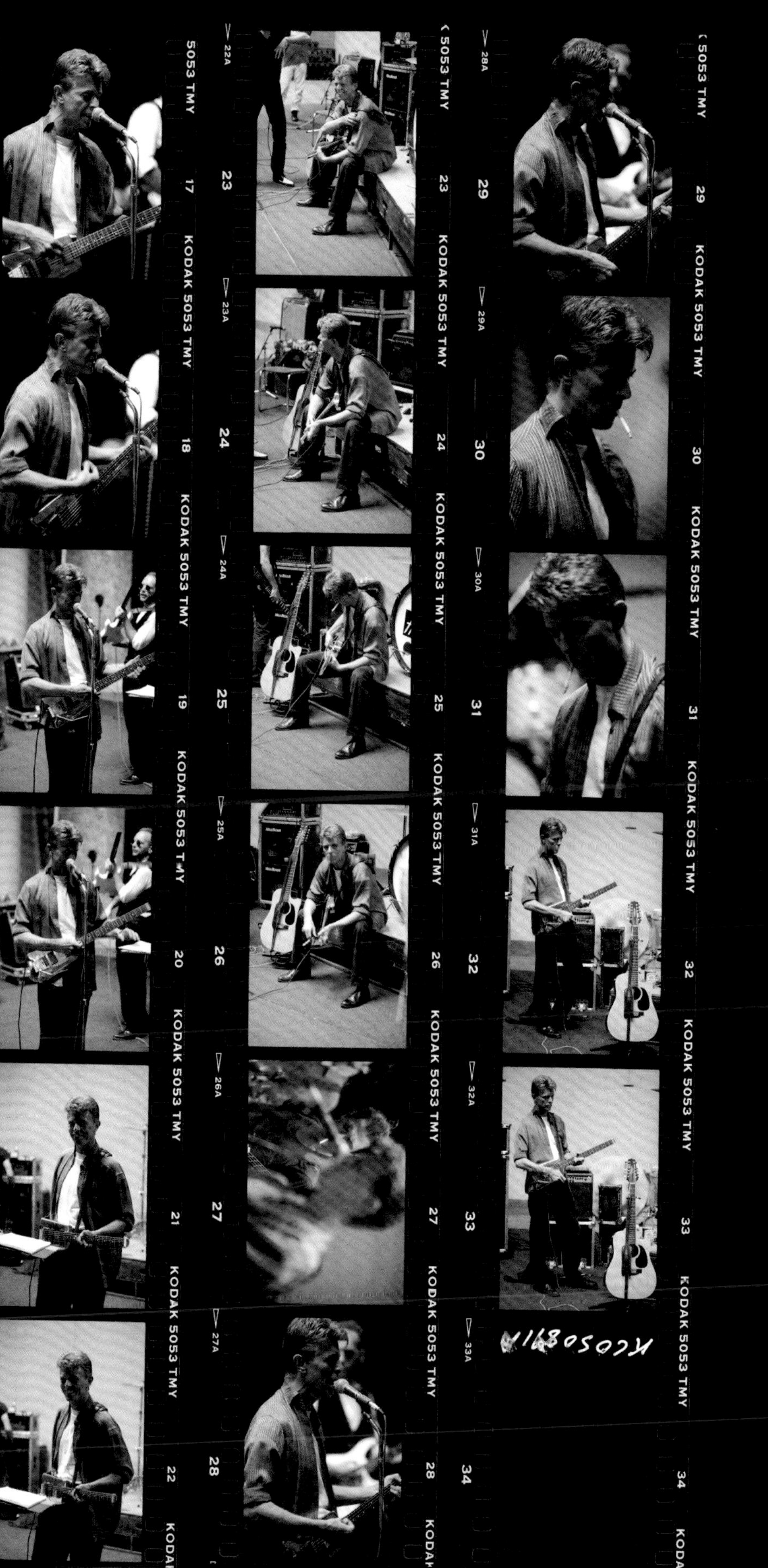

8 NOVEMBER 1995
SLY STREET, LONDON

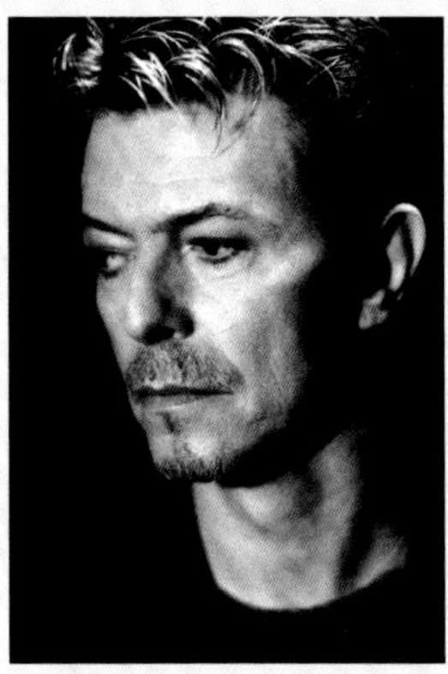

The following series of photographs were taken in a scruffy East London studio where I photographed many *NME* covers – including those featuring Björk, Oasis, Suede, Courtney Love and PJ Harvey. It was an unprepossessing space, usually untidy, a little bit dank with white-painted brick walls. I was used to it, in the way that you stop seeing familiar surroundings, but I must admit that changed a bit when Bowie entered the space for the first time. I suddenly saw it through his eyes.

As soon as Bowie arrived, his minder told everyone to move to another part of the room so Bowie could get "in the zone". This resulted in Bowie raising an eyebrow, as if to suggest he would rather get out of the zone as quickly as possible. He was sitting on a battered old sofa with most of the stuffing hanging out of it. Nevertheless, he seemed perfectly happy and relaxed.

Of the following images, I took the black-and-white portraits first. I wanted to concentrate on a series of close-ups. Then we had a break for the interview with Steven Wells. I asked if he would mind me shooting during this, since I hadn't seen many interview photos with Bowie. I like to shoot during informal conversations, if possible, because people can be quite animated. But it is also important to be unobtrusive while doing this, given that it is the writer's time with the subject. I think the contact sheet captures Bowie's relaxed demeanour – smoking and chatting and laughing, and showing how he used his hands when he was thinking or expressing himself.

After the interview, I planned to take a series of colour shots. While I was resetting lights for this colour session, one of the rented studio flash units wouldn't work. It was too late to get another one organized, so I had to work with the 60-watt bulbs they had as modelling lamps and pretend I wanted to shoot in fairly low light. If this had happened on my first shoot with Bowie in 1991, I would have been mortified. But, four years later, I think I got away with it.

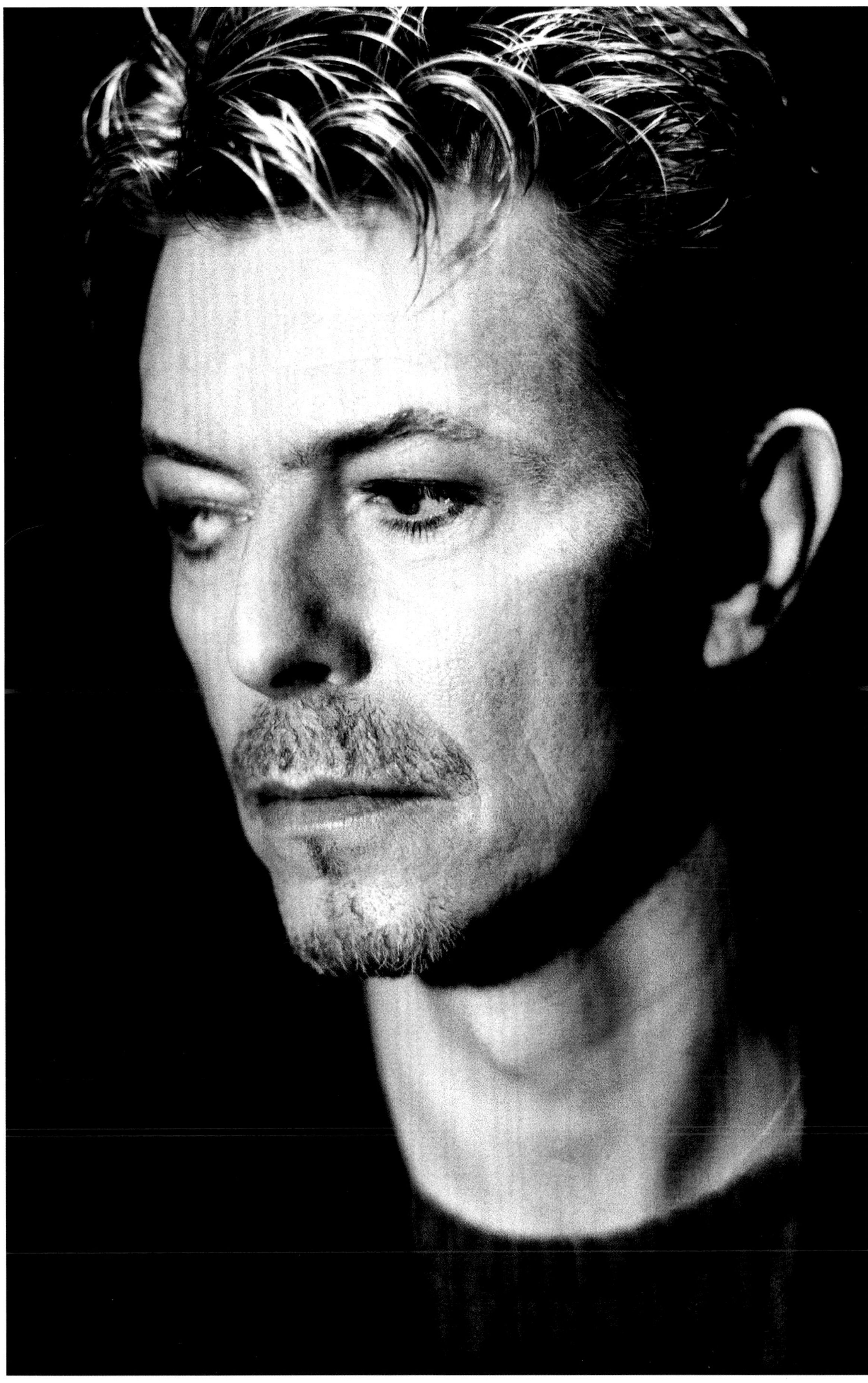

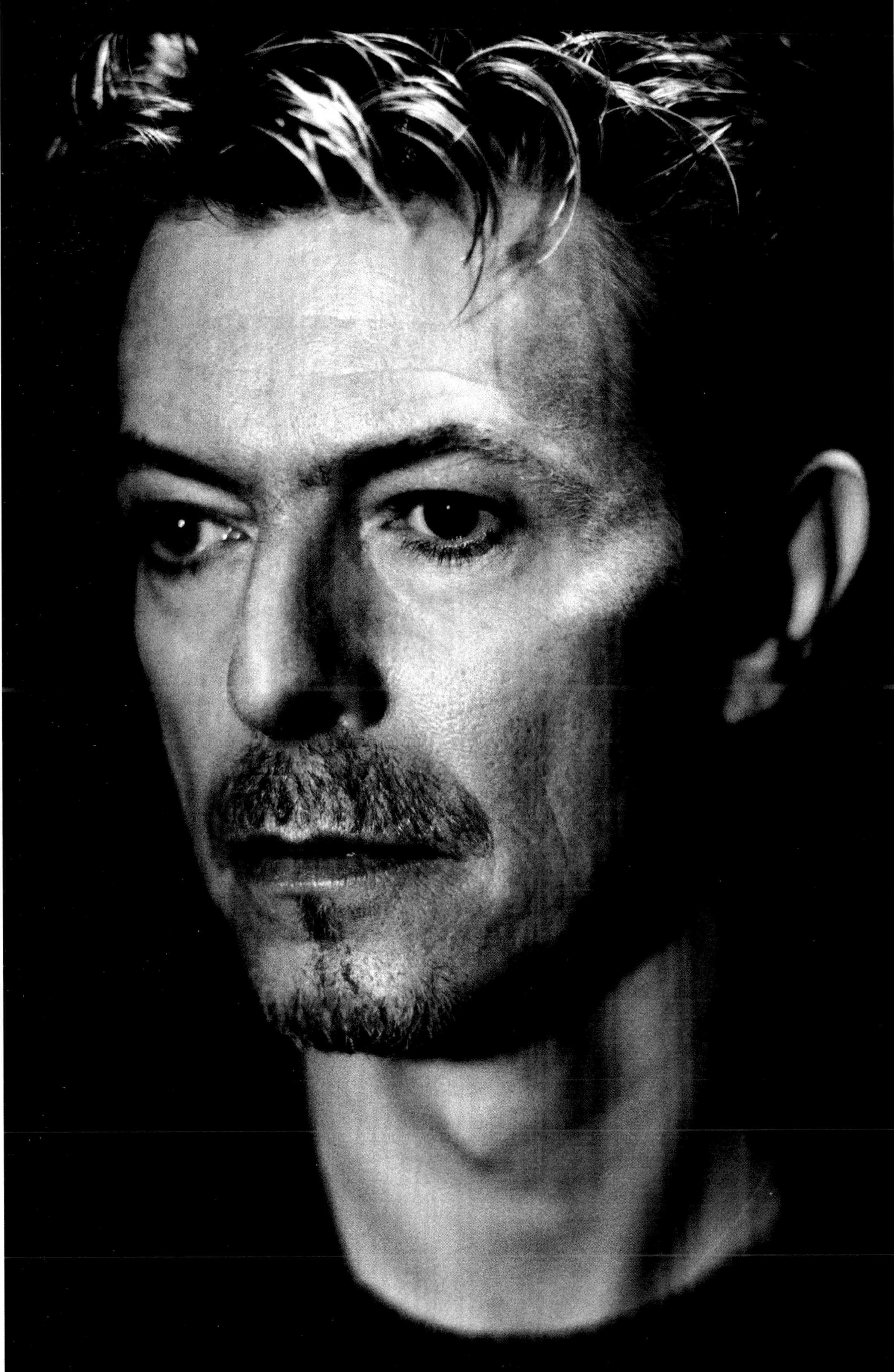

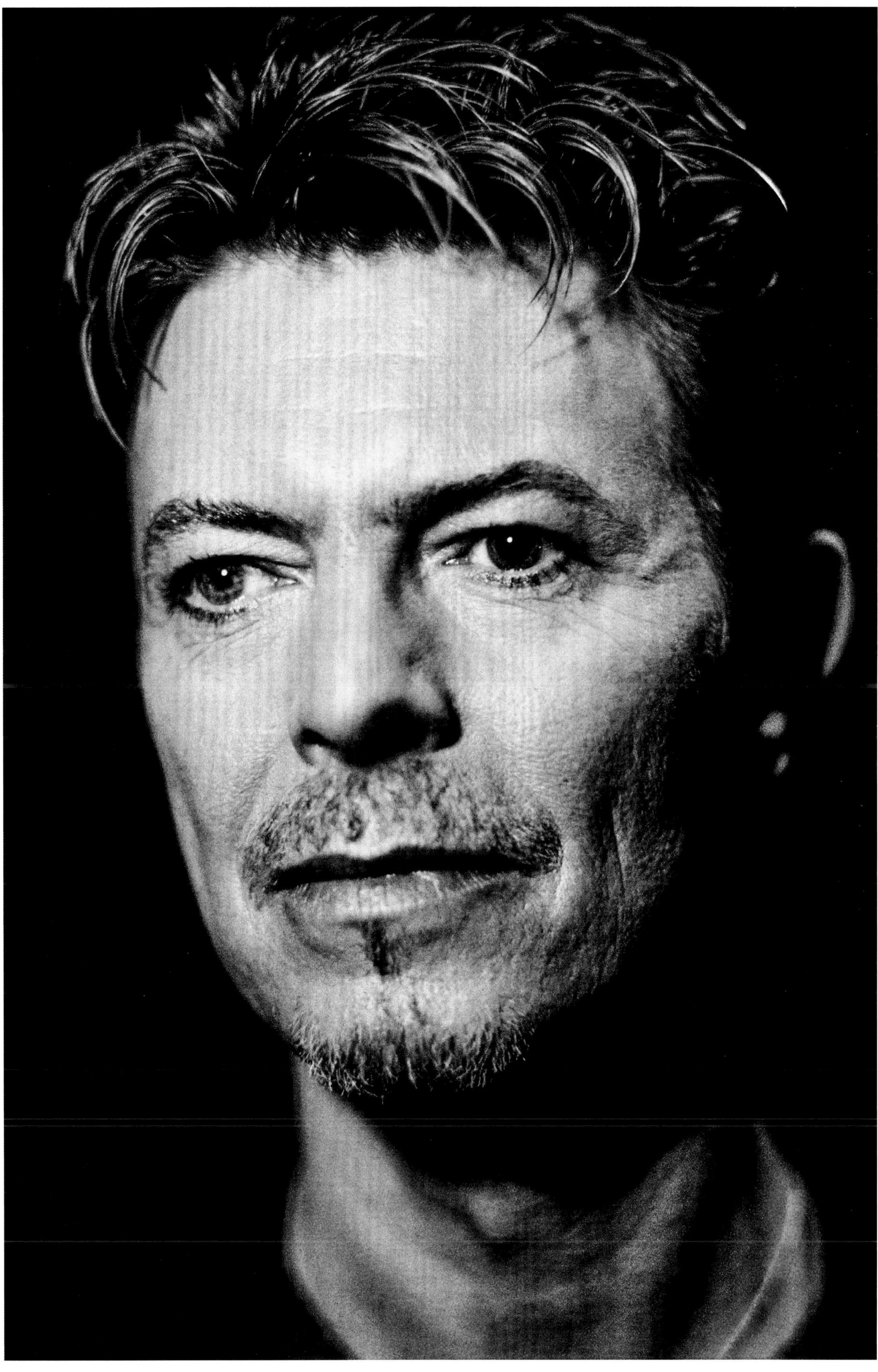

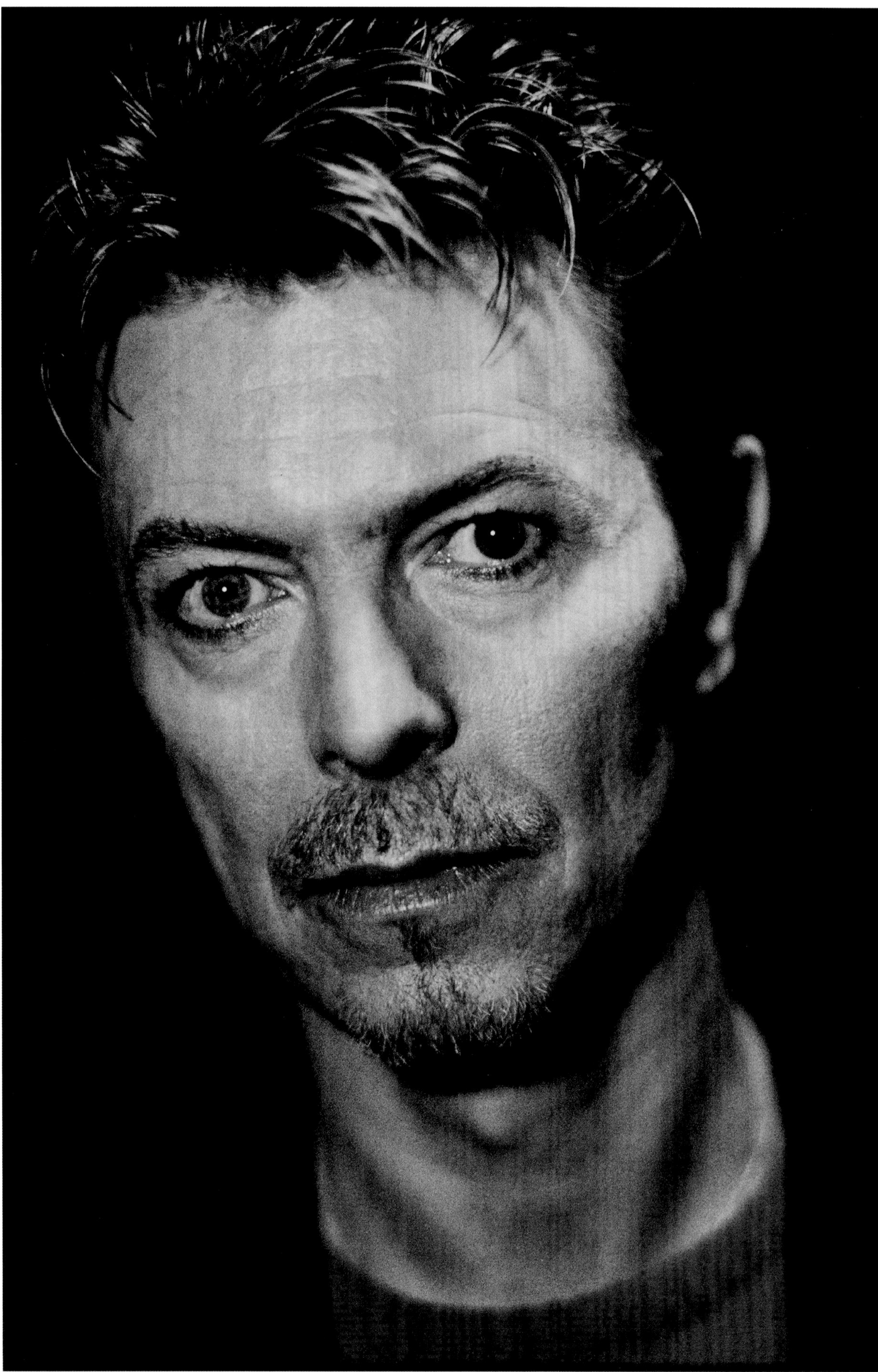

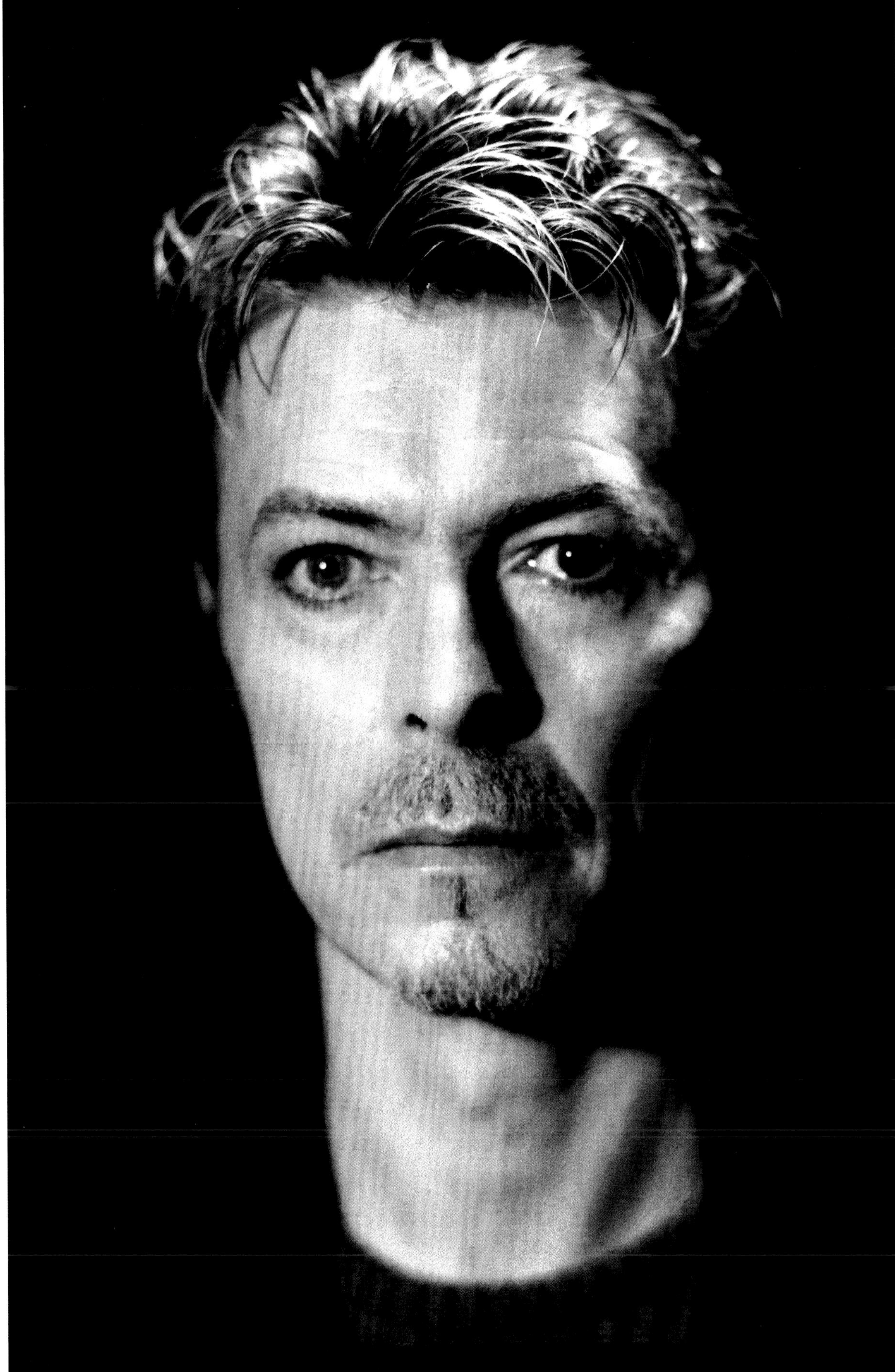

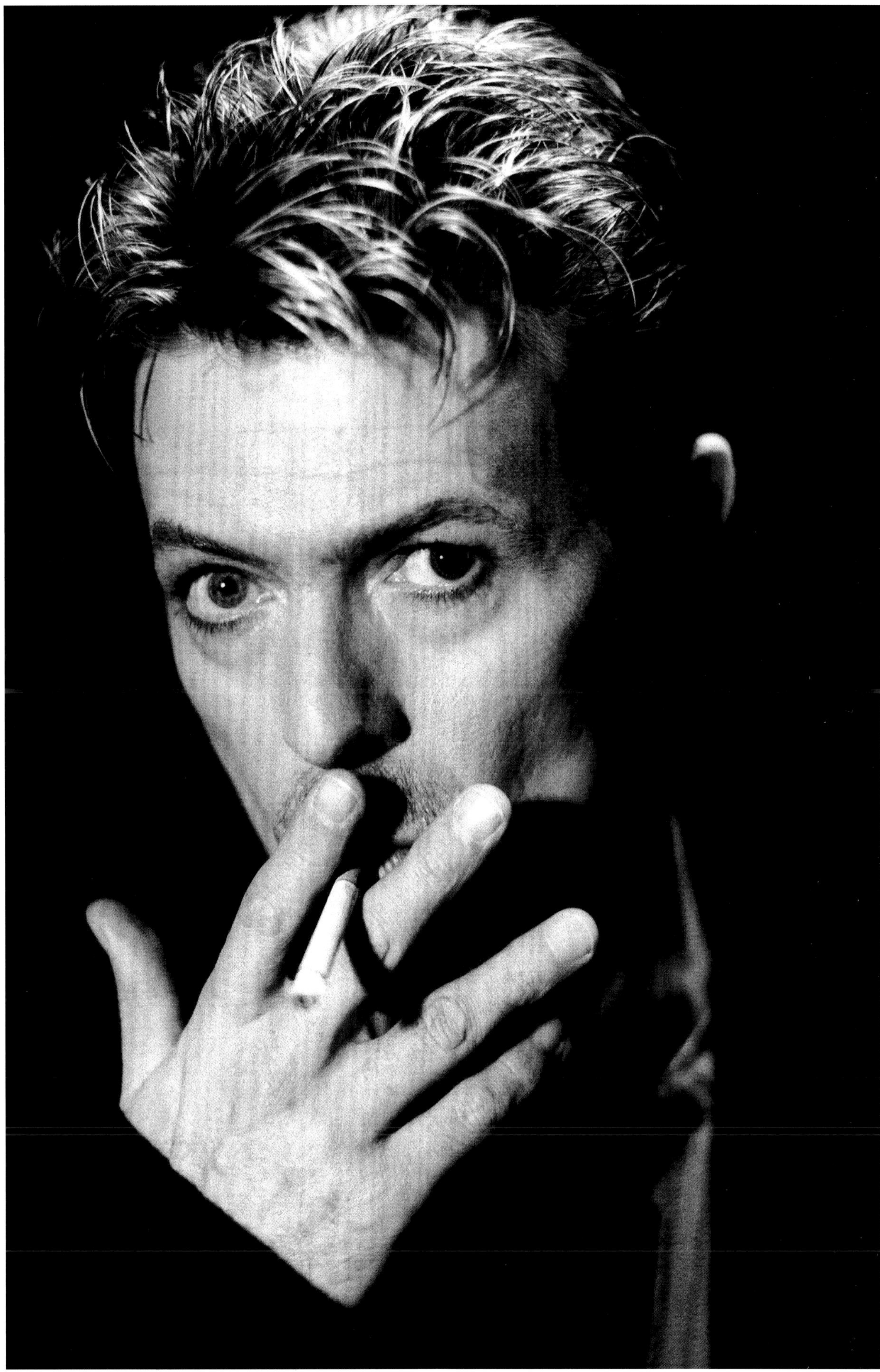

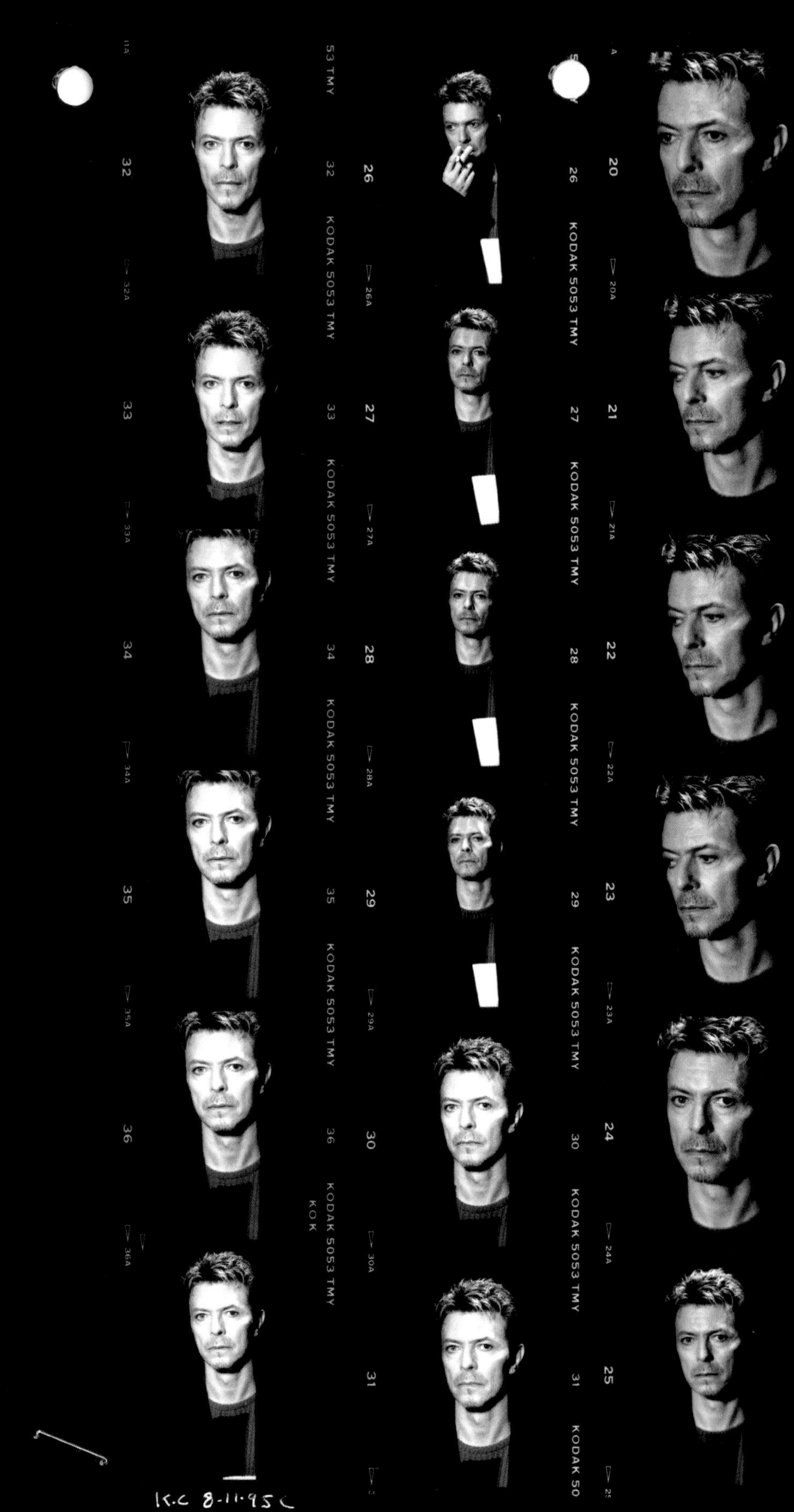

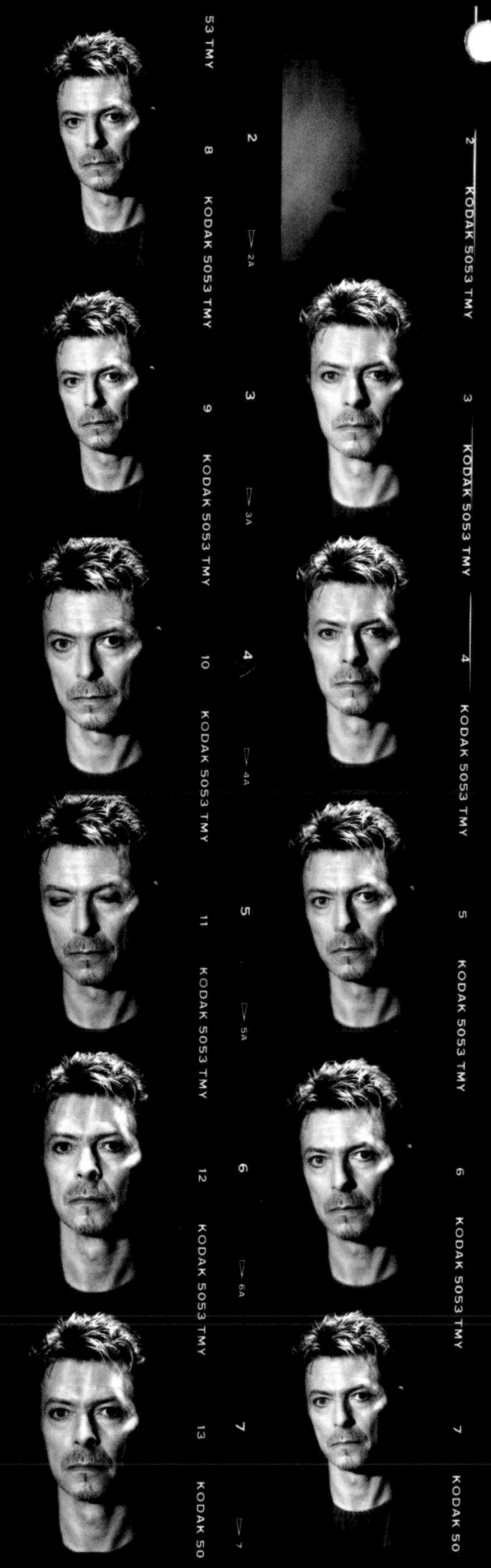

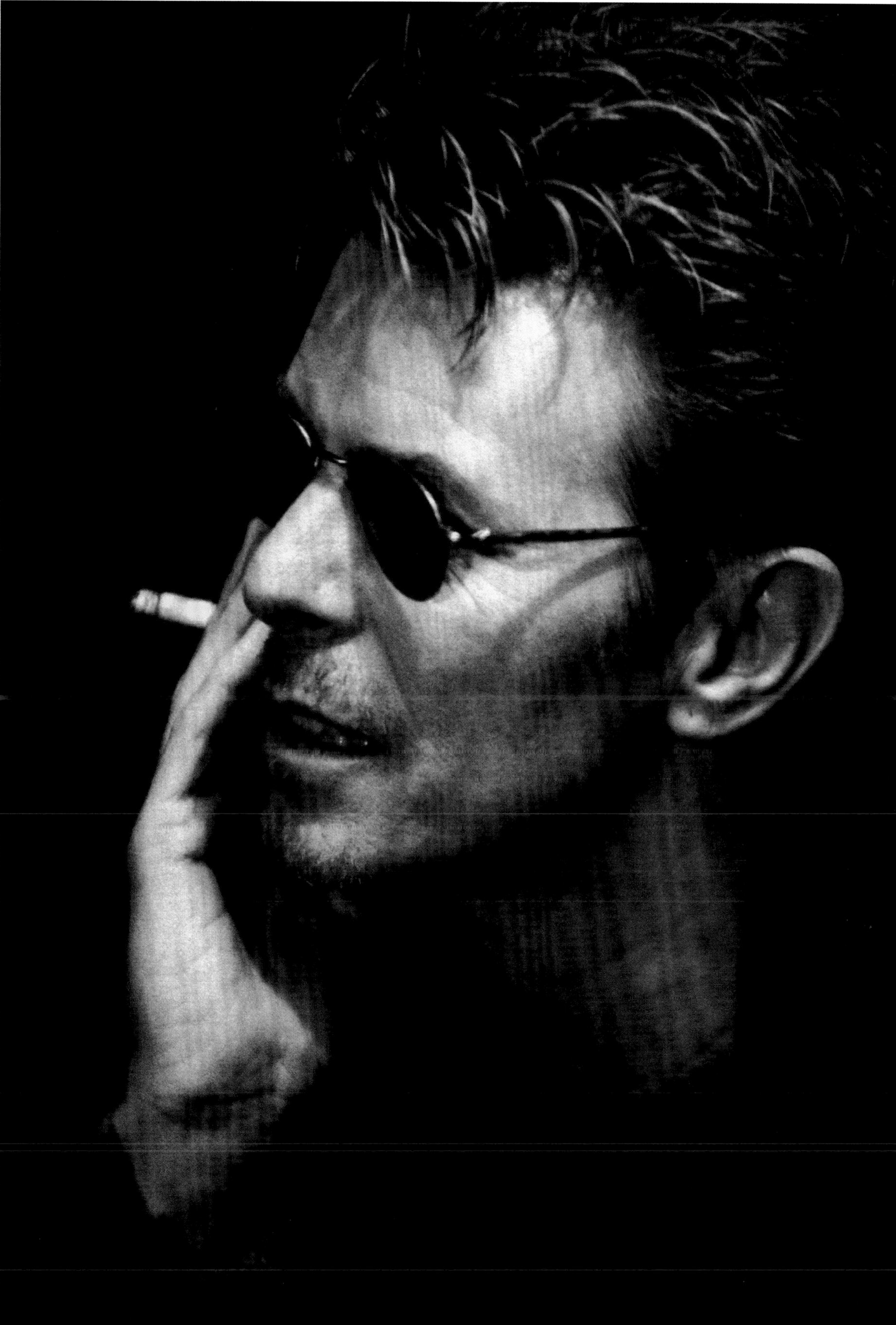

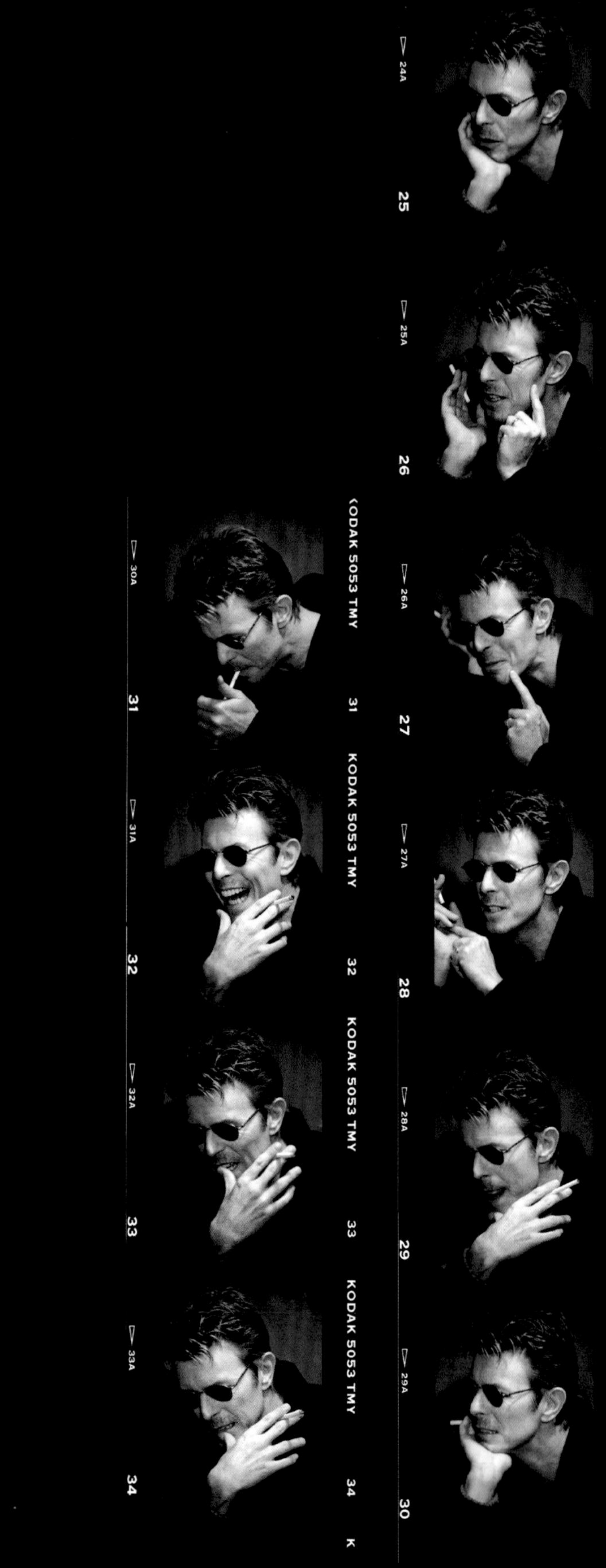

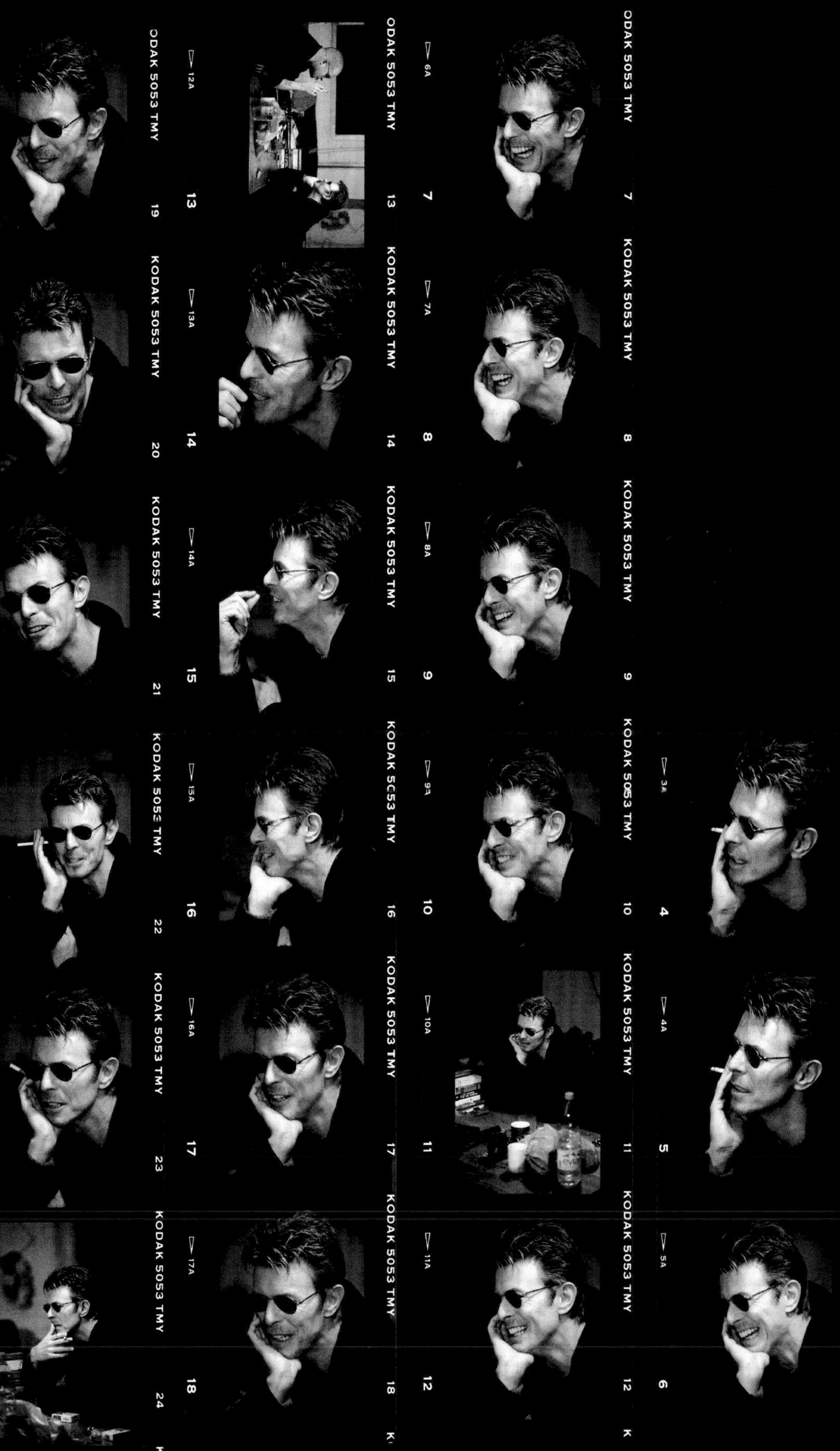

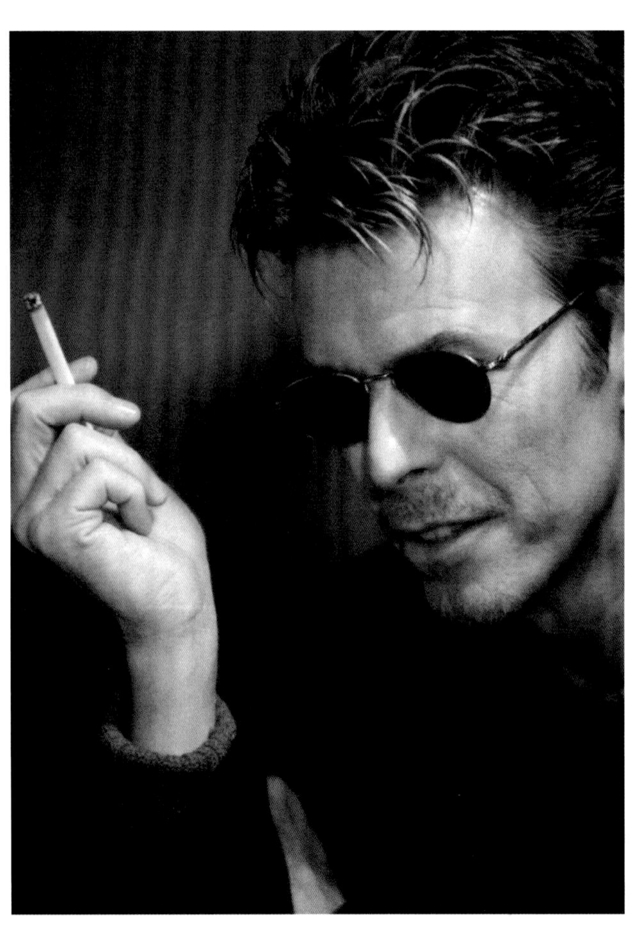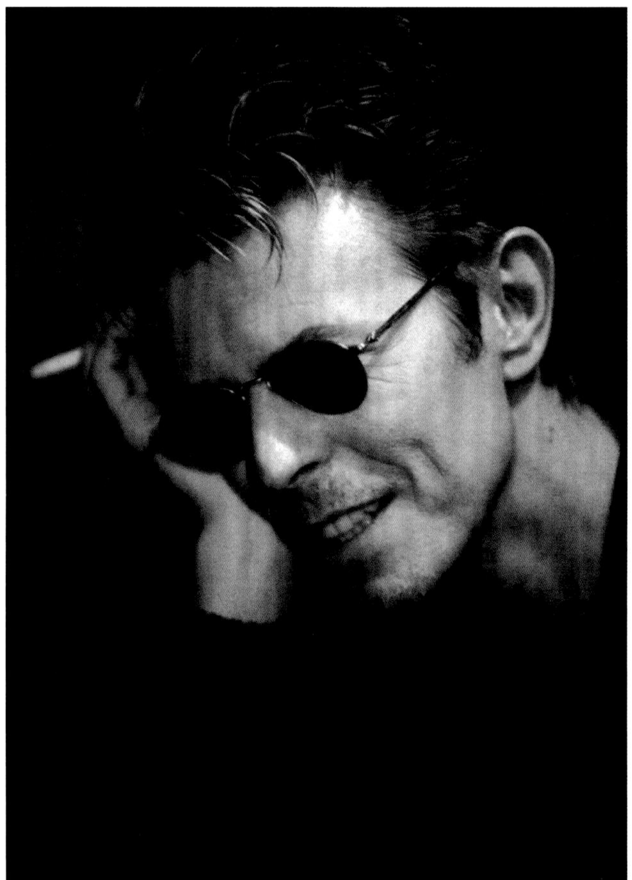

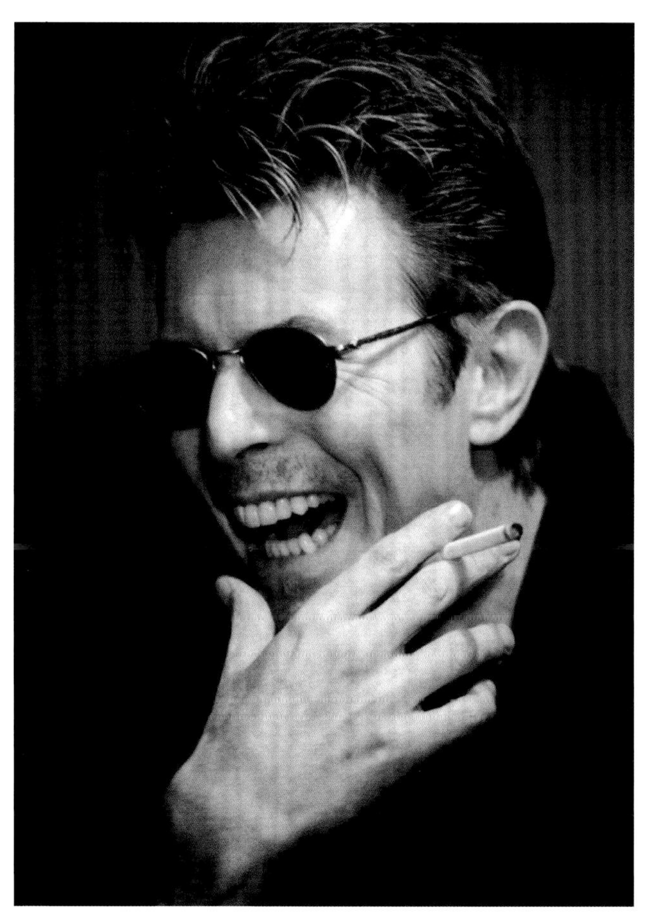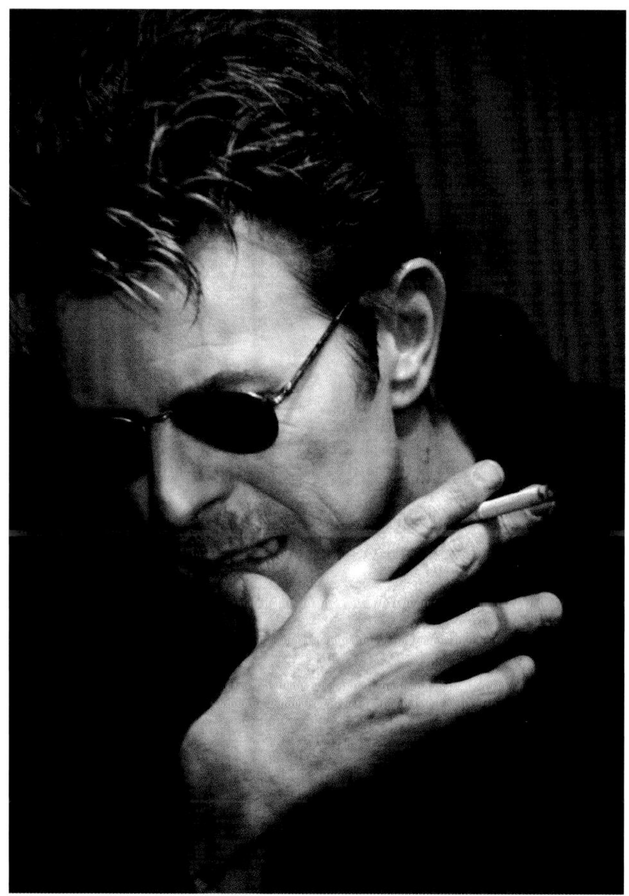

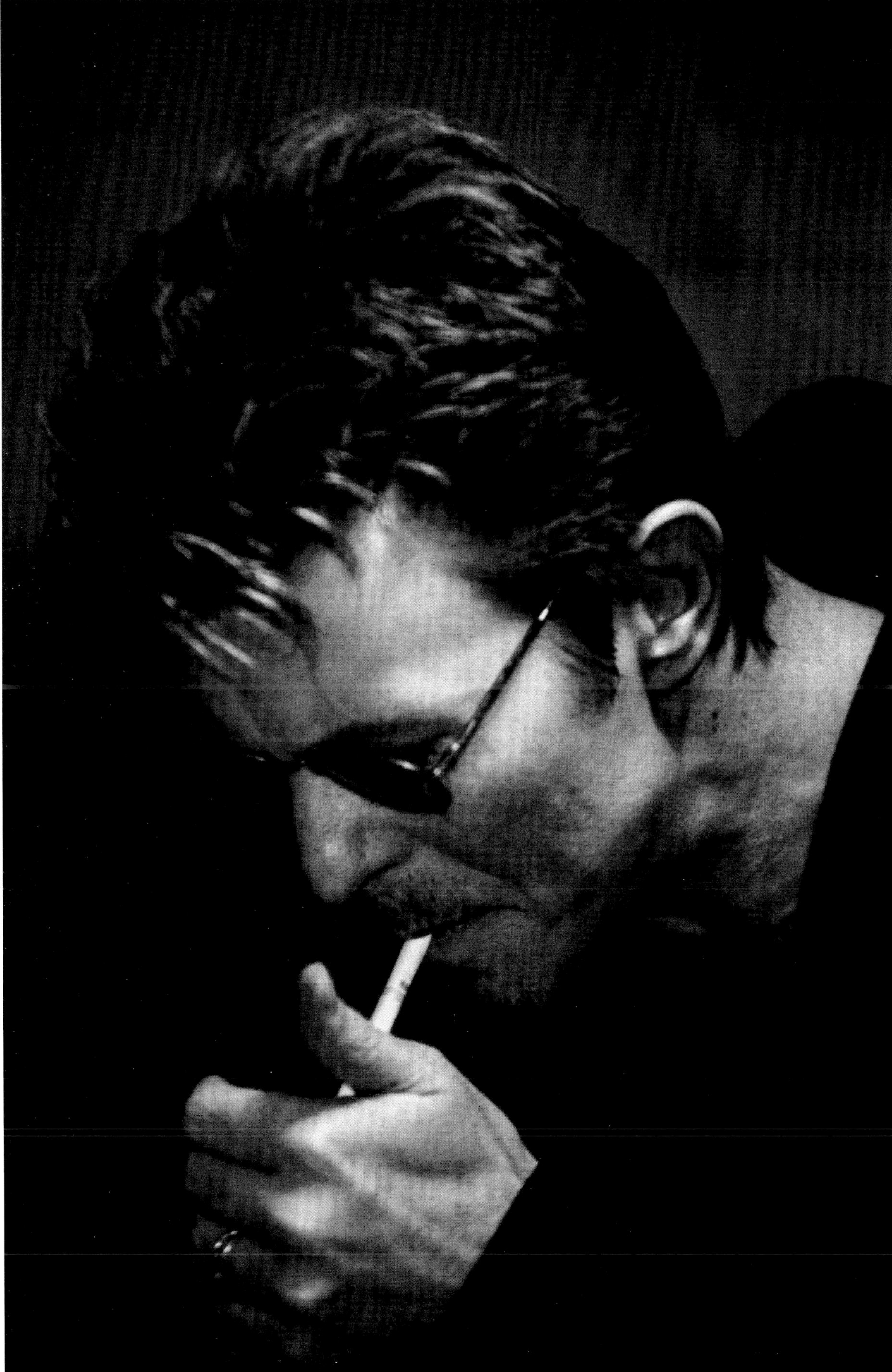

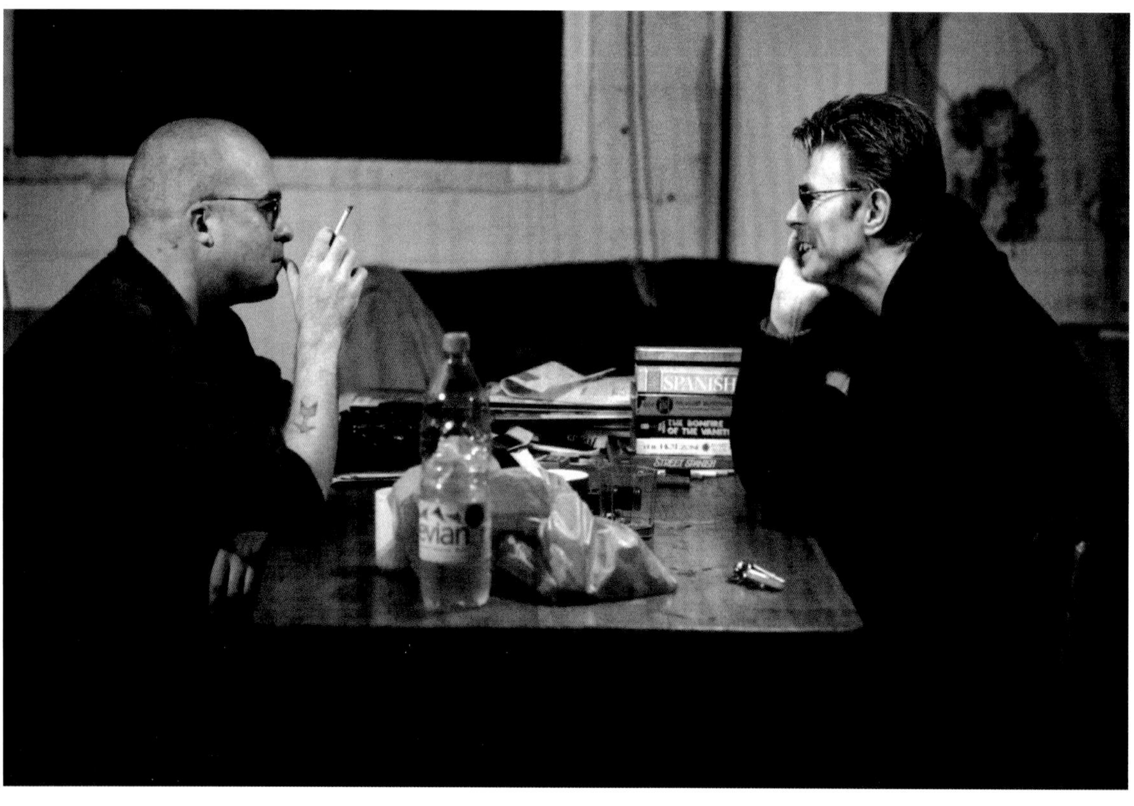

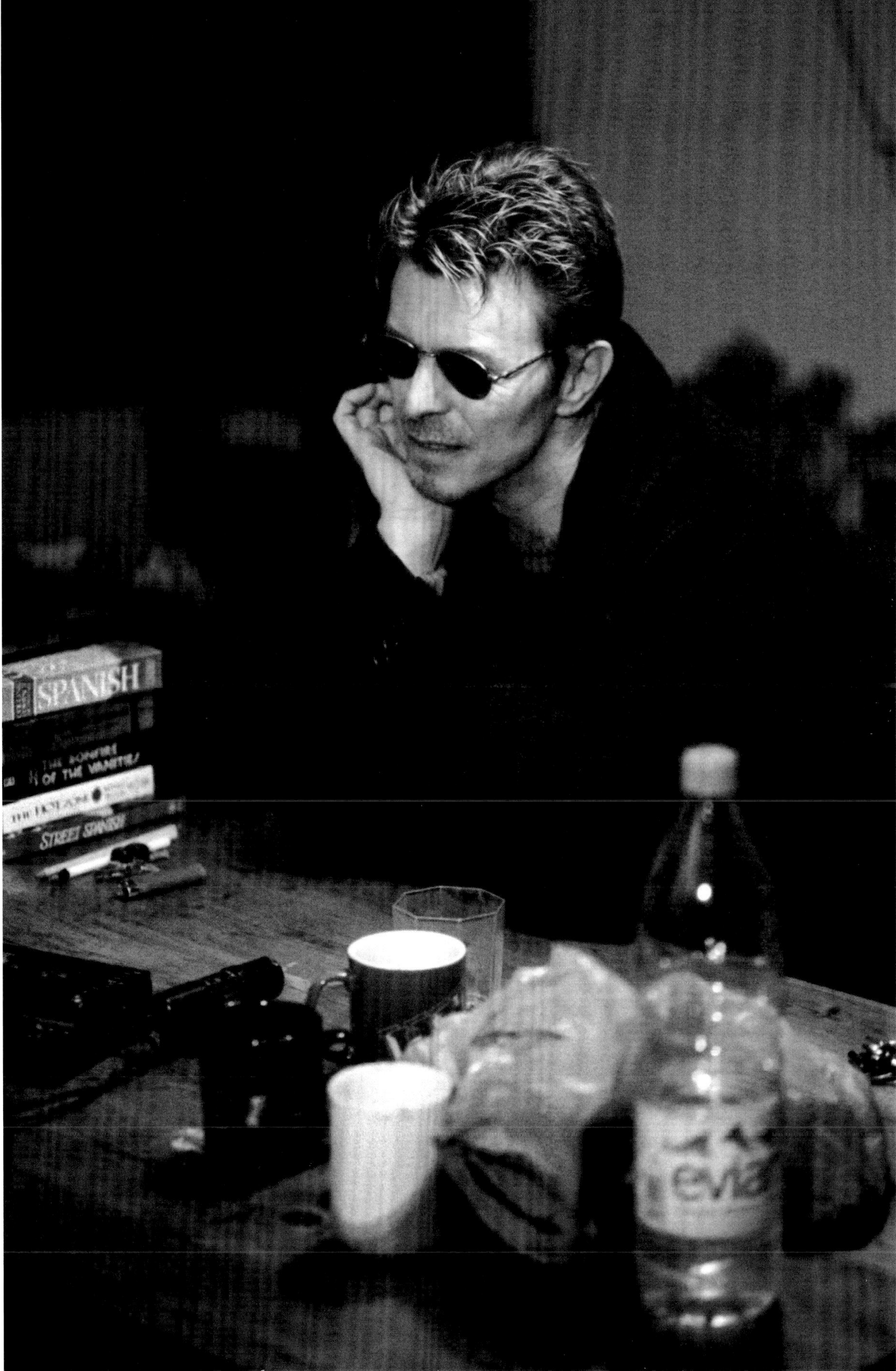

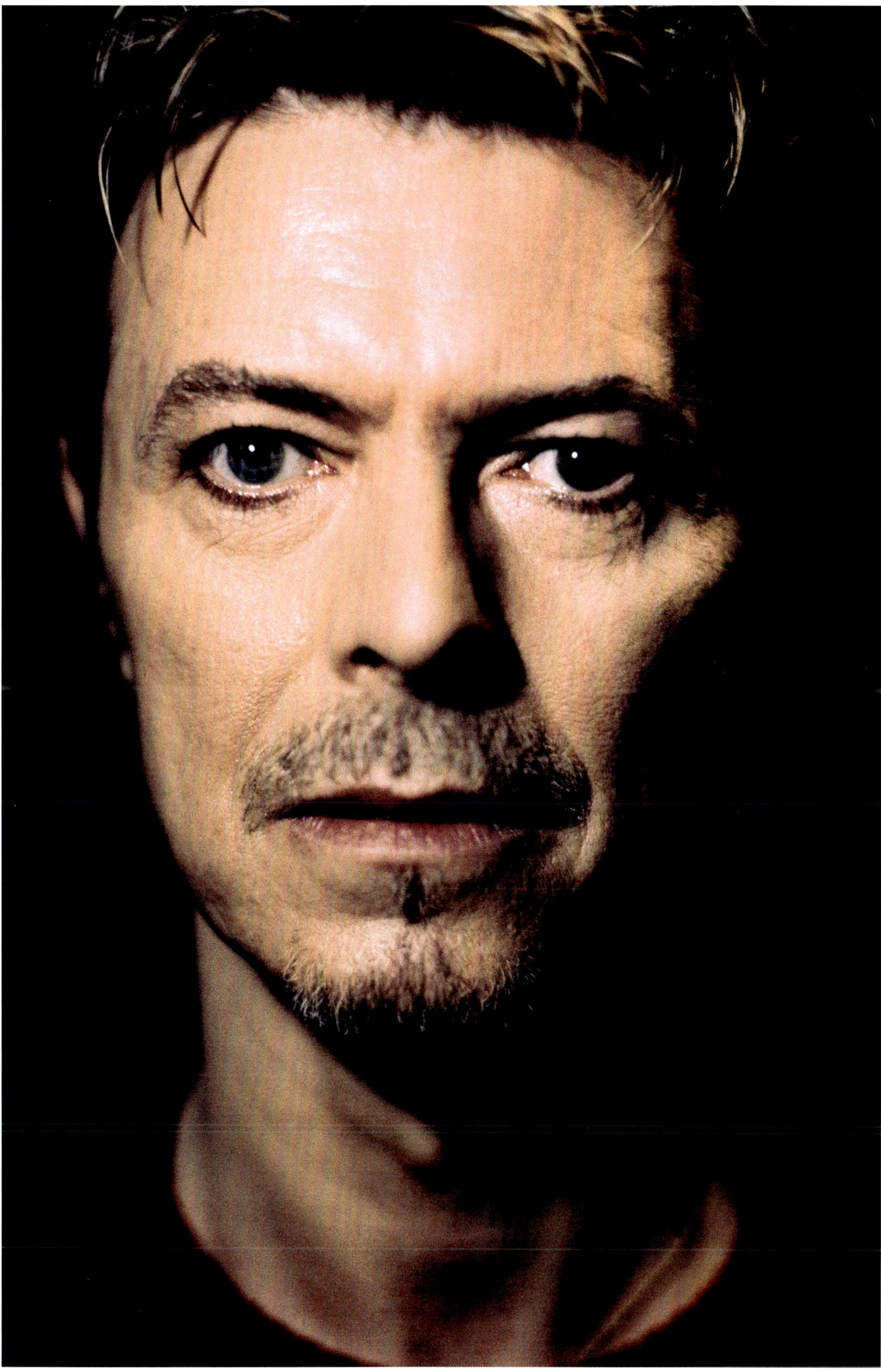

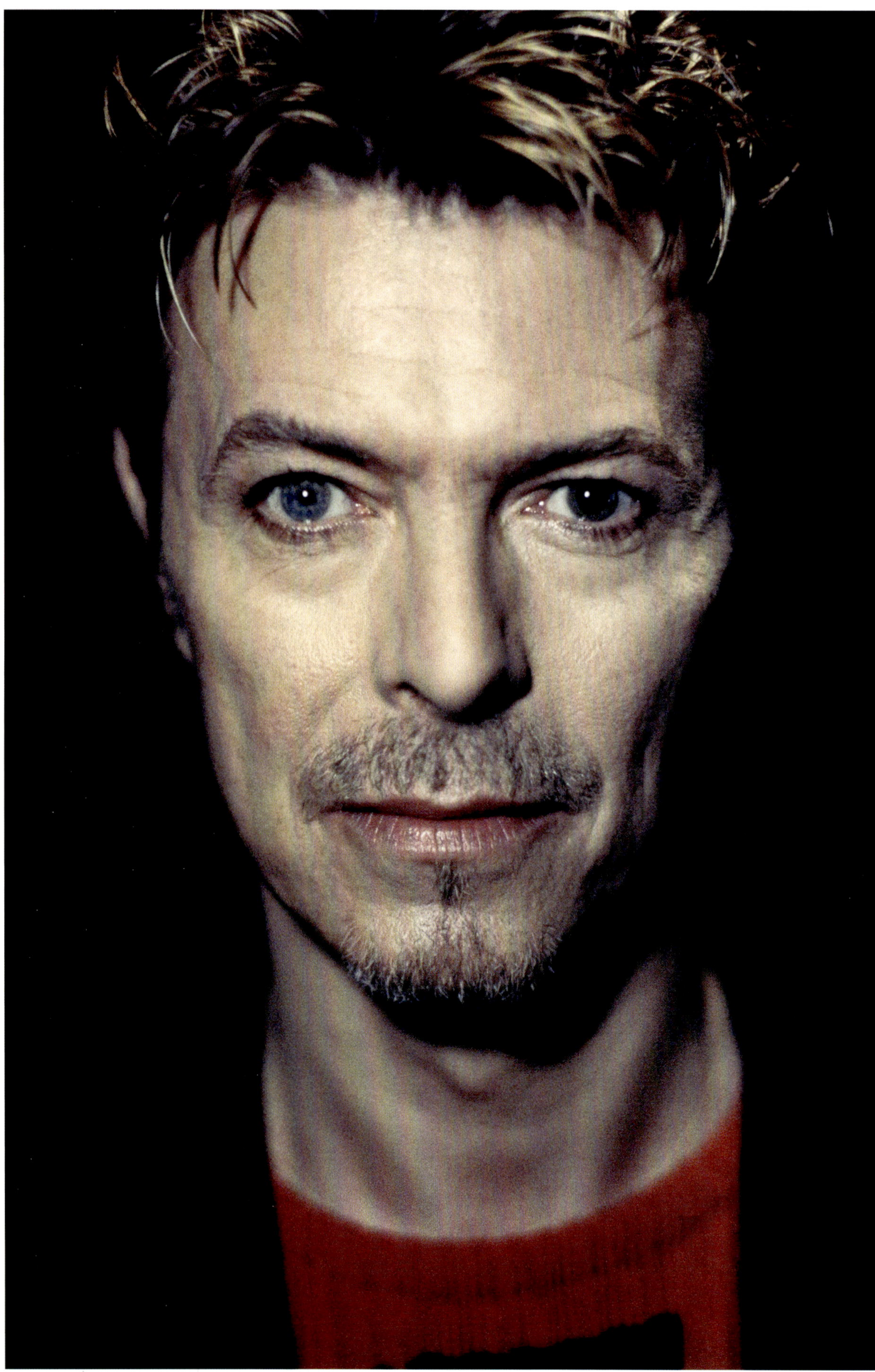

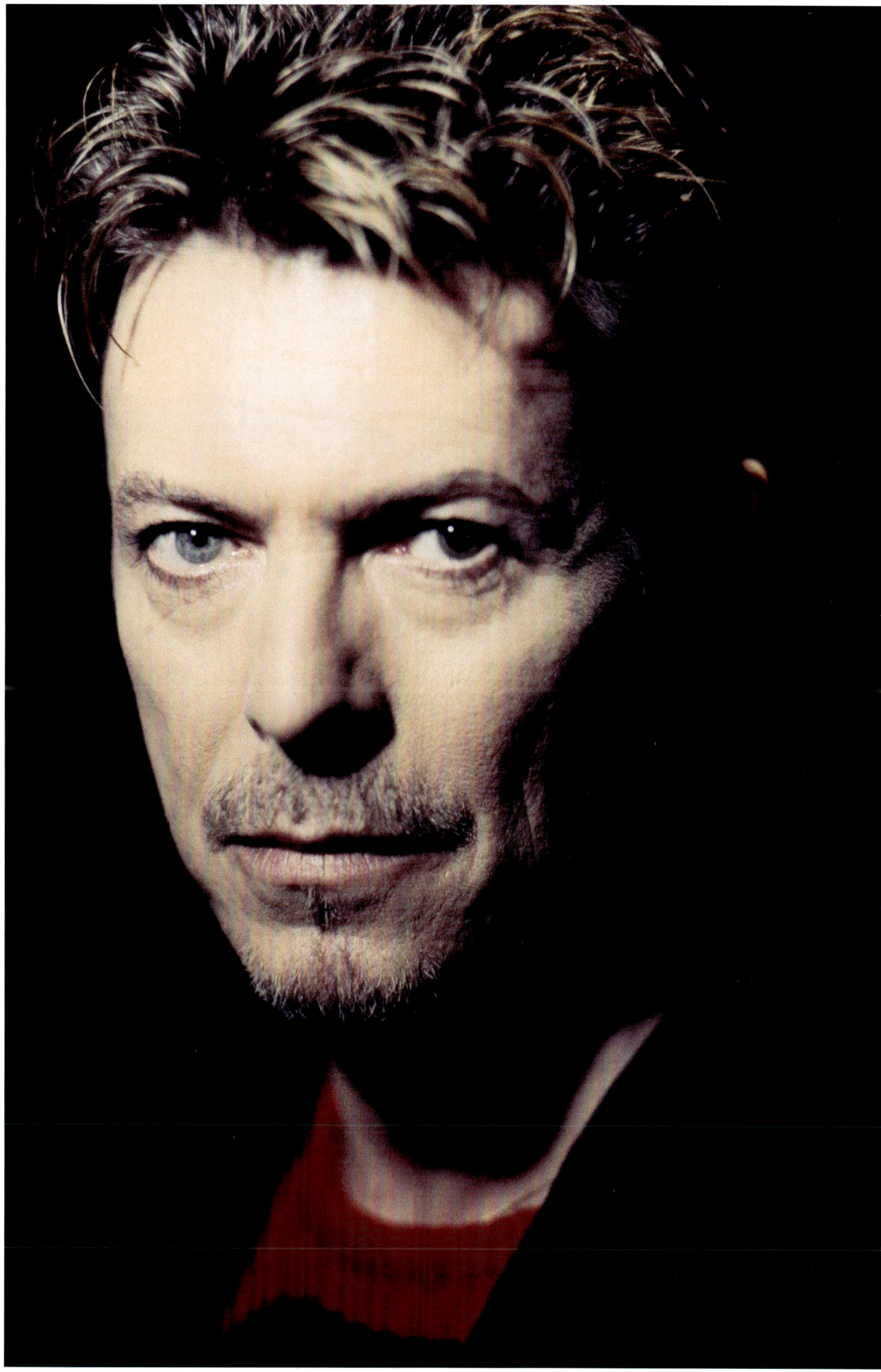

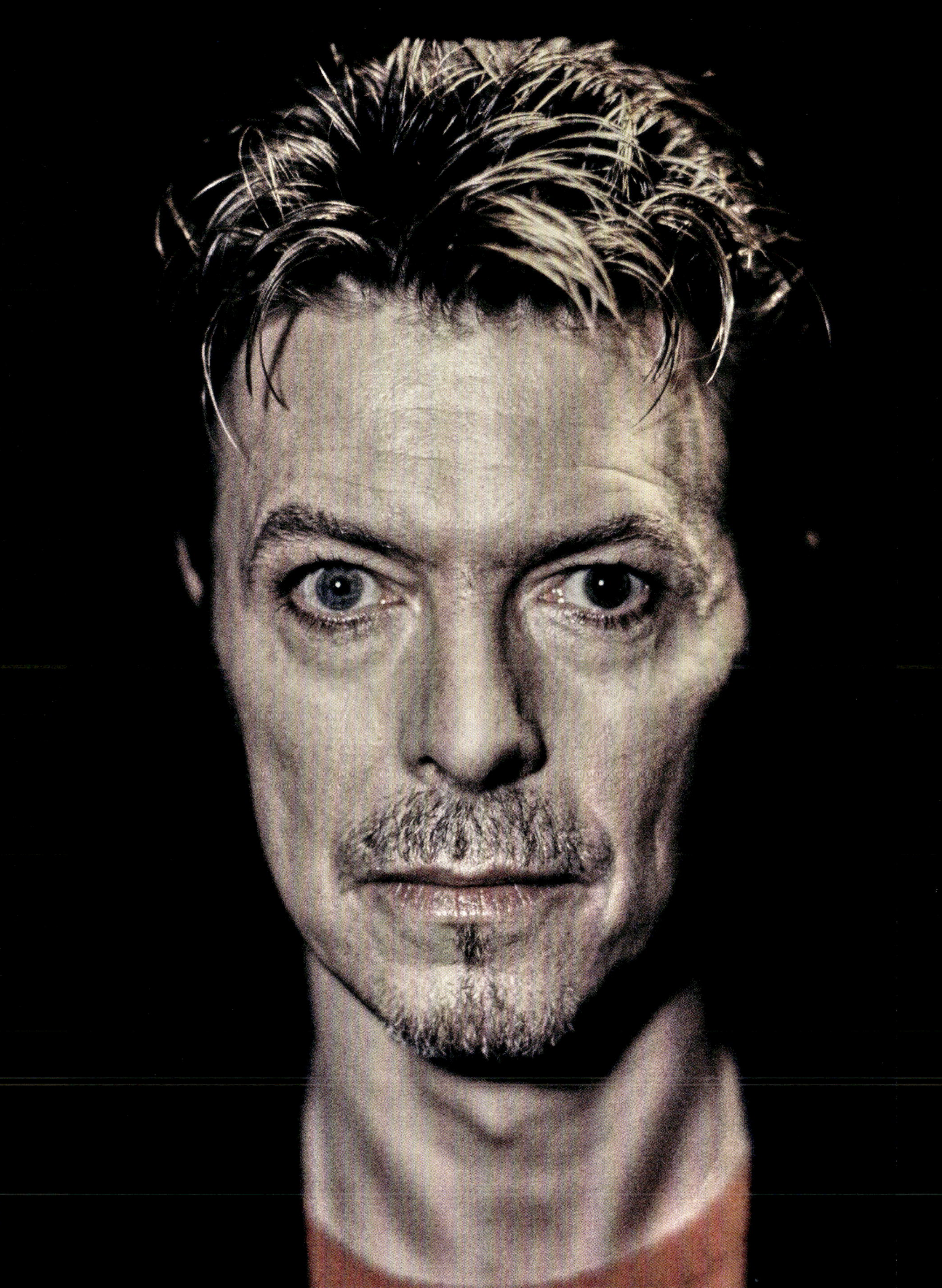

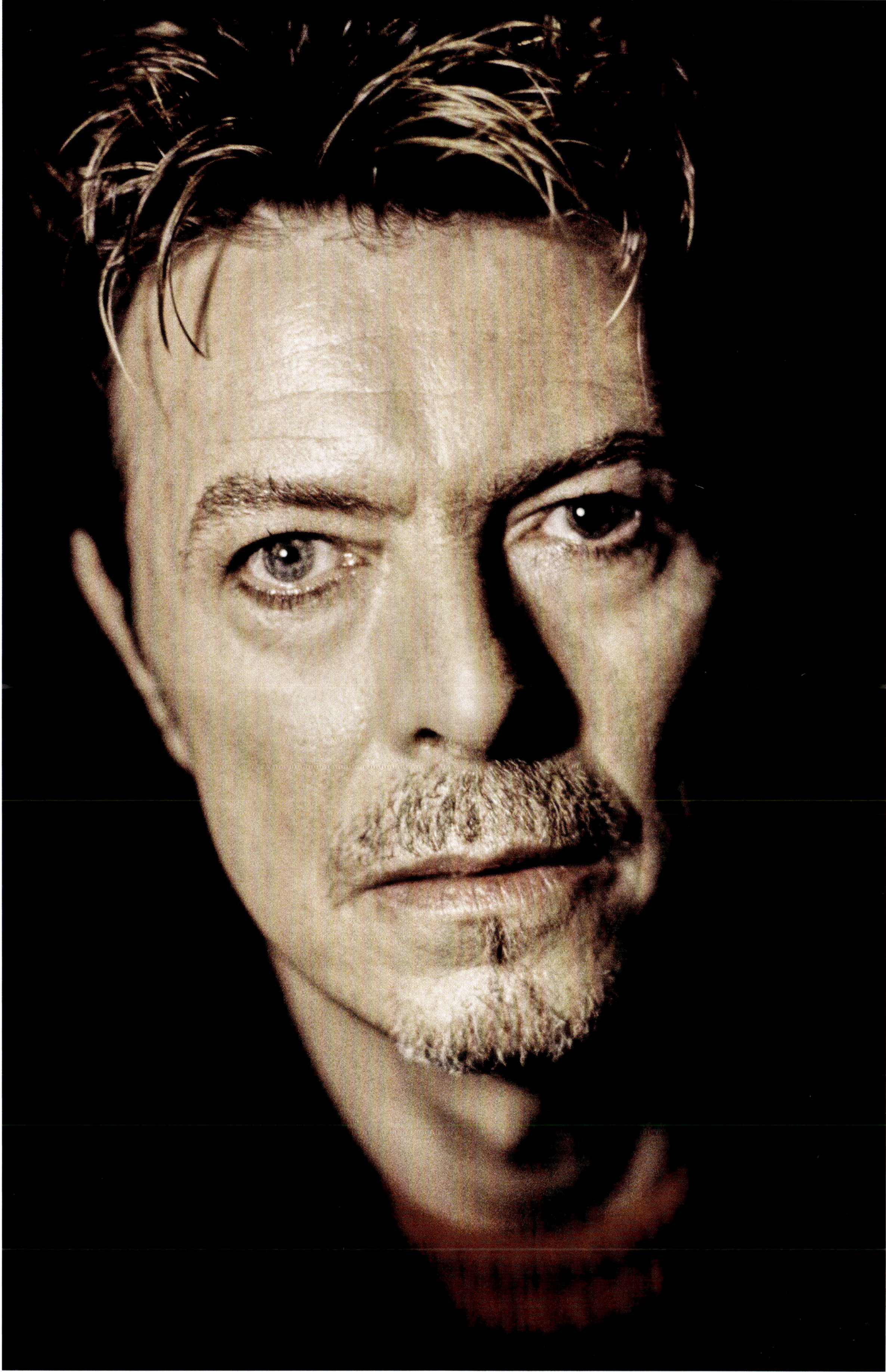

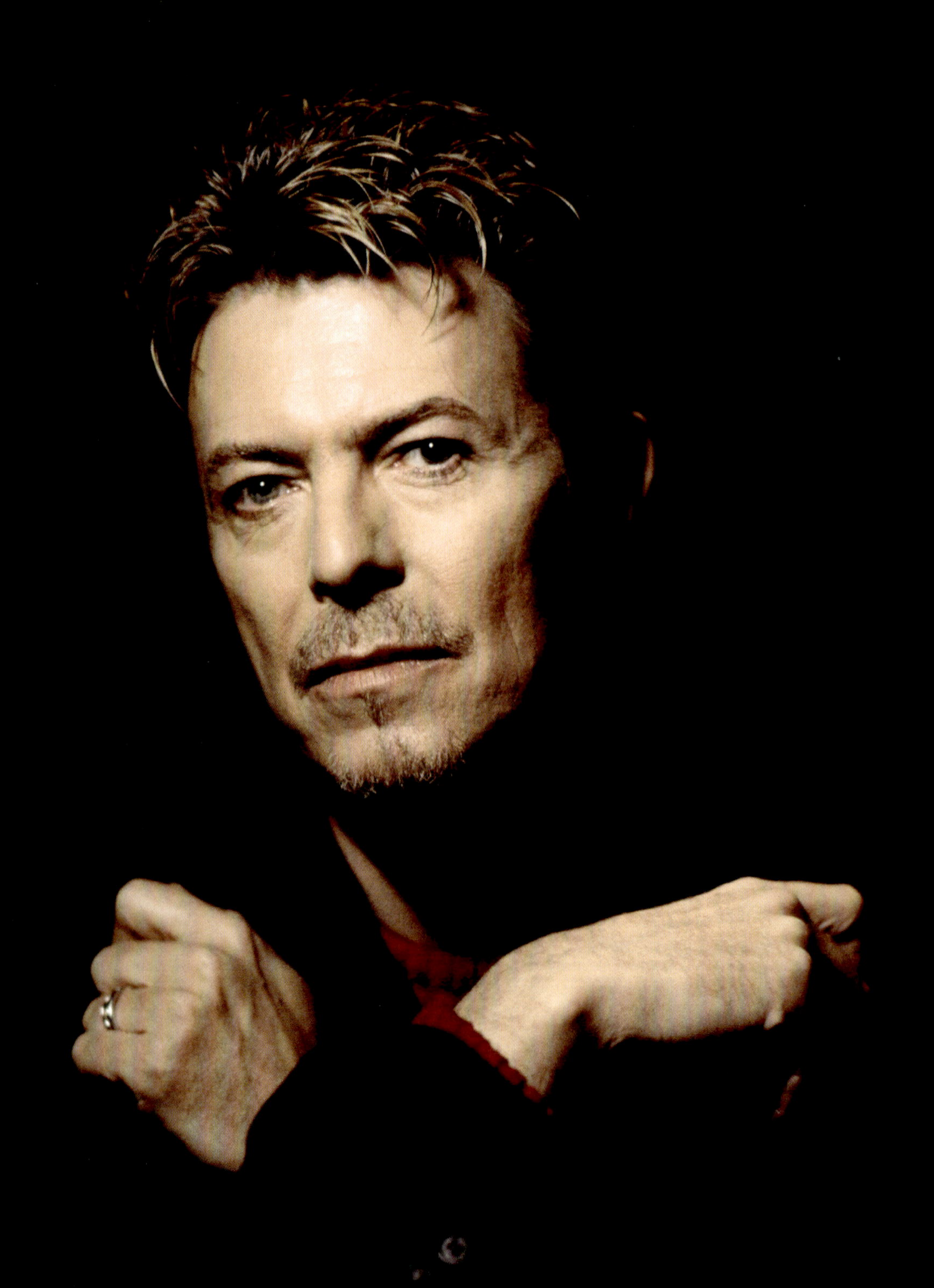

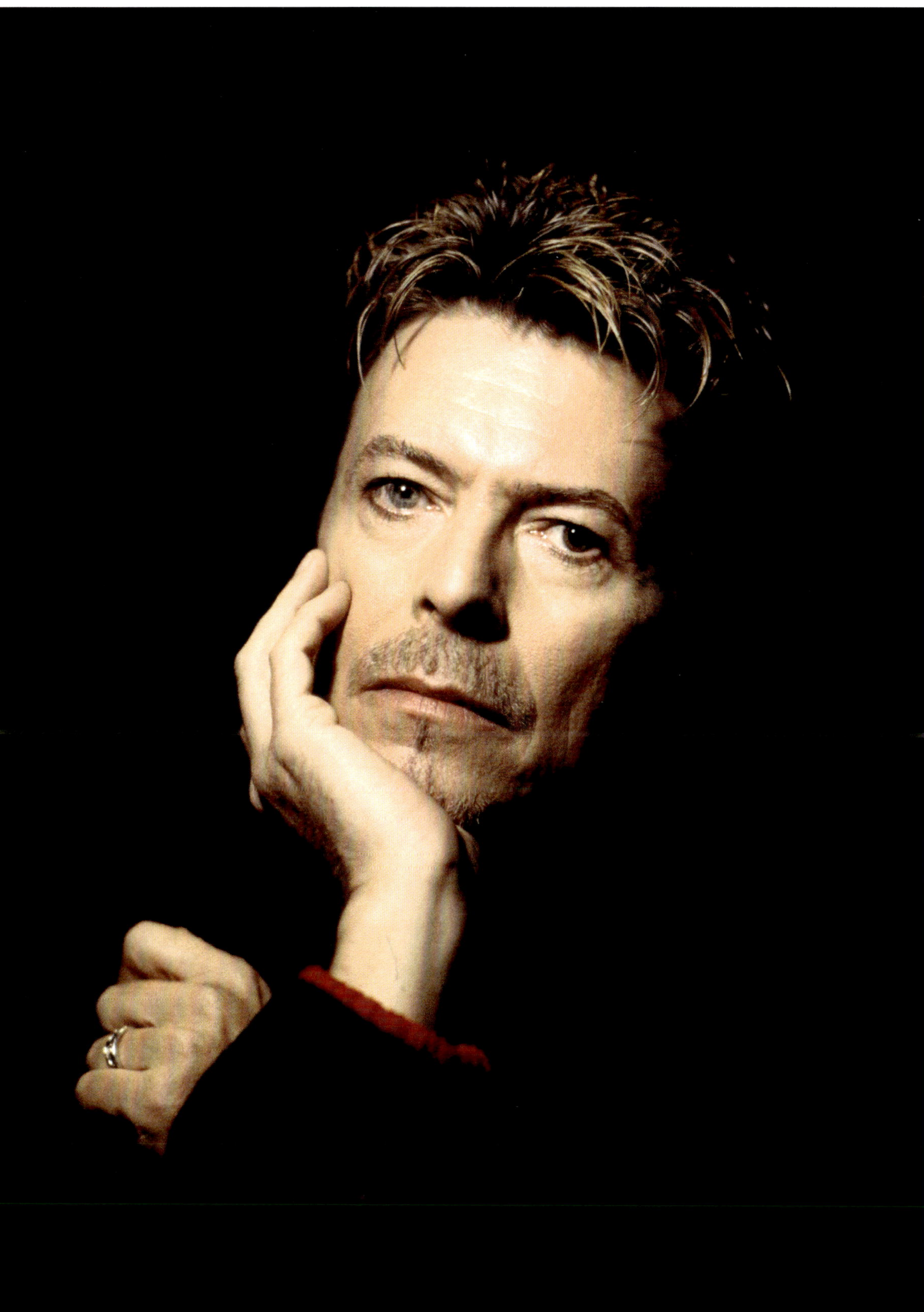

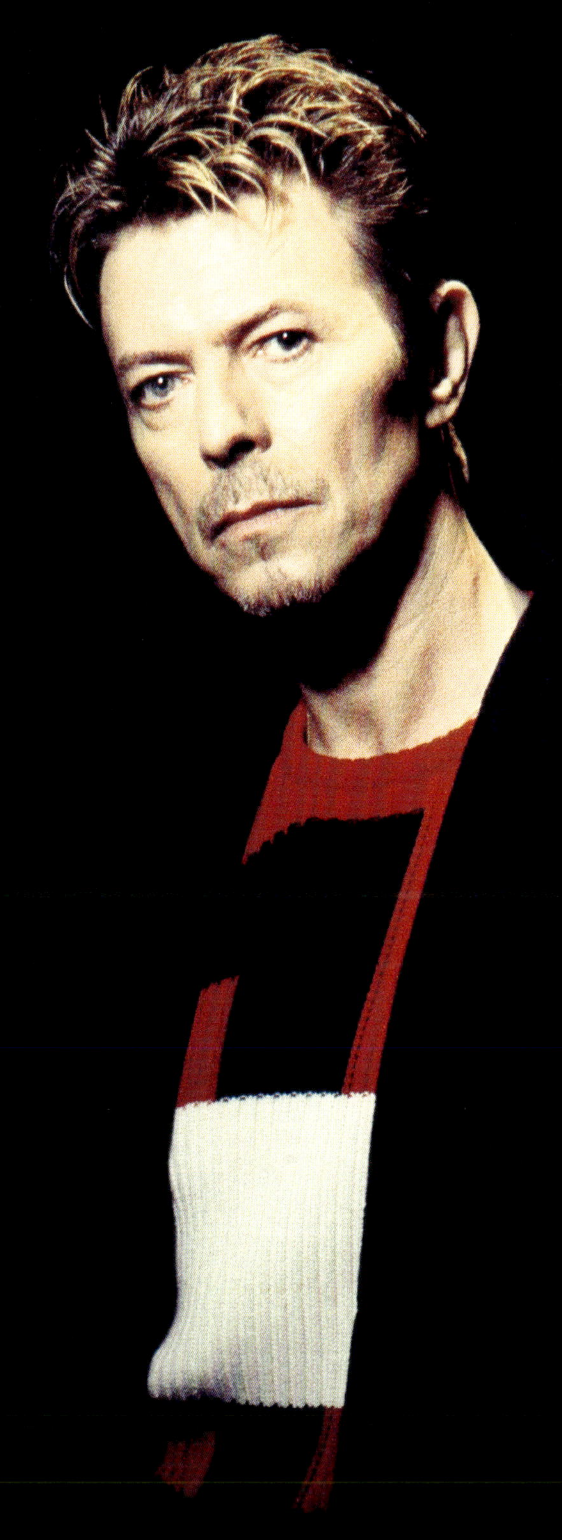

7 JANUARY 1997
MADISON SQUARE GARDEN, NEW YORK

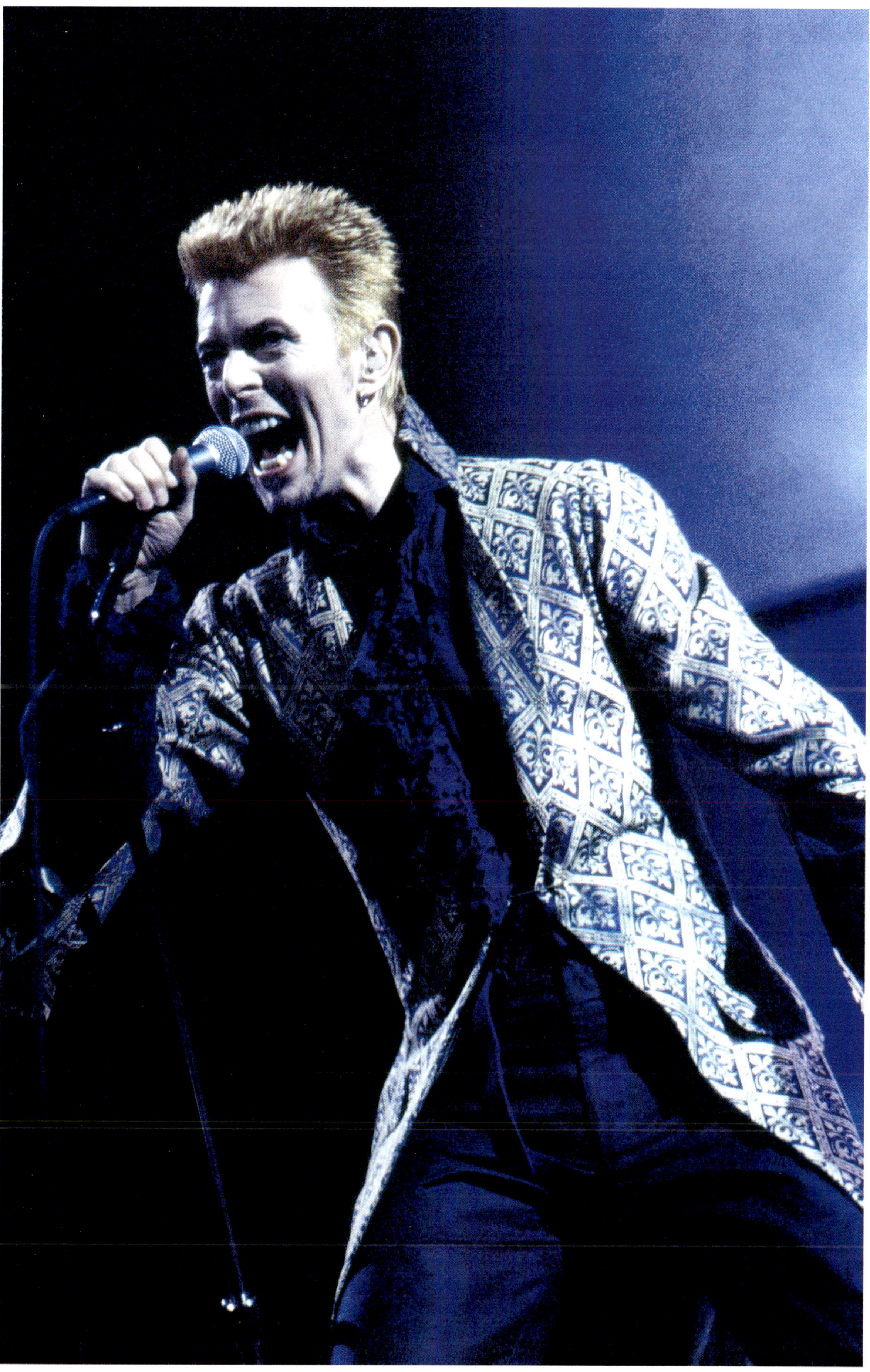

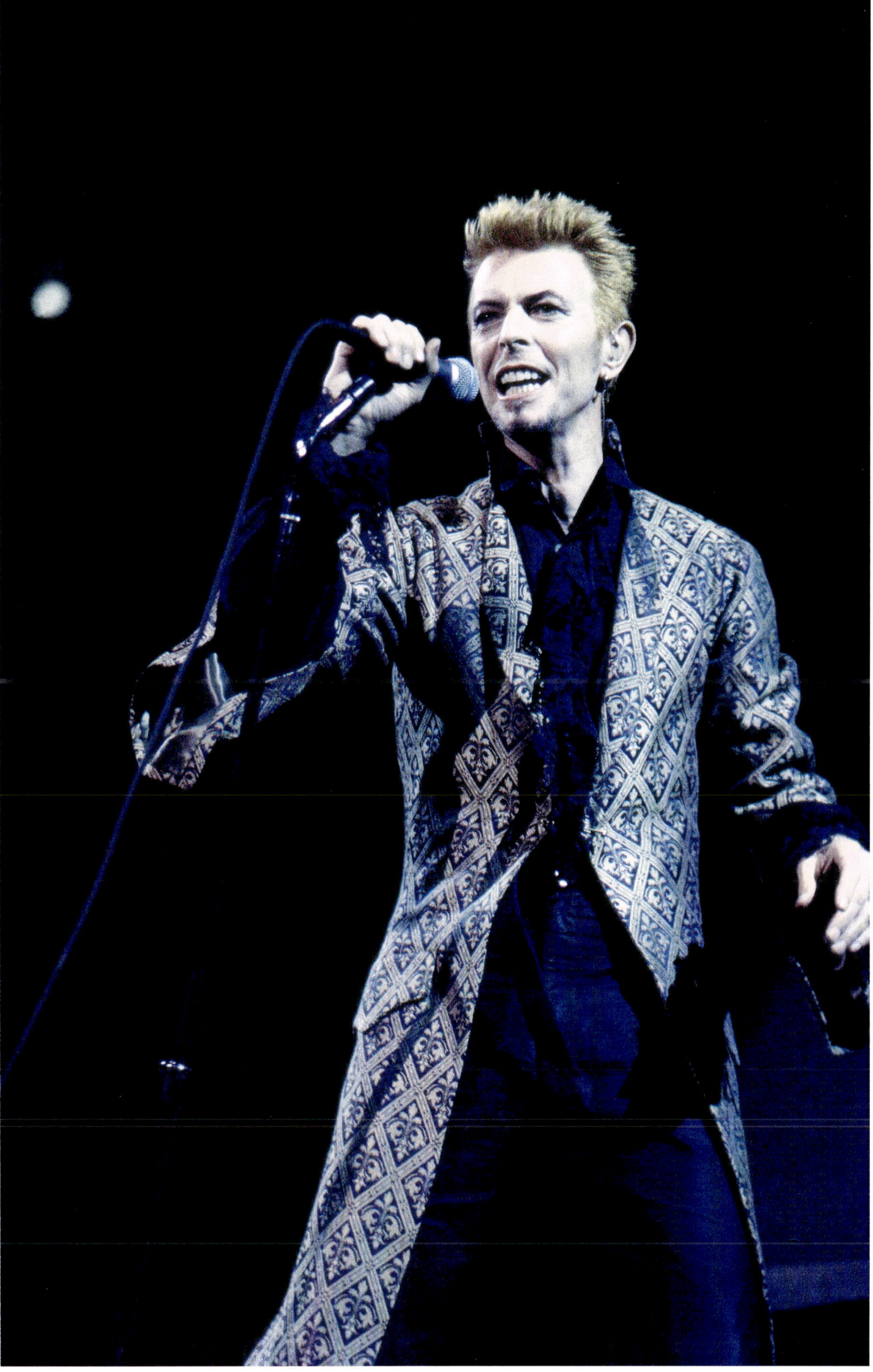

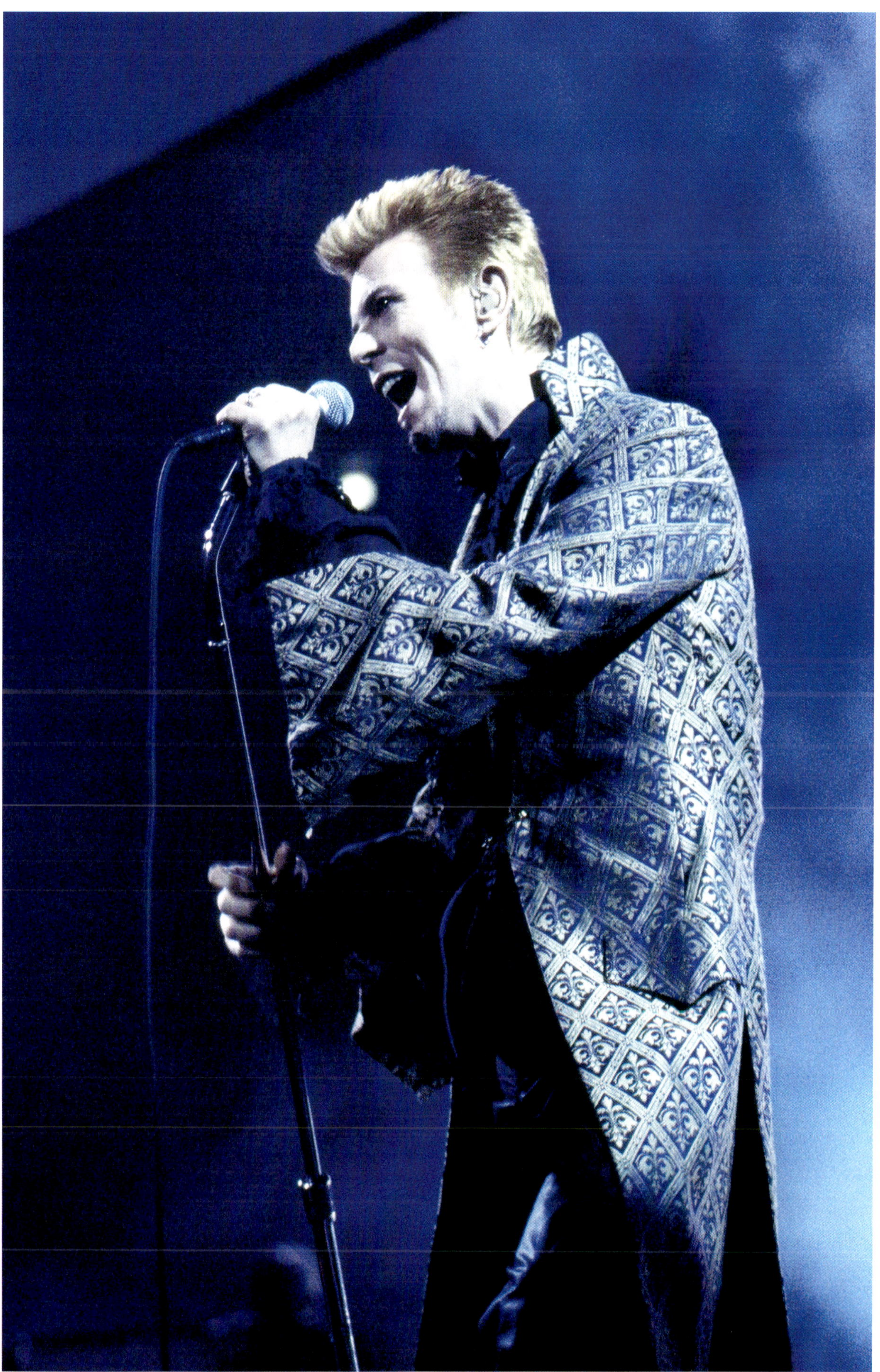

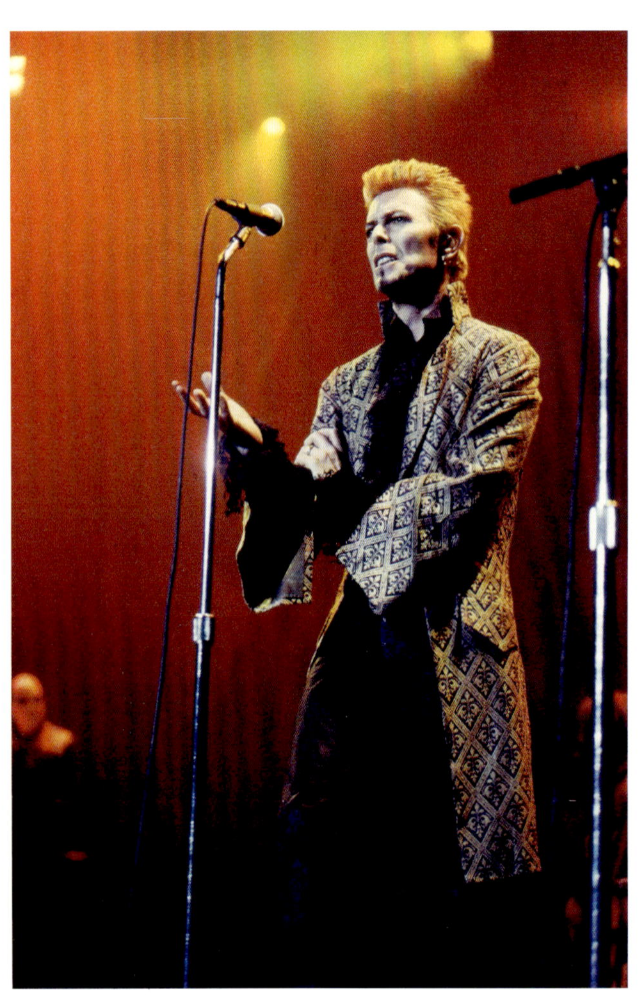
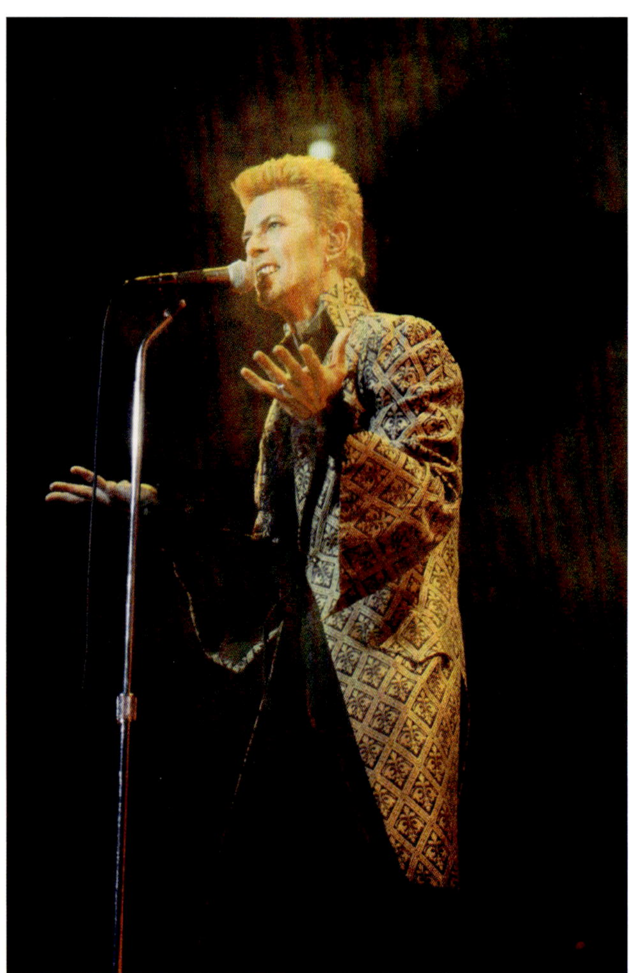

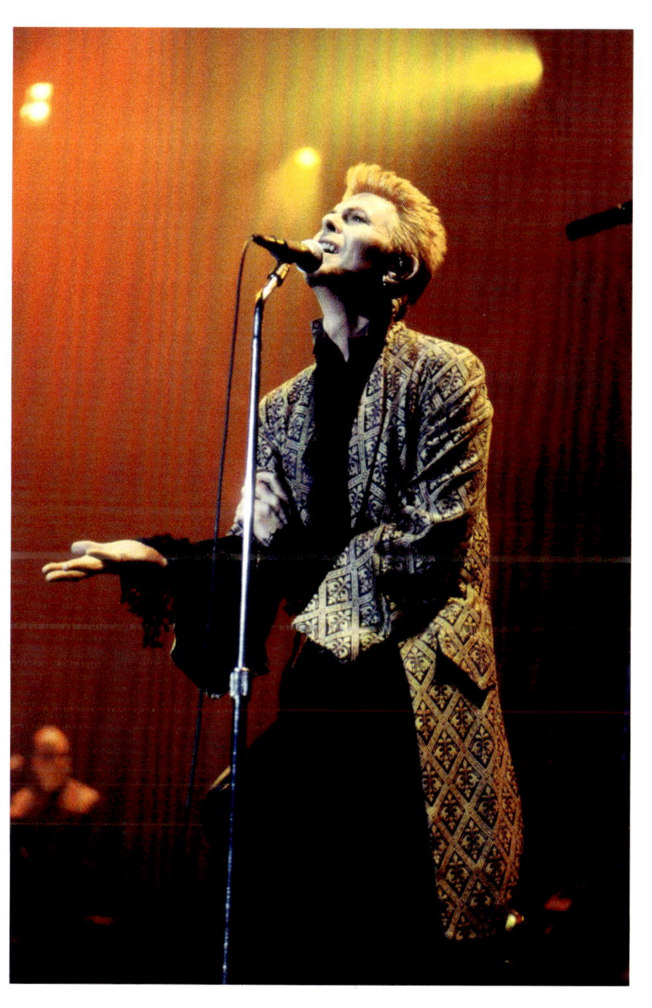
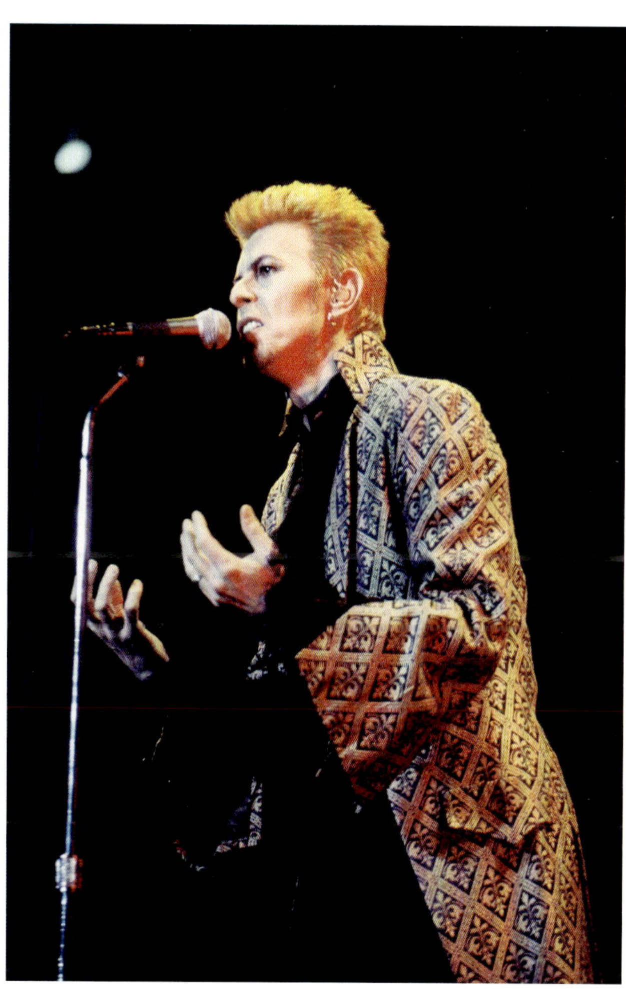

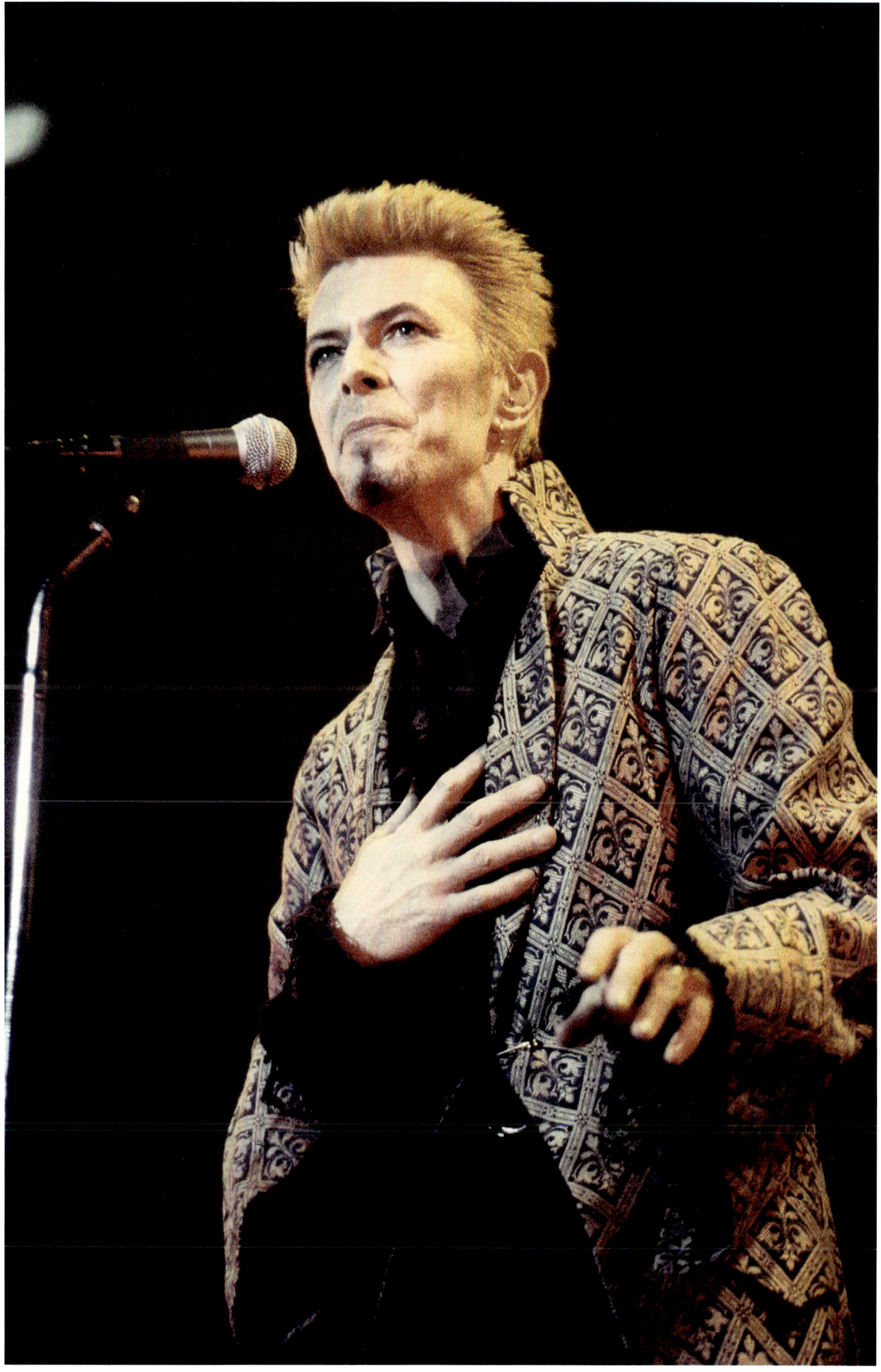

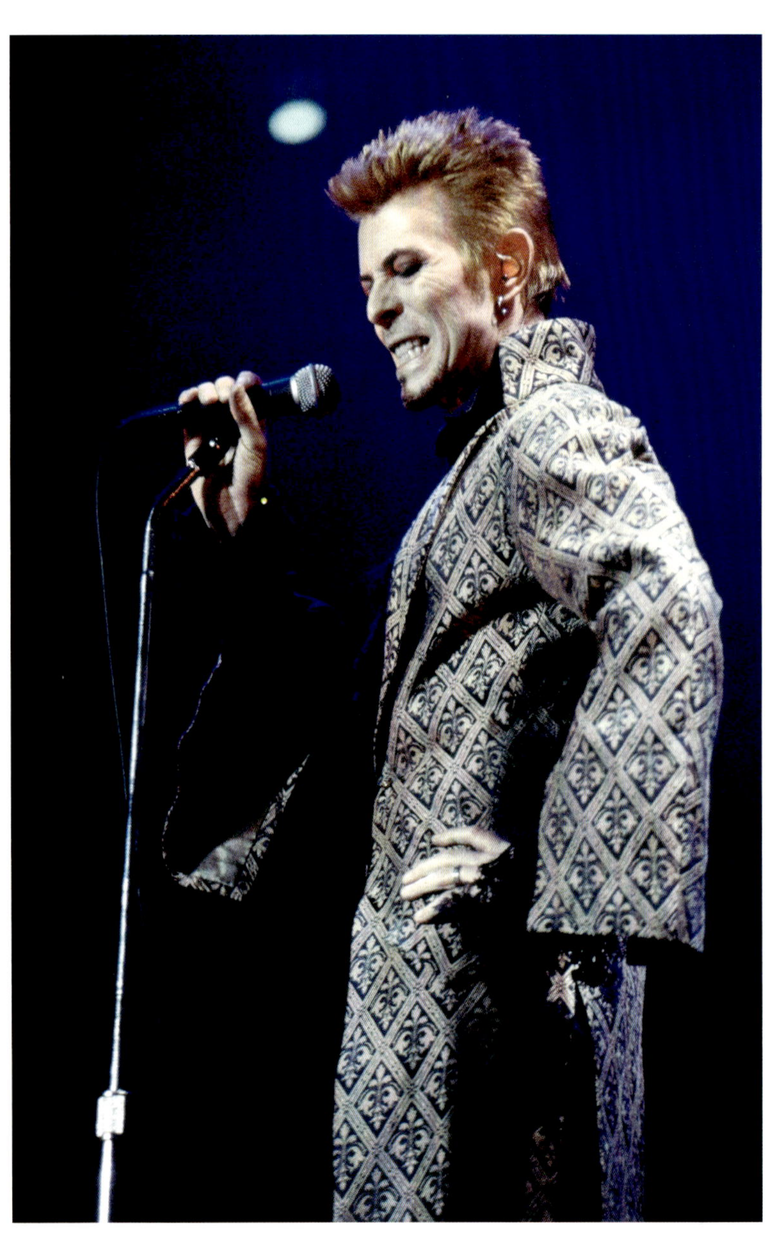

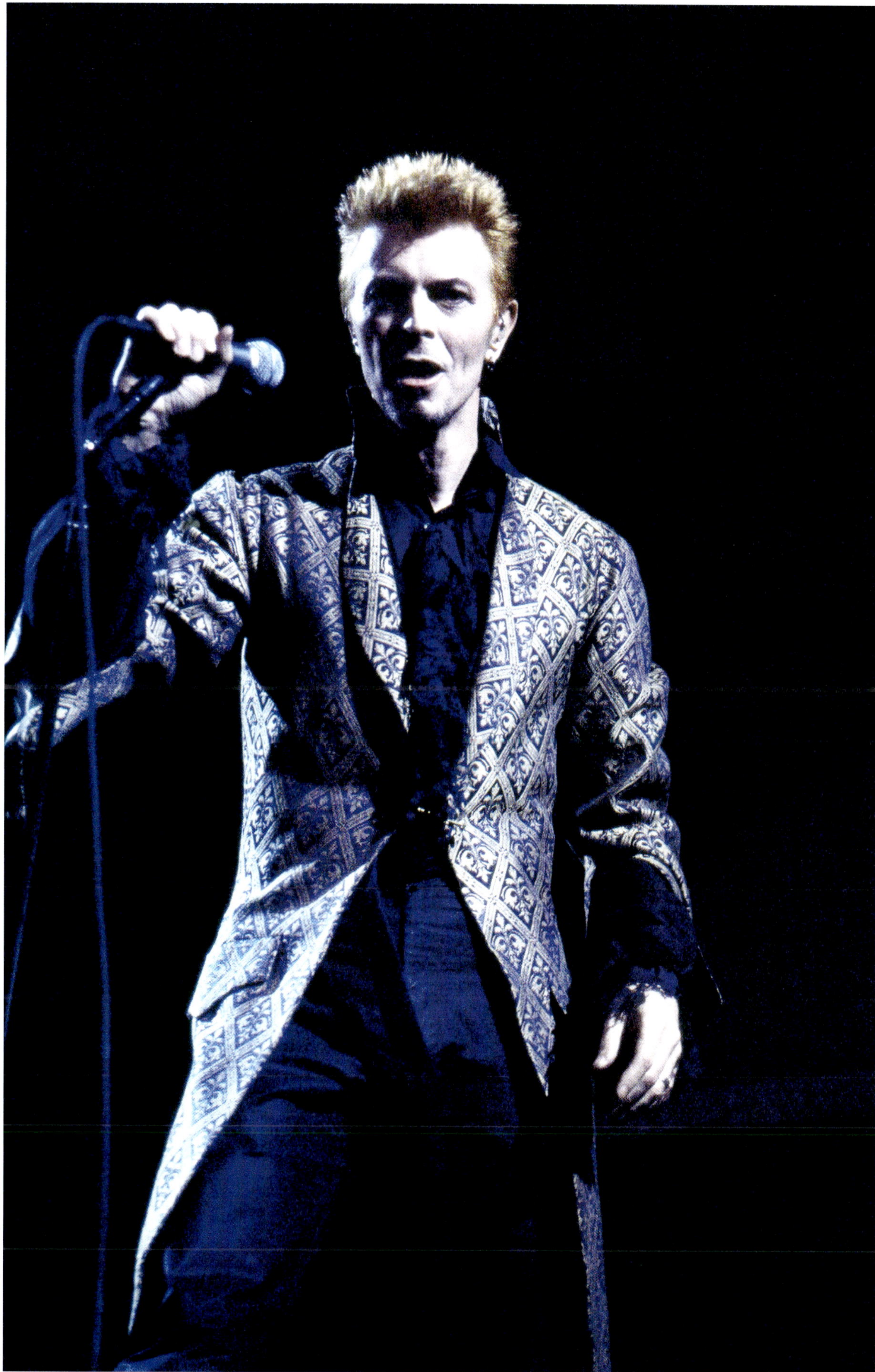

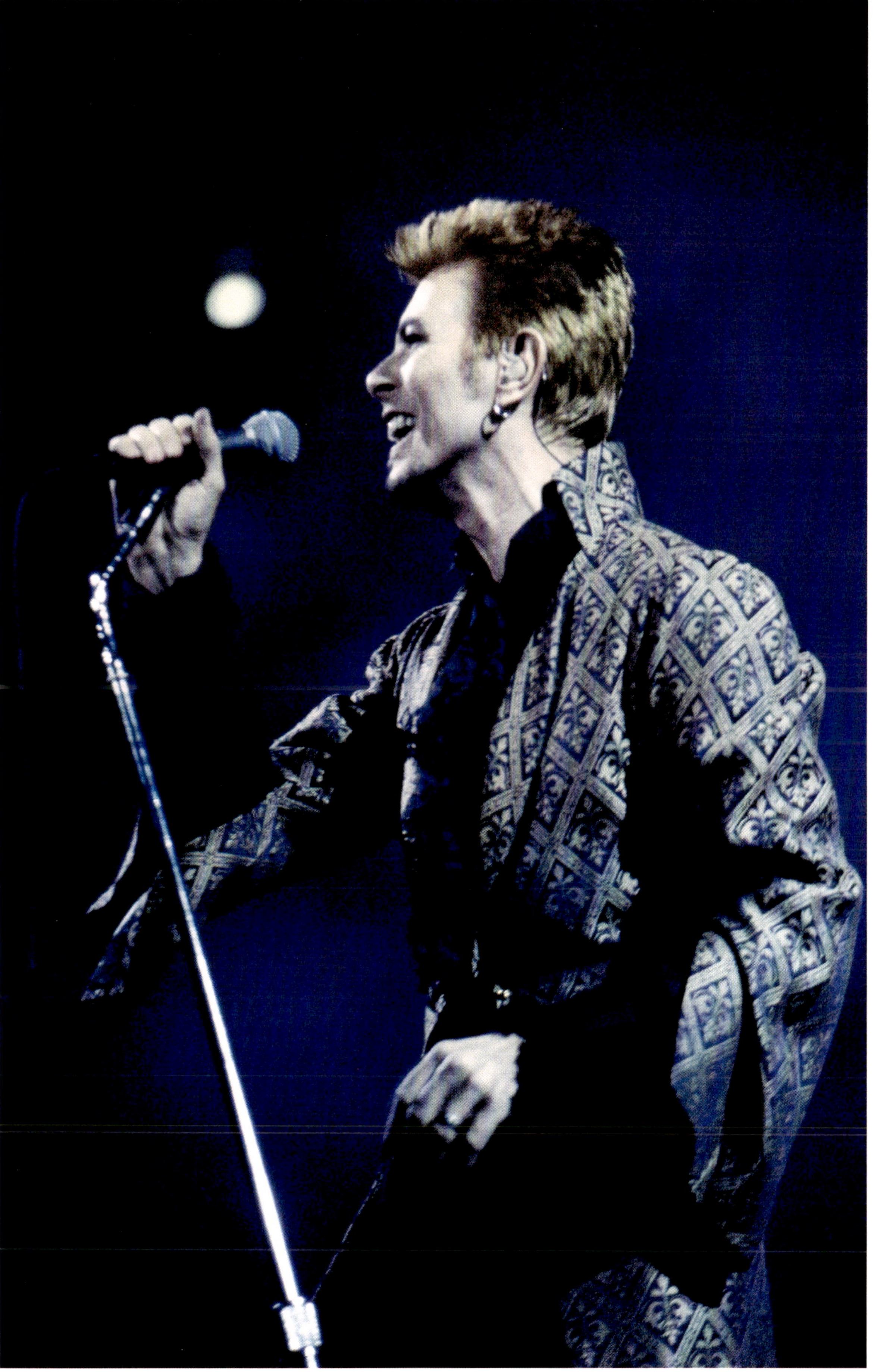

8 JANUARY 1997
TEA & SYMPATHY, NEW YORK

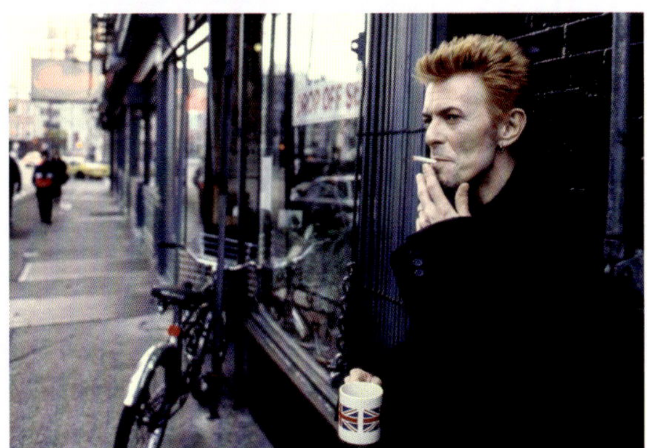

If I had to choose one significant photograph that I took of Bowie, one that had special meaning to me, it would be this shot of him standing outside Tea & Sympathy in New York in 1997. It was commissioned for his fiftieth birthday and taken the day after he played a gig at Madison Square Garden.

We met at his suggestion in the teashop, which was quite small and dark. Bowie was tired from the gig the night before (or, more than likely, the after-party) and I found him with a cigarette and cup of tea in hand. He wanted me to take the photographs inside, but I knew the light simply wouldn't work. It is interesting to think of my own progression at this point. Six years earlier, I had been too scared to ask him to remove his unphotogenic Versace jacket. Now, here I was cajoling him into the street, promising it would take no more than 15 minutes.

Like so many artists, Bowie knew and understood what made a good picture and he reluctantly trudged outside, still holding his cup of tea. He stood against a black wall wearing a black jumper and jacket. The only colour was the Union Flag on his mug, his orangey hair and the smoking tip of his cigarette. I took a roll of close-up portraits. Then I loaded another roll and decided to take some pictures from the side to put him in context, showing a wide shot of the street. He seemed oddly shy being photographed, looking for distractions, and yet no one approached us, nobody bothered him. Although it seems incredible now, prior to the advent of digital cameras it was possible to photograph one of the most famous people on the planet and actually be left alone.

This session is significant to me because I not only felt the most confident I have ever felt photographing Bowie, but it was also the last time I saw him. Such oddly parallel lives; both of us learning our art, occasionally meeting, then reaching the point where we were both old and wise enough to finally know what we were doing. All there, on his birthday, that January day on a cold street in New York.

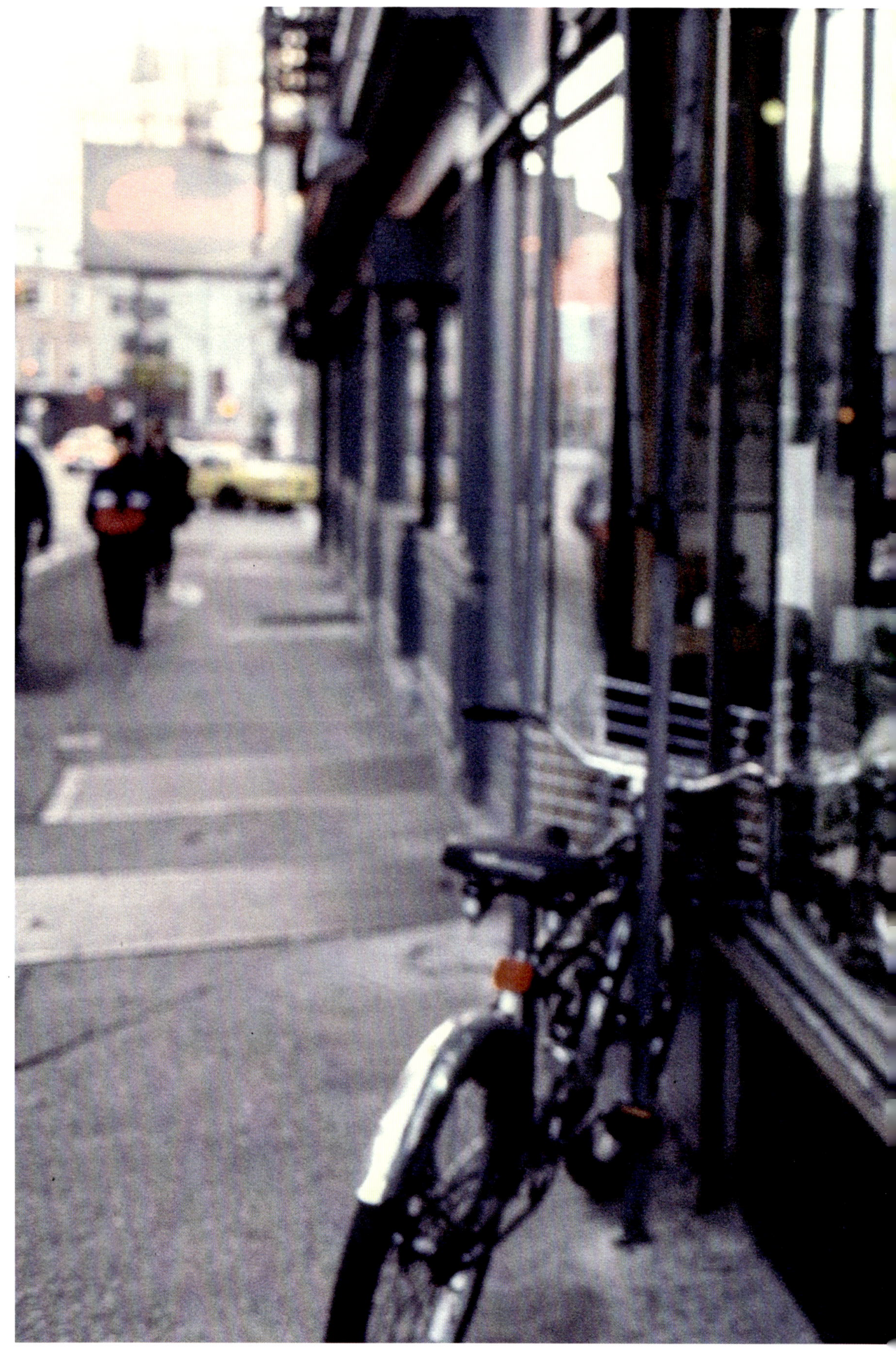

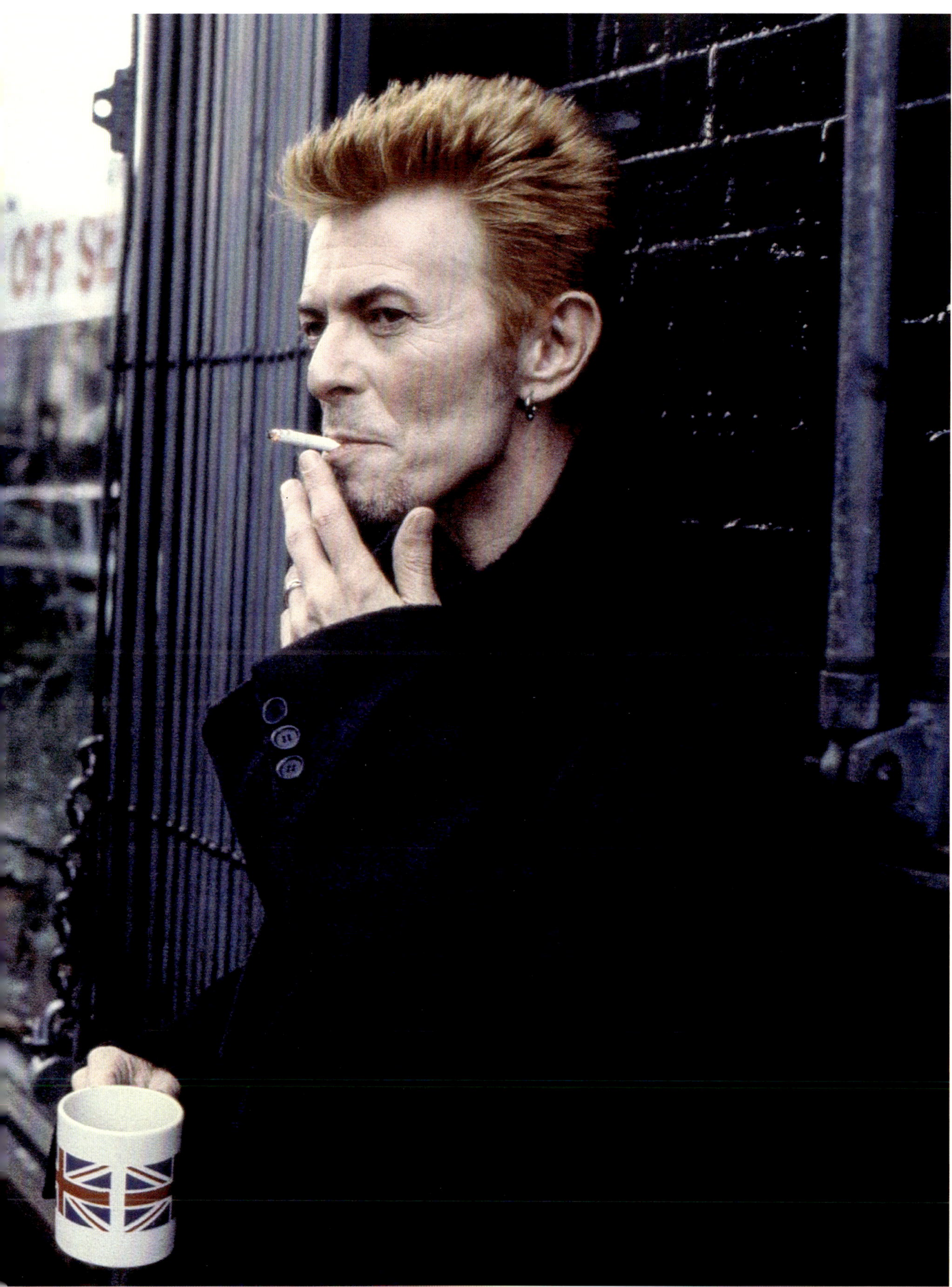

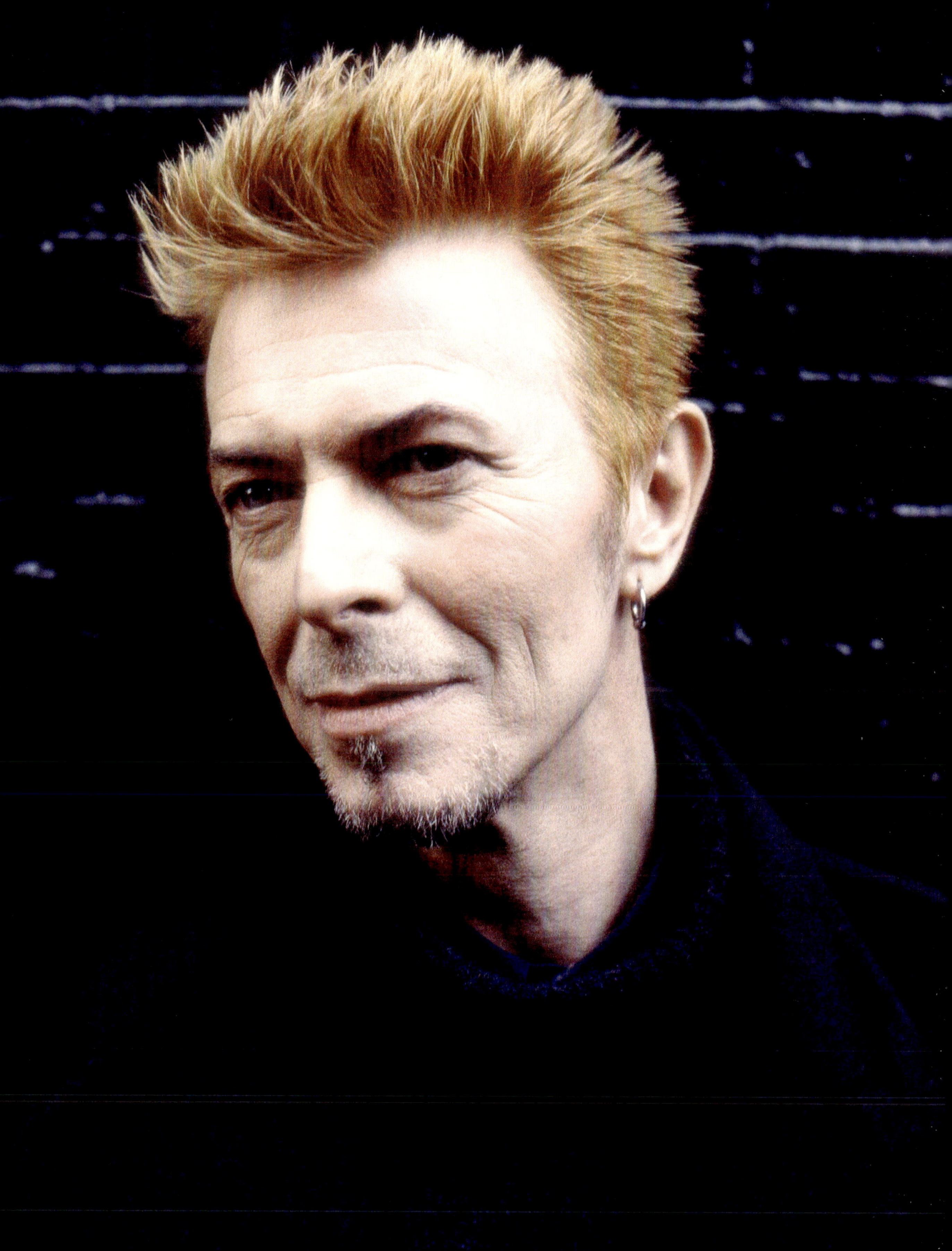

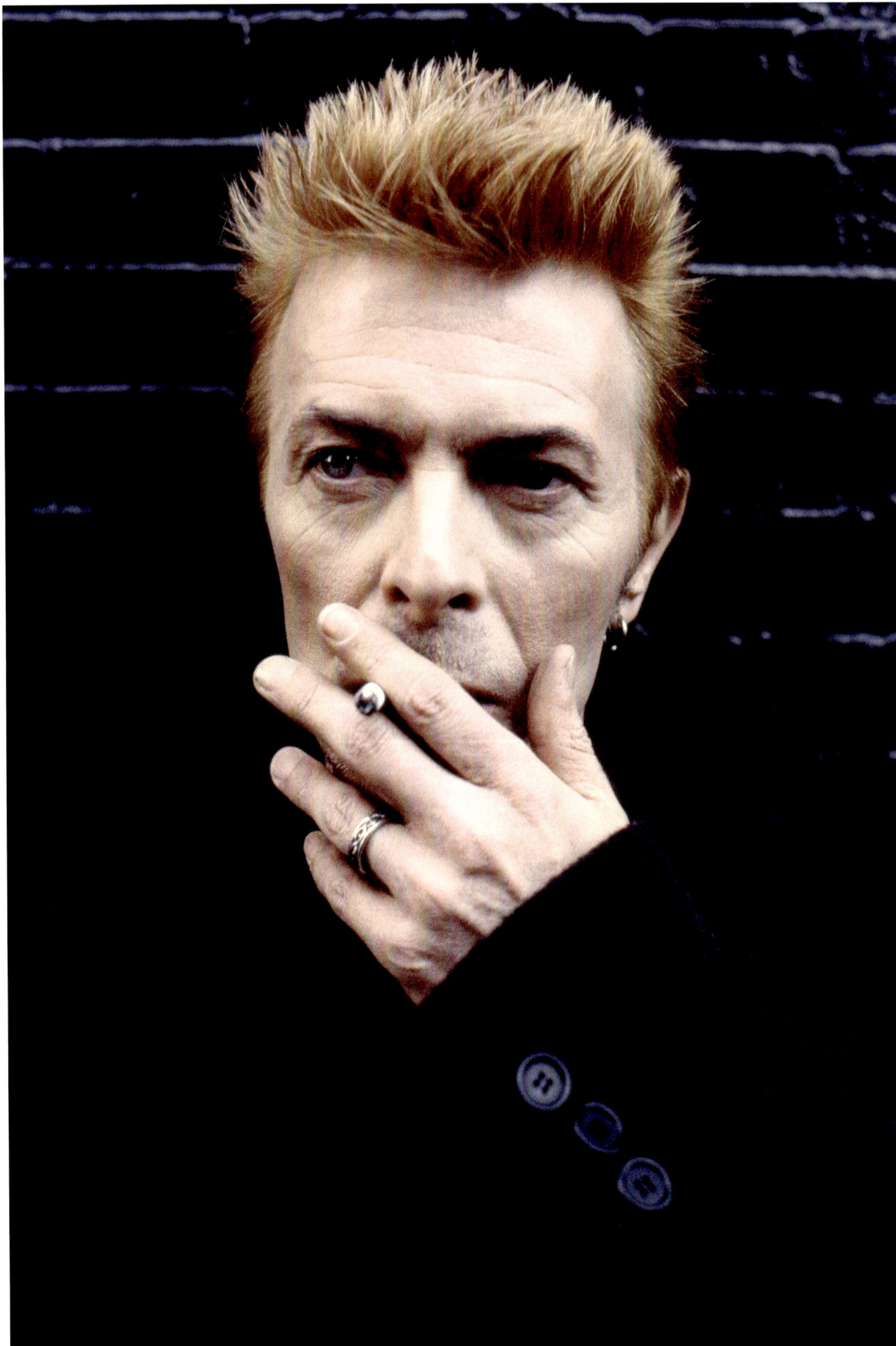

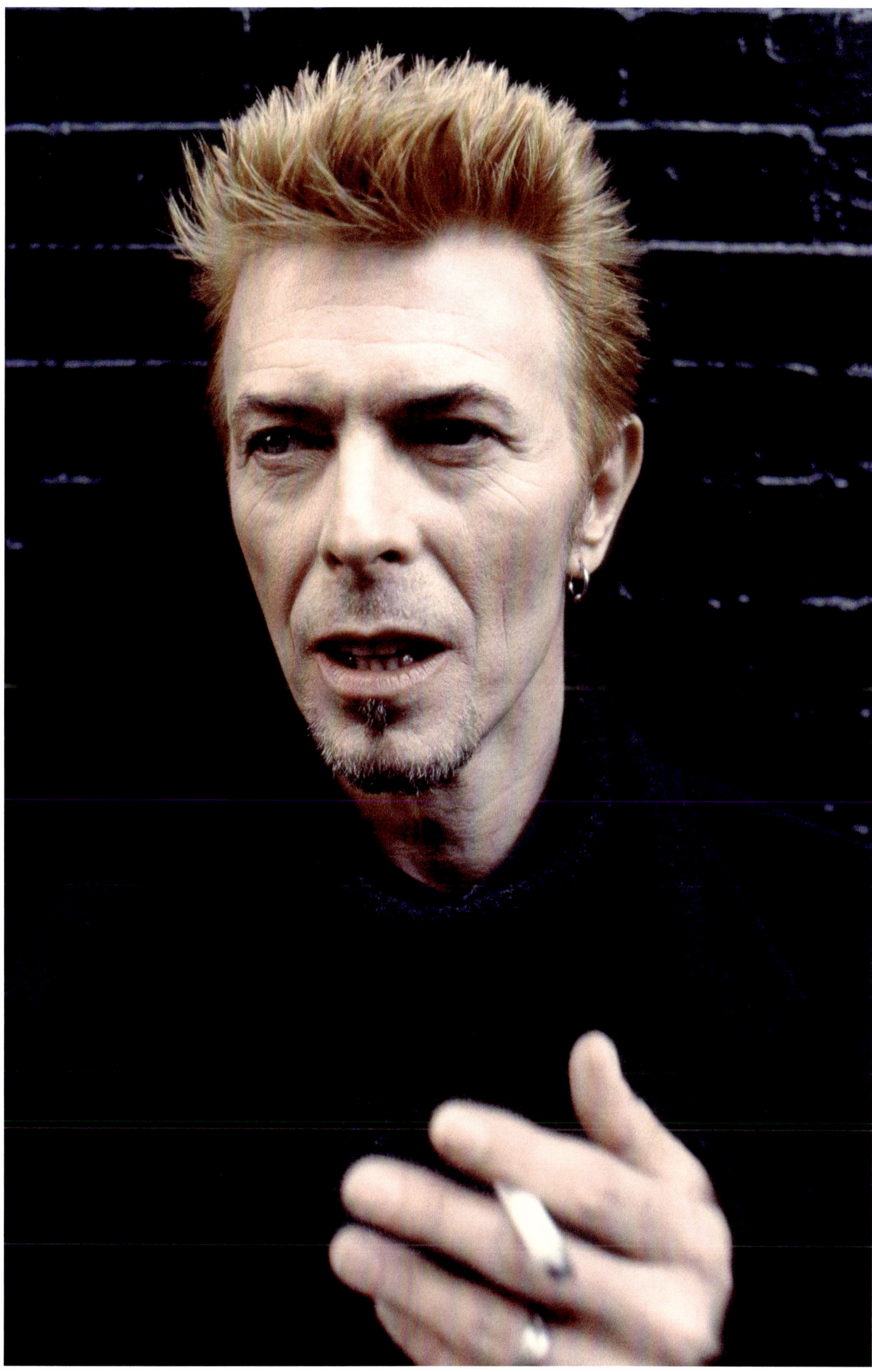

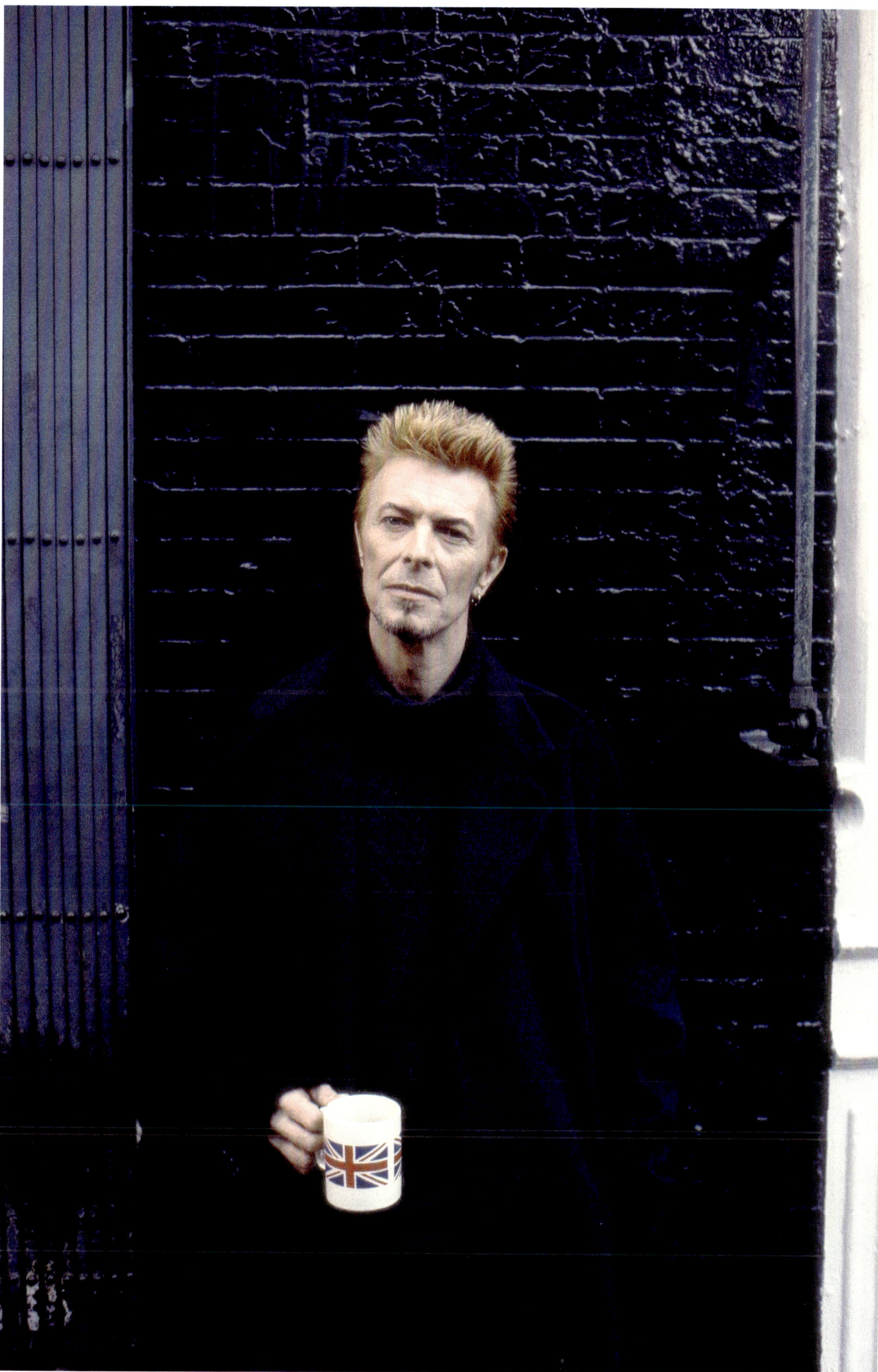

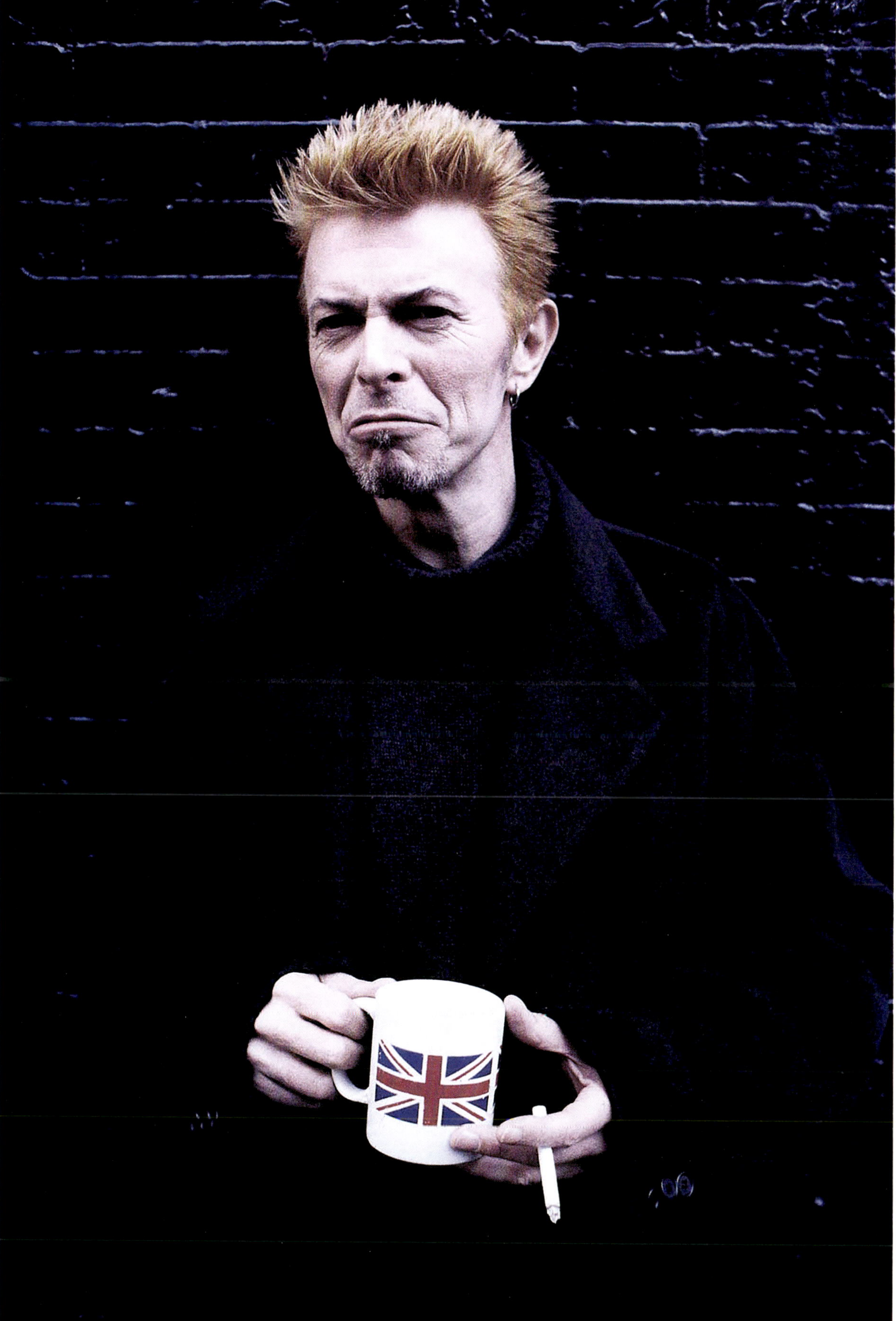

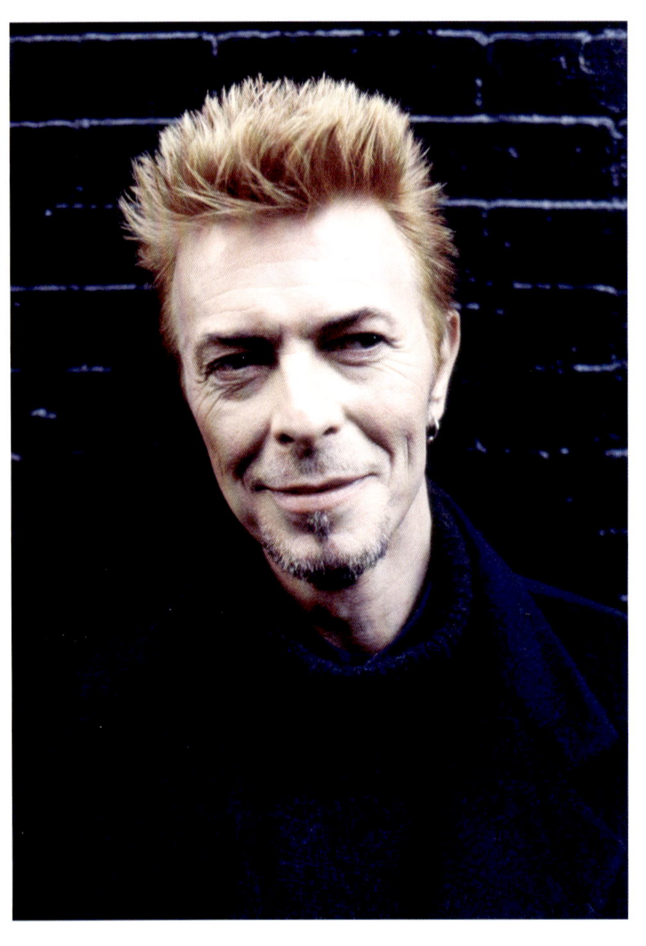
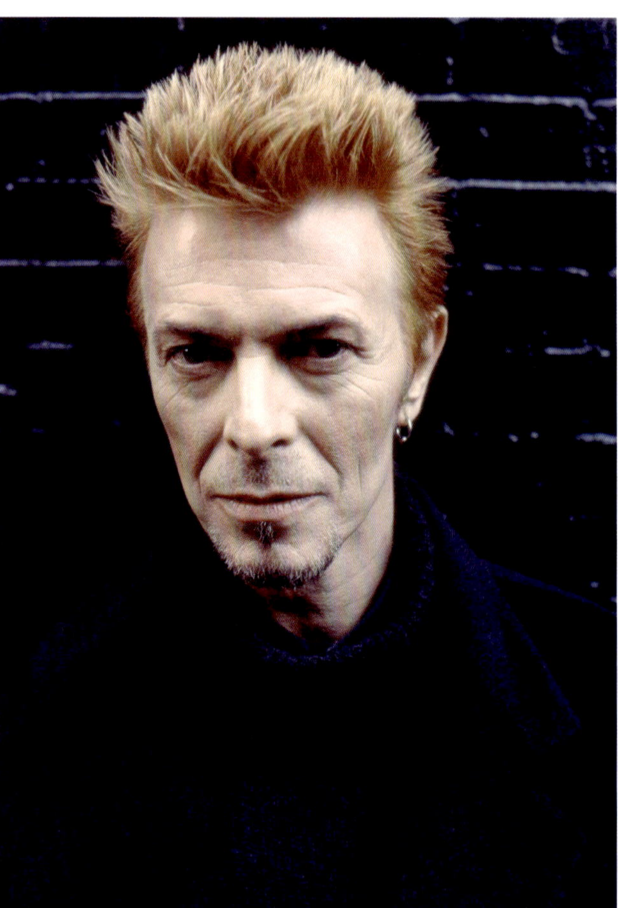
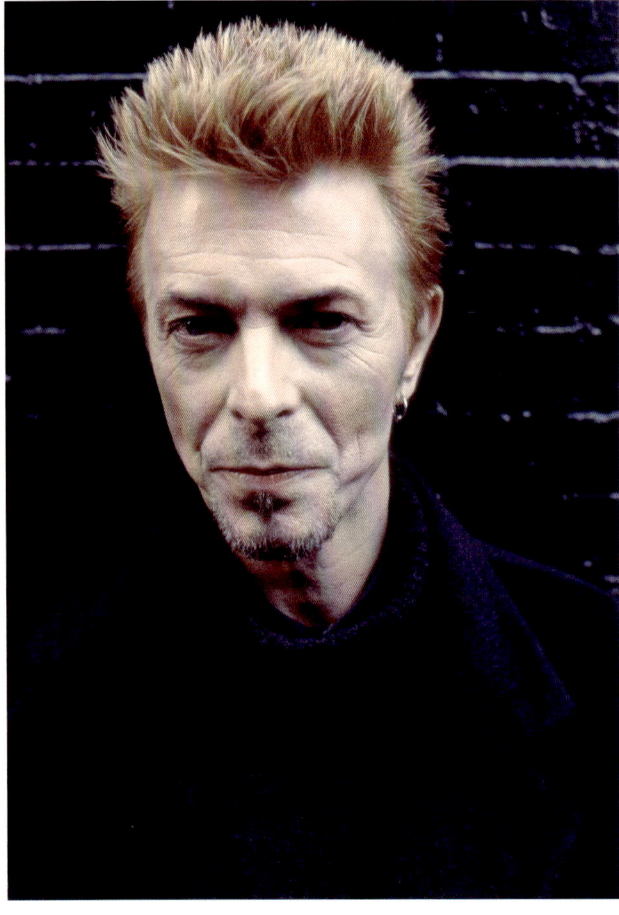
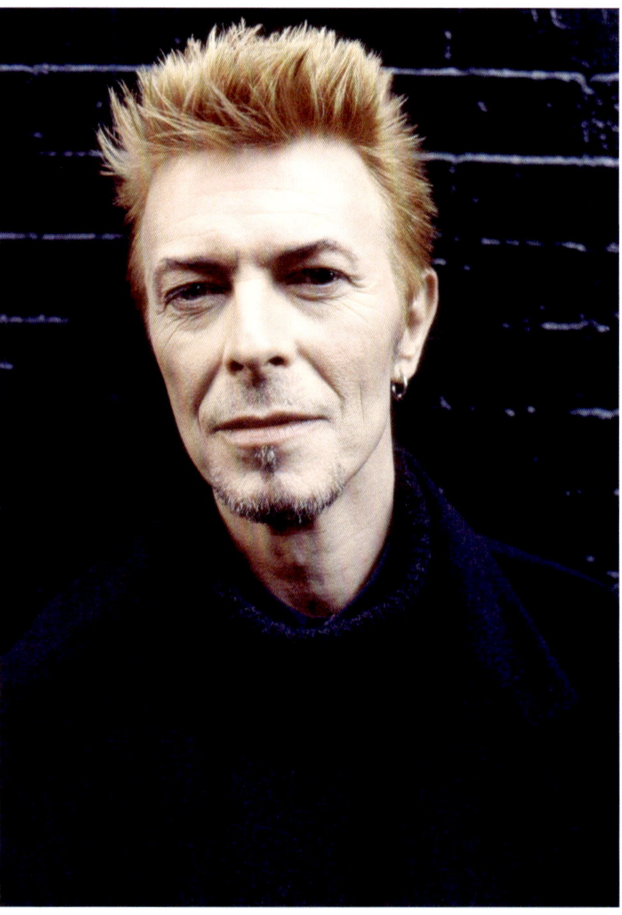

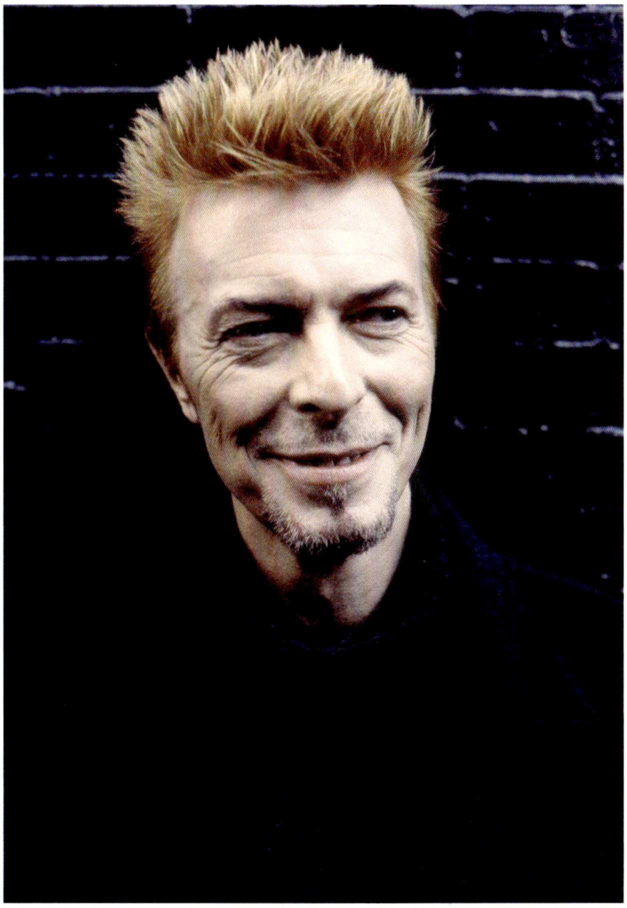

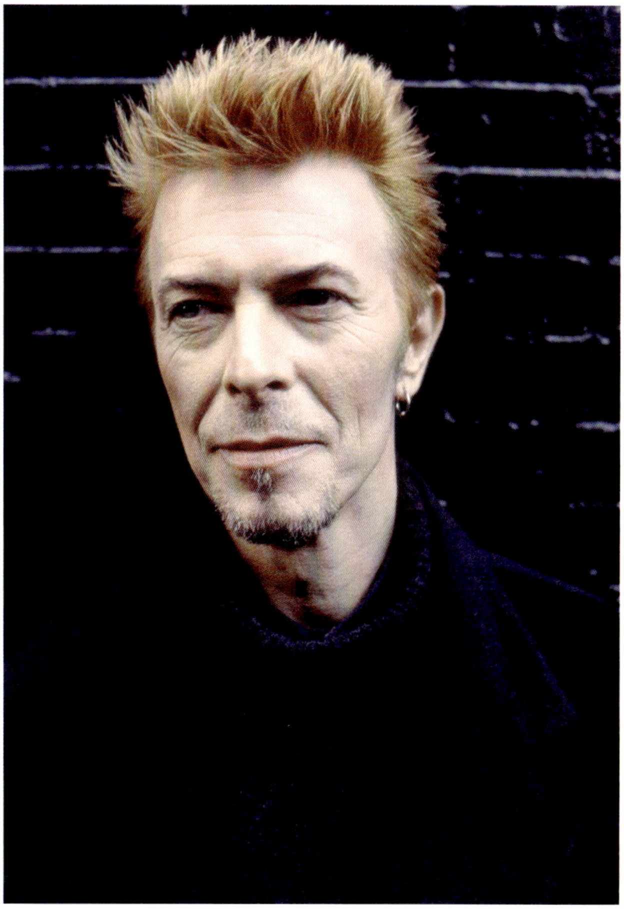

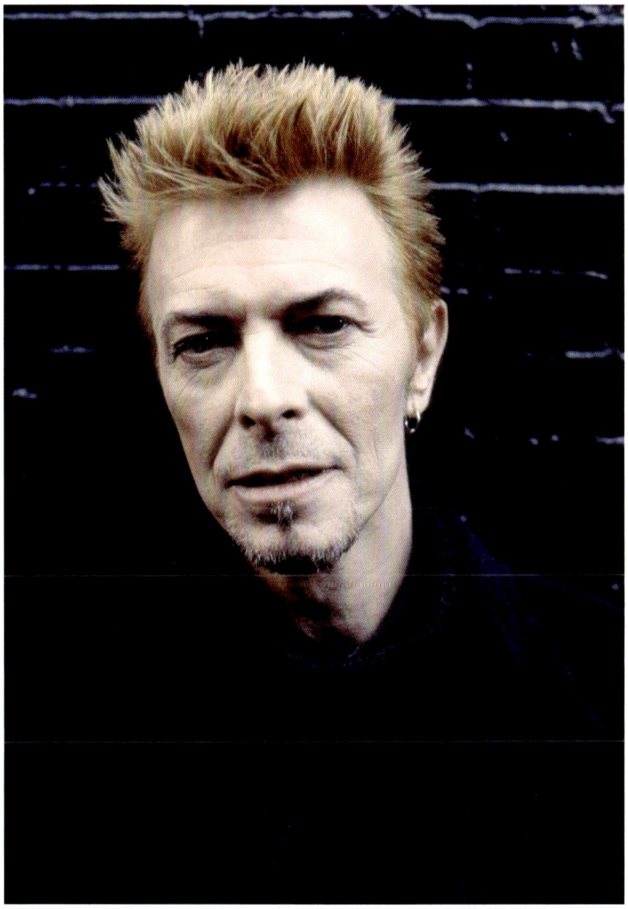

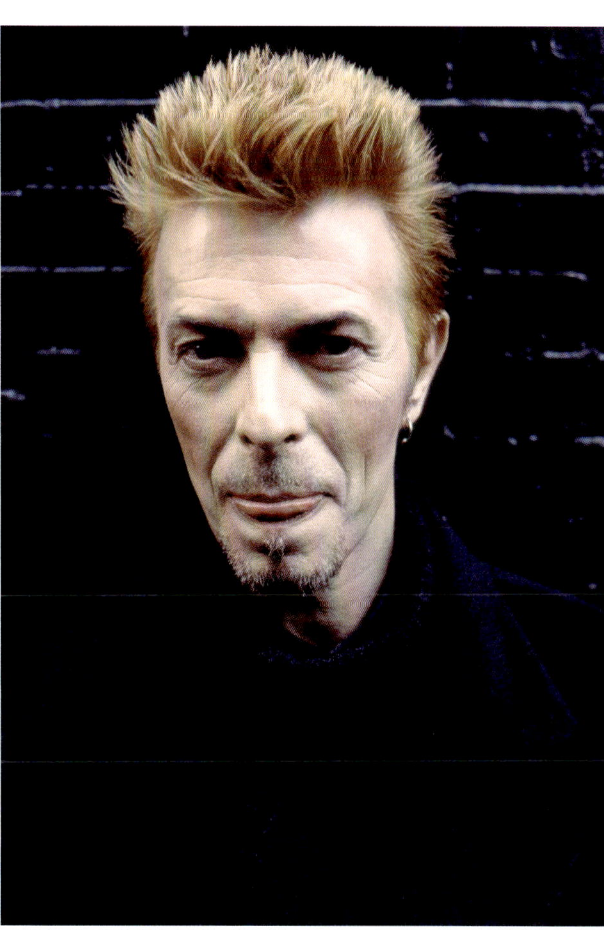

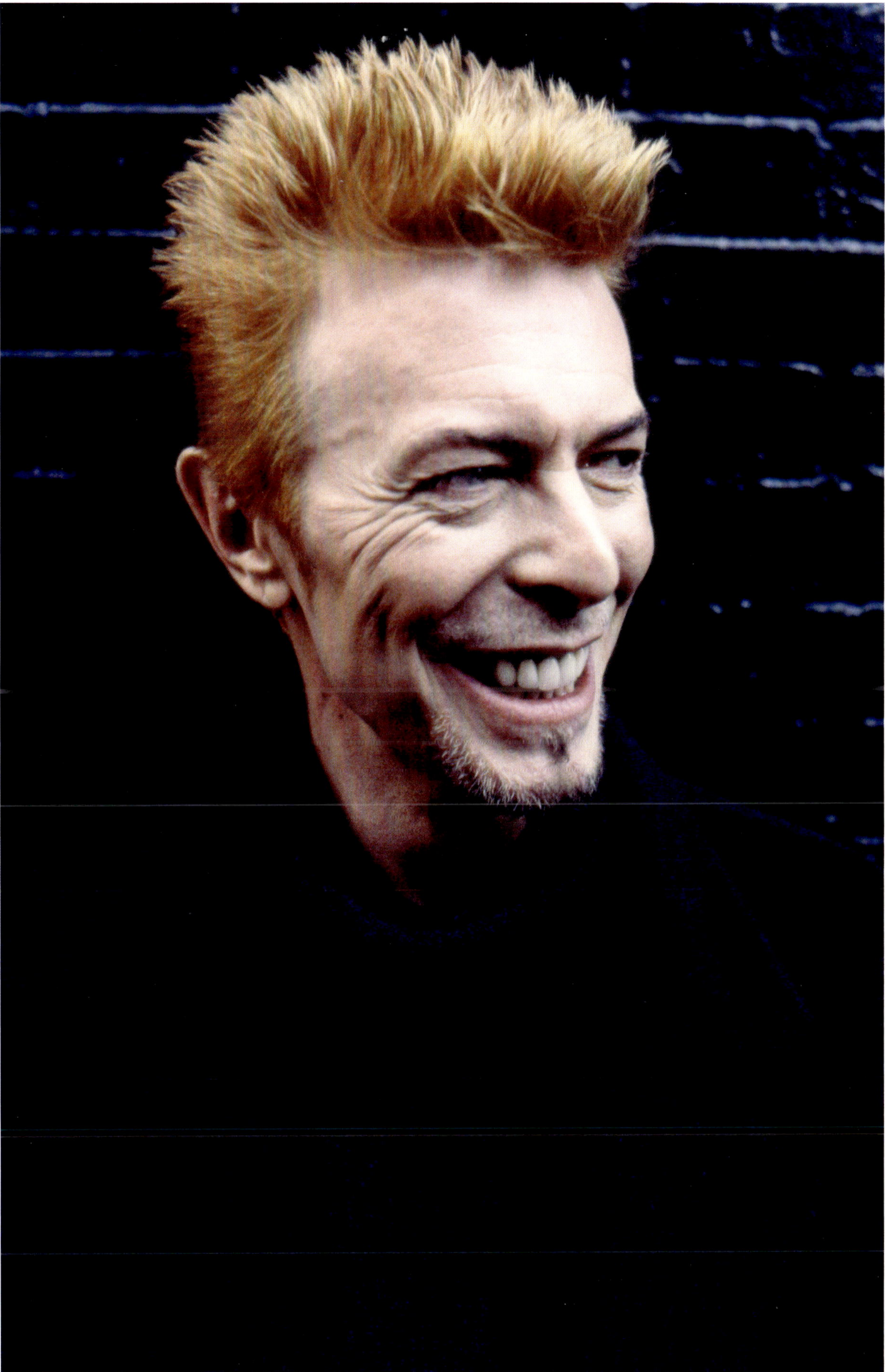

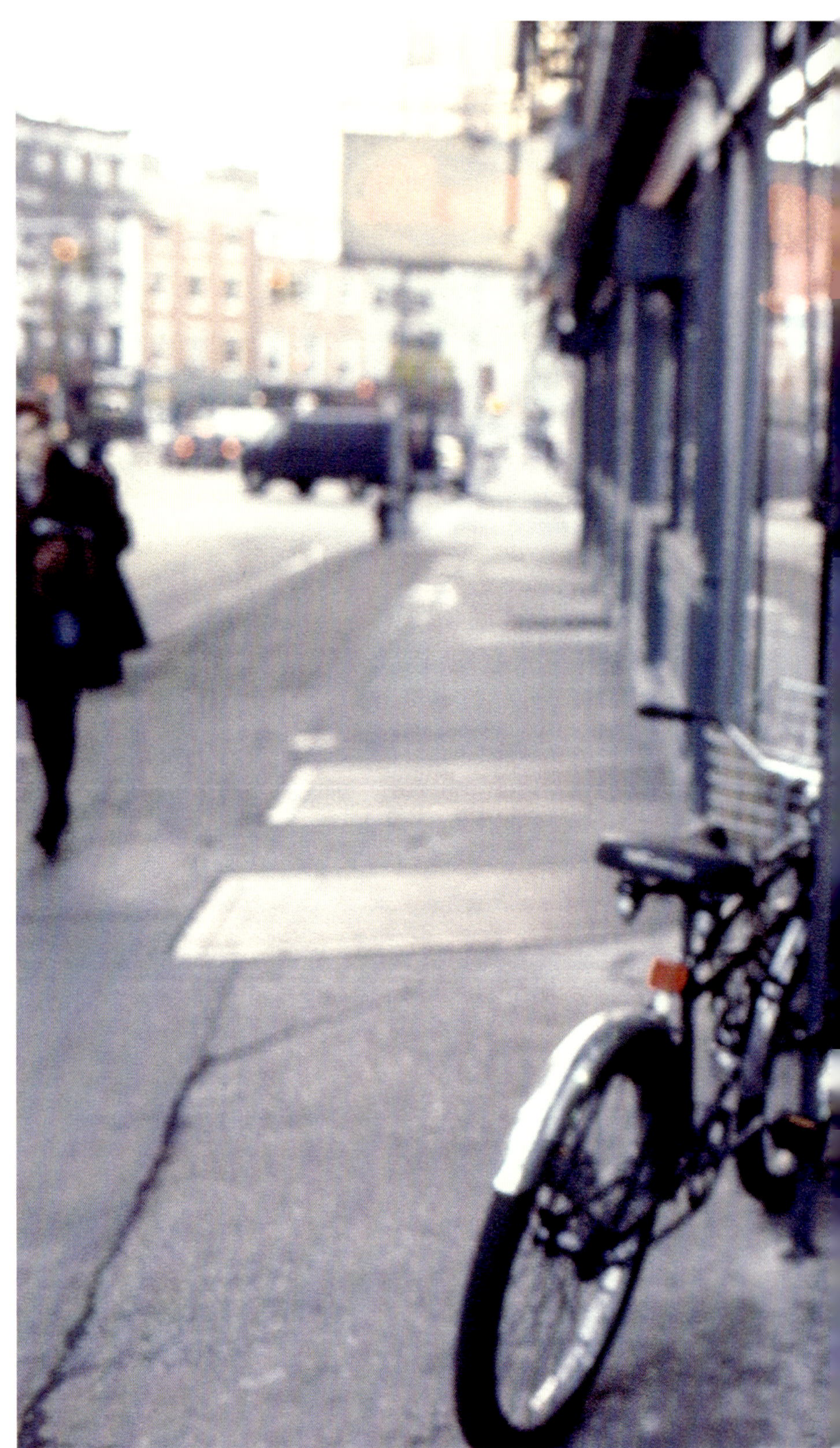

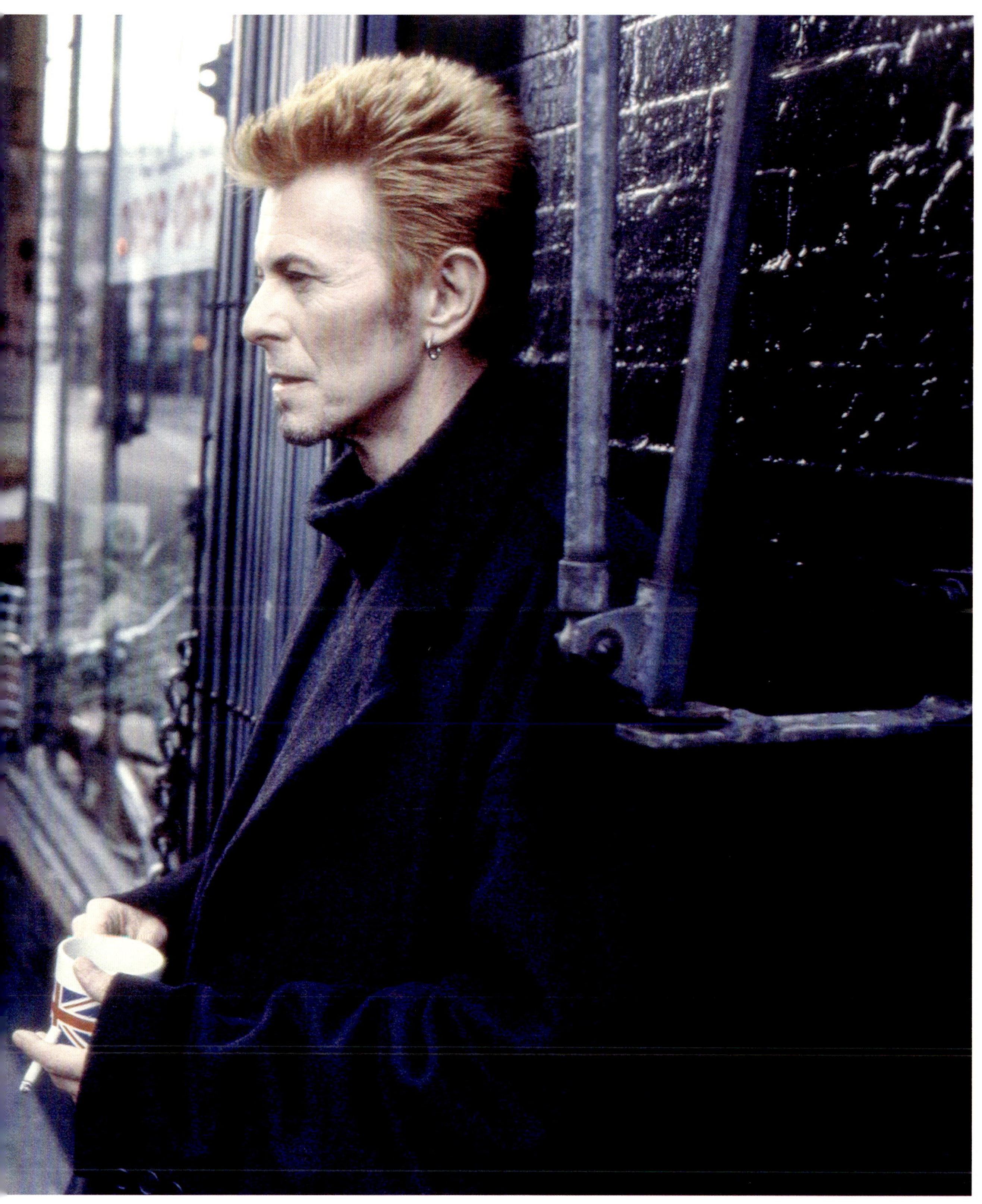

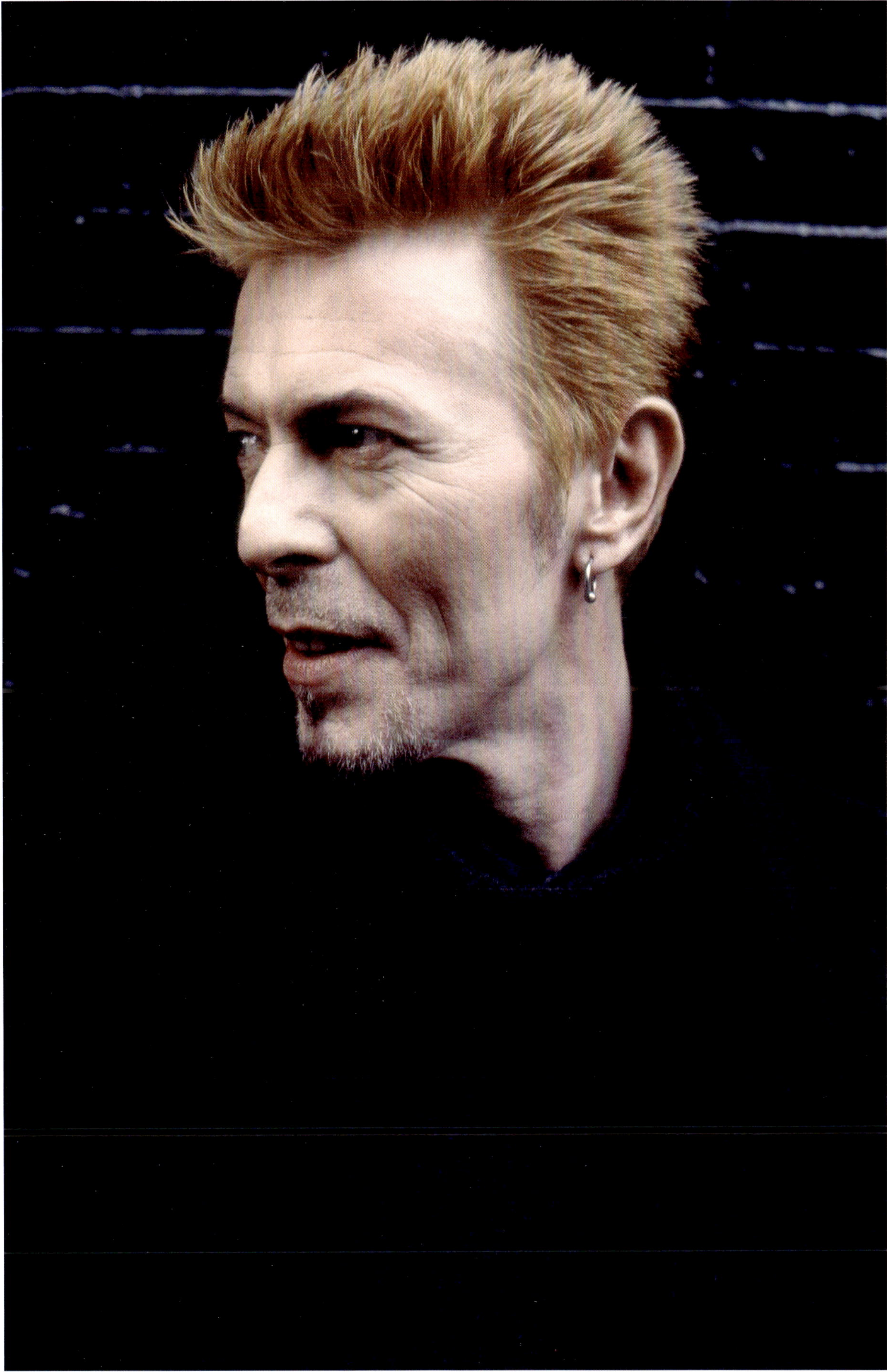

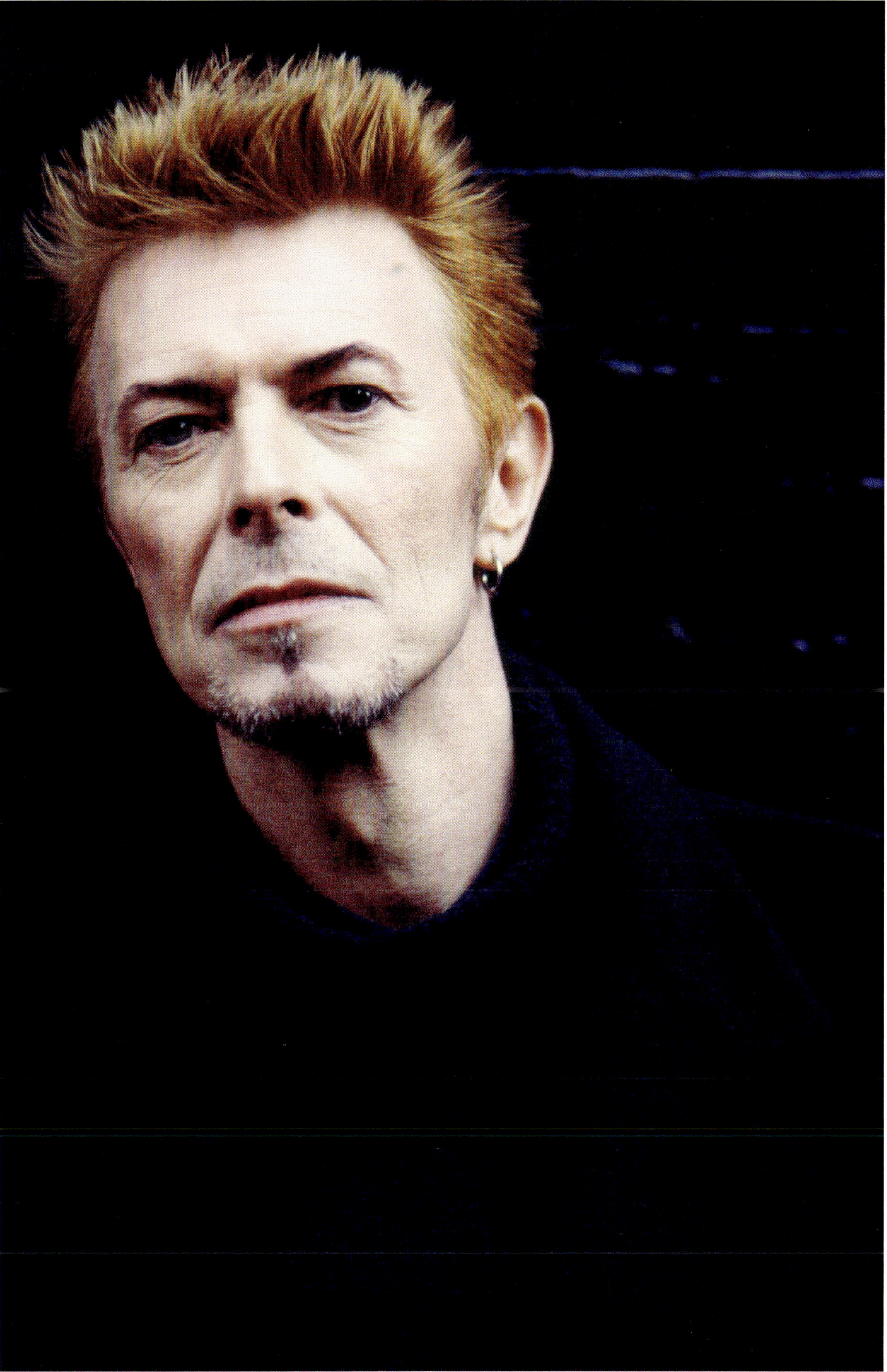

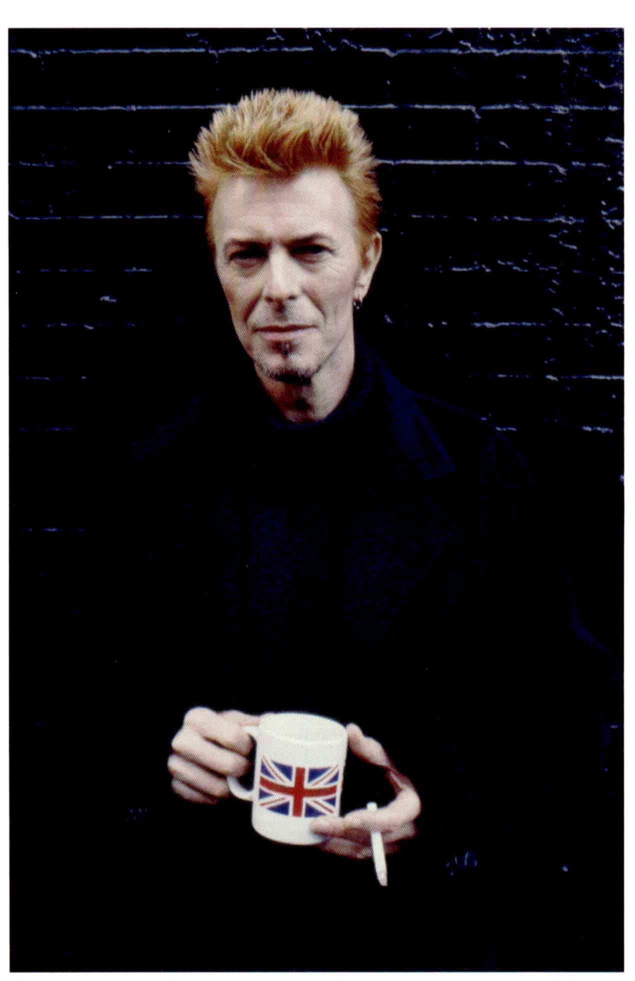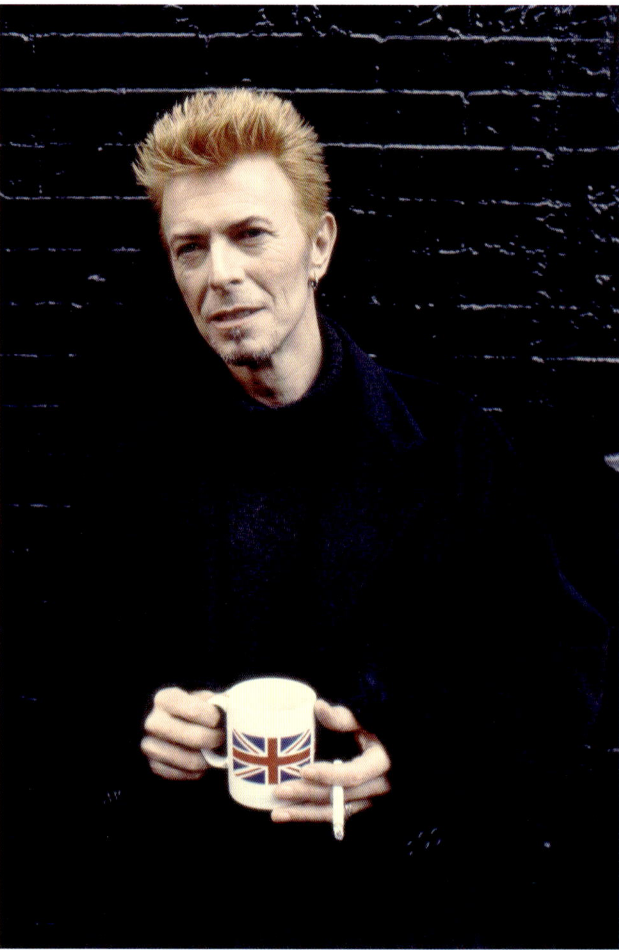

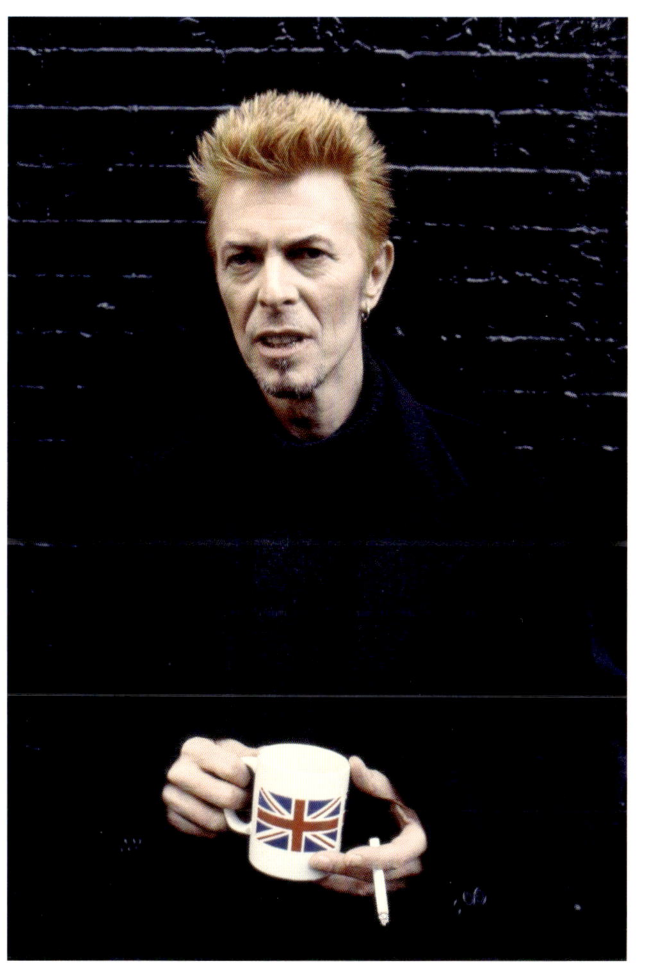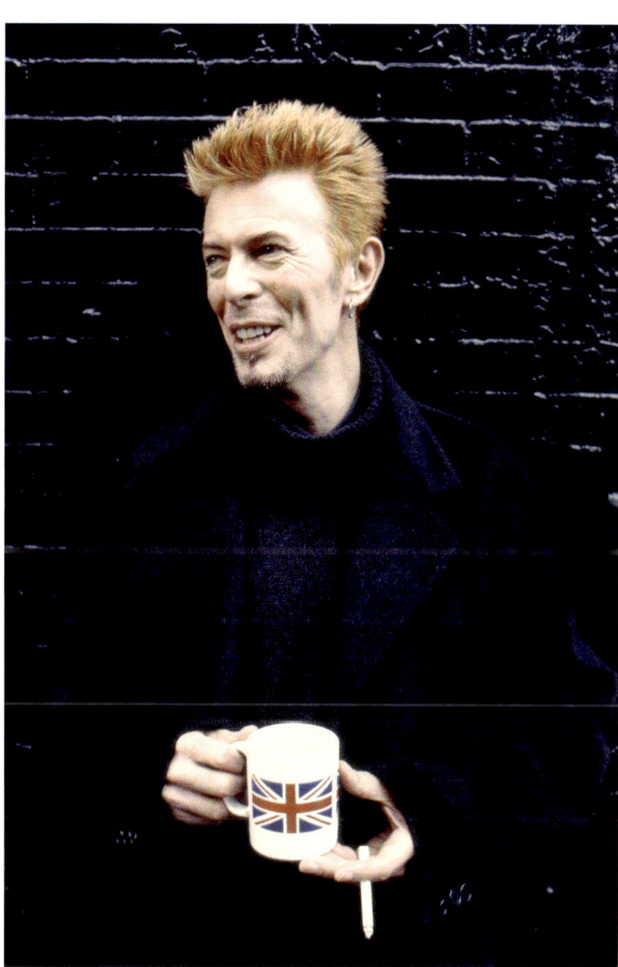

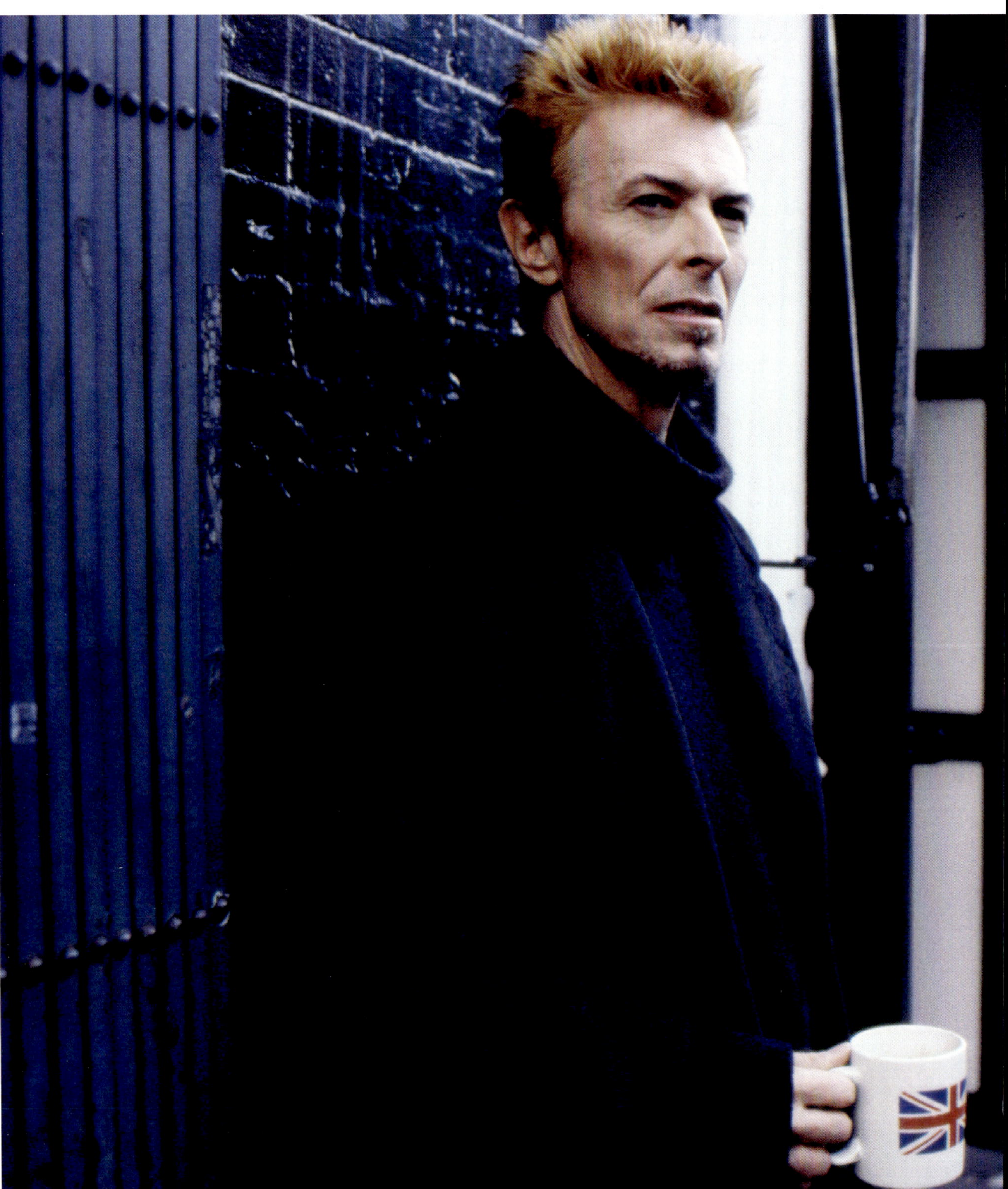

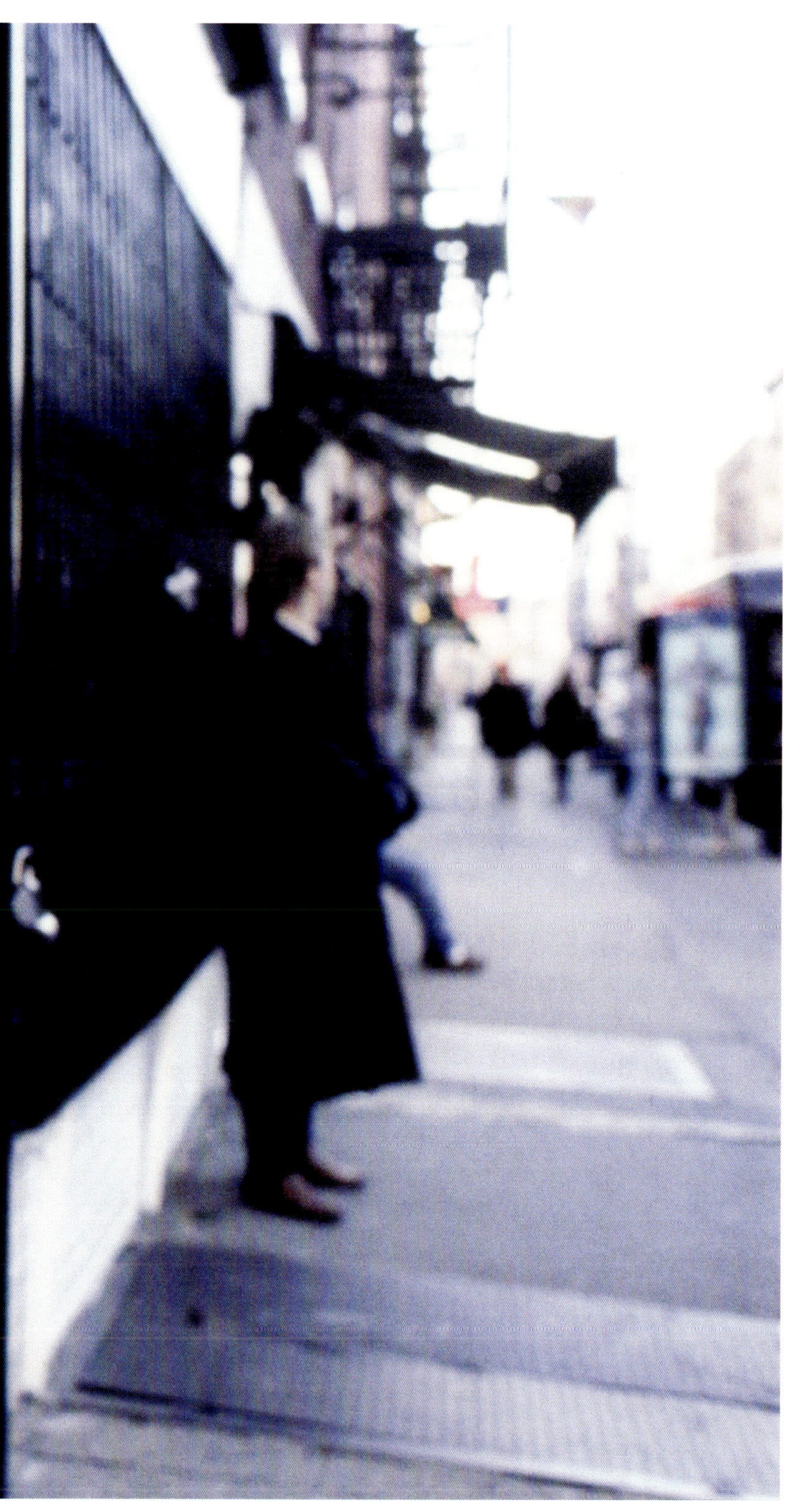

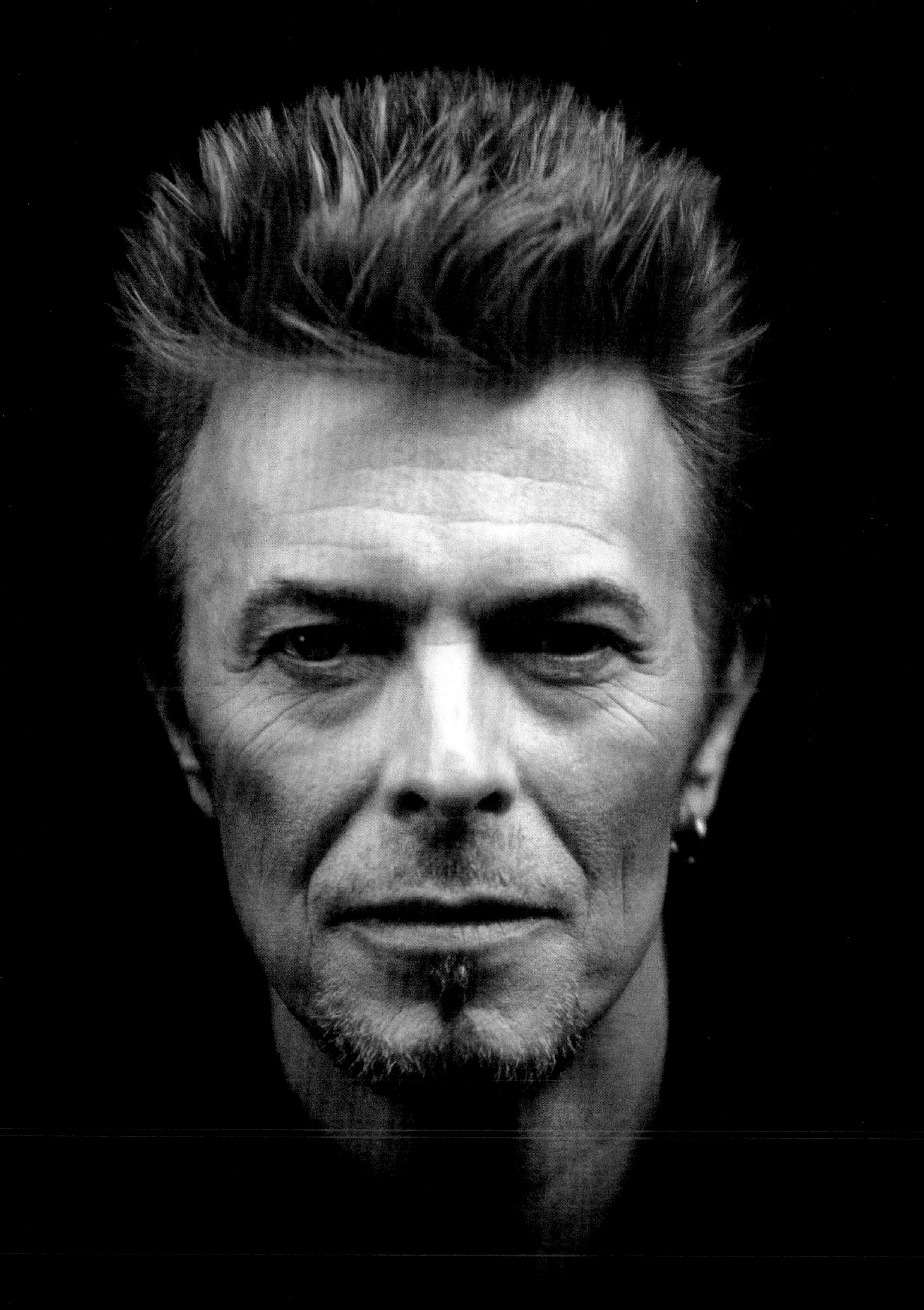

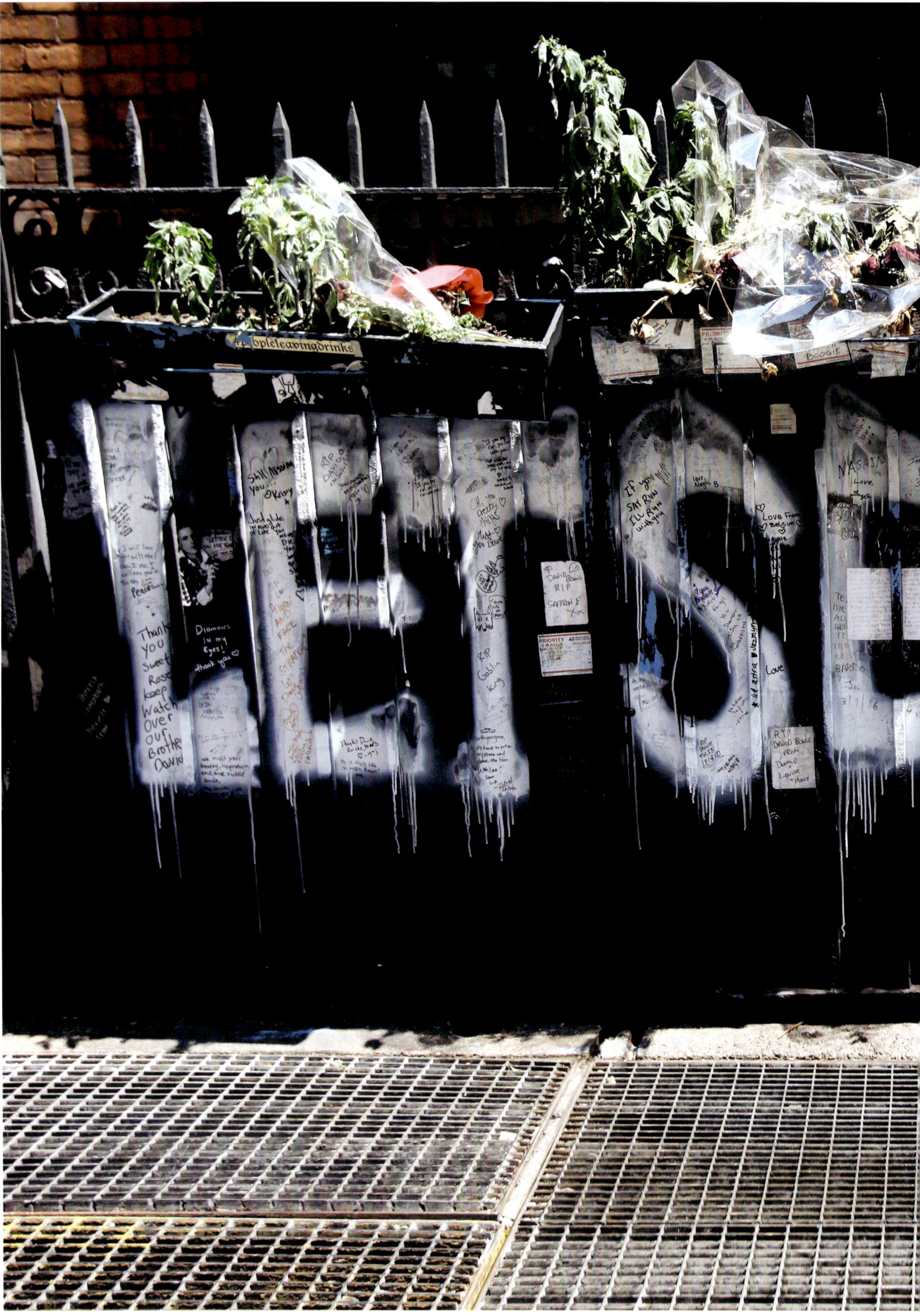

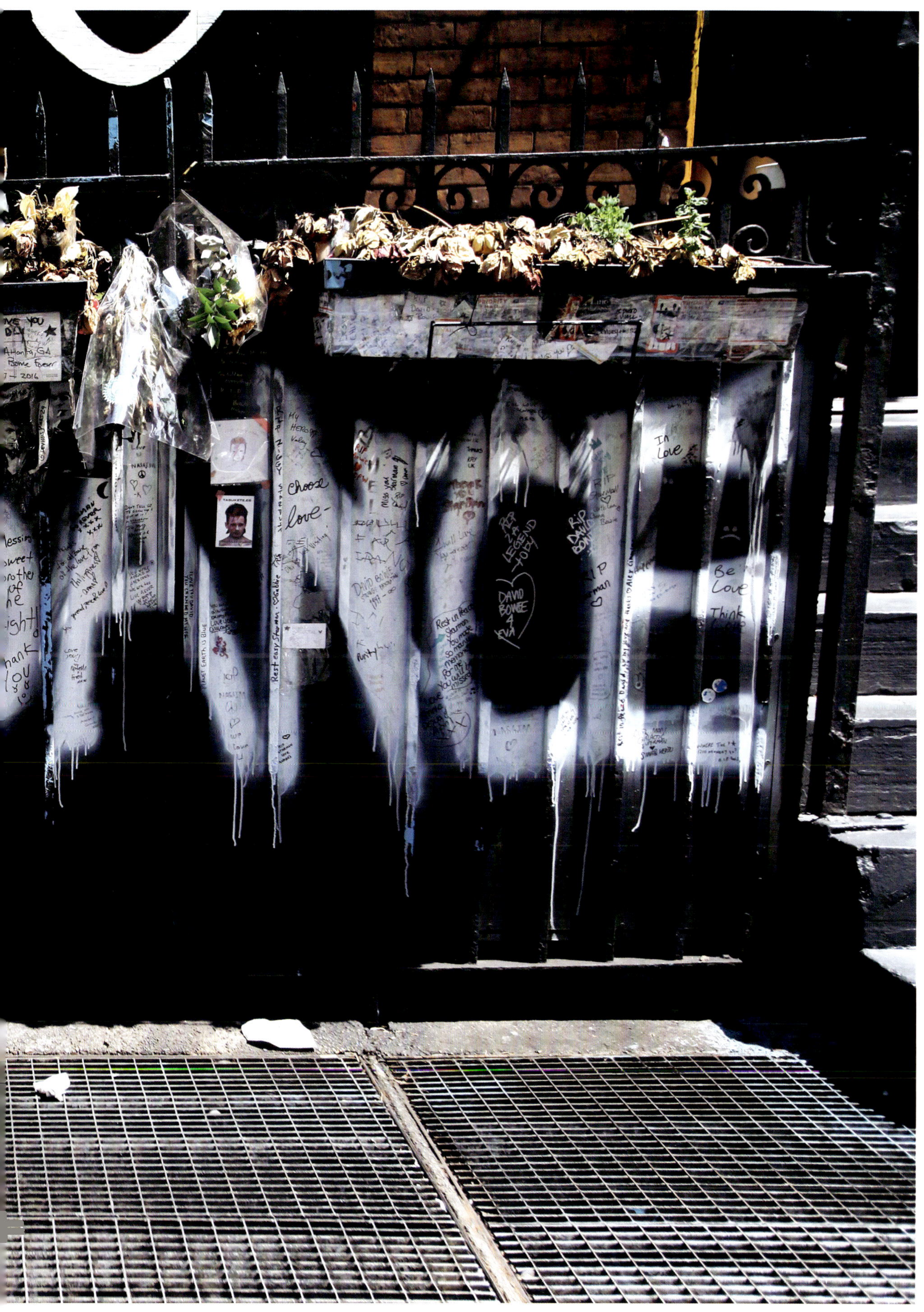

DAVID BOWIE:
"A LITTLE LARGER THAN THE ENTIRE UNIVERSE"

GAIL CROWTHER

The black spikes of the iron railings swelter in the ripple and buzz of a New York summer. Since January they have seen snow, rain and sunshine. Something astonishing has been occurring too. Each spike has begun to tell a story: black ink, blue ink, torn pieces of paper, photographs, drawings, letters, cards, flowers and the dripping, melting spray-paint of the words LET'S DANCE. The stories are from all over the world. Some talk of being saved, some express disbelief, others are prayers and lyrics. Most are about loss, grief and gratitude.

The death of David Bowie on 10 January 2016 resulted in this shrine outside his home. But soon similar shrines began to appear all over the world: London, Berlin, Los Angeles, Milan, Rio de Janeiro. A senior cardinal in the Vatican announced his grief. NASA tweeted, "The stars look very different today." The German Foreign Office thanked Bowie for helping to bring down the Berlin Wall. British astronaut Tim Peake expressed sorrow as he orbited Earth on the International Space Station. Bowie's death felt bigger than the world, a little larger even than the entire universe. With no grave to tether him to the ground, it felt as though his ashes would be forever floating, part of the ether.

Perhaps the biggest shock of Bowie's death was the rupture to continuity, familiarity. For many, he had just always been there, tightly woven with personal histories and key moments, a part of so many emotional lives, providing a soundtrack to the big events or the mundane lying on a bed daydreaming. Suddenly, imagining Bowie as a permanent absence,

somehow everywhere and nowhere all at the same time, felt unthinkable. In those post-death days, shock prevented understanding; there seemed simply chaos and fragmentation, rather Bowie-esque in itself, but nevertheless disorientating.

Mourning was not confined to the real world either. There is nothing more solid or real than a rose tied to a railing, but shrines began to appear in the virtual world too. Pixels and particles networked and connected. It was a different sort of mass mourning, one with no spatial challenges because there were no time–space boundaries at all. "Total fragmentation," Bowie had called the Internet, with possibilities beyond what we could ever imagine, yet in the days after his death, this fragmentation pulled together like cracked mercury into a cohesive whole. Eulogies, reflection, introspection. The lit candles in Brixton echoed the electronic flames flickering in virtual space, each offering their own unique form of grieving.

Even in those early days it seemed as though a separation was occurring, and one that likely would have pleased Bowie – the separation of body and persona. Bodies are finite, they cannot stay for ever, but personas never die. For a while, these two things can exist simultaneously. But once the body has gone, we are left with the part that never really goes away. It is hard to describe what this might be, certainly fragments. Most obviously this is music, but photography plays its part here too. If we can still hear Bowie, it is just as important to still be able to see him.

Lots of photographers see death as an integral part of

their work. In fact, it is often argued that photography exposes the vulnerability in all of us – "flat death" – the fact that that one day we will all pass away. Yet, just for a second, we are captured and immortalized in a moment when all our futures are unknown and unknowable. Bowie was captured in this way more than just about anyone. Despite being so elusive and private, his face has a comforting familiarity. Here he is with an eternal cigarette, with orange hair, or as words scrawled on the iron railings outside his home say, with that subtle smile. The photograph itself becomes a sort of surrogate living entity and performs a bringing back, a remembrance, a certainty that will never allow us to forget.

Kevin's photographs of Bowie anaesthetize time. Each frame allows then and now to merge. Memories can fall into the image and Bowie stays just as he always was. In one photograph, the year is always 1991 and Bowie is always in Dublin, in a large rehearsal warehouse. He will always be standing in front of a dark wall artificially lit by an indoor light. It is with this certainty and comfort that we can engage with the image. In silhouette it seems initially that there is nothing much to see, until you notice the luminous cigarette, centre-frame. Like eyes adjusting to a darkened room after a bright light, the gaze then travels to the curve of Bowie's ear, to the tips of his hair. Look closely and you can even see his eyelashes all bathed in the same silvery, ethereal light. Part of his face has fallen into blackness, but this hardly matters. How much of Bowie do we really need to see to know Bowie is Bowie?

Or the year might be 1973 on a June night in Leeds. You can almost sense the heat and smell of the concert. Bowie is captured perpetually in flight, arms outstretched, as though he is about to launch himself from the stage. Two silver bracelets dangle from his left wrist. He remains animated, real and alive within the confines of the frame. Often we encounter these photographs as pure and uncomplicated images. And in many ways this is the art of photography. We would never know, although we do now, the preparation that this scene required. Looking at the image, we would have no idea that it exists only because Kevin had taken a previous shot at a different concert that he felt he could improve. Which means that another photo exists from a little earlier in the month, when Bowie is also captured in flight but not quite as perfectly framed or suggestive of the moment. This sudden seizure of time stamped into an image is why Roland Barthes called cameras "clocks for seeing" in *Camera Lucida*. But while time is stopped within the frame, it isn't beyond it. One day people who were not even alive at the same time as Bowie will look at these photographs. Yet, despite this, he will be there, waiting for them.

This means that a book of Bowie photographs is a powerful contextual document. Not just to preserve, but to provoke too. Each page brings a different image, yet it is likely that each of us will respond in different ways to certain pictures. Why does one photograph move us more than another? Why, when it is the same person in each image and the same person taking each photograph, do some haunt us so? It is quite mysterious,

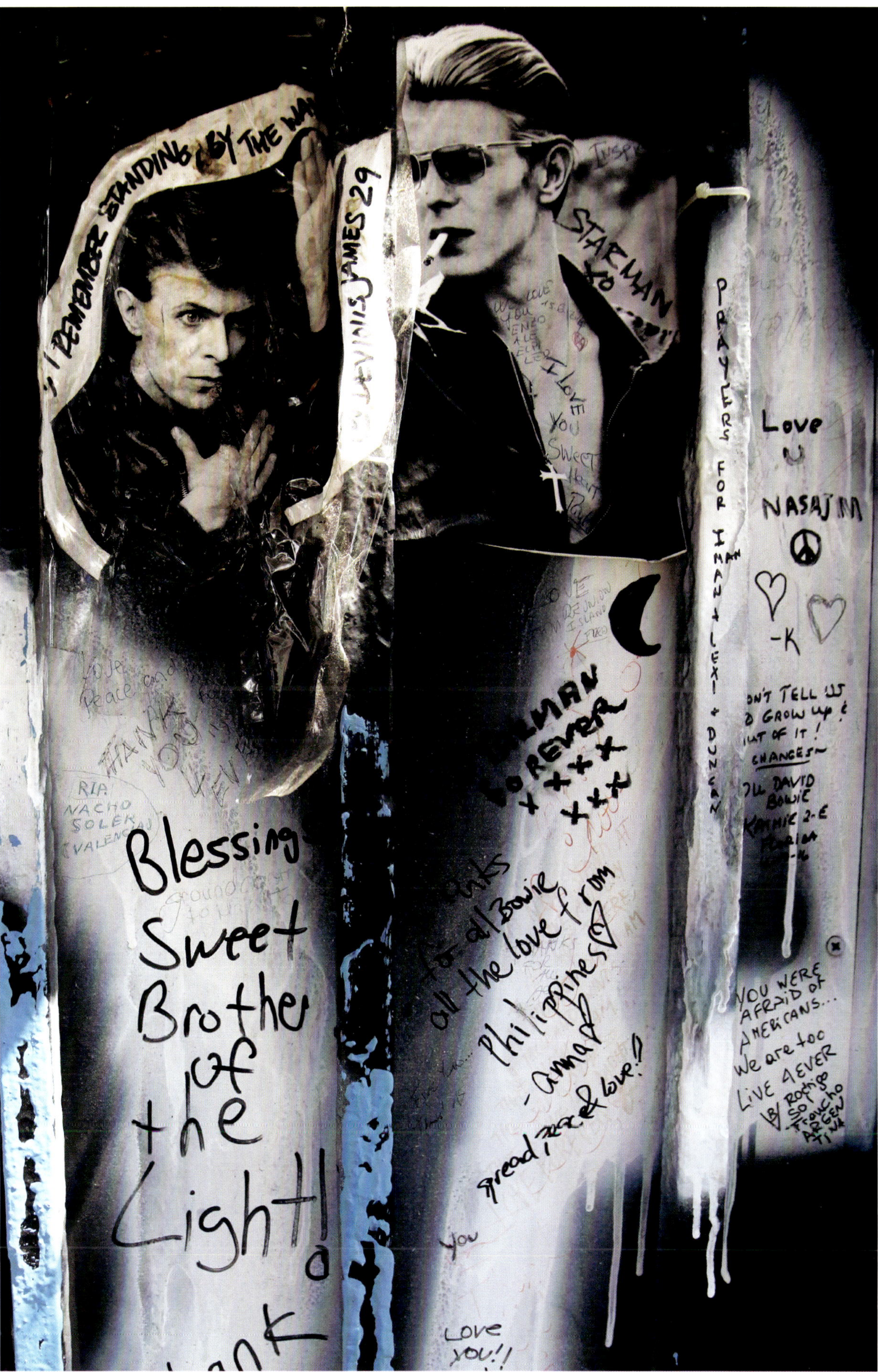

I REMEMBER STANDING BY THE WALL
LEVINUS JAMES 29
STARMAN XO
INSPI
WE LOVE YOU
ENZO
ALE
ELI
LEN
I LOVE YOU SWEET HEART
PRAYERS FOR IMAN + LEXI + DUNEAN
LOVE U NASAJM
-K
LOVE FROM REUNION ISLAND
RIP
BOWMAN FOREVER
XXX
XXX
XXX
YOUR PEACE AND
THANK YOU
RIP
NACHO
SOLER
VALEN
Blessing
Sweet
Brother
of
the
Light!
to all Bowie
all the love from Philippines
- Anna
greatness & love!
you
LOVE YOU!!
DON'T TELL US TO GROW UP & OUT OF IT!
CHANGES
I'LL DAVID BOWIE
KATHIE 2-E
FLORIDA
YOU WERE AFRAID OF AMERICANS...
WE are too
LIVE 4EVER
Rodrigo
SOLEDAD
TROUCHO
ARGEN
TINA

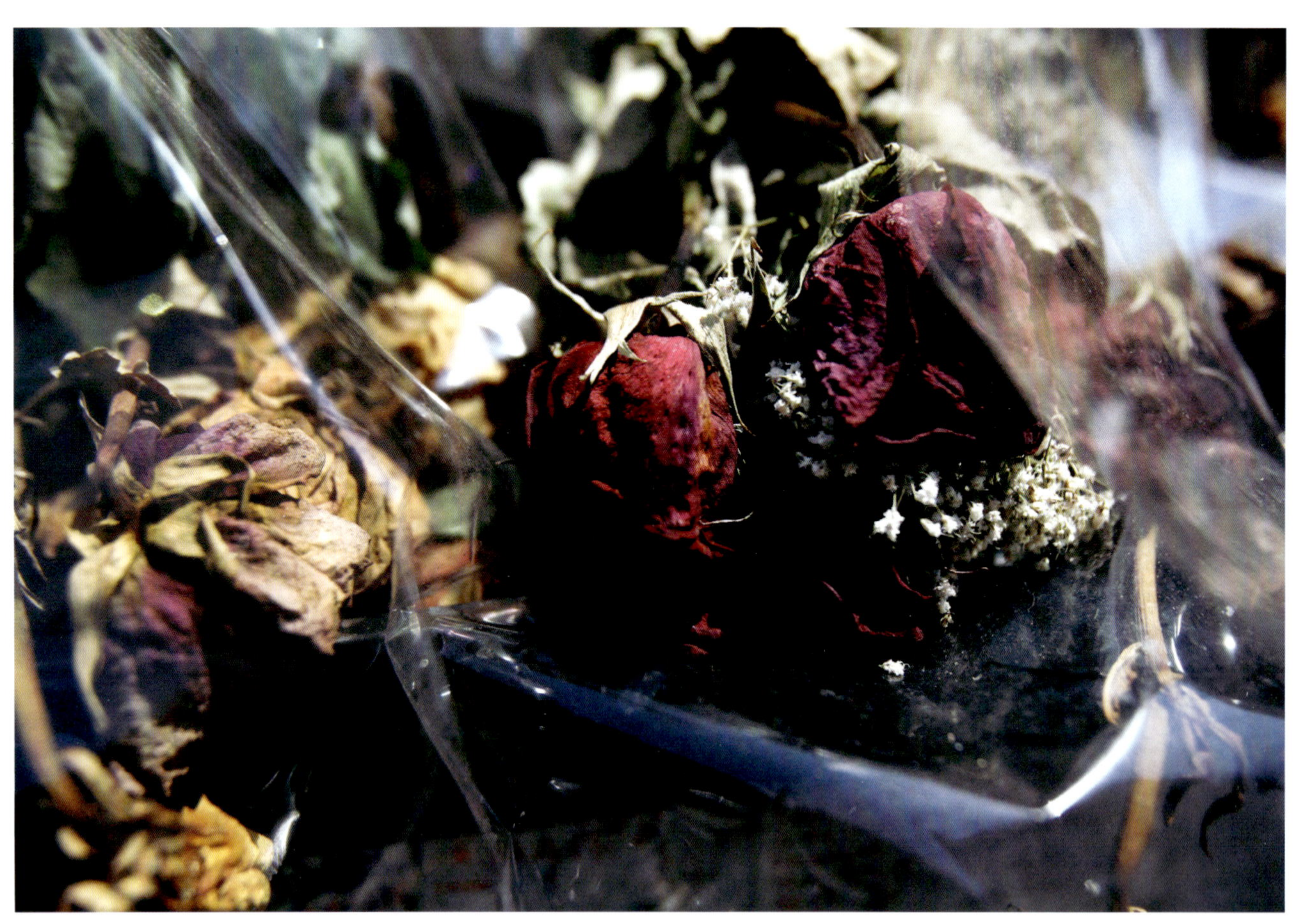

BUT THE IMAGES PROVOKE TOO. THEY REMIND US THAT BOWIE DARED TO DEFY TRADITIONAL AND DOMINANT BOUNDARIES

but perhaps it is because we all bring different histories and memories, different pleasures and desires. Perhaps it is the perfect illustration of the title of this book, taken from one of Bowie's favourite poems by T S Eliot, *The Waste Land*, Part 1 "The Burial of the Dead" – we mix memory with desire. And then through this lens our eyes see what they are instructed to see.

But the images provoke too. They remind us that Bowie dared to defy traditional and dominant boundaries. And there is empowerment in this subversion and rebellion, not just for Bowie but for us too, looking and listening. The stories that unfolded on those iron railings in New York throughout 2016 were testament to Bowie's power to liberate people, at least from their own cages, if not from society's at large. He offered so many the confidence to construct an identity that seemed to simply not fit in the world in which they found themselves. The refrain "Turn and face the strange" from "Changes" was pure defiance. Bowie had much to say about the ruinous fragmentation of a modern, industrialized society, so there is something pleasing – and it is tempting to think it may even have been *deliberate* on his part – about him becoming a cultural figure to subvert this fractured isolation and unite. Bowie fans are some of the most productive in the world: forums, fanzines, books, websites. If modern society truly is atomized, then what happened after Bowie's death refuted this, and instead unveiled a true community coming together in a moment of mass mourning, trying collectively to make sense of their loss. Bowie was a man, a musician, a husband, a father,

an artist, but he also was and remains a cultural figure who offers optimism, hope, pleasure, passion and transformation.

Bowie will never truly leave us. We have his music. We have footage. We have his films and artwork. We have clothes and costumes. The zoot suit designed by Peter J Hall for the Serious Moonlight tour. The striped body suit designed by Kansai Yamamoto for the Aladdin Sane tour stands ever ready for Bowie to leap back into those sculpted, flamboyant trousers. We know that he never will, but his bodily outline is there forever waiting. We have his endearingly handwritten lyric sheets. "Rebel Rebel" captured in blue and purple ink, showing that he started and went back to it repeatedly. "They put ~~you me~~ you down" – each thought process changed with a strikethrough. There are his diaries and notebooks, extraordinary musings jotted in such ordinary spring binders. How is it possible for them to hold these words, these ideas?

And ultimately we have these photographs. Little pockets of immortality that somehow simultaneously remind us of loss while offering some sort of resurrection. As we career through time, Bowie is stilled and steady, travelling with us. Maybe, in the end, that is the true art of photography. It stays with us when everything else passes away. This book, too, enters a sort of immortality, surely echoing the words by the Portuguese poet Fernando Pessoa that could have been written about, or by, Bowie himself: "I pass and I remain, like the Universe."

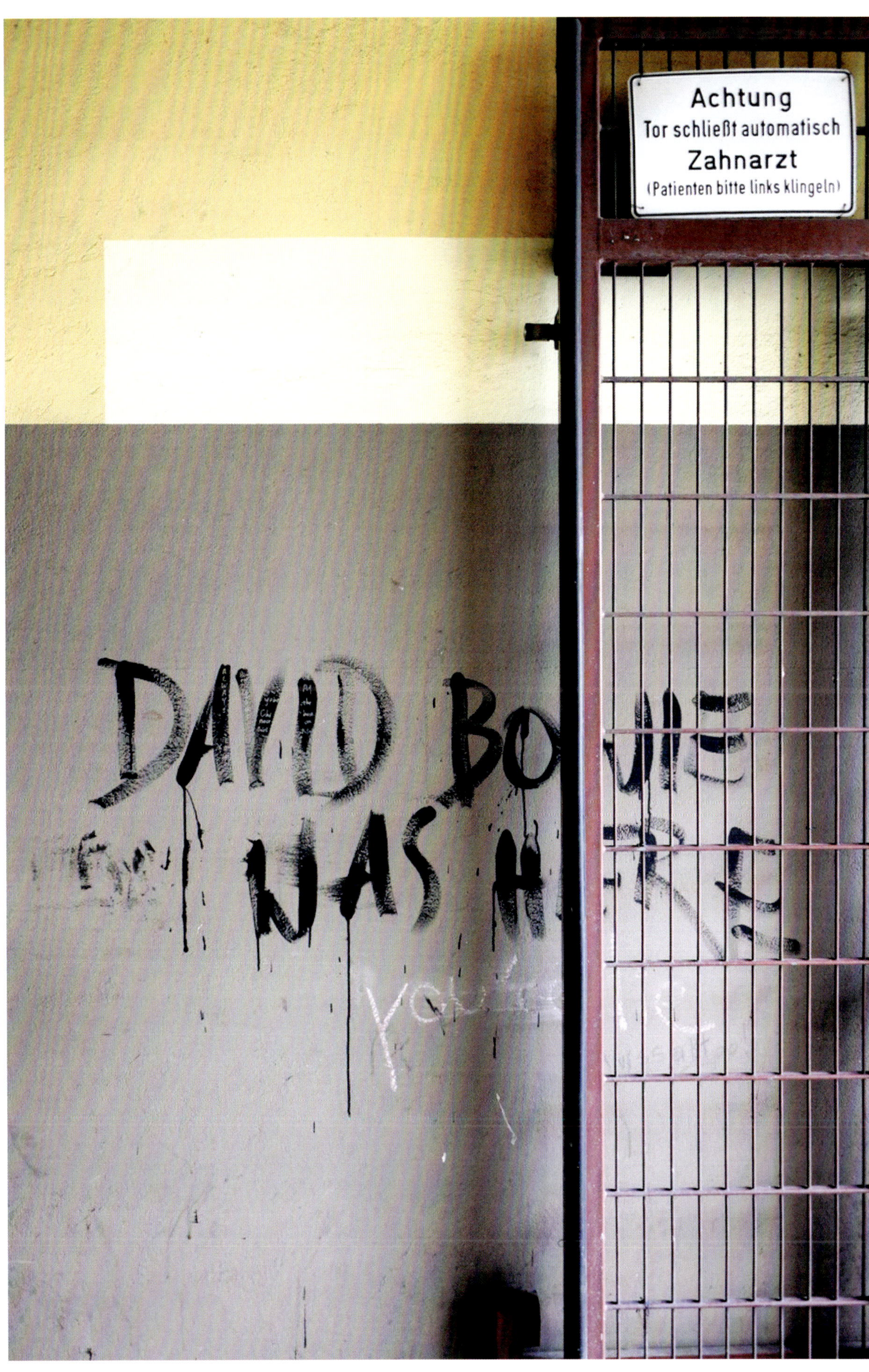

Achtung
Tor schließt automatisch
Zahnarzt
(Patienten bitte links klingeln)
DAVID BOWIE
WAS HERE

ACKNOWLEDGEMENTS

Putting a book like this together is impossible without a good team around me, and once again I'm lucky to be working with the same core of people at Cassell who I've worked with now for several years.

Thanks to my long-suffering publisher, Alison Starling, whose ideas and support proved invaluable as ever. Her ability to remain relatively calm when deadlines come and go is quite remarkable.

Thanks also to Karen, Matt, Jonathan and Pauline for all helping to make this work – as ever. You're all great to deal with, even if my deadline surfing gives you all nightmares. Thanks also to Blake Lewis and Adam Powell at Iconic for all the scanning. "Kevin, did you have to take so many photographs of Bowie?"

Massive thanks to my agent, Carrie Kania, whose constant support, encouragement, and Champagne kept me going through the tough winter months; The French House in Soho does a roaring trade every time I'm working on a new book. Although, to be fair, I don't really need an excuse to while away the days there.

I couldn't have produced this book without Gail Crowther. Gail's ability to turn an average piece of prose into something of beauty is one of her many strengths, she sees things much more clearly than I do and has been invaluable in helping to give this book a true narrative flow, instead of it just plodding along. Gail is also more concise than I am and can strip back most of my multi-clause sentences into precise ten-word sentences that make sense. And finally, she also suggested telling stories to run alongside many of the sessions. Thanks a million, and the Champagne's on ice.

Thanks also to friends old and new who I've been to countless Bowie gigs with; to Noel Gallagher, Paul Morley and Goldie for their kind words adorning the back of this book; and to Alan Edwards, who made sure I got to as many of the gigs as I did and that my accreditation was always spot on. Also, a huge thanks to my commissioning editors at the NME, for believing that I'd always come up with the goods. It generally worked out well – er, didn't it?

A big kiss for my daughter Ella, who, I think, still likes going to gigs with me.

Finally, a huge thanks to David Bowie. I doubt my career would have followed the same path if I hadn't taken that photo of Ziggy in Leeds.

And boy, could he play guitar.

weldon**owen**

an imprint of Insight Editions
P.O. Box 3088
San Rafael, CA 94912
www.weldonowen.com

CEO Raoul Goff
VP Publisher Roger Shaw
Editorial Director Katie Killebrew
Executive Editor Edward Ash-Milby
VP Creative Chrissy Kwasnik
Art Director Allister Fein
VP Manufacturing Alix Nicholaeff
Production Manager Joshua Smith
Sr Production Manager, Subsidiary Rights
    Lina s Palma-Temena

First published in Great Britain in 2023
by Cassell, an imprint of
Octopus Publishing Group Ltd
Carmelite House
50 Victoria Embankment
London EC4Y 0DZ
www.octopusbooks.co.uk

An Hachette UK Company
www.hachette.co.uk

Text and photographs copyright
© Kevin Cummins 2023

"David Bowie: 'A Little Larger than the
EntireUniverse'" text copyright
© Gail Crowther 2023

Design and layout copyright
© Octopus Publishing Group 2023
The Waste Land by T S Eliot quotation
used with permission of Faber & Faber Ltd

Publisher: Alison Starling
Senior Editor: Pauline Bache
Creative Director: Jonathan Christie
Assistant Production Manager: Allison Gonsalves

Endpaper photograph: Potsdamer Platz, Berlin,
22 February 2023

Frontispiece photograph: David Bowie's childhood
home, Plaistow Grove, Bromley, 6 February 2023

Pages 242, 247 and 248 photographs: Lafayette Street,
New York, June 2016

Page 251 photograph: Hauptstraße 155, Berlin,
23 February 2023

All rights reserved. No part of this book may be
reproduced in any form without written permission
from the publisher.

ISBN: 979-8-88674-095-0

Manufactured in China
10 9 8 7 6 5 4 3 2 1

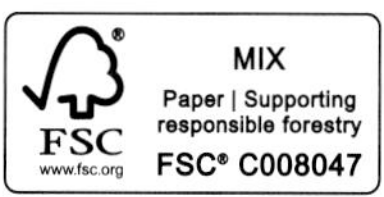

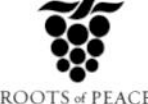

ROOTS of PEACE   REPLANTED PAPER

Insight Editions, in association with Roots of
Peace, will plant two trees for each tree used in
the manufacturing of this book. Roots of Peace
is an internationally renowned humanitarian
organization dedicated to eradicating land mines
worldwide and converting war-torn lands into
productive farms and wildlife habitats. Roots of
Peace will plant two million fruit and nut trees in
Afghanistan and provide farmers there with the
skills and support necessary for sustainable land use.

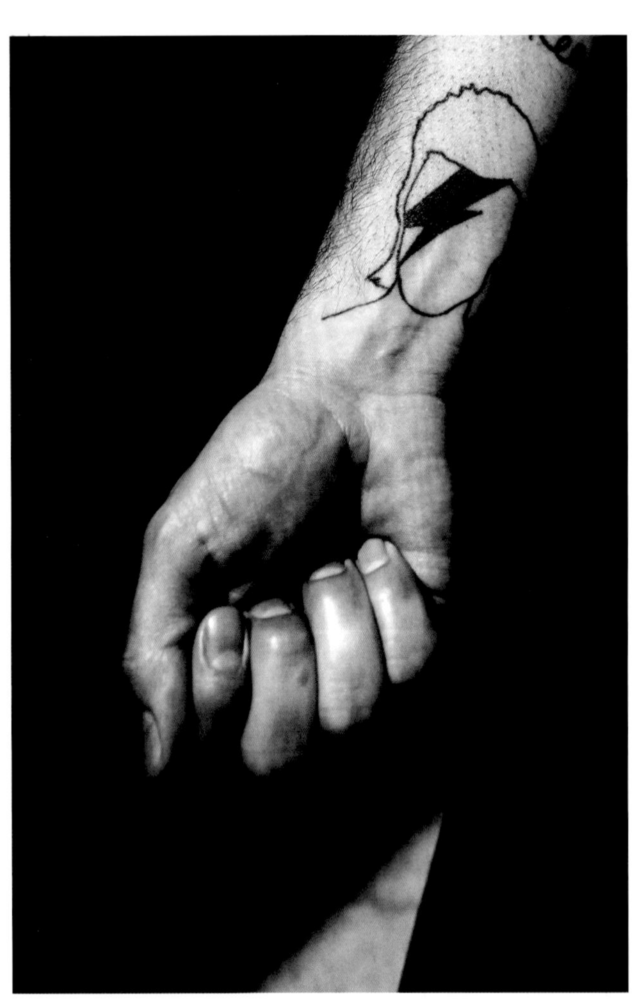

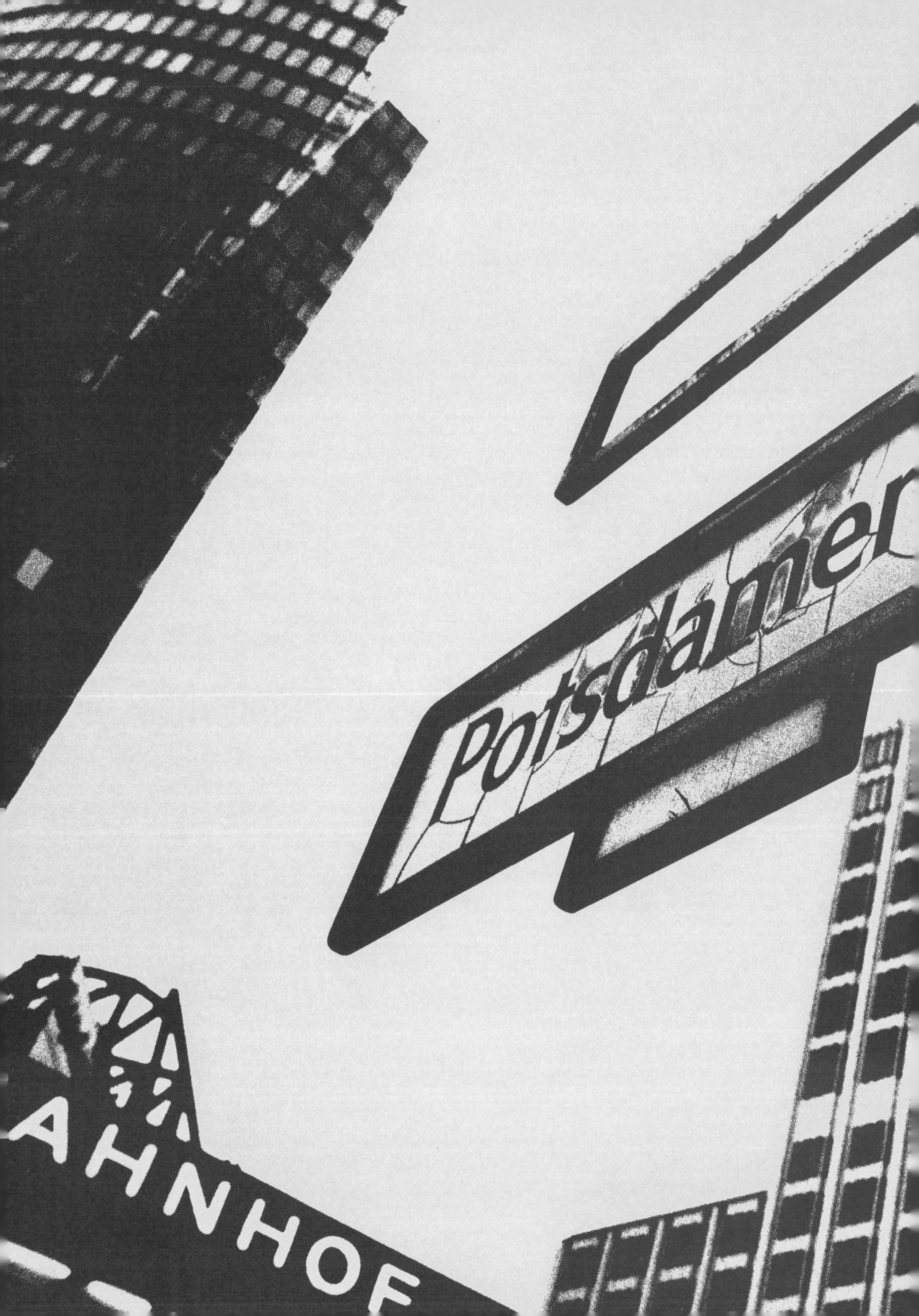

Potsdamer
AHNHOF